Rhythms of Recovery

Rhythm is one of the most important components of our survival and well-being. It governs the patterns of our sleep and respiration and is profoundly tied to our relationships with friends and family. But what happens when these rhythms are disrupted by traumatic events? Can balance be restored, and if so, how? What insights do eastern, natural, and modern western healing traditions have to offer, and how can practitioners put these lessons to use? Is it possible to do this in a way that's culturally sensitive, multidisciplinary, and grounded in research? Clients walk through the door with chronic physical and mental health problems as a result of traumatic events—how can clinicians make a quick and skillful connection with their clients' needs and offer integrative mind/body methods they can rely upon? *Rhythms of Recovery* not only examines these questions, it also answers them and provides clinicians with effective, time-tested tools for alleviating the destabilizing effects of traumatic events. For practitioners and students interested in integrating the insights of complementary/alternative medicine and 21st-century science, this deeply appealing book is an ideal guide.

Leslie E. Korn, PhD, MPH has worked for over 35 years in private practice and community mental health specializing in integrating psychotherapy and complementary and alternative medicine for the treatment of traumatic stress and chronic physical illness. She introduced somatic psychotherapy at Harvard Medical School where she was a clinical fellow and faculty in the department of psychiatry. She teaches in the Mental Health Counseling licensure program at Capella University, USA.

Rhythms of Recovery
Trauma, Nature, and the Body

Leslie E. Korn

Routledge
Taylor & Francis Group

NEW YORK AND LONDON

First published 2013
by Routledge
711 Third Avenue, New York, NY 10017

Simultaneously published in the UK
by Routledge
27 Church Road, Hove, East Sussex BN3 2FA

Routledge is an imprint of the Taylor & Francis Group, an informa business

Library of Congress Cataloging in Publication Data

Korn, Leslie E.
Rhythms of recovery : trauma, nature, and the body / Leslie E. Korn.
    p. cm.
  Includes bibliographical references and index.
    ISBN 978-0-415-80749-4 (hardcover : alk. paper) —
ISBN 978-0-415-80750-0 (pbk. : alk. paper)   1. Biological rhythms.
2. Chronobiology.   I. Title.
QP84.6.K67   2012
612'.022—dc23   2012015353

ISBN: 978-0-415-80749-4 (hbk)
ISBN: 978-0-415-80750-0 (pbk)
ISBN: 978-0-203-14812-9 (ebk)

Typeset in Times New Roman
by Apex CoVantage, LLC

To Nancy Avery

If the body had been easier to understand, nobody would have thought that we had a mind.

—Richard Rorty

Contents

List of Figures, Tables, Exercises, and Online Materials

FIGURES

TABLES

EXERCISES

ONLINE MATERIALS

http://www.routledge.com/books/details/9780415807500/

Assessments

3.1   The Nijmegen Scale
6.1   Trouble with a Client?
6.2   Body/Pain/Visual Analogue Scale
6.3   Food Diary
6.4   Thyroid Test

Discussion Questions

Glossary
Resources
CE Exam

Acknowledgments

Like most writers of books such as this well know, the process of putting a book together is a solitary endeavor, the final product of which is possible only with the help and support of many other people. I am deeply grateful for the generosity and support of friends and colleagues who, when I reached out to them, always responded with good cheer. Many excellent practitioners, researchers, and scholars responded openheartedly to my questions and provided their careful reading and thoughtful ideas for improving many of the chapters. I am deeply indebted to John Chitty, Renee Levine, Lisa Mertz, LizAnne Pastore, Marilyn Piper, Ethan Russo, and Jose Vasquez for their scholarship, knowledge, and commitment to the success of this project. I am especially thankful to Gray Graham and Dr. Nicholas Gonzalez, who have been generous with their time and knowledge in support of my work. While I have followed the weather and thus relocated frequently between homes in Massachusetts, Washington State, and Jalisco, Mexico, I am blessed to have long-time and steadfast friends who remain personally supportive and interested in my work. I am grateful especially to Jill Charney, Laurel Gonsalves, Diane Aronson, Brooke Beazley, and Janet Schreiber, whose loving support over the years has nurtured me personally and emboldened me professionally. When I arrived in the jungle at the age of 20, my friends and clients in west Mexico introduced me to a way of life that led to my career. Friends in the villages have invited me to share in countless adventures on what I can only believe has been a predestined path. Marlene Bremner, my assistant of many years, cheerfully helps me stay organized and gently lets me know when I am making no sense at all. I am indebted to my late parents, Barbara and Richard, whose consistent and loving nurturance ensured that I was able to survive and thrive in spite of rough times, and to my loving and always kind brothers, Stephen and David, with whom I am proud to walk along the family path. My faithful dogs Bodhi, Flip, and Saba are constant models of "positive psychology" and enthusiasm for our family and for my clients. The late Elizabeth D. Wagner taught me the essence of being a healer, and she is always close in my heart. Finally, I am grateful to my husband, Rudolph Rÿser, the most generous and loving spirit, who is always willing to edit my misplaced syntax and continually makes me laugh with his songs and poetry.

Introduction

This book is a reflection of my own clinical experience, garnered during 35 years of practice. My first introduction to catastrophic human experiences came during clinical work in rural Mexico, where natural disasters as well as family violence brought adults and children to the clinic I founded. These cross-cultural experiences nourished my curiosity about alternative approaches to health care. I thus began my studies of traditional forms of healing with *curanderas* (*curar* means "to heal") who relied on the gifts of nature to heal. I underwent initiations by fire that only life in the jungle can offer. As a result, I observed and often experienced nature's theft of health along with its powerful effects on restoring health.

When I returned to the United States in 1983, I had been living in the jungle for 10 years, practicing polarity therapy and massage therapy as well as yoga, nutrition, and herbal medicine alongside *curanderas*. I undertook the study of parasites; first the intestinal, at the Harvard School of Public Health, then human, in the department of psychiatry. Following my training in psychotherapy, I began integrating both bodywork with psychotherapy treating chronic pain, illness, and (complex) posttraumatic stress arising from sexual and physical violence and war. I have been fortunate to provide clinical care for diverse individuals from many cultures and geographical locations and economic backgrounds. It was perhaps the lessons learned from "jungle medicine" that taught me not to be afraid; that suicidal people might just need to be touched in order to "hold them" here on earth; that a survivor of sexual abuse suffering excruciating pain from an anal sphincter spasm will benefit from gentle manual release of the perineum more than a muscle relaxant; or that just because someone has been on antidepressant medications for 15 years does not mean that she cannot withdraw and thrive without them. The courage shown and trust given by all the people I have worked with who have experienced great adversity contributed to the ideas in this book.

In 1997, I was fortunate to return to Mexico, where I again lived and worked with the same indigenous population for 5 years. There, I coordinated a team that conducted the women's traditional medicine community trauma research project, which inquired into the synergistic effects of intergenerational trauma and community stress arising from neocolonial development and its contribution to chronic illness. During a hiatus from Mexico between 2004 and 2007, I conducted traditional foods and medicine research and trainings with American Indians of the Pacific Northwest, with a focus, once again, on the intersection of stress, trauma, and chronic illness. Currently I divide my time between private practices in the Pacific Northwest and west Mexico and continue to integrate the many modalities I explore in this book.

The ubiquity of traumatic experience worldwide suggests that a broad range of health practitioners and human service professionals will meet and work with trauma victims as well as have trauma experience themselves. It is essential to understand the universal and culture-specific impact of trauma in a world where migration is extensive. The act of migration itself is often a result of, or fraught with, violence. Likewise, response to trauma is influenced by differing cultural values about verbal or somatic expressions of pain, suffering, and victimization. The practitioner's basic knowledge about and awareness of the interface between culture and somatopsychic expressions of distress can determine efficacy or stagnation in the treatment process.

Because the symptoms of trauma often go undiagnosed, a patient's symptoms may be disguised, unrecognized, or misunderstood by both client and clinician. This book focuses on reliable methods for diagnosing posttraumatic stress disorder (PTSD) and extends the clinical lens to incorporate the often "hidden in plain sight" presenting symptoms: the somatic voice.

Over the past 30 years, feminist and multicultural clinicians and educators, war veterans, and pioneers in the mind/body fields have all contributed to a shifting paradigm in conceptualizing posttraumatic stress. Theories and treatment approaches have changed radically from the early-20th-century models of psychopathology and intrapsychic conflict. These models often stressed therapeutic interpersonal neutrality and the separation of mind and body; they developed in a social climate that ignored or repressed the role of gender, race, class, and family socialization patterns in psychological development. I review some ways in which this early development of psychology informed many of our ideas today and ask the reader to continue to question our current assumptions about practice.

Many clinicians will agree that the field of posttrauma therapy promotes an integrative approach. Traditional psychodynamic and cognitive-behavioral approaches are informed, refined, and enhanced by feminist, relational, and family systems, along with energy psychology and body psychotherapy models. Likewise, our clients consult with complementary and alternative medicine practitioners for their symptoms of trauma. These methods include acupuncture, massage and bodywork, nutrition, herbal medicine, curanderismo, homeopathy, shamanism, yoga, and naturopathy. It is essential to develop a common language for communicating across disciplines and to know what each discipline has to offer.

Traumatic stress is a mind/body health problem, and some of the methods of treatment presented in this book have come of age during the revolution in our understanding of the complexity of mind/body interrelationships. Traumatic experiences, the unexpected catastrophes of life, affect the functioning of the whole being physically, emotionally, mentally, and spiritually. Underlying the integrated functions of mind/body/spirit, in humans and animals alike, are natural rhythms that pulsate, oscillate, and vibrate. This book focuses on how these natural rhythms are affected by trauma and how they may be restored by a holistic approach to recovery. Nature provides the means of restoring a person's psychobiological equilibrium, often lost through trauma, even as it also precipitates traumatic stress through floods, storms, and quakes. To elucidate how nature can balance the psychophysical seesaw characteristic of traumatic stress, I draw on ancient and contemporary cross-cultural principles of medicine and healing and show how they integrate naturally with psychotherapy and counseling.

The ancients of many cultures considered gaining control over the autonomic nervous system, and hence over the mind, integral to health. Many of these traditions arose out of the need to heal people from experiences of trauma, ubiquitous throughout history. Traditional initiation rites are often stressful and were developed as inoculation strategies to increase resiliency among community members exposed to life's traumas. For this reason, I examine the role of ritual. My purpose is to provide a context for understanding and integrating the conventional principles of the psychotherapeutic treatment of traumatic stress within a holistic framework. The holistic principles presented are rooted in accessing and utilizing the natural life force of dynamic, changing polarities. As this book explains, these concepts are ubiquitous across cultures and prominent in both Western and Eastern medicine. Normally, these natural, oscillating rhythms are orchestrated synchronistically by the central and autonomic nervous systems. In response to trauma, these rhythms are severely disrupted, affecting all aspects of healthy function.

The healing rhythms of nature that I explore here occur at three interrelated levels: the innate capacities within the individual, or forms of psychophysiologic and biological self-regulation; the rhythms exchanged in relationships between people, in particular between practitioner and client, which can occur at many levels, including one that I call somatic empathy; and the rhythms and resources that people derive from the natural world.

Treating survivors of trauma is both labor-intensive and a labor of love. The practitioner is constantly challenged to listen and to believe as well as to avoid unduly influencing or interfering. She is compelled to do no harm, to self-reflect, and to protect the safety and boundaries of the professional relationship. Posttrauma therapy is a young and growing specialty that draws from all the human service disciplines and calls upon the enduring universal values of human connection, community, and restoration of social supports. Practitioners will find here principles that undergird the task of any professional working with a survivor of trauma; sustaining hope, patience, compassion and courage through the often arduous but rewarding task of helping another human to heal.

Ultimately, healing is a mystery of the heart. The capacity to listen deeply requires access to the voice of one's own heart. A client's story emerges from strength and courage and must be met with clarity, creativity, and equal courage on the part of the practitioner. The joint partnership of constructing a meaningful narrative requires a practitioner to extend the range of her own voice. To help a client to locate herself, to enter fully into an embodied life, requires that I locate my own life and physical body as the foundation for my work. Since the ideas in this book arose during the early years I spent living and working in Mexico, I begin my discussion of trauma in the setting that nourished my discoveries about the healing rhythms of nature.

HOW TO USE THIS BOOK

A companion website provides a variety of resources to complement this text. There you will find a Continuing Education (CE) exam, appendices containing exercises from this book for both therapist and client in downloadable handout format; audio, a list of hyperlinks to resources, additional reading including nutritional protocols and recipes, a glossary of terms used in the book, and discussion questions for each chapter to stimulate further study for practitioners, their students and interns.

http://www.routledge.com/books/details/9780415807500/

1　The Rhythms of Life

He who makes an enemy of the earth makes an enemy of his own body.
—Popol Vuh: The Mayan Book of the Dawn of Life

I began touching people therapeutically in Mexico beginning in 1973, when I lived in the jungle. The first people who came to my *palapa*, which over-looked the Pacific, did so because they were in pain or hoped to relax their mental strain. *Palapas* (thatched roof houses) get their name from the coconut palm fronds, which the men cut, measure, and then drag down the mountain by burro. They weave and tie the fronds to handcrafted ironwood frames, forming a huge straw hat over an open space. The roof sways and lifts with the wind, breathing and absorbing moisture like nostrils, mediating the inside and the outside, which often merge during the wet months in the jungle.

I first worked with the Mexican-Indian women, whose childbirths I had at-tended and who, because of the burden of multiple births and relentless work under the sun, often looked more like the mothers of their husbands than their wives. They brought their widely flattened sore feet and muscular shoulders, indented by ironlike bras that cut deep grooves across the top of the trapezius muscle. We shared village gossip and they were both honored and amused at my interest in traditional ways of healing. They told me that dried cow dung rubbed on the head cured baldness and then offered to demonstrate on me. They told me stories they had themselves been told about snakes that lived near the *cascadas* (waterfalls) and were known to be so dexterous that they could unzip your dress, get inside your pants, and get you pregnant. As we got to know each other better, they shared the trauma of their lives and loss of fam-ily members to the hardships of the jungle and sea: drowning, tetanus, amoebas exploding the liver, rape, and incest.

The women brought their little ones in when they fell off horses and hit their heads or fell out of hammocks or over the bow of the 40-horsepower *pangas* (small, outboard-powered fishing boats) as they hit the beach on an off wave, bruising the ever so tender sacral bone at the base of the spine. The men came in for treatment accompanied by their wives for the first session, just to make sure nothing untoward would take place. They sought relief for a variety of problems that usually had to do with occupational accidents: diving and the residual effects of too much nitrogen in the blood. Some of the men did not survive. Those who did rarely went diving again, nor did they ever walk the same way again.

One night Ezekiel, an ever-grinning, gold-toothed carpenter whose wife Ophelia made the best coconut pies in the village, was brought ashore. I was asked to his house where he lay in bed, inert and unable to urinate. I arrived amid the crowd of neighbors ritually dropping emergency money onto his bed, body, and clothes. No one needed to mention that the delay in reaching the charter medical flight to Acapulco, still an hour's boat ride away over rough, full-moon seas, was due to lack of money. And while Zeke's pockets were stuffed with pesos, his pants half on, belly exposed and scarred from previous battles unknown to me, I placed needles in his abdomen according to Chinese tradition to help him relax while he waited.

They said it was a miracle that Zeke survived. When he returned from the decompression chamber in Acapulco, 800 miles down the coast, he came for treatments and I worked on the firmly muscled legs, which betrayed him only when he walked. As I pressed hard into the core of his calves and the fascia lata on the outside of his thighs, he talked of the terror when he and his cousin Ruben were diving deep in search of sleeping lobsters and the 100-foot hose choked off the air at the same moment the *panga* stopped vibrating because the generator in the hull faltered too long.

A few years later, after my thatched roof house had burned to ashes, Ezekiel had fully recovered. I asked him to take a buzz saw and climb the 200-foot coconut palm, which grew out of the center of the *zalate*, the dying strangler fig tree that had given my house its name years before I arrived. Invariably, when passersby saw this symbiotic site for the first time, they would cry out with an astonishment that reflected their confusion about which tree came first, the *zalate* or the coconut. It was difficult without knowing their history, or nature itself, to tell by looking. The coconut tree appeared to rise straight up out of the middle of the fig; or was it the other way around? Like other parasitic intertwinings, the exact nature of their relationship was not evident upon first glance. However, the strangler fig, whose shape and skin was like elephant bark, got its name because its seed popped down into the coconut, which was already quite old when it ineluctably became host. The fig then proceeded to wrap its way around the palm and the landscape, its roots ruling the hectare of hillside like huge thighs and forearms elbowing their way through all my attempts to make steps from rocks on the path to my door. Twice yearly, the *zalate* bore fruit, dropping a hailstorm of green fig balls as quickly as they popped open. They tapped upon my roof around the clock, appreciated only by the bats, which, as they made their nightly pass through my house to see if the *raicimo* (bunch) of bananas were perchance left uncovered, left their sticky, fig-filled droppings on my floor.

The *zalate* died a slow giant's death after the fire in 1983 and I missed cleaning up the thousand-figged parade that signaled another half year gone by.

However, with the shade veil from the *zalate* gone, along with the garden, which now served as a burial ground for the shards of my grandmother's heat-burst china, there was sunlight all day long. This prompted Ophelia to bring me several flowering bushes from her garden, some of them sweet red and pink cabbage roses to plant near my gate, which needed some color and a stubborn hold on its steep, eroding side. The last of the *zalate*'s roots did not dry and merge with the earth it had faithfully served until 6 years after the fire. By then, the roses were strong and in full bloom, and Ezekiel was able to climb the Coco to amputate the remaining limbs of the *zalate*. Then, sadly, as he shimmied down the smooth gray skin, he had to cut the still-live coco herself, who now without the support she had grown accustomed to, threatened to topple over onto my new roof whose dried fronds, barring another unthinkable fire, would not need replacing for another 4 years.

The majestic coconut is never willingly toppled, being the source of roof, oil, milk, and soap. But when she comes down her bounty is as rich in death as in life. My neighbor Alicia asked for two dozen thick, rippled *rajas* (slices) whose scratchy center resembles the scruff of the nut; when faced inside the house and tied side by side, they form walls against the sea air. The *zalate* then proffered her base as a table and six 3-foot stools for my kitchen, with four more going to Ophelia and Zeke. Finally, we ate her heart of palm, to which we added oil and lemon and gave thanks as we ate.

Over the years, I have come to understand the story of the *zalate* and its hold on my imagination in several ways. The relationship between the coconut palm and the huge strangler fig is not unlike the psychic intertwinings that occur between abuser and abused. One, a strangling parasite, takes over; the other, helpless to stop it, loses its identity and fears surviving on its own.

Having talked with many victims of psychological abuse or physical domination, I hear repeatedly the metaphor of possession and suffocation. One woman said of her long-term childhood abuser: "I felt that he was like a virus that had entered my bloodstream—and would be there always—even if and when I recovered."

The need to cut the coco down even after it had stood for several years after the *zalate* had burned speaks to the inevitability of loss endured as a result of the psychological surgery that is often required to recover. Like the limbs wrapped around the coco, personality development takes place around and within the traumas of early life; extrication is never clear-cut and always entails loss. Yet the story of the *zalate* and the coco also contains images of hope. With the shade cover from the *zalate* now gone, I had a sprouting garden and light streaming into the house. Ezekiel recovered from his own pain and near paralysis to live a full life. The trees are also an image of healing; vines wrapped (helix-like) around a bold straight stalk remind me of the caduceus, also called the staff of Hermes, the cross-cultural icon of medicine and healing, representing the nervous system, the helix of descent into the underworld and ascent to the light of awareness (see Figure 1.1). Like the tree, the caduceus is a universal image of change and transformation.

The Caduceus

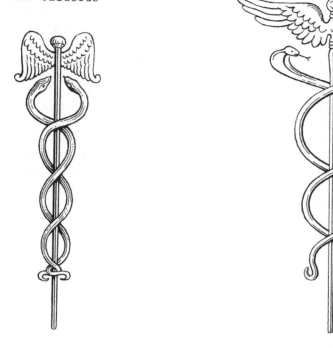

Figure 1.1 Caduceus.
Source: Adapted from *Polarity Therapy: The Complete Collected Works* (Vol. 1), by R. Stone, 1987, p. 33. © 1987 by CRCS Publications. Reprinted with permission.

This image of the caduceus is of a strong central pole around which are wrapped two serpents that, representing consciousness, are a universal image of transformation, a symbol of shedding old skins. The caduceus serves as an image of the nervous system for many cultures. It is the central spinal cord and autonomic ganglia in allopathic neuroanatomy. For the kaballists, the mystical sect of Jews, it takes form as the tree of life. The *Borgia Codex* of Mexico displays a serpent and a centipede entwined, signifying the polarities.

For the Hindus this same image portrays the Kundalini, the she-serpent who sleeps at the base of the spine in the sacrum (sacred bone) and is awakened by the practice of yoga, bringing awareness and integration to the individual. Its closest analog in Western depth psychology is the unconscious. In the Greek myths, it is Hermes, messenger of the Gods (known by the Romans as Mercury) who travels to the underworld at the behest of Zeus to bring back the maiden Persephone (Kore), who is abducted and raped by her Uncle Hades. This myth of death and rebirth through pain and suffering is the enduring theme of healing from trauma. The caduceus symbolizes the archaic knowledge of yogis and shamans who access innate psychophysical capacities that are rooted in controlling the autonomic nervous system. Thus the individual controls the staff (spine) of Hermes by sending and receiving messages from the (inner) gods and transmutes the underworld of pain into the freedom of a chosen life.

THE RHYTHMS OF LIFE

The experience of trauma is as old as humankind itself. One can only imagine the early hominid's evolutionary urgency to fight or take flight—the response that lies at the heart of the autonomic nervous system's response to trauma by increasing heart rate, blood flow, and oxygen levels. The emotion of fear primes the pump and energizes hormones like epinephrine, which clear the mind, sharpen the vision, and light the fire that excites the muscles to move quickly out of harm's way. Escape from trauma brings (temporary) victory; the alternative is to freeze in inaction, leading to injury or death. Some of the functions of the autonomic nervous system, so called because they are "automatic" and instinctual, include the pulses of heart and breath, the periodic flush of gastric acids, the electrical charges of the brain, and the eliminative waves of bowels, which open and close the ileocecal "gate." In health, these organs function rhythmically without conscious control, giving rise to the ebb and flow of life. The heart beats 40 to 220 beats a minute, depending on condition and activity. The breath cycle is completed 4 (yoga) to 20 times (aerobic) a minute, more or less. The brain emits electrical signals measured in cycles per second or hertz (Hz)—from approximately 2 to 3 cycles per second during deep sleep (delta), 4 to 7 Hz (theta), 8 to 12 (alpha), 13 to 18 (beta), and above 40 (gamma). Whether electroencephalographic (EEG) patterns actually drive the brain (Evans, 1986) or consciousness drives EEG, as the renowned psychophysiologist and physicist Elmer Green insists (E. Green, personal communication, November 11, 1998), we have capacities to gain control over these processes. This forms the basis for self-regulation practices such as meditation or the modern technological equivalents, biofeedback, neurofeedback, or devices such as musical or electrical stimulation devices that entrain alpha-theta brainwave patterns. Though traditionally it has been believed that people are in one or another state, such as alpha or theta at one time, it is now thought that people are in all EEG frequencies simultaneously in different areas of the brain (Wilson, 1993).

This timely ebb and flow of natural rhythms—the polarized dynamic of opposites represented as sleep and wakefulness, inhalation and exhalation, systole and diastole, beta and delta—are severely compromised by trauma. An understanding of the methods that affect consciousness and brainwave function is useful for both the clinician and client in the treatment of trauma. Many of the methods proposed in later chapters address ways to regulate states of consciousness and their brainwave analog for the purpose of healing.

Healing is rooted in the rhythms of reconciliation: forces that shift shapes as inner and outer, darker and lighter, hotter and colder, closer and farther. In Chinese tradition and many tribal cultures, the rhythms of the body are considered one with the natural world. Disease or illness results when one becomes out of balance with these forces. Practitioners of traditional Chinese philosophy and medicine refer to these dynamic polarities as yin and yang, mediated by a transitional third energetic phenomenon, called Tao or Balance. Rooted in concepts dating back to the 4th century BCE, yin and yang originally referred to "the shady side of the hill" and "the sunny side of a hill," respectively (Unschuld, 1985, p. 55). Ayurvedic medicine, the practice of Hindu culture in ancient India dating as far back as 2300 BCE (Amber & Babey-Brooke, 1966; Rao, 1968) refers to these concepts as the *ida* and *pingala*, mediated by a third principle, *shushumna*. Both traditional Chinese and Ayurvedic healers refined the art of diagnosis by palpating the pulses—considered to be the rhythms that are "witness of the soul" (Amber & Babey-Brooke, 1966). Randolph Stone, the cranial osteopath and originator of polarity therapy, detected three pulses, which he called frog, snake, and swan (Stone, 1986), ostensibly due to the quality of the feel and movement of blood and the significance to health of these variations.

The reconciliation of opposing yet complementary forces has particular import for the treatment of posttraumatic stress. Trauma disrupts endogenous rhythmic cycles of function and cyclic movement is replaced by a state of fixation. This is well established by conventional medicine as reflected in the concepts of autonomic hyperarousal and hyper/hypoactivity of the hypothalamic-adrenal-pituitary axis. The autonomic nervous system is composed of three branches, the sympathetic, the parasympathetic and the most recently identified, the ventral vagal complex or social nervous system (Porges, 2011). The restoration of balance within these forces—whether called yin and yang, ida and pingala, or parasympathetic and sympathetic—is at the heart of Eastern and Western medical traditions alike.

Rather than sustaining the natural flow of oscillating life force, trauma causes autonomic fixation and loss of the normal range of body regulation, including extreme, uncontrollable cycles of response characterized by opposing fluctuations of cognition, behavior, and kinesthetic perception. It is the restoration of flexible movement instead of fixation by balancing these extremes that poses the central dilemma for the integrated mind/body treatment of traumatic stress. Drawing on this theme from both Eastern and Western traditions and identifying and balancing the oscillating rhythmic functions provides a unifying approach to holistic therapy.

The convergence of traditional and contemporary healing approaches that has been catalyzed during the past 30 years has antecedents from a rich historical past. The centrality of balance to healing is found in the word *medicine*, which derives from the Sanskrit verb *maa*, meaning "mother" and "to measure," and *manya*, meaning "to move back and forth; to align in the middle" (Frawley, 2001). The principal icon of balance in both Eastern and Western modes of medicine is the caduceus, or staff of Hermes. It signifies the reconciliation of polarized forces in nature and, in the 16th century, became the alchemical symbol for the evolution of the soul. It serves as a visual icon of modern medicine and represents the role of the autonomic nervous system in the transmutation of trauma.

Alchemy was the first chemistry of the Western world concerned with the esoteric science of transmuting the two subtle energies of sulfur and quicksilver into gold. Alchemy's subtext is the esoteric art of transforming spiritual consciousness. It was mercury, associated with the mind, that facilitated the action between the two energies. The alchemical association with mercury was the mind, "forever darting about to and fro" (Evans, 1986, p. 116). Gaining control over unconscious or automatic functioning is the basis of many healing traditions, and is an important key to healing the mind/body split that results from trauma. The caduceus is first associated with the Babylonian mother goddess about 4000–1955 BCE and is later identified with Ishtar—the goddess of fertility, love, and war—and Aphrodite, the Greek goddess of love and beauty. The word *caduceus* is Latin, derived from the Greek word *Kerykeion*, which is associated with the word *keryx*, meaning "herald" or "to announce" (Friedlander, 1992). Hagens (personal communication, January 7, 1996) suggests the etymological *kha* (Egyptian aspect of body) = ca, duo = du, duco = duceus, or "two spirits lead the body." The Greek messenger of the Gods, Hermes (the Roman god Mercury), was said to have come upon two snakes fighting and then threw his staff between them to break up the fight. The snakes became entwined around his staff. Herein lies the symbolism of the "mind," which serves as the "messenger" of the gods. The mind mediates the fight between the dual nature of the self: the conscious and the unconscious, the automatic and the regulated. The upright staff represents *shushumna*, the cerebrospinal energy. The two snakes represent dual functions of the autonomic nervous system: the sympathetic and parasympathetic. Each serpent "represents part of the double chain of ganglion of the sympathetic nervous system descending on each side of the spinal column" (Stone, 1986, p. 37). The right serpent is the sun essence, the heat, yang, or pingala; the left, the lunar essence, is the cooling yin or, ida. The last open loop and the lower part of the staff are the cauda equina. The crossing over in the center denotes the nerve plexus, called cakras or chakras, in Hindu esoteric anatomy. These plexi or nerve networks link the cerebrospinal and central nervous system with the peripheral system (Stone, 1986, p. 33). The wings of the caduceus represent the two hemispheres of the brain. The knob at the center signifies the pineal body, the most subtle endocrine gland of Western anatomy and until recently considered by modern scientists to be vestigial. The pineal is referred to as the crown chakra wheel by the Hindus and together with the pituitary is considered the "third eye." The name *pineal* comes from *pinus*, or pine cone, so named because of its shape. It sits in the center of the brain and develops during the fifth week of human embryonic life. Though we assign blame these days to Descartes for the schism of mind and body that we are so desperately trying to unify, Descartes considered the soul to reside in the pineal gland:

> In man, [*sic*] the brain is also acted upon by the soul, which has some
> power to change cerebral impressions just as though those impressions in
> their turn have the power to arouse thoughts, which do not depend on the
> will. . . . Only (figures of excitation) traced in spirits on the surface of
> (the pineal) gland, where the seat of the imagination and common sense
> (the coming together of the senses) is. (Gregory, 1987, p. 724)

The pineal gland is referred to as the third eye perhaps because it was believed to be an organ similar to the external third eye found in some fish and
lizards. Regarded as the organ of intuition in occult philosophy, it is seen as
"the link between objective and subjective states of consciousness, the visible
and invisible worlds of nature" (Hall, 1972, p. 210). The pineal is also represented in the Greek stories of the one-eyed Cyclops (Hall, 1972) by which the
higher ego can see into one's own animal nature; it is also referred to as Janus,
the two-faced god and keeper of the gates of the sanctuary. Sansonese (1994)
writes:

> The pineal body is located under the fornix—Latin for vault—a structure
> of the midbrain described in anatomy texts as having four pillars. Both the
> fornix and the pineal body are closely hemmed in from above by the optic
> thalamus. Thalamus means wedding chamber in Greek. (p. 154)

This "wedding" or union Sansonese refers to is between the conscious and
unconscious mind. The pineal gland has long been considered by spiritual ad-
epts to be the center for the transmutation of consciousness. Its location in the
center of the brain is the focus of yogic, Taoist, and alchemical meditation,
all of which focus the external eyes on the third, inner eye in the center of the
forehead.

The relationship of the eyes to consciousness and exercising the eyes is
an ancient method of healing. Eyes have long been considered integral to
self-awareness and lead to access of the unconscious as evidenced throughout cross-cultural meditation and shamanic "insight" practices. The eye is
associated with Mercury (Hermes) as the catalyst for alchemical transformation (Reader, 1994). According to Hirschberg (as cited in Reader, 1994), the
Greek name for pupil, *pupilla*, also means child, or *kore*, meaning "the young
maiden." Kore is another name for Persephone, who leaves the darkness of the
underworld of trauma to emerge into the light of rebirth. One of the traditional
meanings of the story of Persephone and Demeter signifies the worship of
agriculture and its seasonal rhythms. Persephone goes underground during the
fall, taking with her the light and vegetation, and reemerges with the budding
of new flowers in the springtime.

Nature is redundant and provides abundant ways to alter vision in states of
consciousness. The psychiatrist Rick Strassman (2001) suggests that mystical experiences, with their accompanying visual and auditory hallucinations,
are biologically mediated by the pineal secretion of the "spirit molecule,"

N,N-dimethyltryptamine (DMT), a serotonin/melatonin analog. He further proposes that microsecretions of DMT are released into the bloodstream during the rapid eye movement (REM) stage of sleep, accounting for the vivid imagery and visions of dream states. Whether DMT is sourced from within the brain or via the shamanic vision-producing "spirit vine" brew, "ayahuasca," used ritually by indigenous peoples of South America and more recently by seekers of healing from the addictions, there can be no doubt that visions mediated from within or without play a central role in healing.

The symbolism of the eye is common to both Europe and Mesoamerica in a variety of ways. Building on Wasson's research (1980), Ott and Wasson (1983) identify the "disembodied eye" as a motif found throughout Mesoamerican pre-Columbian art as well as in ancient (3500 BCE) Crete. Both of these ancient cultures incorporated entheogenic substances into their ritual traditions, suggesting that the "disembodied eye" represents the seeker under the visionary influence of mushrooms that produce psilocybin, which has a high affinity for serotonin receptors in the brain. Another theory about Persephone's journey is that she "disappeared" while picking flowers, and her ingestion of an entheogen, a common practice among women of ancient Greece, took her to the underworld. "There can be no doubt that Persephone's abduction was a drug-induced seizure" (Wasson, Hofmann, & Ruck, 1978, p. 13). The hallucinogenic Psilocybe mushrooms were known to the Nahua of Mexico as *teonanácatl*, the "divine mushroom," because they caused one to see or know god. Whether serotonin/melatonin is enhanced by entheogens or selective serotonin reuptake inhibitors (SSRIs), brain chemistry is central to trauma recovery. Gimbutas (1989) suggests that the eyes and the serpent are joined together in Europe in an ancient association:

> The pictorial association of eyes with snakes and the representation of eyes by snake coils was a widespread phenomenon in both southeastern and Western Europe. . . . The dynamism of the serpent is a very ancient and recurrent human preoccupation. The snake's energy, it was believed, was drawn from water and the sun. (p. 58)

The caduceus image is also found in Mesoamerica, where Tlaloc, the Nahua rain god and counterpart to Hermes (de Santillana & von Dechend, 1969) has two serpents passing through his eyes and, like the caduceus, signifies "en-light-en-ment." That is, the capacity to "see" or to be the seer comes with transformation mediated by the eye/brain connection (see Figure 1.2).

Practices such as crossing the eyes induce a parasympathetic state by the oculocardiac reflex (Reader, 1994) and may explain the neurological mechanism underlying Kriya yoga, meditation and yoga poses that focus the eyes on the bridge of the nose, cross them, or roll them into the back of the head. For example, the lion pose (*Simhasana*) of Hatha yoga involves focusing on the, ājñā or third eye while sticking out the tongue, one of children's favorite yoga poses and one that relieves tension. It is noteworthy that this pose is very

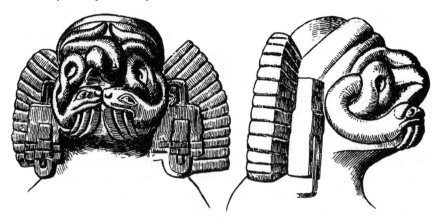

Figure 1.2 Tlaloc, the Nahua Rain God (and counterpart of Hermes).
Source: Adapted from *Hamlet's Mill: An Essay Investigating the Origins of Human Knowledge and Its Transmission Through Myth,* by G. De Santillana & H. Von Dechend, 1969, p. 291. © 1969 by David R. Godine, Publisher, Inc. Public Domain.

similar to an Olmec (1100–600 BC) figurine depicting the "Tattooed Jaguar," which Goodman (1990) suggests represents a ritual trance posture leading to metamorphosis. Meditating while crossing closed eyes triggers the *vagus* nerve and slows the heart, setting the stage for a trance state. Eye movement desensitization and reprocessing (EMDR) is a variation on these ancient practices. The saccadic eye movement is hypothesized to mimic REM brain states during sleep, when information is undergoing processing and integration. The Tibetan practice of using specialized exercises is another consciousness-training aid that involves a complex process of crossing and moving the eyes throughout the range of motion allowed by the orbital muscles (see Figure 1.3).

Tibetan monks use it to improve physical sight as well as inner vision or insight. The Dutch yogi Jack Schwarz, who collaborated with Alyce and Elmer Green at the Menninger Foundation Voluntary Controls Lab in Topeka, Kansas, has outlined similar exercises designed to increase the activity of rods and cones in the retina and increase the range of light spectrum visible to the human eye (Schwarz, 1980), thus enabling vision beyond the normal spectrum. Eyes are also central to developmental psychology and object-relations theory. The mirroring gaze of a loving parent upon an infant ensures early bonding and healthy development and, through the meeting of the eyes, the "windows of the soul," trust is learned and exchanged between the practitioner and client during the course of therapy.

The importance of light to health is of particular concern to the trauma survivor and cannot be overestimated. Light is central to the synthesis of melatonin, which in turn converts to serotonin. Low levels of serotonin and melatonin are bidirectionally associated with posttraumatic stress disorder (PTSD), depression, sleep disorders, rage and irritability, seasonal affective

Figure 1.3 Tibetan eye chart.
Source: Public Domain.

disorder, premenstrual syndrome (PMS), and bulimia. People who are chronically stressed are often sensitive to bright light, especially sunlight, and often wear sunglasses for protection, though this is the opposite of what is helpful.

THE PINEAL GLAND, CIRCADIAN RHYTHM, AND LIGHT

PTSD, chronic pain (fibromyalgia), and sleep problems are all characterized by circadian rhythm imbalance (Scaer, 2001). In order to understand more fully the disruption of rhythm and time perception caused by trauma, it is useful to explore briefly the role of circadian rhythm, light, and the pineal gland. Circadian rhythm underlies the endogenous, 24-hour cycle of human function. The central nervous system regulates adrenal function via the hypothalamic-pituitary-adrenal axis, and stress disrupts the balance. Circadian rhythm is present each step of the way in this process. Circadian rhythm and the resulting secretion of endocrine hormones and neurotransmitters depend upon the transmission of light through the eyes. We can observe the importance of this function to human health by the disruption that occurs as a result of crossing multiple time zones (jet lag), and by working at night and sleeping by day ("the night shift"). The pineal gland holds the largest stores of serotonin in the brain. Melatonin is synthesized from serotonin. Melatonin is central to the cycles of sleep and wakefulness, puberty, and the aging process. Melatonin levels are lower in some women with Pre Menstrual Syndrome (PMS) and mood disorders, such as seasonal affective disorder (SAD) and seasonal PMS are common among peoples living in the northern hemisphere where light is scarce during many months of the year (Shafii & Shafii, 1990). Exposure to 2 hours of bright evening light resulted in decreased levels of depression among women with PMS (Gallagher, 1993). Elevated levels of stress hormones have been observed in people sitting under cool white lights, leading the German government to ban these lights in hospitals (Liberman, 1990). Exposure to standard cool white-light fluorescent fixtures has been implicated in hyperactivity, fatigue, irritability, and attention deficits in some schoolchildren (Liberman, 1990). Increasing exposure to natural sunlight or full-spectrum indoor lighting can ameliorate these symptoms (Liberman, 1990; Shafii & Shafii, 1990).

Human rhythmicity depends upon internal clocks or timekeepers called *zeitgebers* (*zeit* = time; *geber* = givers) or pacemakers. The pineal responds to the pacemaker functioning in the suprachiasmatic nuclei (SCN) in the hypothalamus by secreting melatonin. When light is received through the retina of the eyes, it travels via the retinohypothalamic tract to the SCN and a signal is sent to the pineal gland (Strassman, 1991). Ablation or scarring of the SCN eliminates circadian rhythm. Trauma causes a disruption in the function of the hypothalamus (Rossi, 1986) and attachment traumas of early life result in low levels of melatonin (Reiter & Robinson, 1995; Shafii & Shafii, 1990). Research on the psychobiological substrates of traumatic stress and the symptoms of anxiety, depression, and insomnia implicates depletion of serotonin, which metabolizes to melatonin. The most popular antidepressant medications for traumatic stress, obsessive-compulsive disorder, PMS, and eating disorders are the selective serotonin reuptake inhibitors (SSRIs), drugs such as Luvox (fluvoxamine), Paxil and Paxil CR (paroxetine), Prozac (fluoxetine), Celexa (citralopam), Lexapro (escitalopram), Effexor and Effexor XR (venlafaxine), and Zoloft (sertraline) (Friedman, Davidson, Mellman, & Southwick, 2000). SSRIs prevent the reuptake of serotonin in the brain by "pooling" more at the brain synapse. By understanding the biochemical disruption of rhythmic cycles in trauma, we may find a path by which circadian rhythms can be reestablished by stimulating natural processes using nature's methods.

One example of nature's therapy is found in the mineral lithium; as lithium carbonate, it is often used for the treatment of bipolar disorder. However, the long-term use of lithium carbonate has serious side effects. It lengthens the circadian rhythm (Moore-Ede, Sulzman, & Fuller, 1982), accounting in part for its positive effect on mood disorders. A 10-year study of lithium in the drinking water of Texas counties found that the incidence rates of suicide, homicide, rape, and addictive behaviors were lower in counties where the drinking water was lithium-rich (Schrauzer & Shrestha, 1990). Lithium is naturally present in water supplies including streams and hot springs throughout the hemisphere. Traditional soaking pools such as Ohanepecosh, also known as Laughing Springs by the local Indians, run at the base of Mt. Tahoma and have long served indigenous peoples of the Northwest, just as Mexican Indians have soaked, giggled, and healed in hot springs outside of Guadalajara and throughout the southwestern United States.

THE RHYTHMS OF TIME

Time stops for the victim of trauma. The traumatic moments of the past become suspended like a still life that keeps flashing the same pictures before the mind's eye. These somatosensory images, called flashbacks, repeat themselves visually, aurally, and kinesthetically. They intrude upon the present, making it difficult and often impossible for the sufferer to locate herself or himself in time. This inability to distinguish the present moment from the past is experienced simultaneously in a variety of ways. Often, the person feels as if it were the past but knows cognitively that it is the present. Yet the patient nonetheless shakes physically, in fear of the present or future. The experience of the past trauma is like a nagging, subcutaneous patch of poison that prevents the future from coming into focus. The future under normal circumstances is a vista filled with hope and plans; in trauma it is frozen by the past, for the future holds the ever-present fear that the past will be lurking. Thus the victim lives in a timeless *bardo*, a netherworld, of neither here nor there, what the Hindus call the world between worlds where the soul travels during its passage through the various stages of consciousness at death. Not actively participating in the rhythmic and changing course of life can lead to a sense of being swept along, as if out of control. Thus it becomes apparent how a person's spirit can be crushed by trauma. The perception and experience of time provides the scaffolding about which meaning and purpose in life are constructed. Ordinarily, change is given coherence and meaning as we actively participate in the passage of time. This personal and collective creation of coherence and form refers to spirit, a word whose Greek derivation *respir* means, "to breathe." In Hippocratic texts we read, "Breath is the rhythm of life" (Fried & Grimaldi, 1993). In trauma, the individual "holds the breath in fear" or "has the wind knocked out of him," as his spiritual scaffolding shakes and sinks under the burden of traumatic experience. Our individual rhythms and the perception of time are also interpenetrated with those of other human beings, animals, and the natural world.

The movements of seasons and stars intersect and interact with human rhythms. Life is oscillation and pulsation, attuned to and entrained by the geomagnetic pulse. The predominant frequency range of magnetic pulsations around the earth is about 7.8 Hz (cycles per second) (Evans, 1986). The 7.8-Hz brainwave frequency is the boundary between alpha waves and theta waves just on the border of waking up or falling asleep. The theta wave is frequently observed in the EEG patterns of experienced meditators, who learn to pass from alpha to theta without falling asleep (Evans, 1986), and is considered the brain wave analog of creativity and reverie (Green & Green, 1989). It is this rhythm of 7.8 cycles per second (cps) that is often sought during the treatment by neurofeedback of PTSD and traumatic brain injury (TBI). One study using neurofeedback demonstrated that the 7.8-Hz frequency brought about the largest cerebral blood flow of all frequencies between 1 and 60 cps (Budzynski, Budzynski, Evans, & Abarbanel, 2008). These low-frequency oscillations are also theorized to serve as a carrier for anomalous logarithms or telepathic information (Mishlove, 1993), which may account for why meditators and healers who cultivate this frequency are often known to have extraordinary or anomalous cognition (Krieger, 1979). In addition to its role in transducing light for the regulation of circadian rhythms, the pineal gland has been suggested as the physical organ of consciousness (Strassman, 1991) in the human body, believed to transduce geomagnetic and bioelectromagnetic energies (Mishlove, 1993; Roney-Dougal & Vogl, 1993). For this reason, it has also been suggested as the organ of anomalous cognition, which is "the acquisition of information about the world without the mediation of the known senses" (Spottiswoode, 1990, p. 91). Although the neural mechanism of information transduction is not understood, a correlation between anomalous cognition and very low frequency magnetic field variation has been demonstrated. The stress of certain electromagnetic frequencies has a profound effect on the functioning of the pineal gland and the nervous system in general. Exposure to electromagnetic frequencies associated with computers and other electronic devices at the 60-Hz range decrease melatonin levels (Reiter & Robinson, 1995). The neural structures of mice showed stress responses after exposure to 60-Hz fields, and another study using short-term exposure to low-intensity nonthermal microwave radiation produced alterations in benzodiazapine receptors. These receptors play a central role in mediating anxiety and stress (Becker, 1992). Valium is a benzodiazapine used for the treatment of anxiety; it is also well known to suppress REM sleep and cause nightmares.

The most important wavelength for melatonin effects appears to be the green to blue-green range of the light spectrum (Strassman, 1991). This suggests the role of nature's colors—the ocean, woods, trees, and sky—in regulating melatonin levels in the brain. It is possible that pavement and buildings, along with the destruction of trees, promoting loss of contact with the blue-green light of the forests and ocean, obscure the wavelength of the light spectrum most beneficial for brain function. Might chronic stress and separation from the rhythms of nature, including alterations in exposure to light in the industrialized world, be altering the capacity of the brain to secrete and regulate the neurotransmitters? Is the epidemic in industrialized societies of depressed, anxious, and traumatized people (and children) who take exogenous chemicals to regulate brain chemistry related to light source degradation? What then are the effects of artificial light and longer workdays on the brain receptors and neurohormones that govern our states of consciousness? Wehr (1992) conducted experiments in which men slept under light conditions and sleep cycles similar to those of prehistoric peoples who were exposed to only 10 hours of light daily, living in the middle latitudes in the middle of winter. The "modern" men experienced increased levels of melatonin and a "waking trance" for several hours during the middle of the night. This waking trance provided the ancients with a restorative, creative, and affiliative experience with the cosmos, much as dreams provide access to the inner self. What does it mean to large societies of people if they no longer have these experiences? When the men in the study returned to their previous schedule, their melatonin decreased and their chemistry and sleep returned to their usual patterns. How has industrialization and the widespread exposure to artificial low-frequency electromagnetic fields contributed to the unremitting levels of stress and chronic depression observed in the United States and other industrialized countries? Might we consider this environmental trauma: the natural world traumatized by an overwhelming disruption of natural cycles and rhythms? Coupled with interpersonal violence and intergenerational trauma, perhaps we are left without much resilience to respond to trauma and realign with nature's subtle healing forces.

What is the relation, then, between humans, animals, and the cycles of nature and the rhythm of healing? The oldest methods of healing are the hands. Manual stimulation of the superior cervical ganglia (the autonomic nerves in the neck) produces changes in pineal biochemistry that mimic changes produced by environmental light-dark cycles (Strassman, 1991). This may provide clues to the role and efficacy of therapies like massage, chiropractic, and osteopathy, which are known to stimulate the nervous system (and increase serotonin levels) via manipulation of the cervical spine. Gentle contact on this area of the spine often induces deep relaxation and sleep (Stone, 1986, 1987) and is part of established bodywork protocols to reduce stress, pain, and depression (Korn, Loytomaki, Hinman, & Rÿser, 2007; Korn, et al., 2009).

Upon descending to the Paleolithic caves of Pech Merle in southern France, I was astounded to see the (female) red-ochre hand prints alongside a column of eight red dots and a sacral image, leading me to wonder how the ancients of 15,000 years ago thought of the spinal column and touch (Figure 1.4). Could this be the first representation of the energy centers later depicted as the Kundalini and the caduceus by the Hindus and Greeks respectively? Gimbutas (1989) has suggested that the hands and feet of these caves symbolize the "touch of the Goddess," and together with representations of animal and insect life, "promote the process of becoming" (p. 306). Hagens (personal communication, January 7, 1996) asks whether the Cro-Magnon practice of ingesting human brains included ritual ceremonies designed to utilize psychoactive, cerebrospinal substances, ostensibly contributing to the process of becoming. This suggests the ancient role of organs and ritual foods used to balance our systems that I explore later on.

For ancient peoples, survival in a world where nature had the upper hand was rooted in their capacity to regulate their connection to nature and its

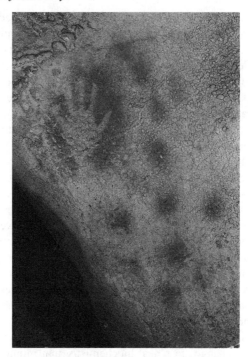

Figure 1.4 Pech Merle: cave painting of human hands in southern France, 18,000–
        27,000 BCE.
Source: Public Domain.

complement of unforgiving forces. This is contrasted by much of contemporary civilization (civil = cities), which is marked by attempts to dominate even
the most extraordinary of natural forces.

SUMMARY

The social dissociation from the exogenous rhythms of nature embedded in
modern life often prevent access to a wide array of curative methods that directly reset our natural rhythms. Trauma is a universal and historic experience;
we are often called upon to "envision" healing for our clients, even when they
cannot do so. As we contemplate how the metaphors and methods we use today
derive from an ancient legacy, redrawn by time and "progress," we likewise
place in perspective the evidence so often required in our halls of practice.

2 Paradigms of Dis-ease and Diagnosis

> The Oedipus complex does not have the status of the cholera bacillus, or even the charmed quark.
>
> —Robin Lakoff

Dis-ease communicates distress, and distress occurs within complex sociocultural and political environments. The cluster of symptoms now diagnosed as posttraumatic stress have a long history of other names, the most enduring of which is hysteria. For centuries, hysteria was a catchall diagnosis that encompassed many of the symptoms we now recognize as posttraumatic stress disorder (PTSD).

In this chapter I provide a brief historical context for understanding the diagnostic categories of hysteria and traumatic stress and thus consider how paradigms of the past continue to influence our attitudes about PTSD today. In the late 20th century, the Vietnam War veterans returned home and fought for recognition of the debilitating symptoms resulting from the disasters of war. This occurred simultaneously with feminists' demands that the reality and effects of violence in the domestic sphere be recognized; thus a new official mental health nosology created the category of PTSD in 1980. Today clinicians continue to clarify new categories of dis-ease resulting from exposure to traumatic experiences. These include disorders of extreme stress (complex posttraumatic stress disorder, or CPTSD) (van der Kolk & Pelcovitz, 1999) and developmental trauma disorder (van der Kolk et al., 2009).

In this chapter I shall

- explore hysteria as a diagnostic category
- explore the names and symptoms assigned to what today is called posttraumatic stress
- identify ways in which culture informs diagnosis
- explore how gender attitudes influence diagnosis

TRAUMA AND ANCIENT CULTURE

What indeed was traumatizing to ancient peoples? What did these events mean and how did the people respond? How do their rhythms resonate within us? Moreover, what secrets of theirs survive in forms that may be meaningful to us today? For the ancients, measuring shadows, coping with the vagaries of the unexpected, and making the unseen visible must have taken a sharp turn for the worse when surprise, shock, or terrific loss first occurred at the hands of other humans.

Large-scale invasions, massacres, and cultural upheavals resulting in slavery and population shifts occurred with the Kurgan invasions of "old Europe" around 6000 years ago (Eisler, 1988). The first city-states in Mesopotamia developed about 3500 BCE as a protective response to organized violence, during the same period that the first caduceus is identified with the mother goddess Ishtar in Mesopotamia. Thus emerged the important link between traumatizing disorders and civil and domestic violence that plague patriarchal cultures (Herman, 1992). Eisler (1988) dates the emergence of the "dominator model" in Europe to approximately 4000 BCE with the Kurgan migrations that led to warfare and dominance over women and children. It was, "not metals per se, but rather their use in developing ever more effective technologies of destruction that played such a critical part in what Engels termed 'the world historical defeat of the female sex'" (p. 46). Around 700 BCE, Homer detailed the tolls of war on men, the symptoms of which are indistinguishable from PTSD in veterans today (Shay, 1992). In *The Iliad*, the Trojan prince warrior Hector says "war is men's business" and grief is universal in its cry when Hector is killed and Andromache recites, "all the days and nights of my weeping for you" (Blundell, 1995, p. 48).

HYSTERIA IN ANCIENT GREECE

A woman of ancient Greece felt a terrible pressure rise from her belly, move up through her diaphragm, and suffocate her speech as it rose to her throat. The diagnosis made by Galen, the 4th-century physician, was *hysterike pnix*, or the "suffocating womb." *Hyster* ("womb") becomes woman's emblematic attribute, and "hysterical" is codified into the language of her reproductive organs. The suffocating uterus was deemed the cause of hysteria, for which prescriptive treatment included massage, venesection (the cutting of veins), and inhalation of essential oils, whose healing properties altered moods, much like today's aromatherapy. The early association of possession, paralysis, and prostration with woman, womb, and hysteria codified the origins of medical misogyny that permeated rational Greek culture and later became a tenet of Western medicine (King, 1993). The consensus was that women's sexuality was at the root of her pathology. Martial (CE 40–104) refers to women feigning hysteria in order to have intercourse with young doctors (then an established treatment for hysteria) (King, 1993). This reference to women's sexuality is reintroduced in the 16th century when Van Forest states "some women simulate hysterical suffocation by imagining sexual intercourse" (King, 1993, p. 62). The relationship between women and hysteria becomes linked to demonology during the Middle Ages (Rousseau, 1993). Evidence is found in their (perverse) sexuality, their worship of nature, their use of hallucinogenic plants, and their communion with animals (all of which ran counter to church canons). They were "witches" who "talked to plants and animals" and whose "numbed patches of skin" signified their demoniacal nature (Rousseau, 1993, p. 98). (This tactic is apparently alive and well in the 21st century: A woman who brought criminal charges against a psychiatrist who had drugged and raped her was similarly subjected to questions about whether she "talked to plants and animals," as though that might signify that she was what? A witch? A lying borderline personality? [anonymous, personal communication, November 30, 2003]). The names may change but the need to define behaviors as female, sex-crazed, aberrant, and dangerous to male clinicians persists. Hysteria, witchcraft, shell shock, borderline personality, and posttraumatic stress are among the names used to describe similar behaviors and reactions.

Loss of speech and its various permutations throughout the ages is an important symptom of hysteria. Today, while men and women do not as often lose function of their vocal cords, they often have "no words" to describe their experiences. As their trauma stories begin to emerge, they are often so disjointed or frightening that they are often disbelieved. The current clinical vernacular focuses on girls and women "finding their voice" or not losing their voice (Belenky, Clinchy, Goldberger, & Tarule, 1986). This cultural phenomenon is rooted in patriarchy's deafness to the experience of girls and women (Gilligan, 1982; Gilligan & Richards, 2009; Machoian, 2006; Taylor, Gilligan, & Sullivan, 1997). The loss of voice by abuse survivors is quite literal: many are threatened with death or the death of loved ones if they speak the truth. Still others are murdered.

HYSTERIA IN CHINA AND JAPAN

The symptoms and diagnosis of hysteria were not limited to ancient Greece and the Western world. Ilsa Veith (1965), one of the first contemporary historians of hysteria, suggests that the major difference between hysteria as a diagnosis in Western cultures and the hysteria of possession that grew out of the animistic religions of Japan and China was that no "personal responsibility (and therefore no blame) attached itself to the victims of such forces" (p. 75; see Figure 2.1).

In ancient China, scholars theorized that mental disorders developed as a result of the imbalance of yin and yang in those who had lost the way of the Tao or the correct path of life. According to Veith (1965), popular beliefs in Asia centered on the supernatural. Stories told of how "apparitions, described

Figure 2.1 Hysteria treatment in China, 1834.
Source: From Sokei Dojin, Byo ka su chi ["Health Handbook for the Patient"], 1834. Adapted from *Hysteria: The History of a Disease,* by I. Veith, 1965, p. 93. © 1965 by The University of Chicago Press. Reprinted with permission.

as hairy, of monstrous height, and intent on violating maidens were known to cause madness in those that beheld them" (p. 78). Perhaps these "supernatural" stories were but cloaks around the reality of assault in women's lives. Cures, carried out by the *Wu,* a male or female healer designated to expel evil influence, took the form of exorcisms during the T'ang dynasty (CE 618–906). One such cure describes a daughter with "fits of madness, in which she sometimes inflicted injuries on her own self, jumping into fire or running into water; and meanwhile she became pregnant as if by sexual commerce with men" (Veith, 1965, p. 79). The healer, Veith (1965) goes on to say, "succeeded in inducing a deep slumber in the patient and the next day she was released from her obsession" (p. 78). This clinical picture shares much in common with the symptoms of today's victim of sexual assault who reenacts the trauma through self-mutilation or prostitution. Likewise the reference to "inducing a deep slumber" may refer to hypnotic induction.

HYSTERIA IN EUROPE

The psychological revolution in the 19th century began with the stories of "hysterical" women: Marie Wittman ("Blanche"), Bertha Papenheim (Anna "O"), Ida Bauer ("Dora") are among those whom their doctors—Martin Charcot, Josef Breuer, and Sigmund Freud, respectively—chronicled. The stories these women told contributed to an understanding of how the (unconscious) psyche finds a language through somatic expression. This led to Freud's theory called *somatic compliance*. The body (soma) tells the story that the mind (psyche) cannot put into words. However, these women's stories were filtered through the reigning paradigm of the day, so that much was misunderstood and ultimately (re) codified into the male model of development that underlay psychoanalysis. Rousseau (1993) suggests, "What had presented itself to the Greeks as a fiery animal, an overheated, labile, voracious, and raging uterus, was now, in Charcot's world, diagnosed as a sexually diseased and morally debauched female imagination" (p. 185). Numbness is the signature of hysteria, along with demons, traumatic stress, and countertransference!

The 17th-century physician Thomas Sydenham, who adhered to the adage *vis medicatrix naturæ* ("the healing power of nature"), brought hysteria out of the dark ages of its demonological associations when he observed "hysteria imitates culture" (Rousseau, 1993, p. 102). However, even though concepts of woman have changed since medieval times and the Victorian era, images and beliefs about her debauchery still influence the practice of modern medicine; the resulting persecutions have merely become mutated.

Charcot, the 18th-century neurologist, referred to the bodily signs of hysteria as "the stigmata," drawing on the Inquisition's *stigmata diaboli,* which marked the bodies of witches. Charcot wrote:

> You will meet with [simulation] at every step in the history of hysteria, and one finds himself sometimes admiring the amazing craft, sagacity, and perseverance which women, under the influence of this great neurosis, will put in play for the purposes of deception—especially when the physician is to be the victim. . . . It is incontestable that, in a multitude of cases, they have taken pleasure in distorting, by exaggerations, the principal circumstances of their disorder, in order to make them appear extraordinary and wonderful. (Gilman, 1991, p. 61–62)

In 1909, Carl Jung wrote Freud for advice about his patient, Sabina Spielrein, a brilliant young Russian Jewish medical student whom Jung had diagnosed with hysteria. Spielrein was perilously distraught by Jung's betrayal of her as a result of his adulterous and abusive sexual relationship with her. Jung wrote, "Since I knew from experience that she would immediately relapse if I withdrew my support, I prolonged the relationship over the years. . . . She was, of course, systematically planning my seduction, which I considered inopportune. Now she is seeking revenge" (Kerr, 1993, p. 218). To which

Freud replied, "The way these women manage to charm us with every conceivable psychic perfection until they have attained their purpose is one of nature's greatest spectacles" (Kerr, 1993, p. 219).

Pierre Janet, the French neurologist whose work on hysteria and dissociation has been resurrected as seminal (van der Kolk, 1989), suggested while lecturing at Harvard in 1920 "that hysteria was frequent only among the French women, which astonished nobody, on account of their bad reputation" (as cited in Showalter, 1993, p. 314).

Today we continue to see this type of misogyny manifested in modern medicine. For example, the majority of patients diagnosed with borderline personality disorder are women. The diagnosis is also assigned to patients who have been (sexually) abused by practitioners, and it has been used as a defense in the courts. In spite of some gains within the professions, clinicians still use language that betrays pervasive professional attitudes about the role of women's sexuality as a cause of their own "betrayal." Gutheil (1989) writes,

> Patients with borderline personality disorder are particularly likely to evoke boundary violations of various kinds, including sexual acting out in the transference-counter-transference. Patients with borderline personality disorder apparently constitute the majority of those patients who falsely accuse practitioners of sexual involvement. (p. 597)

If what Gutheil means by "the majority" is the estimated 4% of accusations that are false (Pope & Vetter, 1991) compared to the estimated 10% of male psychiatrists and psychologists who sexually abuse their patients an average of eight patients each (Burgess, 1981; Holroyd & Brodsky, 1977), then the patriarchal arbiters of rectitude are in trouble. The use of borderline personality disorder continues to serve as the diagnostic bucket into which "difficult" (read "annoys the clinician") patients are placed. Isn't it time that we rename this diagnosis for what it is: CPTSD?

MALE HYSTERIA

Rather than representing a static syndrome, hysteria has long been considered a dynamic disease category that reflects the mores and attitudes of the culture around it. Yet precisely because hysteria (and CPTSD) mirrors culture back to itself that societies across national and cultural boundaries have a difficult time recognizing and believing the realities of the victimization. While hysteria has been associated predominantly with women over the centuries, it has also been recognized in men, though often under different names during different epochs (Showalter, 1993) and also associated with men's "aberrant" sexuality. The recognition of victimization and hysteria among men has also been fraught with denial. Today, denial about male victimization is reflected in the dearth of data about male sexual abuse (Holmes & Slap, 1998; Lisak, 1993), which is estimated to occur in 16% of men (Dube et al., 2005), and the ongoing failure to protect young men from institutionalized abuse, as seen in recent cases involving clergy, sports coaches, and school teachers. Yet, throughout the ages male hysteria could not be denied. The voiceless permutations of distress were expressed through the centuries via somatic complaints wherever culture was pitted against gender and behavior. Showalter (1993) suggests:

> [T]hroughout history, the category of feminine "hysteria" has been constructed in opposition to a category of masculine nervous disorder whose name was constantly shifting. In the Renaissance, these gendered binary oppositions were set up as hysteria/melancholy; by the seventeenth and eighteenth centuries, they had become hysteria/hypochondria; in the late nineteenth century they were transformed into hysteria/neurasthenia; during World War I they change yet again to hysteria/shell shock; and within Freudian psychoanalysis, they were coded as hysteria/obsessional neurosis. (p. 292)

But after all, hysteria was a wom(b)ans disease—or was it? The term *shell shock* was coined during World War I by the British psychologist Charles Myers, who observed that the symptoms of hysterical women were similar to the "amnesia, impaired vision and emotional distress among British soldiers in France" (Showalter, 1993, p. 321).

Since the dominant nosology leading into fin de siècle medicine suggested that hysteria was a feminine complaint, the soldiers' symptoms had to be traced to a physical injury, from the shock of an exploding shell (Showalter, 1993). Gender-role oppression and the stoic silence it demanded hurt men as well. Myers' diagnosis was rejected for years, and he often tried to defend many of these war-wounded men from execution by the military they had served. As Showalter (1993) points out, "If the essence of manliness was not to complain, then shell shock was the body language of masculine complaint, a protest against the concept of manliness as well as against war" (p. 325).

Karl Abraham, a prominent turn-of-the-century analyst, articulated that shell shock or male hysteria occurred in "passive, narcissistic, neurotic and latent homosexuals" (Showalter, 1993, p. 324), an attitude that even persists today as Iraqi and Afghan war veterans request alternative diagnoses from their psychiatrists, like "sleep disorder," rather than being labeled with the "unmanly" and career-ruining PTSD. Even as these 19th- and early-20th-century practitioners identified the realities of victimization, most wilted under the various influences that distorted their theories and therapeutic outcomes. W. H. Rivers, a psychologist and anthropologist known for his compassionate and successful treatment of traumatized World War I British soldiers (Showalter, 1993, p. 325), may have had a more accurate understanding of "difference" than did doctors such as Abraham because his own somatic symptoms (Showalter, 1993) and homosexuality had prepared him for the turf of difference.

Fears of (sexual) difference embedded in the culture of Victorian Europe defined diagnosis as well as treatment. These fears extended beyond gender relations to its epistemic twin of "race" relations. Psychiatric historian Sander Gilman (1991) has written persuasively about how anti-Semitism profoundly affected Freud's development of psychoanalysis, suggesting that Freud's internalization of oppression as a Jew was projected onto women. While Freud was attempting to unravel the mysteries of the symptoms of hysterics in the early 20th century, he was subject to the pressures of his professional milieu. He was ridiculed and threatened with censure by his colleagues when he suggested that hysteria was based in early childhood sexual trauma (Kerr, 1993). The effect of this scorn was overdetermined, however, for, as Gilman (1991) points out, Freud was already an outsider by virtue of being a Jew.

The dominant European attitude of the era was that Jews (especially Jewish men) were subject to hysteria by virtue of their (genetic) effeminacy and debased (incestuous) sexuality (Gilman, 1991). As it turned out, Freud's mentor, neurologist and hypnotist Martin Charcot, was a rabid anti-Semite. This revelation compelled Freud to distance himself from Charcot, who also believed in the traumatic sexual etiology of hysteria. Freud charted a separate course: he went to study with Bernheim, a Jewish physician living outside of Paris whose hypnotic technique was devoid of the theatrical showmanship that ultimately discredited Charcot. However, this, in turn, contributed to Freud's negation of his seduction theory and led to his theory that little girls (and boys) desired their parents sexually (the Oedipus and Electra complexes)—a ruinous idea that resulted in more projection than proof. Gilman (1991) suggests that indeed much of the basis for psychoanalytic theory and, I suggest, the modern reaffirmation of woman-as-hysteric rests with Freud's displacement of his own sense of pathology (the "otherness" of being a Jew) onto woman-as-other. From a somatic perspective, Gilman points out, this took form in the psychoanalytic method of lying on the analytic couch and being "heard" and not "seen," for the couch assured that one lay (or sat) out of visual, physical range. With the late-19th-century diagnostic emphasis on "looking like a Jew," the substitution of verbal (for somatic) language assured a "raceless" neutrality. The results, however, pervade current clinical attitudes to this day; Lakoff and Coyne (1993) suggest that "The short-sightedness of those parts of psychoanalytic theory that concern female psychology not only so permeates the whole that it is impossible to expunge, but also informs and indeed creates the backbone of all individual, insight-oriented therapies" (p. 38).

During the early 20th century, the symptoms of hysteria (which was the predominant neurological disease of the time) were separated into several categories. Today, these symptom clusters may be found in PTSD, somatization disorder, dissociative disorders, conversion disorder, anxiety disorder, borderline personality disorder, and histrionic disorder. The current consensus that hysteria no longer exists is taken up by Rousseau (1993) who, following Sydenham's lead, argues that hysteria imitates culture, suggesting that it may just have donned a new costume:

For if the medieval hysteric's geographical locale was the farm on which she toiled and conversed with family and neighbors; if the Georgian woman's world was the Ranelagh and Vauxhall Gardens where she paraded, and the town and country houses where she sought pleasure; if the Victorian woman's interior purview was the dark bedroom in which she pretended to see nothing at night, certainly not her husband's naked body and aroused sexual organs; then today these locales have not disappeared but have been transformed into other social locations: the health club, the bedroom with its paraphernalia of biofeedback machines, the practitioner's waiting rooms, the pain clinics, even the beauty salons and ever-proliferating malls. Paradoxically, it seems today that these are the locales of health and therefore of pleasure and happiness. Yet it may be, upon closer observation, that they are merely the places where modern hysteria—what our vocabulary calls stress—has learned to disguise itself as health. (p. 100)

There are two intersecting historical parallels to this current ethos of controversy: women's rights and the publicity about child sexual assault. Controversies about "false memories" and "memory implantation" by practitioners in both the United States and Europe, which predominated in the 1990s, are an example of society's denial of the prevalence of sexual abuse. When Freud first presented his theory of the etiology of hysteria in 1896 to the Society of Physicians in Vienna, Krafft-Ebing said that it sounded "like a scientific fairy-tale," and still others accused him of suggesting the repressed memories of abuse to his patients (Kerr, 1993, p. 38). Of this dilemma Kerr (1993) writes, "Understandably, Freud's claim [of the abuse etiology of hysteria] raised epidemiological eyebrows. Hysteria was enormously widespread. It simply did not seem possible that child abuse had occurred in every case" (p. 37).

As today, these struggles took place in an era in which feminism and the women's rights movement posed a challenge to patriarchy (Tomes, 1994) (not to mention the animal rights/vegetarianism and abstinence movements that feminists were involved in, alongside the rise of spiritualism among women).

However, with Freud's disavowal of the seduction theory came the ammunition for a counterrevolutionary backlash; it deflected feminism's challenge back on its proponents by labeling them neurotic and maladjusted and sending them to the analyst's couch.

Solomon (1995) suggests that contemporary mental health professionals deny sexual abuse because "[they] are unable to transcend prevailing cultural and social norms; they are 'blinded' by professional theories; and because of a fundamental human difficulty in comprehending and acknowledging our own vulnerability" (p. 271). Challenging the taboo of silence about incest in the early 1980s, psychiatrist Judith Herman (1981) raised social and professional awareness about the long-term effects of exposure to violent physical and sexual behaviors. Socially codified denial behaviors in private practice, various agencies, the government, school gyms, and church confessionals continue unabated. This denial extends to the failure to deliver treatment and disability benefits to Iraq and Afghan War veterans. Soldiers report lack of treatment, overmedication, and a focus on unnecessary therapies. There is no dearth of denial; Gulf War syndrome, the assignment of the bipolar disorder diagnosis to children living in violent homes, and the failure to systematically identify the role of violence as the major cause of mental illness and then to act on it. This is a startling sort of denial given the findings from a large U.S. health maintenance organization that 34% of those surveyed reported adverse childhood events such as emotional, physical, and sexual abuse (Edwards, Holden, Felitti, & Anda, 2003) and that these exposures predicted significantly increased rates of PTSD, depression, completed suicide and suicidality, mental illness, psychotropic drug use, addiction, and early death.

SUMMARY

Conceptions of disease and clinical practice are informed and prescribed by cultural context. Understanding the cultural and historical foundations of current diagnostic and treatment methods adds breadth and perspective to understanding and utilizing current nosology. Categories of the past reflect cultural beliefs and continue to exert influences on current diagnostic and treatment paradigms. Our tendency as clinicians is to be ahistorical and to consider our current techniques as the "latest and greatest" and the older categories as ancient and ignorant. But do our diagnostic categories still reflect cultural and gender biases? How does gender bias merge with cultural expectations to determine treatment? An understanding of the impact of socially ordained beliefs helps to prevent a static definition of the individual and the community and contributes to more humane and effective treatment. Knowing the history that has led to the current paradigm of treatment may lead us to question whether current approaches to assessment, diagnosis, and treatment are in the best interest of our clients. This awareness may also prevent us from repeating patterns of power imbalances, betrayal, and poor treatment resulting in iatrogenic disease. By identifying some of the recent cultural and historical foundations that have informed treatment over the past hundred years, I have contextualized the range of theories, often invisible or unspoken, and the often compartmentalized assumptions in the practice of therapy.

3   Soma and Psyche

The truth about our childhood is stored up in our body, and although we can repress it, we can never alter it. Our intellect can be deceived, our feelings manipulated, our perceptions confused, and our body tricked with medication. But someday the body will present its bill, for it is as incorruptible as a child who, still whole in spirit, will accept no compromises or excuses and it will not stop tormenting us until we stop evading the truth.

—Alice Miller

Posttraumatic stress disorder (PTSD) is the quintessential mind/body *disorder* that alters physiological, biological, and psychological homeostasis. Clinical observation and research point to a complex pattern of dysregulation that impairs physical, affective, and cognitive function. People who have been traumatized often present with distressing and frequently intractable psychosomatic symptoms, often without knowing consciously that the source of their symptoms is the trauma they experienced.

In this chapter I shall

*   define the psychosomatic symptoms of PTSD
*   define state-dependent memory, learning, and behavior
*   explore how understanding the somatic mechanisms underlying traumatic stress facilitates effective treatment
*   explore the role of hyperventilation and anxiety
*   identify the role of integrative methods to balance endogenous opioid systems to restore balance and health

Knowing how the body-mind interacts in trauma enables the practitioner to make appropriate and timely referrals for somatic therapies, including psychopharmacological support; provide psychoeducational support to the client about somatic symptoms and help the patient to gain greater control over her or his life; and identify patterns and strategic methods to reduce physiological hyperarousal and state-dependent memory and behavior.

THE BIOLOGY OF TRAUMATIC STRESS

Traumatic stress precipitates a condition of physiological and psychobiological imbalance in the nervous system and in the endocrine, immune, and neuropeptide systems. In response to trauma, the individual experiences two coexisting responses that are conditioned by a hyperaroused nervous system: one of over-reaction (*intrusion*) and one of underreaction (*avoidance/numbing*) to actual or anticipated environmental stimuli. The victim must cope with conditioned responses that are psychophysiological in nature and if untreated are often impossible to control. These stimuli serve as reminders of the trauma through sensory cues; visual, auditory, and olfactory perceptions that trigger profound reactions that often perplex nontraumatized people who witness them.

Whatever the source of arousal, a response cycle of intrusive and avoidance symptoms are set in motion by the *autonomic nervous system* (ANS). ANS dysregulation is a major hallmark of posttraumatic stress. The traumatic battles that were experienced externally have now been recorded internally. These experiences are engraved semantically and somatically by a host of known and as yet undiscovered mechanisms. These include *stress hormones* that are believed to encode memory, learning, and behavior while an individual is in a particular state of consciousness. This is referred to as *state-dependent memory, learning, and behavior* (SDMLB), discussed below in more detail.

In addition to psychosomatic symptoms, a victim of trauma often copes with changes to self-identity resulting from the lifelong effects of direct assault on the physical body. This may include disabilities such as loss of a limb, loss of capacity to bear children, and chronic pain. Grief over loss of control, self-efficacy, and functional capacity will be a recurring theme in treatment. The constant state of hyperarousal is akin to always being "on edge" and results in a compensatory response that includes avoiding activities and numbing feelings and sensations. This overreaction to subsequent normal life events, as well as withdrawal from active participation, becomes a secondary loss—often a diminished or lost future. Successful treatment includes integrating approaches that enable the client to achieve better affective and somatic self-regulation. In order for one to do this, it is helpful to understand how the ANS responds to extreme stress.

THE STRESS RESPONSE

The *stress response* may be considered to exist along a continuum: eustress, stress, and traumatic stress. *Eustress*, a term coined by Dr. Hans Selye, refers to a positive stressful challenge, such as that occurring when one is training for a marathon or learning the skills required for a new job. It is the interaction between the normal daily stressors of life with the individual's personality that defines the way a person perceives and makes meaning of the event. This leads to the perception of the stress as positive or negative and determines the degree and type of response. For example, normal life events such as attending school, job changes, relocation, and marriage or partnerships all constitute normal life stressors that, when coupled with an individual's sense of control and purpose, determine the level of perceived stress. The perception of an event coupled with individual control, self-efficacy, and meaning influences psychological and physiological function.

Stress traumatizes when stressors overwhelm the individual's capacity to cope. The idea that every person has a "breaking point" is based on the observations of the limits each person has to withstand stress. Traumatic stress is by definition an experience in which the survival of the whole organism is at stake, and it responds with the "fight, flight, or freeze" response. Selye first defined this *general adaptation syndrome* as a predictable psychophysiological response to stress. During experiments he began in the 1930s, Selye observed that after rats were exposed to toxic chemicals or frigid waters, they displayed a common psychophysiological reaction arising from the nervous system's response to overwhelming shock. Regardless of the type of stressor, he found a common generalized reaction in the animals. This included gastrointestinal, cardiovascular, and respiratory dysfunction as well as generalized depression and distress. Selye observed a three-stage response resulting in psychosomatic dysfunction: *alarm*, *resistance*, and *exhaustion*. In the first stage of alarm, stress results in ANS arousal and activation of the sympathetic response. The adrenal glands release the hormones epinephrine and norepinephrine, causing a rise in heart rate, blood pressure, and respiration, which enables the organism to fend off the threat. These stress hormones are considered to play an important role in the storage and consolidation of state-dependent memory, learning, and behavior.

Roger, a 45-year-old Iraq War veteran, illustrates the experience of hyperarousal and state-dependent memory, learning, and behavior: "I live near an auto mechanic and when I am in my yard gardening and hear a car backfire, I dive for the bushes. My wife finds me crouching and shaking and crying, afraid to come out because I am surrounded by mortar fire. When will this go away?" The hypervigilance and exaggerated startle response prevalent in PTSD occurs because the "alarm" keeps going off and is in a constant state of alert to the perceived threatening environmental stimuli. Such a stimulus may take the form of a *trigger* that reminds the person of the original threat. For Roger it is the backfire of a car that sounds like mortar fire; for Joelle, it is seeing a man in daylight walking toward her, reminiscent of the man who raped her. Joelle, a 25-year-old student who was raped 2 years earlier, said: "Whenever I'm walking down a street and a man is walking towards me on the sidewalk, my whole body starts to shake uncontrollably. I tell myself this is the present, but at these moments my body is living in the past and the past rules my life."

However, a trigger may also be unrelated to the trauma and nonetheless stimulate a sensory response. It is theorized that stress hormones released as a result of arousal by an external reminder of the original threat are the biological substrates of the *flashbacks* experienced during the intrusive cycle. The alarm stage is followed by the resistance stage, in which the repetitive psychosomatic response to the stress leaves one "stuck in a groove" (Rossi, 1986) and unable to break free of the cycle. Following a period of hyperactivity, "fighting off" the stress, the individual may lapse into the third stage of exhaustion, which is associated with chronic unresolved symptoms. This stage includes symptoms such as the chronic tension and pain associated with whiplash months and years after an accident or chronic pain in the pelvic region years after a rape. Selye was the first researcher to demonstrate the relationship between exposure to stress, the subsequent release of hormones from the hypothalamic-pituitary-adrenal (HPA) axis, and the development of psychosomatic symptoms. Building on Selye's work, researchers have determined that exposure to stress and violence during childhood adversely alters the normal development of the brain and nervous system. This results in enduring changes in psychophysiological and psychobiological function and leads to chronic health problems throughout adulthood.

GROUP STRESS AND TRAUMA

Exposure to chronic stress occurs among individuals but also in members of whole groups by virtue of their membership in those groups. *Cultural trauma, historical trauma,* and *intergenerational trauma* are among the concepts used to explain the response to chronic stress among whole groups of people and how this stress is "transferred" across generations.

The roots of the terms *historical trauma* and *intergenerational transmission of trauma* derive from observations that the sociohistorical experience of cultural groups exposed to prolonged stress and suffering resulting from war, genocide, and interpersonal violence initiates the transfer of a psychobiobehavioral template of stress to offspring and subsequent generations. Seminal research conducted among survivors of the Nazi Holocaust (Nadler, Kav-Venaki, & Gleitman, 1985; Yehuda et al., 1998), the Khmer of Cambodia (Sack, Clarke, & Seeley 1995), American Indians (Brave Heart & DeBruyn, 1998; Whitbeck, Adams, Hoyt, & Chen, 2004) and Aboriginal peoples (Gagne, 1998) of North America and Mexico (Korn & Rÿser, 2006) suggest identifiable patterns of trauma and health dysfunction. Historical trauma among American Indians refers to the legacy of colonization and genocide (Whitbeck et al., 2004) resulting from European contact in the United States, the effects of which persist today. The clinical significance of historical trauma and its interaction with exposure to lifetime traumatic events is unclear and has yet to be definitively elucidated. Recent attention has focused on the putative role of historical trauma in neurobiological function (Yehuda et al., 2005) and there is some evidence that these effects may be passed on at the neurobiological developmental strata via the HPA axis system (Gunnar & Donzella, 2002) in response to intergenerational trauma (Strickland, Walsh, & Cooper, 2006).

Yehuda et al. (2005) found that adult offspring whose parents had survived the Nazi Holocaust and developed PTSD had low cortisol levels, which reflects Selye's exhaustion stage discussed earlier. The intergenerational transmission of trauma is hypothesized to occur during the prenatal (Yehuda et al., 2005) and perinatal stages of neurobiological development (Schore, 2003), suggesting a theoretical basis for the predisposition to the development of PTSD, depression, anxiety, and vulnerability to substance abuse (Schore, 2003). Yehuda et al. (2005) report that infants born to mothers who were pregnant and developed PTSD following their witnessing of the 9/11 terrorist attack in New York City had significantly lower cortisol levels, suggesting the effects of HPA axis transmission on the fetus.

Persistent changes in HPA axis are also seen in subjects with a history of child sexual abuse and with current major depression. Findings from several studies suggest that chronic exposure to traumatic experiences reduces hippocampal volume and that hippocampal damage extinguishes the awakening cortisol response without affecting the rest of the cycle (Buchanan, Kern, Allen, Tranel, & Kirschbaum, 2004). Understanding how stress affects the 24-hour cortisol rhythm is central to making intervention decisions using nutritional and botanical medicine, which can restore cortisol rhythm and balance.

Acute stress can enhance *immune* function whereas chronic stress suppresses it (McEwen, 2000). Chronic stress produces cardiovascular reactivity, immunological, and endocrinological alterations (Kiecolt-Glaser, Malarkey, Cacioppo, & Glaser, 1994) and can negatively affect functional and structural changes in the brain (McEwen, 2000) and increase immune activation in patients with PTSD. For example, it is well known that stress can trigger autoimmune diseases such as rheumatoid arthritis and that people with PTSD are at higher risk for autoimmune function (Boscarino, 2004). In these cases the body's immune system becomes hyperreactive, reflecting another level of systemic overreaction to perceived threat after the trauma events have passed. People with PTSD have increased levels of inflammatory markers and increased reactivity to antigen skin tests (Pace & Heim, 2011). The separation of nonhuman primate offspring from their mothers (grief) results in suppression of the immune system (Cohen, 1994). Widows and widowers are also found to be more susceptible to illness during the first year of the loss of their spouse. By contrast, high levels of social attachment behaviors appear to be protective against immunosuppression (Cohen, 1994).

The effects on health arising from traumatic stress experiences is amplified by the effects on immune function of actual exposure to chemicals, biological, and waste products that occurred following the nuclear accident at Chernobyl in the Ukraine, the Gulf War, and the inhalation of toxic fumes and air by rescue workers following 9/11. These effects are further exacerbated by the delays or denial of the reality of exposure by government officials that affect victims. Of the psychological and physical trauma of radioactive exposure at Hanford nuclear reservation, which was built on Yakima Indian land, Russell Jim, director of the environmental restoration project, says:

> During the fifty years of Hanford's operation, especially when the [Columbia] river was highly contaminated by the reactors, the site managers knew full well that tribal people were being poisoned. But they simply ignored their own data and considered us to be expendable. (R. Jim, personal communication, September 12, 2004)

Environmental disasters are multifocal and not easily addressed in the short or long term (Goldstein, Osofsky, & Lichtveld, 2011). The mental and physical health effects of the stress of environmental contamination on Akwesasne Mohawk Indian land persist (Papadopoulos-Lane, 2010) and interact with historical trauma. The *Exxon Valdez* oil spill in Prince William Sound, Alaska, in 1989 ruined traditional fishing grounds and food sources for Alaska natives and nonnatives alike. Hurricane Katrina struck the southeastern United States in 2005, displacing thousands from their homes. The effects of such events are felt for years and often generations. The *Deepwater Horizon* oil spill of 2011 affects ways of life, with bodies, lands, seas, and wildlife exposed to neurotoxins. The stress does not end with the event but persists for years during attempts to receive reparations, which are often inadequate. PTSD is not limited to residents of these locales. First responders, both residents and visitors, are also vulnerable to high rates of secondary trauma. With the increasing contribution of climate change to adverse effects resulting from disasters, the trauma clinician will be called upon to work with individual, social, and environmental causes of PTSD, which affect all aspects of individual and community function and induce extensive losses. Addressing loss and grief as a result of disasters is central to coping and surviving with trauma.

ALLOSTATIC LOAD

The observations that repeated exposure to stress whether it begins in childhood or as an adult accumulates and builds over time in life, affecting physical and mental health has led to a model called *allostatic load*. This term refers to the price the body pays for being forced to adapt to the effects of chronic stress (McEwen & Seeman, 1999). Some evidence suggests that discrimination may constitute a stressor and contribute to a greater lifetime allostatic load. Cumulative stress across the lifespan is often associated with low socioeconomic status and chronic discrimination and may provide a psychophysiological model for minority health disparities. Conversely, social relationships mitigate the effects of allostatic load (Seeman et al., 2004). This intersects with a new model of stress response called "tend and befriend."

TEND AND BEFRIEND: THE FEMALE STRESS RESPONSE

Whereas Selye's model has dominated the concepts of stress response, Taylor et al. (2000) posit a female stress response model they call *tend and befriend*. This model adds a dimension to the flight or flight/freeze concept and suggests that women (and other female animals) respond to stress by engaging in activities of care and connection; that is, tending to the care of offspring and family and engaging in behaviors that support social connection, affiliation, and attachment. Oxytocin is considered to mediate this response biologically; it is the main neurohormone responsible for social behaviors and empathy. It is produced primarily in the hypothalamus and is associated with the thymus and immune function (Carter et al., 2005) and has been shown to promote trust and well-being while reducing fear and blood pressure (Ishak, Kahloon, & Fakhry, 2011; Olff, Langeland, Witteveen, & Denys, 2010). Dysfunction of the oxytocin system may be involved in the development of PTSD (Ishak et al., 2011), and combining nasal administration of oxytocin with cognitive-behavioral therapy may be useful in reducing fear, enhancing safety and trust, and supporting social engagement (Ishak et al., 2011; Olff et al., 2010). As I explore later, the role of touch therapies and massage and interaction with animal companions has many positive effects for treatment, including the increase of oxytocin levels. This research reinforces the importance of integrating psychological, biological, and physiological methods and their role in establishing and maintaining strong social connections for the recovery of physical and psychological health after trauma.

LEARNED HELPLESSNESS

What happens, however, when we cannot successfully fight or take flight or tend and befriend to ameliorate shock or stress? As clinicians, we often treat individuals who appear unable to act in their own best interest or to mobilize to make change, and we wonder how to help them. The research of Seligman and Beagley (1975) may illuminate the complex response to *inescapable stress*. During the 1960s, Seligman and Beagley conducted experiments on dogs that were exposed to stressors they could not escape. During the experiments, in order not to receive an electric shock to their paws, Seligman and Beagley trained the dogs to jump from one compartment in a shuttle avoidance box to an adjoining compartment. When the dogs had mastered this task, a barrier was put in place that prevented some of them from escaping the shock. Two thirds of the animals could not escape and subsequently experienced depression, disruption of normal defecation, and generalized distress. More interestingly, when the barriers were removed and the animals were allowed to move to escape the shock, they remained passive. Seligman and Beagley's attempts to drag the animals across the grid to teach them that the cage was now safe were only partially successful: some dogs mastered the new task but most remained helpless and passive. This loss of self-efficacy and the inability to mobilize change observed in the animals exposed to inescapable stress, which mimicked depression and posttraumatic stress in humans, led to the development of a behavioral analog called *learned helplessness* (Bremner, Southwick, & Charney, 1991). The enduring somatic tug-of-war we so often see in traumatized people and the failed attempts to balance the extremes result from the original helplessness in the face of terror. Feeling helpless to change the present, the trauma survivor believes that there is no future. The persistent and pervasive effects of self-harming behavior, somatic dysfunction, and self-medication, however, only reinforce a sense of being out of control.

Subsequent research reformulated the *attributional theory* of learned helplessness, hypothesizing that "mere exposure to an uncontrollable event is not sufficient to produce helplessness. Rather, it is the expectation that the future cannot be controlled that results in learned helplessness" (McCann & Pearlman, 1990). Why some dogs were able to mobilize, relearn, and resist the development of learned helplessness is an important question to answer if we wish to understand the role of resiliency in the prevention of post-traumatic stress. Seligman's work evolved into "learned optimism" and "positive psychology," leading to the development of a program called "comprehensive soldier fitness," a resiliency training program.

STATE-DEPENDENT MEMORY, LEARNING, AND BEHAVIOR

Learned helplessness intersects with the central assertion of state-dependent memory, learning, and behavior: what we learn and remember is dependent upon our psychophysiological state at the time of the experience (Rossi, 1986). The theory of state-dependent memory, learning, and behavior (SDMLB) includes the study of hypnosis, dissociation, information systems theory, and psychosomatic illness (Rossi, 1986). SDMLB refers to a complex system of mind/body communication that attempts to answer the following questions:

- What are the mechanisms of mind/body information exchange?
- How are overwhelming emotions transformed into physical symptoms?
- How does "broken" mind/body communication heal?

Conditions of intense sensory experience such as intense pleasure or pain underlie SDMLB. We are often transported back in time by a special song or the smell of perfume or aftershave that evokes in us the complexity of that personal historical memory. However, a sensory cue that triggers a traumatic memory may be overwhelming, intrusive, and painful. Recall that when Roger heard a car backfire, it brought back a state-bound memory of mortar fire. As one client who was violently beaten by her mother said to me, "When I walk into your office after your previous client, I get nauseous and feel like throwing up because she wears the same perfume as my mother."

How do physical symptoms express emotions and become reintegrated into adaptive modes of functioning? When stress is transduced into psychosomatic symptoms, Rossi (1986) refers to this process as *information transduction*: the conversion of information and/or energy from one form to another. He proposes that the limbic-hypothalamic-pituitary system is the major anatomical mechanism that acts as a mind/body transducer. This area of the brain is concerned with emotional experiences and reactions and includes the hippocampus, the amygdala, olfactory regions, and the hypothalamus. The hypothalamus controls the ANS, which integrates the basic regulatory systems of hunger, thirst, sex, temperature, heart rate, and blood pressure. SDMLB is rooted in the limbic-hypothalamic-pituitary system response (Rossi, 1999), and molecules of the body modulate mental experience and mental experience modulates the molecules of the body.

One task of all therapies is to help a client decondition from SDMLB leading to the ability to:

- exert control over "automatic" responses
- decondition reactivity due to memories and experiences
- change maladaptive behaviors acquired during a traumatic or altered (dissociated) state of consciousness

---

Laura experienced multiple childhood sexual and physical traumas and is now struggling to establish physical intimacy with her partner. She illustrates the difficulty of deconditioning from SDMLB:

> I learned how to use my mind to control the pain in my body. I would just leave my body. But now I want to stay in my body, to feel. Why can't I get my body to do what my mind says? I keep thinking that I should be able to—that it's a moral failure that I haven't succeeded by now.

Laura reveals feelings of futility, frustration, and shame that are common to people who have been victimized. Since many of the victim's functional difficulties arise out of dissociative symptoms that include amnesias and hyperamnesias, helping her to understand and decondition triggers, along with resymbolization, forms an important part of therapy. Rossi (1986) asserts that therapies work by accessing state-bound memories and reframing cognitive beliefs, and that "every access is a reframe."

SOMATIC SYMPTOMS OF TRAUMA AND ADDICTION

People with PTSD experience a nexus of symptoms that include somatization, depression, anxiety, and dissociation. They may experience musculoskeletal pain that alternates with lack of feeling and sensation, gastrointestinal problems, and heart, respiratory, and reproductive problems. Nightmares invade their sleep, and their waking life is affected by recurrent visual images of the trauma itself. They feel out of control. This perception, in turn, drives them to remain on guard—to be hypervigilant and overly controlled. Affective outbursts that include irritability, aggression, and fear lead to withdrawal and detachment from activities and interpersonal connections. Imbalances of neurochemicals in the brain; they contribute to the negative feedback loop of depression, irritability, self-mutilation, and eating disorders.

Because the causes of somatic symptoms cannot always be diagnosed, treating these conditions can be difficult for the general practitioner, who may lack knowledge of the extent of PTSD's effects on physical health. On the other hand, the practitioner may call these symptoms psychosomatic (which

---

Sara, a 14-year-old young woman, had been sexually abused and had a diagnosis of oppositional defiant disorder. She abused drugs and alcohol, which brought her into treatment, and she was disruptive, thus annoying her teachers and milieu therapists. She had very painful periods and kept complaining of pain in her pelvic region, but medical exams and testing revealed no precise cause. I told her that we were going to treat it and asked her to describe her pain in detail, to describe when it began, what she thought the cause was, and what she thought would help reduce the pain. She spoke in detail about the abuse she had experienced, and I asked her to touch the areas of her pain as she spoke. We limited these discussions to 15 minutes each session over a period of four sessions. I suggested that we move slowly and that each time the pain might have something new to reveal, so that as we discovered what the pain had to say, we would have more knowledge about how to treat it.

Setting limits on the exploration of pain created safety for Sara, and this approach honored her focus on the physical pain, which was the story her body was telling about her experience. Simultaneously her "oppositional behavior" abated and she made progress. Together, we wrote a report to the physician about the nature of the pain and its cause.

---

technically they are, for they involved both psyche and soma), leading only to the prescription of an antidepressant.

SELF-MEDICATION

In order to cope with somatic symptoms, trauma victims will often resort to self-medicating behaviors. This contributes to the high rate of addiction among trauma victims: 75% of Vietnam War veterans with PTSD developed problems with alcohol, and 19% to 59% of individuals seeking treatment for substance use disorders are estimated to have PTSD (Back, Sonne, Killeen, Dansky, & Brady, 2003).

In one large study, one in three of the women with PTSD developed alcohol dependence; however, women who experienced trauma but did not develop PTSD also had similar rates, suggesting that it is the trauma and not the PTSD that leads to alcohol dependence (Sartor et al., 2010). One third of female veterans met lifetime criteria for substance use disorder, with about half reporting rape during their lives and one quarter reporting rape within the military (Booth, Mengeling, Torner, & Sadler, 2011). Self-medicating behavior—like the use of alcohol and drugs, food fasts, binges, and self-injury, such as cutting and burning the body—reflects attempts to alter brain chemistry and affect dysregulated by trauma.

Animals exposed to inescapable stress develop analgesia when exposed to another stressor shortly afterward (van der Kolk, 1989). Stress-induced analgesia is due to the production of endogenous opioids and endocannabinoids. These contribute to complex cyclical patterns of affective and behavioral responses, including the addictions. Endogenous opioids are neuropeptides found in the brain and in receptors throughout the body. Their discovery has furthered our knowledge about the relationship of emotions to chemistry and has begun to illuminate some of the channels by which the brain, mind, and body communicate with each other. Dr. Candace Pert discovered the complex pathways of the endogenous opioids (endorphins, enkephalins) and suggests that they are the biochemical correlates of emotions. Endocannabinoids and their receptors exist in the brain, where they affect mood, pain, and behavior throughout the body; they are crucial modulators of the ANS and the immune system.

Chronic and persistent stress appears to decrease the effectiveness of the stress response and to induce desensitization. For many victims, this leads to the inability to react appropriately to danger and underlies the observation that people who have been repeatedly traumatized cannot utilize affective cues to activate the appropriate response.

Risk-taking behavior or reenactment is another type of addictive behavior. Reenactment refers to behaviors where the individual reenacts and relives (unconsciously) parts of the trauma. This behavior suggests a biological analog to what Freud called the repetition compulsion. For example, a high percentage of female and male prostitutes also have histories of child sexual abuse. Most women begin prostitution as sexually abused adolescents. Veterans often return to war as mercenaries; for some, the Vietnam War did not end, it just relocated to the jungles of Mexico and Hawaii. I have met and worked with dozens of veterans, living as expatriates, wandering in the rainforests of Mexico and living as though the Vietnam War had never ended. Most of these men are addicted to alcohol, drugs, and danger. Thousands of former veterans of the Iraq and Afghanistan Wars work throughout the world for private contract companies to carry out a range of war-related activities, and many have PTSD (Feinstein & Botes, 2009). Reenactment appears to arise in part from a psychobiological imperative to produce endogenous opiates that alleviate pain, numb feelings, and rage and have a tranquilizing effect. Researchers speculate that these naturally occurring opiates are chronically depleted in people with PTSD (Hoffman, Burges-Watson, Wilson, & Montgomery, 1989) and that chronic opioid depletion contributes to substance abuse, self-mutilation, eating disorders, and dissociation. Chronic stress exposure and PTSD likely lead to clinical endocannabinoid deficiency and the associated functional pain symptoms of fibromyalgia, migraines, and irritable bowel syndrome (Russo, 2008b). Heroin, an exogenous opioid that temporarily reduces physical and emotional pain, supplants opioid production. This explains why recovering addicts are very pain-sensitive and respond well to acupuncture, which stimulates the endogenous opioids and endocannabinoids. Painful states result in (unconscious) efforts by the victim to stimulate opioid/endocannabinoid production, either by reexposure to trauma, which activates brain opiate receptors in the same way as exogenous opioids like heroin, or by other self-harming behaviors, like cutting or burning the body. Prior to self-injury, victims report the overwhelming urge to feel and to relieve anxiety (Favazza, 1987; Villalba & Harrington, 2003).

There is some research on the efficacy of substituting acupuncture for cutaneous self-injuries like cutting and burning. One study demonstrated that acupuncture reduced self-injurious behavior (SIB) but not depression in adolescents (Nixon, Cheng, & Cloutier, 2003). Interestingly, researchers have identified SIB in nonhuman primates targeting known acupuncture analgesia points (Tiefenbacher, Novak, Lutz, & Meyer, 2005). Nixon, Cheng, & Cloutier (2003) suggest teaching self-acupuncture as an alternative to SIB. Combining these therapies with counseling links listening to oneself, the body-voice, and being heard by others to self-care activities and can be very effective. Machoian (2006) has worked extensively with teen girls with SIB, emphasizing the relational underpinning of self-harm: the cry of "not being listened to." Introducing therapies that pierce the skin, like acupuncture, or apply heat, like moxa, provide an alternative to self-harming behaviors. While these therapies stimulate similar sensations and psychobiological responses, they are enacted in the context of healing and self-awareness. They are easily integrated into cognitive-based mindfulness and provide a bridge to other self-regulation strategies. The patient learns new behaviors, is better able to manage affect, and develops new options for physical relaxation.

In 1971 I met Dr. Ho Kuan-Chuang, an elderly Chinese scholar who was a descendant of early-20th-century Chinese revolutionary leaders and who, like many of his generation, went to France to study before his final transit to the United States. While in France, he was influenced by the work of Paul Nogier, a neurologist who developed auricular acupuncture (see Figure 3.1) and advanced what is now known as the vascular autonomic signal, is a sympathetic vasculocutaneous reflex that responds to various immediate stressors (Chalmers, 2007).

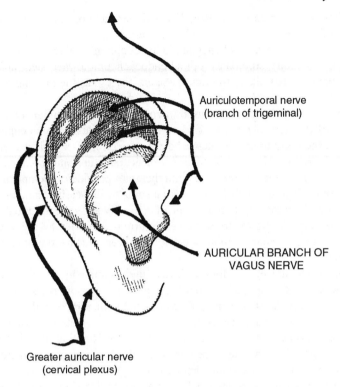

Auriculotemporal nerve
(branch of trigeminal)

AURICULAR BRANCH OF
VAGUS NERVE

Greater auricular nerve
(cervical plexus)

Figure 3.1 Vascular autonomic signal (VAS).
Source: Adapted from *Science and Human Transformation: Subtle Energies, Intentionality and Consciousness,* by W. A. Tiller, 1997, p. 164. © 1997 by Pavior Publishing. Reprinted with permission.

Dr. Ho taught me needle insertion, clinical indications, and Chinese meditation from *Tai Yi Jin Hua Zong Zhi* ("The Secret of the Golden Flower"), methods that I am grateful to have learned early in my life, for it set me on a path of study and the practice of energy medicine.

Acupuncture is a 5,000-year-old traditional Chinese medicine approach to healing. It works by stimulating specific points of the body to interact with the body's energy, called *qi*. In the biomedical world, acupuncture has found a niche working with conventional medicine in the area of pain management and has proven to be very effective. Auricular acupuncture is a more recent innovation and applies small needles, magnets, and even "seeds" to the ears. It is a powerful physiological intervention that induces deep relaxation and reduces cravings and addiction withdrawal symptoms. Anatomically, the vagal nerve comes close to the surface in the auricle (which also accounts for the application of cranial electrical stimulation electrodes placement on the earlobe). Acupuncture, both auricular and full body, is effective for conditions of dissociation, substance abuse, pain, SIB, and the addictions in general. A study conducted by Hollifield, Sinclair-Lian, Warner, and Hammershlag (2007) found that acupuncture was beneficial in the treatment of PTSD. Acupuncture (and moxibustion) stimulates opioid/endocannabinoid-mediated analgesia (McPartland, 2010), likely through the same process as the burning and cutting associated with self-injury.

Moxibustion, which often is used in conjunction with acupuncture, is the burning of the herb *artemis vulgaris* directly on or just above acupuncture points on the body to create intense heat. In my clinical experience with patients who self-mutilate, the application of acupuncture and moxibustion as well as deep massage and pressure point therapies provides a therapeutic transition from self-injurious behavior via the soma to self-caring therapy. These therapies address the psychobiological addiction by allowing a titrated period of therapeutic withdrawal from the self-injurious activities by replacing the activity with a similar method, located, however, outside the spectrum of self-injury.

Behaviorally it is helpful for the client to understand why he or she behaves in this way; identifying the need to achieve a state of consciousness as a physical need reduces the shame and guilt associated with SIBs and also increases adherence to a program of alternative modes of self-regulation. Auricular acupuncture is also effective for nicotine withdrawal. Nicotine blocks the HPA axis reaction; when they quit, people with PTSD experience an increase in PTSD-like symptoms, including depression.

The triple warmer meridian in Chinese medicine flows through the western anatomic region of the hypothalamus in the brain. The triple warmer governs the endocrine system and the autonomic system as well as addictions and is associated with family relationships (see Figure 3.2).

In working with survivors of sexual trauma I have observed that while acupuncture (electrical and needle only) provides a significant option for altering endogenous brain chemistry, pressure point/touch therapies provide a tactile-affective quality that needling generally does not. Where needling remains more "medical," touch returns one to the somatic-emotional template of attachment. Individual needs and the meaning of needle insertion should be explored. Many people, most notably people addicted to heroin and abuse survivors, do not want an "oily" massage without clothing, nor do they want someone to "penetrate" them with a needle. Combining psychotherapy with the somatic-emotional therapies and acupuncture can provide an effective approach. Whereas each method alone has its limitations, all three become synergistic and support withdrawal from the addictions at different stages of recovery. Body and auricular acupuncture also reduces the severity of withdrawal symptoms associated with rapid opiate detoxification (Montazeri, Farahnakian, & Saghaei, 2002), reduces cravings, increases the rate of participation of patients in long-term treatment programs, and reduces recidivism rates (Bullock, Culliton, & Olander, 1989). Public health programs

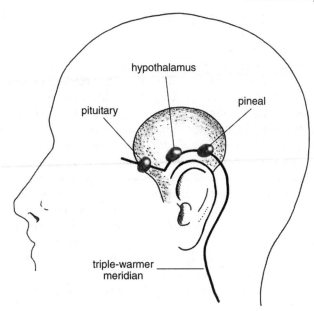

Figure 3.2 Triple warmer meridian and hypothalamus/pituitary glands.
Source: Adapted from *Mind, Body and Electromagnetism* (2nd ed.), by J. Evans, 1992, p. 114.
© 1992 by Ross-Evans.

recognize the relationships among chronic exposure to violence, depression, substance abuse, and cyclical acts of crime and have instituted models in prisons and clinics that combine counseling and acupuncture detoxification therapy. One such is the Community Addiction Recovery Association (CARA) in Sacramento, California. Many of these programs follow the protocol of the National Acupuncture Detoxification Association (NADA), an auricular acupuncture treatment that involves fine needles being inserted just under the skin at five different points on the outer ears (National Acupuncture Detoxification Association, 2010). Benefits of the treatment include reduced cravings and anxiety, and improved sleep (National Acupuncture Detoxification Association [NADA], 2010). The NADA protocol is used in prisons as well as in post-9/11, post-Katrina treatment and in refugee and border camps worldwide. The NADA protocol is available for lay acupuncturists, and many states allow individuals to train in this simple six-point treatment program without going through the 3-year acupuncture licensure track. The NADA protocol is simple and quick; it can be done daily for addiction treatment. If needle penetration feels too invasive, electroacupuncture or meridian pressure therapies can be beneficial alternatives. The NADA conducts training for nonacupuncturist professionals to conduct the NADA protocol and certifies acupuncturists and physicians in this specialized method. The NADA protocol, also known as acu-detox and the five-point ear acupuncture protocol, was developed by the physician/acupuncturist Michael O. Smith and has been widely used in urban and rural settings for the treatment of alcoholism and chemical dependency.

There are other acupuncture traditions that much like theoretical models in counseling, vary in technique and relational emphasis. I particularly like "Five Element Acupuncture," developed by J. R. Worsley, for it actively integrates emotional and spiritual well-being and values extensive history taking. Traditional Chinese medicine is more commonly practiced in the United States, and Japanese acupuncture has a gentle approach that is often very light; the penetration is pain-free, making it suitable for young or sensitive individuals. Most schools of acupuncture have free or low-cost clinics in major cities where advanced students intern, making it an affordable choice. Many native Chinese practitioners do not practice what in the West is considered a "bedside manner," so when that is important to the client, look for it carefully among Five Element practitioners. As with any method, the relationship and connection between healer and client is vital to the healing response. Chinese medicine also has a comprehensive repertoire of herbal medicine, which is often used in conjunction with acupuncture.

Traumatized people engage in reenactment behaviors both psychologically and biologically, and both aspects must be treated integratively. Helping clients to gain control over their behaviors requires both their ability to understand the psychobiology of their reactions and to substitute positive sources for the production of endogenous opioids. Therapeutic methods such as acupuncture, massage, exercise, and shamanic rituals are effective partly because they stimulate natural brain chemicals; the opioids and cannabinoids and help people find healthy ritualized substitutes for unhealthy behaviors. These methods also facilitate deep rest and engage the natural rhythms that restore health.

EXERCISE 3.1: SELF-CARE EXERCISE: AURICULAR ACUPRESSURE (ONLINE EXERCISE)

Two simple self-care auricular acupressure exercises that I teach to my clients can be done at home and with a partner to increase energy and relaxation (see Figure 3.3).

THE ULTRADIAN RHYTHM

The mind/body has a natural rhythmic healing response via the *ultradian rhythm,* the 90- to 120-minute cycle of rest and activity that occurs within the larger 24-hour circadian rhythm discussed earlier. This rhythm corresponds to the shifts that occur every 90 to 120 minutes in natural brain

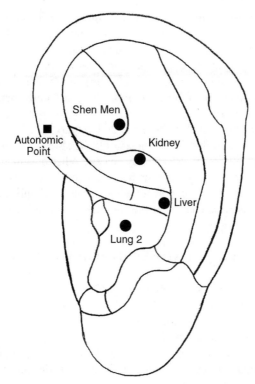

Figure 3.3 Auricle showing acupuncture points.
Source: Adapted by Fatima Moras.

hemispheric dominance, and these shifts correspond to nasal dominance. During a 90-minute (ultradian) cycle, one hemisphere of the brain is more active and the opposite nostril is more "open" (less congested) than the other. Werntz (1981) demonstrated that the "open" nostril correlated to the opposite side of the brain during its dominance phase and thus were "windows" that revealed the phase of rest/activity—or parasympathetic/sympathetic oscil-lations—of the brain hemispheres (Rossi, 1986) at any point in time. This observation provided an important physiological link to the ancient science of yoga *pranayama*, which is based on nostril-specific breathing methods to alter consciousness, mediated in part via the activation of either the right or left hemisphere. This discovery also provides insight into healing mecha-nisms of trance, hypnosis, and meditative states. The word *pranayama* comes from the root word *prana*, meaning "life force." More than just oxygen, it is considered the force of Spirit: the breath of the gods and goddesses. Appar-ently Anaximenes, a Greek philosopher of the 6th century BCE, held a similar view, suggesting that as our souls, being air, hold us together, so breath and air embrace the entire universe. In Spanish, the words *espiritu* and *respirar* mean "spirit" and "to breathe," respectively, and are linked to "inspiration."

The Hebrew mystics call it *ruach*, the Chinese call it *chi*, and the Greeks call it *pneuma* (*pneumon*, meaning "lung"). Prana is said to flow through the body in channels called *nadis*, which correspond to acupuncture meridians. The main nadis are the *ida*, the *pingala*, and *shushumna*, mentioned earlier in relation to the caduceus. In yoga, the *ida* (yin) corresponds to the left nostril and the right hemisphere of the brain. *Pingala* (yang) corresponds to the right nostril and left hemisphere.

According to yoga scholars from the 2nd century BCE, "If you control the breath, you control the mind." Gaining control of the breath via specific exercises is central to regulating the ANS. Pranayama and other breathing exercises provide a foundation for self-care and the restoration of rhythm. Even when breathing is not the focus of restoring the ultradian rhythm, a simple 20- to 40-minute rest period once or twice a day when the body asks to stop all activities is advised.

DISORDERED BREATHING AND HYPERVENTILATION

Disordered breathing is very common in PTSD and exists along a spectrum of function; hyperventilation syndrome (HVS) is at one end of that spectrum. Disordered breathing often goes undiagnosed; most symptoms of hyperventilation are not the typical rapid, shallow breathing that occurs during panic attacks. People who overbreathe often complain of headaches, neck pain, jaw pain, leg and body cramps, and tension in the shoulder muscles. Posturally, such people may present with their jaws jutting out, as if gasping for air even as their shoulders slump forward. Unconscious attempts to restore posture by pulling the neck posteriorly, like a turtle pulling her head into her shell, results in a muscular "tug of war" in the neck and leads to chronic neck pain.

The postural changes that occur in HVS are as much emotional as they are physical, and we can often sense the oppression our clients feel by observing

EXERCISE 3.2: SELF-CARE: TURTLE EXERCISE (ONLINE EXERCISE)

An effective practice for breath- and posture-related issues is the yoga "turtle" exercise, which reconditions and stimulates the neck muscles while one is breathing through the diaphragm.

the patterns of their muscle contraction. Dysregulation of respiration may begin with birth trauma or can develop in response to chronic anxiety. Abuse affects posture and posture affects breathing. Women (more commonly than men) experience thoracic outlet syndrome, which may derive from a physical trauma, such as a car accident; an athletic injury, such as triceps pushups; or repetitive trauma due to computer work that strains ergonomics and thus posture. However, a number of sexually abused women I have worked with reported thoracic outlet syndrome as a part of a matrix of chronic pain, anxiety/breath/upper chest and neurovascular compression. The thoracic outlet (it is really an inlet) is an area at the top of the rib cage, between the neck and the chest. Contraction along this pathway leads to compression of the brachial plexus (the heart or fourth chakra) and subclavian artery. Many of these women report the experience of unwanted attention or abuse related to their breasts. Chronic scalene muscle tension in the neck, which co-occurs with associated breathing dysregulation (and asthma), exacerbates this syndrome. In hyperventilation, the neck muscles are often overdeveloped because they do most of the work, leading to chronic neck pain. The scalenes, through which the brachial nerve bundles pass, are often contracted from this overuse. Certainly many women have described receiving abusive attention to their breasts as children and have therefore undergone breast surgery. Many of these women also experience body dysmorphic disorder, which involves a preoccupation to the point of impairment with imagined or slight defects in appearance, resulting in surgeries that bring no relief (Didie et al., 2006). All of this occurs within the respiratory matrix of muscle and memory. In his analysis of the whiplash model of pain, Scaer (2011) suggests, I believe correctly, that the chronic pain syndrome often resulting from mild motor vehicle accidents does not correspond with the actual events—that it more likely represents dissociated memory that was laid down at the time of impact due to intense fear (Scaer, 2011).

With chronic hyperventilation or overbreathing comes brain hypoxia, which in turn contributes to depression and headaches. The occurrence of overbreathing, or HVS, is estimated in the general population at 10% and likely more, for it is often undiagnosed. Like dissociation, hyperventilation can be difficult to detect because, without the symptoms of a full-blown panic attack, the signs are often subtle. While the client is often aware of symptoms such as chest tightness, tingling, or excessive yawning or gasping for breath at times, he or she usually does not understand dysregulated patterns or why they occur. Overbreathing may develop as a conditioned fear response that occurs first at the time of trauma or it may occur later in life—for example, in latent PTSD. Asthma and PTSD are highly associated (Goodwin, Fischer, & Goldberg, 2007), and overbreathing commonly co-occurs with asthma, chronic bronchitis and chronic laryngitis; indeed, these may be symptoms for many years before the causes are identified. Hyperventilation can occur without anxiety and anxiety can be caused by hyperventilation. In its chronic form, it is a conditioned behavior that responds to guided deconditioning, breathing retraining, and nutrition.

YOGA AND BREATHING

Pranayama exercises involve the alternation of breathing patterns to facilitate control of the ANS, brain hemispheric dominance, and thus states of consciousness, including mood. These methods may vary among different disciplines, including Hatha yoga, Kundalini yoga and Kriya yoga; however, whatever discipline is used, the practice of pranayama leads to brain hemispheric synchrony in which neither hemisphere dominates but both function together. This contributes to trance states and integrated hypothalamic function (Rossi, 1986), the balanced state of healing. It is only during deep trance states or integrated right/left hemispheric function that both nostrils are fully open (Sansonese, 1994).

The nasal cycle marks physiological states. Greater airflow in the left nostril correlates with the resting phase, and greater airflow in the right nostril correlates with the activity phase. The hypothalamus integrates and regulates these two physiological states of rest and activity. With disruption of the HPA axis, the rest activity rhythms are also disrupted. This suggests that activities which reregulate these rhythms—such as specific breathing exercises associated with yogic pranayama, specifically forcing the breath through only one nostril—stimulate the contralateral hemisphere and ipsilateral sympathetic nervous system via the hypothalamus (Shannahoff-Khalsa, 2006).

By ascertaining which hemisphere is dominant at any moment, we can also choose to change it though breathing exercises. By teaching these methods to clients, we can enable them to relax more easily or to focus attention. A more active left hemisphere is more conducive to intellectual activity. For example, lying on the left side of the body enhances intellectual or work-related activities. Lying on this side helps when people feel "spacey" or dissociated. Lying on the right side of the body opens the left nostril and hence activates the right side of the brain for inner work, creativity, relaxation, and sleep. Yoga breathing methods have shown significant efficacy for the treatment of PTSD and depression among people who experienced the 2004 Asian tsunami (Descilo et al., 2010).

The basic method of pranayama is taught in yoga classes and involves breathing through one nostril while holding the other closed. I explore specific techniques in later chapters.

EXERCISE 3.3: THERAPIST EXERCISE: EVALUATION OF ULTRADIAN RHYTHM DOMINANCE

With a client lying down on the table, observe the size of the nostrils' openings. They are often uneven in size, with one smaller than the other. This represents the nostril that is used less or is more often congested and reflects the fact that the opposite side of the brain is less active. Recommending increased breathing through only the smaller nostril (while keeping the other nostril closed with a forefinger) during pranayama a few times a day for several minutes will balance brain activity.

ASSESSMENT

Mental health clinicians do not routinely assess for physical symptoms; however, every effort should be made to assess for disordered breathing, especially where breathing retraining will be taught. Some of the signs of hyperventilation may be assessed while the therapist is sitting with clients and are obvious during the first session. These include repeated yawning, sighing or breath hold-ing, irregular breathing cycles, noises related to breathing (Chaitow, Bradley, & Gilbert, 2002) and may also include complaints of not being able to take a deep breath or feeling tight in the chest. The inability to hold the breath for more than 30 seconds may be indicative of HVS; chronic hyperventilators can rarely hold the breath for more than 10 to 20 seconds (Chaitow et al., 2002). Speech may sound strained, particularly at the end of a sentence, which often cannot be finished without taking another breath at which time in extreme cases gasping for breath or contraction of the vocal cords may be heard. Visually, clients may appear to take shallow breaths, have neck muscles that are tight, and have com-plaints of chronic fatigue or pain in the neck, particularly common in the trape-zius and scalene muscles. The scalenes are respiratory accessory muscles and are often overused in people with both asthma and anxiety; shallow breathers benefit from stretching these muscles. The Nijmegen Scale (van Dixhoorn & Duivenvoorden, 1985) is a short survey that can be integrated into the initial intake to identify HVS and related symptoms (see Online Assessment 3.1).

Effective treatment of anxiety and disordered breathing incorporates the use of breathing exercises, cognitive-behavioral therapy, nutrition, and specific bodywork/massage techniques. Working with a professional to man-ually release the chronic contraction of the diaphragm and the accessory re-spiratory muscles such as the scalenes, sternocleidomastoid, and trapezius is very effective because it helps to make unconscious functional patterns con-scious. Massage of these muscles also feels good, and the sense of pleasure where there had been pain reinforces the capacity to change and may enhance self-care compliance. Because HVS and anxiety always have a biochemical substrate, I address approaches to nutritional management in Chapter 8.

Breathing also has beneficial effects when done outdoors in the forest or next to moving bodies of water, like the sea or streams. A thousand years ago, the Greek physician Galen advised patients to breath by the sea to improve health. The positive effects of breathing at the ocean are believed to result from the high concentrations of negative ions in the air. Air ions are either positively or negatively charged molecules surrounded by fewer than 10 water molecules (Fried & Grimaldi, 1993). Exposure to negative ions increases serotonin levels in the brain, which has a positive effect on mood, learning, performance, reac-tion time, and perception of pain (Fried & Grimaldi, 1993). Treatment with a high-density negative ionizer (and bright light) appears to act as a specific antidepressant for patients with major depression (Terman & Terman, 1995, 2005). Exposure to higher concentrations of negative air ions can be part of a holistic program for recovery. For people who are housebound or have limited access to negative ions in nature, the use of an air ionizer is recommended.

Yet another application of oxygen to the treatment of trauma is the use of hyperbaric oxygen therapy (HBOT) which is the inhalation of 100% oxygen in-side a hyperbaric chamber that is pressurized to greater than 1 atmosphere (atm). HBOT causes both mechanical and physiological effects by inducing a state of increased pressure and hyperoxia. HBOT is typically administered at

1 to 3 atm. The duration of an HBOT session is typically 90 to 120 minutes, and it is being used to increase oxygenation of brain tissue for the treatment of PTSD and traumatic brain injury. Originally designed as a treatment for decompression illness experienced by divers and for healing burns and wounds in hospitals, innovative "off label" uses include for cardiovascular health, autism, stroke and cognitive decline, and TBI. A pilot study of veterans with mild to moderate TBI, postconcussion syndrome, and PTSD showed significant improvements in physical exam findings, cognitive testing, and quality-of-life measurements, with concomitant significant improvements in brain scans using single-photon emission computed tomography (Harch et al., 2012). Hyperbaric oxygen reduces cerebral oxidative stress, inflammation, vasogenic edema, and hippocampal neuron death (Eovaldi & Zanetti, 2010; Huang & Obenaus, 2011). Evidence suggests that HBOT is neuroprotective and will likely be the next widely integrated physical medicine treatment for PTSD and TBI.

STRESS AND THE HEART

Across all cultures, the heart is considered the psychophysical organ of love, grief, and compassion. The Chinese word means both heart and mind, reflecting the belief that consciousness resides in the heart. Chinese medicine identifies the main function of the heart as acknowledging "momentary reality as it occurs, unimpeded by the mind's interpretations of events" (Jarrett, 1995). American Indian trauma is also referred to as heart sickness (Duran, n.d.). Of the ancient Mexicans' associations with the heart, Leon-Portilla (Waters, 1975) writes, "life symbolized by the heart (y-ollo-ti), was inconceivable without the element which explains it, movement (y-olli)" (p. 121). The "bleeding heart" is a cross-cultural image of invasion, suffering, and the potential to transform suffering through the development of compassion. The bleeding heart is an image of postcolonial Mexican Catholicism, representing love and courage, and a pre-Columbian icon representative of sacrifice connected with fertility (Sussman, 1991). The modern celebration of Valentine's Day derives from the German and English transformation of the bleeding heart into a symbol of romance (Sussman, 1991). A "broken heart," "the bleeding heart," or "loss of heart" all speak to the traumatic nexus of grief along with rage, anger, and pain. These acute and chronic states are autonomically mediated and manifest in high rates of heart disease in people with PTSD. Especially when associated with anger, chronic stress leads to heart disease, and PTSD is associated with the development of coronary atherosclerosis and myocardial infarction (Ahmadi et al., 2011).

One of the most effective approaches to measuring how stress affects heart function before it manifests gross symptoms is by measuring 24-hour heart rate variability (HRV). HRV is a standard cardiac measure that has led to brain/mind/heart technologies for healing. HRV provides a noninvasive measurement for understanding how heart-focused meditation and interpersonal exchange may help to heal the heart darkened by trauma. HRV refers to the naturally occurring beat-to-beat changes in heart rate (McCraty, Atkinson, & Bradley, 2004) and serves as a window into the function of the ANS. When the sympathetic nervous system is activated, the heart rate increases and the variations in beat-to-beat activity decreases. Greater variability indicates better autonomic and cardiovascular health. With parasympathetic activation, the heart rate decreases, explaining, for example, why activities such as meditation and relaxation, which increase parasympathetic dominance, reduce the heart rate and increase variability. The greater the variability in heart rate, the better a person's health; HRV decreases as a part of the aging process. Studies of people with posttraumatic stress indicate that they have decreased HRV (Cohen, Benjamin, Geva, Matar, Kaplan, & Kotler, 2000), thus providing a psychophysical window into the imbalance between the sympathetic and parasympathetic system. Measures of 24-hour HRV with highly stressed American Indian caregivers who did not have a diagnosis of heart disease found that the majority of the caregivers, nearly all of whom had had at least one major traumatic exposure in their lives, had depressed HRV, suggesting that their autonomic function was affected by their chronic stress (Korn, McCraty, Atkinson, Logsdon, Pollisar, & Rÿser, 2012). McCraty, Atkinson, & Tiller (1993) found that intentional focus solely on the heart leads to improved self-regulatory mental and emotional states, referring to this state as a "psychological coherence" that arises from sustained, positive emotion (McCraty, Tomasino, Atkinson, & Sundram, 1999). McCraty et al. (1993) conducted research using HeartMath, a brain-heart technology with police who had PTSD; results showed an improved capacity to identify and manage stress, manage negative emotions, and improve the vitality and quality of familial relationships. In addition to the use of sensors, one focuses on a feeling of gratitude and meditations and imagery that visualize the heart.

EXERCISE 3.4: LOVING-KINDNESS MEDITATION

For those who prefer low-tech approaches, there is a simple mindfulness meditation, the *Metta Bhavana*, which can be done easily while sitting comfortably. I have shared it with clients who are feeling the pain of a broken heart and who have themselves "lost heart." It may also be used to stop the obsessive, repetitive fears and worries that often plague a traumatized person. While individuals are saying these lines silently, they may envision their hearts and create images that offer healing.

> *May I be filled with loving-kindness*
> *May I be well*
> *May I be peaceful and at ease*
> *May I be happy*

As simple as this exercise seems it can often meet with a lot of resistance. Self-blame and a lack of self-compassion are hallmarks of PTSD. It may feel overwhelming at first or, as one client said, "I am not ready to be loving!, toward me or anyone else!" In this case, I will suggest Natalie Goldberg's (2005) exercise called the "inner critic," where she describes the inner critic as always sitting on the shoulder, criticizing. This exercise is applicable to anyone who is oppressed by the inner critic, who is obstructing access to loving-kindness and compassion toward oneself.

EXERCISE 3.5: ACTIVE EXERCISE

For the inner critic exercise spend 10 minutes writing down all your self criticism and negative thoughts. Then, thank your critic for her advice and fold the paper up and put it on a shelf or basket. By letting these thoughts out of the cage one is free to explore them and also place them aside, so you may proceed more freely, with your tasks at hand.

In recent years, the role and relationship of "the body" in the "body-mind" equation have been recognized and elevated among health practitioners and mental health professionals. Comprehensive healing plans that address the physical, mental, emotional, and spiritual needs of the victim routinely include exercise, biofeedback, and meditation. Besides Judeo-Christian and Asian religious and healing practices, a variety of medical-spiritual rituals, such as wilderness adventures, the American Indian (Lakota) sweat lodge, and shamanic "soul retrieval" practices from cultures around the world have much to teach about integrating spirituality with individual and community healing. The range of somatically based interventions that now supplement traditional psychotherapy, such as therapeutic massage and body-oriented psychotherapy and acupuncture, has expanded substantially, along with the disciplines of nutritional, orthomolecular, and homeopathic/naturopathic medicine. I will address these methods in chapters that follow.

SUMMARY

Traumatic experiences affect all aspects of mind/body function. A paradigm of trauma based on the disruption of rhythmic functions enables the practitioner and client to identify and understand the cycles of affective distress and behavior. Understanding the psychobiology and physiology of stress response helps the client and the practitioner make appropriate treatment choices and helps clients gain control over automatic processes that contribute to their feeling out of control. Integrative practices work with the heart and mind to reestablish coherence and the rhythmic of health.

4   Dissociation

> If multi-vocality is intrinsic to the human condition, then the Western person
> is engaged in a constant process of minimizing or subduing alternate voices.
> —Laurence Kirmayer

A traumatic event induces an altered state of consciousness called dissociation.
Dissociation at the time of a traumatic event appears to predispose a person to
the development of PTSD, either subsequent to the event or later in life (Zatzick,
Marmar, Weiss, & Metzler, 1993). Dissociation is defined as the disruption
of the usually integrated functions of consciousness, memory, identity, sensorimotor control, and perception of the environment (Lewis-Fernández, 1994).
It occurs as a natural protective response to trauma. Prolonged or repeated
exposure to trauma creates lacunae in the fabric of consciousness, alters the
construction of memory in response to the flood of neuropeptides and neurotransmitters, and adversely affects the healthy development and growth of
the personality.

Dissociation is a ubiquitous human capacity, varying by degree and mani-
festation, among people of all cultures. The experiences of dissociation occur
along a continuum, ranging from absorption and imagination to the less common and more psychologically disruptive, amnesia. Case studies of the dissociative disorders in the United States note histories of abuse in 72% to 98%
and 50% to 75% of general psychiatric patients (Steinberg, 1994). Chu, Frey,
Ganzel, and Matthews (1999) studied both the correlation between dissociation and early childhood sexual abuse and also corroboration of recovered
memories, noting that elevated dissociative symptoms were correlated with
early age of onset of physical and sexual abuse. They also found that the more
frequent the sexual abuse, the more common partial or complete amnesia for
the sexual abuse occurred.

Dissociative processes have both negative and positive effects on psychophysical health. Dissociation is part of a symptom matrix associated with PTSD,
including somatization, self-injurious behavior, and eating disorders. Paradoxically, dissociation also involves the capacity for enhanced self-regulation and

pain control. Dissociation is linked to hypnosis, trance states, and metanormal experiences. However, it also has important distinguishing features. The similarities and differences of these various states of consciousness have implications for diagnosis and treatment. Gaining control over dissociative processes and finding a comfortable, person-specific zone of permeability between ego boundaries are two major tasks of treatment.

In this chapter I shall

- define and review the continuum of dissociation and its relationship to trauma
- explore the relationship between dissociation, trance, possession states, hypnosis and metanormal experiences associated with shamanism
- review the research on dissociation and physical health and illness
- examine the relationship between culture and dissociation
- outline the phenomenology of dissociation
- examine the interface between dissociation, somatization, substance abuse, eating disorders, and self-harming behaviors
- present tools for assessment and diagnosis
- review therapeutic approaches to working with dissociation

The experiences of dissociation range from absorption, like the common occurrences of "highway trance" or not being able to remember if you turned off the stove before leaving home, to being "lost in thought," as in the creative reverie of a daydream when you don't hear someone calling. The more distressing and debilitating experiences of not remembering either recent or distant past events, such as not knowing how you ended up in a certain location or with a particular pair of shoes in the closet, or whether or not you attended your high school graduation, occur under more severe conditions of dissociation. This severe type of dissociation generally forms a nexus of symptoms called dissociative identity disorder (DID) (formerly called multiple personality disorder—MPD). I do not explore DID in depth here but refer the reader to the work of Chu (2011), Putnam (1989), Barach (1994), Phillips and Frederick (1995), and Boon, Steele, and van der Hart (2011).

Dissociation is both an experience and a description of a mechanism (Kirmayer, 1994) underlying five core symptoms including amnesia, depersonalization, derealization, identity confusion, and identity alteration (Steinberg, 1994).

The dissociative disorders are generally classified as dissociative amnesia, dissociative fugue, dissociative identity disorder, and depersonalization disorder. Dissociative disorder not otherwise specified (DDNOS) includes those individuals who do not fulfill complete criteria for the other categories. This category is being proposed as unspecified dissociative disorder for the DSM-V and would include dissociative trance disorder.

AMNESIA

Amnesia is the absence from memory of a specific and significant segment of time. Dissociative amnesia is not ordinary forgetting. It is useful to distinguish sleep and hypnotic amnesia from conditions that affect identity and memory of large time segments (Steinberg, 1994). Selective amnesia is a failure to recall events from a specific time period. Localized amnesia involves a complete failure of recall for a specific time. Continuous amnesia is a failure to recall events from a specific time up until the present. Generalized amnesia consists of a loss of memory for one's entire life (Steinberg, 1994). Dissociation occurs as a natural protective response to a traumatic experience, such as being amnesic from the moment of impact during a car crash until finding oneself outside the car several minutes later.

> Jordon came to me for treatment of chronic pain; he had been in a severe auto accident and escaped a burning vehicle and experienced both selective amnesia and depersonalization:
>
> > I began to watch, as though from another vantage point, just as we were about to hit the car in front. Suddenly I felt as though I was watching someone else, that it was not happening to me. The next thing I knew, I was in the ambulance. I don't remember anything during those moments, though witnesses said I pulled myself out of the car.

DEPERSONALIZATION

Depersonalization is characterized by a sense of detachment; an awareness that one is observing the self from outside. It can occur at the moment of trauma, as Jordon described, or following it. People may describe it as feeling "outside their bodies," floating, or watching oneself, devoid of feeling. Some people describe walking around in a bubble or living in a glass cage separated from others. The exploration of traumatic memories can "trigger" depersonalization.

> During the exploration of memories of being raped in high school, whenever Sharon recalled the moment her arms were held down, she became dizzy and felt outside her body. During the process of "working through" the state-dependent memories, the dizziness and depersonalization subsided. She also made important connections to when she experienced the same feeling when making love with her partner, for the same body position "triggered" the memories. While these sensations did not completely disappear, they diminished in frequency and intensity. The affective terror that had often brought an end to her lovemaking, no longer "had a hold on her."

Depersonalization is a state-dependent response. Sharon's dissociation had taken the form of a sensorimotor response. When dissociation is a response to exploring traumatic recollections, it is both a confirmation of the experience and a cue to the practitioner to explore the memories gently with a focus on managing affect. Depersonalization reflects alterations in the sense of personal boundaries, resulting in a distorted body image, eating disorders, and self-injurious behaviors (Cash & Smolak, 2011; Villalba & Harrington, 2003). People often feel compelled to cut or burn themselves to alleviate anxiety, terminate dissociative symptoms, or stimulate sensation in order to be "in their bodies."

People commonly report out-of-body experiences and cultivate and utilize them for personal growth and spiritual development. While these states may invoke fear for some people, they also constitute a paradoxical "controlled letting go" and often signal new periods of personal growth. The ancient Egyptians understood that consciousness could function independently and outside of the physical body and developed extensively their ideas about the *ka*, the body "double" that separates from the physical body and travels at will (Mishlove, 1993). The Eleusian mysteries in Greece (500 BCE to 380 BC) revolved around secret rites that instructed initiates in methods enabling them to separate soul consciousness from the body. These mysteries (often facilitated by entheogens) centered on the worship of Persephone and Demeter and celebrated the goddesses' role in the cycles of the seasons. The "underworld" to which Persephone disappeared refers to her abduction as a call to initiation:

> Persephone would remain as the queen of Pluto's realm during the waking hours, but would ascend to the spiritual worlds during periods of sleep. The initiate was taught how to intercede with Pluto to permit Persephone (the initiate's soul) to ascend from the darkness of his material nature into the light of understanding. (Mishlove, 1993, p. 37)

There are similarities between shamanic practices that engender out-of-body experiences or trance states and dissociation neurologically; both are mediated biologically via the opioid and serotonergic systems. The term *out-of-body experience* is associated with the field of transpersonal psychology and is a form of depersonalization that occurs under either traumatic or non-traumatic circumstances. Meditation, body work, and trance states that arise out of dancing, healing ceremonies, religious rituals, fasting, the channeling of disembodied spirits, and near death experiences all may lead to depersonalization. The main difference in these states is in whether it is a "controlled" loss of control and a desired state of consciousness or not.

Clinical dissociation suggests a fragmentation of consciousness, where the individual is either unconscious of it or not in control of it, nor wanting it; a spiritual or representational framework is generally absent. I have worked with a number of hyperreligious clients (from all traditions) who present with dissociative features in which highly structured religious practices are an adaptive response to traumatic events of childhood. This is particularly evident in circumstances involving mind control or religious or spiritual ideologies. These practices may serve to ground dissociativity or may facilitate it, and this will be unique to each individual. It is also common in clinical practice to hear stories of clients' shamanic journeys or out-of-body experiences, and these can be discussed with knowledge and sensitivity. Dismissing these experiences as nonsense, or pathological, alienates the client and misses the opportunity to help her or him make meaning. The major distinguishing feature between out-of-body experiences and depersonalization is the positive and negative impact these experiences have and whether or not they are under the locus of individual control.

DEREALIZATION

Derealization is closely related to depersonalization and refers to a sense of the external world not being real or being seen though a fog or a curtained window. Like other symptoms, people may move in and out of derealization moment to moment or in cycles during the day or when under stress. Derealization can also commonly occur in response to the use of SSRIs or cannabis.

Mark describes what became a chronic experience of derealization and depersonalization as a result of being raped when he was jailed after an antiwar demonstration:

> I was on the cold cement floor next to my shoes. I just kept staring at them and I no longer felt my body. I felt myself get very small and go into the shoes. I did not feel anything until it was over. Ever since then, I have had trouble feeling anything. I walk around at times touching objects but nothing feels real. Sometimes I can't get a grip on what I'm doing and what my relationship is to where I am.

While dissociation at the time of the trauma is a common adaptive response, repeated traumatic exposures often lead to a style of functioning called *dissociativity*, defined as "the tendency to have dissociative experiences on a day-to-day basis" (Bernstein-Carlson, 1994, p. 47).

IDENTITY CONFUSION AND IDENTITY ALTERATION

Like other symptoms of dissociation, identity confusion and identity alteration occur along a continuum of experience. Identity confusion may involve a time-limited experience of confusion or questioning about who one is at different life stages, especially during nodal change; these experiences are common and integral to growth. The moderate or extreme experience of identity confusion is persistent and associated with depression, conflict, and confusion. Identity alteration is often the hallmark of DID; one assumes different names or obtains possessions that are not recognized or may practice a skill one does not remember learning. Persistent identity confusion and identity alterations lead to ongoing negative effects in one's life interfering with the ability to sustain satisfying work and relationships

One of the defining features of trauma is the experience of helplessness: of losing control over oneself, one's body. Dissociation is a psychophysical response to loss of control.

> Julia, a young woman who had been beaten by her mother as a child said "I decided long ago I wasn't sticking around for that kind of treatment; if I couldn't leave the house, at least I was going to leave my body and not feel anything. I wasn't going to give her that satisfaction!"

Internal and external events change and alter consciousness with both positive and negative results. The control one has over mediating these changes is a primary determinant of whether a state change is innocuous, beneficial, or harmful. Whether it becomes part of an integrated life story or dissociated, split off, forgotten, or remembered as through a haze depends on this control. Because dissociation is a psychophysiological process of encoding state-bound memory, subsequent traumas often catalyze a breakthrough between these compartmentalized barriers to memory.

> Joan, a survivor of childhood sexual assault had never really forgotten her experience, but she was "foggy" on the details. She "never thought it had been much of anything" until she was date-raped 20 years later, and the floodgates of memory and emotion were released: "I had always remembered but it was as though I tucked it in one part of my brain. I could not feel it, so it meant nothing to me. After I was raped, it was like all the walls came down and all the feelings I had never felt about it overwhelmed me. It all converged together."

The task of treatment here is to help Joan to integrate the cognitive, affective, perceptual, and sensorimotor aspects of herself. Altered states are innate to the full range of natural human functioning and, while they are often taught and cultivated under nontraumatic conditions, one of the losses survivors grieve is that they had no control over the adverse conditions that precipitated dissociation.

CONSENSUS TRANCE

> Human groups agree on which of their perceptions should be admitted to awareness (hence consensus), then they train each other to see the world in that way and only in that way (hence trance).

> —Howard Rheingold

The trance state may be under one's control, like a shamanic state or facilitated by hypnotherapy for healing, or it may be unbidden. The concept of trance is also applied to whole cultures or societies that are "en-tranced" by certain ideas and concepts. The continuum of dissociative states of consciousness described above reflects cultural values and modes of perception and expression. The widely accepted clinical ideal that "thoughts, feelings, memories, and actions form a coherent and unified sense of consciousness" (Demitrack, Putnam, Brewerton, Brandt, & Gold, 1990) reflects a culture-bound standard of "univocality, rationality, and consistency" (Kirmayer, 1994). This standard may not be applicable to or even optimal for all societies (Coons, 1993; Kirmayer, 1994; Kleinman, 1988). Dissociation occurs not only as a function of individual behavior, but as a response to social and cultural values as well. Indeed, individual dissociative phenomenology often reflects the range of multivocal idioms sanctioned by societies. Cultural validation often determines whether dissociation is called pathological, normal, or creative. Medical anthropologists suggest that many of the trauma-associated disorders are culture-bound syndromes. For example, Kirmayer (1994) asserts that dissociative identity disorder reflects the limitations on multivocality by Western Protestant societies and that "The rise of DID can be seen not only in terms of individual psycho-pathology, but as the emergence of a new form of social protest against the brutalization and oppression of women and children" (p. 113).

Peters (1994) proposes that the dearth of meaningful rituals of initiation and transition in many Western societies underlies the high percentage of people (estimated at 2% of the population in the United States and 20% of all psychiatric inpatients) diagnosed with borderline personality disorder, suggesting that

> The typical symptoms of borderline disorder (impulsivity, self-harm, dissociation, suicidality, poor interpersonal relations, swings of intense affect) have neither an appropriate culture channel nor symbol system to provide direction and consequently are not fully appreciated by clinicians. However, these "symptoms" may actually be attempts at self-healing gone astray in a culture bereft of an integrative spiritual and ritualistic context, and therefore without an education for transcendent states of consciousness. (p. 35)

Many people diagnosed with dissociative identity disorder are previously diagnosed with borderline personality disorder (Kirmayer, 1994). The borderline diagnosis also has layers of meaning in clinical practice. I have heard numerous clinicians apply BPD as a pejorative term for patients whom the clinician was unable to reach, when they were angry at the patient, or simply when their own countertransference was out of control. Complex traumatic stress may be a culture-bound syndrome, for it occurs only in cultures that tolerate and promote interpersonal violence (Eisler, 1988).

DISSOCIATION, HYPNOSIS, AND TRANCE

Locus of control is an important distinguishing feature between dissociation, hypnosis, and trance states. For example, hypnosis is a therapeutically authorized form of controlled dissociation (Watkins & Watkins, 1990). Many survivors of abuse develop dissociative capacities and as they mature, these capacities evolve into healing or spiritual practices. Without exploration of the boundaries of these states or resolution of the trauma that led to dissociation, these states can become problematic for the individual.

One client with whom I worked told me during her first appointment that she was from the star cluster, Pleiades.

Jane was raised in a Christian charismatic healing family and abused by her mother. Jane made her living as a "trance healer or shaman." When she had told her previous practitioner about her work, he told her that she was delusional, and she left treatment. It was 4 years before she sought another practitioner. Jane was not psychotic. She came for treatment because she had a difficult time separating her metanormal capacities and her need to take care of herself. She said:

> I find myself responding to everyone who asks me to work with them and don't safeguard my own needs. Every time someone asks me to help them it triggers the feelings that I am compelled to help them; it reminds me of my family. Now I see the connection to having lost the right to my needs at the same time as I left my body as a child. My work now is to stay focused on what I want. I still enter a trance, but I do it on my terms.

In my work with complex trauma victims, I note a high percentage of people with metanormal capacities, such as healers, channelers, and medical intuitives. Many people who exhibit metanormal capacities describe a history of traumatic events. These adaptations extend into the "extra-ordinary" range of consciousness and are rooted in psychobiospiritual responses to traumatic experiences.

Shamans or wounded healers are found among all peoples across cultures. Evidence of shamanism is found during the Neolithic period (10,000 BCE) of human development. In traditional and industrialized societies alike the wounded healer has, like Persephone, been to the "underworld" and back;

the journey through trauma leads to knowledge of alternate realities and gifts of guidance that can be used to help others. Today neoshamanism or neurotheology (Winkelman, 2011) is practiced in both rural indigenous cultures as well as in urban industrialized societies, where it represents a renewal of consciousness and reclamation of archaic wisdom. These practices are often syncretic, or they may be linked to "New Age" practices that have become a "panshamanism" deriving from psychological and religious traditions. These practices may or may not involve the use of entheogens. I explore shamanism further in Chapter 7.

In his early work on dissociation and trance, Pierre Janet conducted experiments demonstrating telepathy in subjects under trance (Tart, 1994). The literature on trance and trance possession (Coons, 1993; Winkelman, 2003), anomalous cognition (Jahn & Dunne, 1983), healing phenomena (E. Green, 1990), and parallel universes (Greene, 2011) suggests that multiple, simultaneous realities exist and that metanormal communication occurs quite commonly. Kirmayer (1994) suggests that Western models of education inhibit and devalue the natural reverie of childhood and, with it, the capacity to daydream and become absorbed in images and ideas. Heber, Fleisher, Ross, and Stanwick (1989) compare alternative healers who practiced methods such as channeling, laying on of hands, and metanormal trance-based healing to a group of psychiatric residents. Using measures of dissociation including the Dissociative Disorders Interview Schedule (DDIS) and Dissociative Experiences Scale (DES), they found that the healers had significantly higher levels of dissociation than the psychiatric residents, yet they had no appearance of major psychopathology. The investigators noted that "alternative healers view dissociation as a talent rather than a disorder" (Heber et al., 1989, p. 572). Jack Schwarz was a Dutch yogi and healer who collaborated with Elmer and Alyce Green at the Menninger Foundation. Demonstrating his extraordinary capacity to control his autonomic nervous system, he entered into a trance state, placed a knitting needle through his arm, and then stopped the bleeding (Green & Green, 1989; Schwarz, 1980). The Greens spent decades researching subtle energy fields, meditation, and biofeedback and helped to organize a society of lay and professional researchers called The International Society for Subtle Energies and Energy Medicine.

Research on states of consciousness and dissociative identity disorder in Western psychology has expanded concepts of the full range of human capacities. Rationalism characterized the development of modern psychology during the early 20th century and led to the dominant medical attitude that altered states of consciousness, whether explored through drugs or mysticism, was one of pathology and primitivism. Freud considered that the exploration of meditative states was regressive; this attitude permeated psychoanalytic theory and therapeutic practice and slowed research until the early 1960s. Then, after a brief flowering, altered states research went underground again, and it has been slowly peeking through ever since.

The development of humanistic and transpersonal psychology disciplines expanded the role of researcher-clinicians who experiment with different states of consciousness in order to theorize and apply this knowledge clinically. One of the most influential researchers, experimental psychologist Charles Tart, proposes research based on state-specific sciences (Tart, 2009). State-specific research suggests that the person studying a state of consciousness enter into that state in order to study, observe, and report from within that state and in interaction with the external world. The state-specific research undertaken by many researchers and clinicians has contributed to shifting the paradigm about altered states, including dissociation and trance, and has led to the integration of meditation, yoga, and other consciousness-altering methods into mental health care during the early 21st century. Tart's work is instructive to us as clinicians; just as we undertake psychotherapy as a requisite for conducting therapy, so should we explore altered states of consciousness in order to better understand our clients and ourselves.

Because traumatic stress disrupts balanced patterns of consciousness, victims feel at the mercy of these labile changes and do not understand what they mean or why they occur. To help educate the client and support symptom resolution, the practitioner must be well versed in a variety of states of consciousness in order to help clients define, differentiate, and learn to control these states. Tart (1994) suggests one of the ways for professionals to begin is to share their experiences and fears of the paranormal with their peers. Many people come into treatment having made positive adaptations to the trauma and utilize dissociative capacities successfully for their benefit. It is beneficial to help people make the connections between the development of these "trance skills" and their early childhood experiences of trauma. Because these states of consciousness are intricately interwoven with the development of personality, a gentle process of exploring the meaning, sensory qualities, and behavioral outcomes is required in order to differentiate states of consciousness and gain control over them. This is not to imply that one masters all these states but rather that one can learn ways to achieve more safety, control, and equanimity. By incorporating new frames of reference about how these states developed and using these "shifts," an individual can self-regulate and protect herself or himself better. In evaluating dissociative states and their effects on the individual's life, it is useful to ask whether the individual

- chose to learn and cultivate these innate capacities
- has control over their use and application
- considers them useful, destructive, or a mixture of both

Most complex trauma survivors have varying degrees of control over a variety of kinds of dissociative processes. By exploring controlled trance (dissociative) states clinicians increase their understanding of their clients, reduce fear of these states, and gain the capacity to enter into those states with the client in order to assist them more effectively. This approach can be used with or without hypnotherapy

SOMATOFORM BEHAVIORS, EATING DISORDERS, AND SELF-INJURY

Persistent unresolved physical complaints for which there is no apparent cause form the backbone of physical medicine practice. Many of these symptoms are dissociative phenomena that manifest as chronic pain, somatization, self-injurious behavior, eating disorders, and other addictions. People who develop PTSD as a result of interpersonal trauma as children have higher rates of dissociation and affect dysregulation than do people traumatized as adults (van der Kolk, Roth, & Pelcovitz, 2005). The current concept of somatization (disorder) is rooted in what Freud called *somatic compliance*. This idea arose out of his observation that people with hysteria expressed physical symptoms of distress in a "language" that the psyche could not express in words. When the diagnostic category called hysteria was split into separate categories, the somatic symptoms of hysteria were termed *conversion disorder*; the conversion of psychological distress into physical symptoms. Chronic pain, headaches, digestive and reproductive disorders are among the dominant modes of somatization in current traumatic nosology. This is understandable in the light of these organ systems' connections to autonomic innervation. Delineation and separation of these functions into psyche and soma, mind and body, is an artificial division. Somatization disorder is more appropriately classified as a trauma disorder. Increasingly, as the complexity of mind and body interrelationships is better understood, the somatization category will disappear and become integrated into a more comprehensive, interdisciplinary, and holistic approach that reflects the inseparability of mind and body. The association between PTSD, chronic pain, fibromyalgia, chronic fatigue, and depression is well documented (Raphael & Wilson, 1994). Most patients with fibromyalgia also have a significant history of early childhood stress or trauma. Fibromyalgia, like chronic fatigue syndrome, Gulf War syndrome, chemical sensitivity, and environmental illness is often considered a "somatized distorted belief" on the part of the patient or a displacement of trauma, much as hysteria was in the 19th century. For some clinicians, other vague, multiorgan illnesses are a function of "belief," Staudenmayer (1996) writes,

> Despite the significant therapeutic effort expended, some patients who are imprisoned by a closed belief system about the harmful effects of chemical sensitivities are resigned to travel down the path which ultimately leads to despair and depression, social isolation, and even death. (p. S100)

These are often the traumatized individuals who walk through our clinic door because no one has as yet either listened to or understood the causes of their multiple layers of illness. While dissociativity and somatization are both a response and a coping mechanism, they intersect with profound psychoneuroimmunological and hypothalamic-pituitary-adrenal (HPA) axis dysfunction and together comediate the response that leads to illness complexes such as chemical sensitivity and other less than fully understood complaints. The chemicals or vaccines encountered in war and in the workplace of modern life serve as the "last straw" in which the HPA axis can no longer summon the energy to fight off yet another assault. Illness then progresses, especially when the liver can no longer detoxify and the intestinal lumen can no longer prevent the passage of unmetabolized toxins into the bloodstream. Bell, Schwartz, Baldwin, and Hardin (1996) refer to this response as "neural sensitization," an autonomically mediated sensitivity to a variety of unrelated chemicals, drugs, alcohol, and stressors.

ADDICTION TO SURGERY

As a result of living with chronic pain, the dissociated and traumatized client seeks out surgery, and when one surgery does not eliminate the pain, the surgeries multiply and the survivor is caught between needing help and the cultural imperative to cut. This can result in addiction to surgery.

Ruth described chronic, severe bulimia and self-injury that resulted in repeated hospitalizations. Severe pain in the region of her diaphragm led to several surgeries including removal of the gallbladder, a portion of her intestines, and several additional abdominal exploratory surgeries. She also experienced severe neck pain and had received several spinal fusions. Her surgeon began to believe that surgery might be a form of self-injury in her case, which precipitated his referral to me. When I began working with Ruth I asked her what she felt would be helpful and what her goals were for treatment. She stated that she was considering gastric bypass surgery: she had already had her gallbladder removed and was planning plastic surgery to "tuck" the extra skin. Ruth requested that we do body-oriented psychotherapy, which would integrate touch and talk; she asked me to work in the central area of her body to release the tension in her diaphragm, which was, she said: "tight as piano wires." I gently applied pressure under her rib cage directly into the area of pain as she breathed deeply. As we worked, she had clear images of early life experiences when she felt terrified. During some of these sessions, she experienced some hyperarousal in response to the touch therapy, leading to both new and intensified memories of sexual abuse. We went slowly and gently, processing as we went along. During other sessions, she experienced deep relaxation, saying, "I haven't relaxed this much since I gave up recreational drugs. I didn't know it was possible." After five 1-hour sessions, Ruth said that her physical pain had decreased by 50%, but her memories felt overwhelming and interfered with her ability to work. She decided to take a break from the bodywork segments of our work together and we spent several weeks discussing her memories and bolstering her self-care and self-regulation strategies through breathing and stretching. Ruth was able to release a lot of physical pain and to clarify somatic memories, which had previously seemed to her "like a dream" and prevented her from fully acknowledging the violence that had occurred in her early life. She also experienced what many survivors experience who are undergoing touch therapies: she never knew whether she would relax or become hyperaroused. However, the alliance we developed along with predesignated cues we agreed upon allowed her to signal whether she wished to continue or end the session, and this provided a safety net for her. She was able to take the memories of her experiences and her feelings back into verbal psychotherapy to address them productively. At our last meeting, she said she felt proud and courageous and that she had caught a glimpse of her future— of reconnecting with her body and the pleasure and relaxation she would once again experience. She chose not to go ahead with surgery but to wait while she had fully explored her other options.

Ruth's addiction to surgery is a form of self-harm or self-injury, and in this particular form the medical profession (often unwittingly) participates. People with chronic pain and depression are often desperate and seek help, care, and touch, to "cut the problem out." Self-injury, bingeing, purging, chronic pain, spinal fusions, and the (multiple) removal of organs are all efforts to express, eradicate, or at least endure the anxious speech of the body. These are cries for affiliation, for contact and communication with the first ego, in its own language of touch and holding. This protest against separation is the relentless nightmare of "borderline" patients. The cry goes unanswered as long as medicine withholds help. Injury through surgery allows the patient intimate contact with a healer. Surgeons cut, go inside, and (try to) make it right; for a sexual trauma survivor these surgeries may represent a reenactment of penetration. Rarely do the results address the underlying problem, and often they create additional, iatrogenic problems. How many sexual abuse survivors undergo gastric bypass surgery? How many of these individuals have psychiatric admissions postsurgery (Clark et al., 2007)? How many people who have elective plastic surgery or liposuction have a history of trauma?

Self-injury and addiction to surgery are included in criteria for the diagnosis of borderline personality disorder. Approximately 10% of psychiatric patients injure themselves deliberately (van der Kolk, Perry, & Herman, 1991). There is a significant nonclinical or nonpsychiatric population who also self-injure, such as people who obtain tattoos and pierce their bodies.

There can be a tendency among health professionals to blame the victim. One otherwise sensitive writer notes "some patients 'trick' physicians and dentists into performing unnecessary surgery" (Favazza, 1987, p. 97). I believe that what occurs is not the trickery of patients but the failure of the professional to decipher the patient's story in order to truly address her or his needs along with the willingness of some surgeons to perform unnecessary surgery. Since many of these clinicians are not trained to recognize the relationship among these symptoms and trauma and dissociation, this provides an opportunity for the therapist to educate the medical professional and facilitate a team approach. Surgery for chronic pain most often does not work simply because the trauma cannot be cut out.

Emily's psychiatrist referred her because they both felt therapy was at a standstill and she was concerned about Emily's desire to have additional lipo-suction on her thighs. Emily was an accomplished professional, married, who had a history of bulimia and had debilitating hip, neck, and abdominal pain. Though she had discussed vague memories of having her thighs stroked as a child, she was not fully engaged in her current treatment, and her practitioner felt that a somatic approach might facilitate a change. She arrived for treatment and I palpated the iliotibial band on her outer thighs. Her thighs felt as if they had rope tied tightly around them, wrapped transversely, as in the links of a sausage. As I touched her thighs, she discussed a new visual memory of childhood abuse in detail. These were the areas where the fat bulged, where her hips hurt, where the pleasure and pain were, where she was stroked as a child. She then relaxed deeply. She discussed the memory with her therapist and returned to my office 2 weeks later. During the second appointment, she relaxed deeply, "more so than I have in years," and fell asleep toward the end of the treatment. During the third session, we worked to release the tension in the sternocleidomastoid and scalene muscles of the neck. She had a detailed memory of her father abusing her orally, and she connected her memories of early-morning childhood regurgitations and sore throats with the forced oral sex. We ended this phase of our treatment as she had obtained the new level of confirmation that she needed. She then continued work with her psychiatrist and placed on hold her decisions to have additional liposuction.

CULTURE AND SELF-INJURY

Discussion of self-injury, eating disorders, and somatization must also be rooted in the context of culture. Self-injurious behaviors that occur across cultures can provide insight into the role and meaning of such behaviors. A wide variety of people (and other primates) practice self-injury for many reasons. Primates have been found to practice self-injury in response to isolation and separation anxiety; this accounts for the wide use of SSRIs on dogs, cats, and birds and other companion animals living in industrialized societies who are left alone for too long during the day. Self-injury is also commonly practiced in association with magic, religion, and ritual. Whether these rituals are rooted in conscious choice and have a value to the individual and to the group, as contrasted with rituals that appear only to harm the person, remains an important determinant of their value. The widespread use of tattoos and body piercing is a form of ritual self-injury enacted as part of a larger social ritual of becoming and belonging. We are continually asked to examine our own conditioning and beliefs about the continuum of these acts. Some prominent methods of socially condoned injury include self-flagellation in certain sects of Christianity, male circumcision among Jews and Muslims as well as by allo-pathic medical professionals, female genital mutilation, tattooing, scarification among Pacific Northwest tribes and the American Indian Sun Dance among the

Plains peoples. Among aboriginal culture in Australia, women cut themselves to express their grief. Some practices, like female and male circumcision, are condoned by many cultures and religions (Muslim sects and Jews respectively) but castigated by others. The Sun Dance has long been a religious and purification tradition of the Plains people, and for many, including the Lakota people, involves extended periods of body piercing. This most sacred of rituals occurs during the summer solstice and is a rite of passage signifying both birth and death and the power of the sun. It represents acts of generosity and the giving of that which one controls: one's body. The ceremonies were outlawed until recently by the U.S. government and are currently undergoing a resurgence among the Plains people and their non-American Indian friends.

There is a long history of association between self-injury, hysteria, eating disorders (anorexia), and venesection (the cutting of veins). One ancient Greek treatment for hysteria was venesection. I wonder whether this served a similar purpose then as does self-injury today. A strong relationship exists between self-injury in patients with eating disorders (Cash & Smolak, 2011); one study showed that 50% of females who chronically self-injure having a history of anorexia nervosa or bulimia (Favazza, 1987), which likely results from the anxiety-dissociative-endorphin continuum explored previously. In bulimia (most often associated with carbohydrate bingeing) tryptophan-serotonin would be another final pathway along the continuum in which relaxation is sought as the final outcome.

ASSESSMENT

Dissociation is hard to detect. If you do not look for it, you may not observe it. Assessment begins during the initial interviews. People are more likely to come into treatment complaining of depression, anxiety, eating disorders, or pain. While this may all be true, few people, especially at the beginning of treatment, define dissociation as the presenting problem because they are not aware that they dissociate or that many of their symptoms are manifestations of dissociative processes.

While the following signs and symptoms do not definitively identify dissociative phenomena, they alert the clinician to conduct a more thorough investigation.

- The client forgets what she was saying or suddenly looks "spacey."
- The client is highly responsive to hypnosis.
- A common countertransference reaction is for the therapist to feel sleepy, "spacey," or dissociated while sitting with a client who is dissociating.
- The client shows a lack of affect in describing an emotional response.
- The client describes somatic phenomena such as decreased or limited body movement and a variety of sensations such as dizziness, itching, and shooting pain (Dolan, 1991; Phillips & Frederick, 1995).
- The client has a history of self-injury and addictive behaviors.

TOOLS AND INTERVIEWS

Two tools can be administered as part of the history-taking process: the Dissociative Experiences Scale (DES 1 and 2), which may be used for screening, and the Structured Clinical Interview for Dissociative Disorders (SCID:D). Neither tool asks about traumatic experiences directly because trauma often involves amnesia, where experiences are often not remembered. The DES is a 28-item measure of dissociation designed to elicit information about a range of dissociative experiences in everyday life. Various studies have found mean scores ranging from 43 for people diagnosed with DID, 30 for people with PTSD, and 8.6 to 10.8 in the general population (Bernstein-Carlson, 1994). One study compared healers to psychiatric residents, who scored 15.5 and 3.3, respectively (Heber et al., 1989). However, Kirmayer (1994) suggests that it "remains unclear to what extent high scores on the DES reflect specific psychopathology, nonspecific distress, or simply normal variations in personality and imagination" (p. 97).

Structured Clinical Interview

Steinberg (1994), developed a semistructured interview assessment tool and interviewers guide (1993b), called the Structured Clinical Interview for *DSM-IV* Dissociative Disorders (SCID:D) designed to diagnose and rate the severity of dissociation. The SCID-D can also help to make diagnostic distinctions between dissociative trance disorder, characterized by a temporary state of consciousness involving possession by a spirit, entity, or other power, and acute dissociative (stress) disorder which is distinguished by a duration of symptoms of not more than 4 weeks (Steinberg, 1994).

TREATMENT

Working with the client to identify her priorities and identifying effective treatment strategies should include exploring her personal, social, religious, and cultural values.

The task of therapy is to help the client

- gain control over the dissociative process
- manage the internal and external "cues" which trigger dissociative response
- utilize positive aspects of dissociation, manage the negative aspects
- identify ego states
- form communicative bridges among ego states
- increase control over ego states of consciousness
- grieve the loss of time, memory, and feelings

- grieve loss of control over what should have been naturally arising trance processes
- acknowledge the creative responses that dissociation may have engendered

Guidelines for treatment follow a similar schedule of the three-phase oriented treatment described in Chapter 7: establishing safety, working through, and integration. Insight therapies that integrate additional methods such as eye movement desensitization and reprocessing (EMDR), sensorimotor, cognitive, and behavioral approaches can be used according to client need. Watkins and Watkins (1990) developed an approach to working with dissociation called ego-state therapy, which combines successfully with hypnotherapy to access state-bound memory and resolve conflicts between the various ego states (Watkins & Watkins, 1990). Most psychotherapeutic methods can employ ego-state therapy, which is especially effective in working with the emotion of shame (Phillips and Frederick, 1995). Psychoeducation and skills training is also very helpful and can be conducted with individuals or in a group format (Boon, Steele, and Van der Hart, 2011).

The matrix of psychophysical symptoms can be identified and explored at appropriate stages of treatment by integrating psychological and somatic therapies that focus on

- titrating exposure to new sensations
- managing and tolerating sensorimotor awareness
- reinforcing body image and the sense of body boundaries
- tolerating positive somatic sensations

For several years in Boston I led a small group with women in recovery from CPTSD who experienced significant dissociation and somatic complaints. The group was designed for the later stage of trauma recovery, where the women were not in crisis or experiencing overwhelming affect. Having group members who are at similar stages of recovery enhances group cohesion and avoids the interference of insoluble interpersonal problems. The focus of a body-oriented group for dissociation is to reclaim somatic sensation, sexuality, and self-regulation. This structured 12-week group progresses from reinforcing self-care strategies to include sensory awareness exercises, such as breathing, self-massage, yoga, and homework exercises to build tolerance to body pleasure with or without a partner.

In acute situations I also encourage weight-training exercises with a trainer with time in front of a mirror. Weight training enhances musculoskeletal body awareness, helps define shape, and links movement, muscle, breath, and sensation simultaneously. Done in front of a mirror, it also reflects back musculature during movement.

Often, exploring sensations through visualization and identifying where they are in the body is the first step. Yogic breathing can be useful for its emphasis on moment-to-moment attention to subtle somatic processes.

EXERCISE 4.1: KINESTHETIC EXERCISE (ONLINE EXERCISE)

Homework can include new sensory experiences that create opportunities to experience body boundaries, such as swimming or the use of whirlpools, which focus on the sensations of the water on the body, giving and receiving a hand massage, with or without lotion or oil, and different movement therapies, such as the Feldenkrais or Alexander technique, both of which focus on gentle posture and movement, or Continuum, which is a subtle movement/dance therapy. The kinesthetic exercise may be used to distinguish between the physical body and the energetic or imaginary body.

Focusing on the breath, down to the minutest detail such as the feel of the breath passing through the nostrils, serves to focus attention as well as tuning in to subtle somatic sensations. This approach can also be used with mindful eating; with each mouthful of food, each chew is focused upon. Suggestions for specific activities are derived from cues from the clients that reveal what they want to explore and which sensory process might be engaged; sight, touch, taste, smell, and kinesthetic movement are among those often used. I discuss later the use of therapy dogs for this purpose of safe touch within the office setting. Finally, I work with the individual to define activities to undertake when a patient is feeling dissociated; simple actions like running wrists under cold water or doing skin brushing are among some maneuvers that help to bring the patient 'back in" to the body. The process of including these activities may span several months and is best enacted by titrated experiences that may then be discussed and integrated and that can lead to new challenges.

During group session, participants can discuss their experiences while doing their homework exercises and sharing their growth and challenges. The discussion of traumatic memories is limited to if and when they arise during exercises. This can lead to additional discussions of how to manage feelings or sensations, and the group members play an important role in contributing their own ideas. Therapy dogs (Cleveland, 1995) have also been identified as helpful in treating dissocation, which I explore in more detail in the next chapter.

SUMMARY

Dissociation is a natural response to the experience of trauma. It occurs along a continuum from adaptive to maladaptive. The goal of therapy is to help the client become aware that she or he dissociates, the purpose it serves, when dissociation occurs, to gain control over the process, and ultimately to reduce the "dissociativity" in her or his life. For the clinician, understanding the role of dissociation and identifying the subtle cues that signal dissociation can be pivotal to treatment. When we as clinicians learn the basic principles of these mechanisms and directly experience these states of consciousness through personal activities that generate hypnotic and trance states, it enhances our capacity to assist our clients.

5 Somatic Empathy
The Template of Touch

And what would become of psychoanalytic notions in a culture that did not repress the feminine.

—Luce Irigaray

The indigenous Mexican village where I began my work was a small crossroads of the expatriate world, a gathering place for the wounded who sought refuge from the past and bargained for forgiveness from the future. Vietnam veterans searching for human connection south of the border limped and ached along on disability funds. Some traveled in a stupor of alcohol and painkillers by day, others dived for lobsters and octopus in the quiet of the night. Some expatriates sought refuge from the law, like the drug movers who shifted tons of *mota* from Michoacan, hailing sails at sea during darkened drop offs on the sand. Blackjack gamblers from Vegas and Tahoe downloaded their take into banana plantations and hectares of papaya tree pairings or into elaborately constructed *palapa* houses—all doomed investments that were as ephemeral as the night sky.

I worked with a varied group of people, both indigenous villagers, expatriates and tourists; their bodies were movable installations of pain and stress, where many had stored their memories of trauma for safekeeping. Very early into my work, I discovered that people were talking about important, painful, long-forgotten events in response to my touching the areas that hurt. Many of the indigenous people in the village came to my *palapa* for treatment of chronic pain or because of an accident or emergency. Then, of course, there were *las turista*s who, during their annual sojourn to the sun for relaxation, suddenly found that the time on their hands and the *E. coli* in their bellies lifted the screen off traumatic memories in the form of acute spasms, locked joints, debilitating back pain, and pulled groins, just as their official rites had begun. Artists, adventurers, and travelers who braved rushing cascades of water, the open seas, and travels on horseback through narrow ravines found their way down the steep path to my house, only to discover that their bodies longed to tell the stories that their minds preferred to keep quiet.

When I first began my practice, I was treating people who came because their bodies hurt with intractable pain. As they relaxed on the table, they talked to me of their lives, and it became apparent that there was a relationship between the source of their bodily pain and the content of their words. As I grew in my capacity to listen, people began to trust me and opened more deeply to their own memories, images, and stored pain. Commonly, areas of acute pain were overlays of chronic, ancient pain buried in layers; the first layer was childhood abuse or beatings, followed by accidents associated with high-risk lifestyles, war, or adult rape or violence. These memorable sensations with a history were state-dependent and often waiting to emerge; as with Pandora's box, the contents, once revealed, could not again be shut away.

I had converted my *palapa* into a clinic the year before Rosaria came. Rosaria was the 14-year-old daughter of a couple who lived at the foot of the mountain path. She was 3 years old the summer their thatched house burned down; I first met the family when the village donated funds for a new metal roof. Now I saw Rosaria almost daily when I shopped in the *tienda,* where she weighed out fruit and vegetables for sale. One day she appeared at my door with her mother, unable to move her head or neck. I asked her to lie down on the treatment table and, as I sat at the head of the table, I cradled her skull at the occipital ridge with the cup of my fingers. This hold is known to induce the "still point" in cranial-sacral work; it is called "the cradle" in polarity therapy. It relaxes the cranium and "loosens the lid" held tight by the complex of neck muscles that meet the lower skull. I focused on the layered horizon of the Pacific to the north and listened as the waves crashed against the rocks below.

As I touched the spasm in her neck, I asked Rosaria when the pain started. She replied that several weeks earlier, a man in the village had exposed himself to her and she turned away suddenly. Now she had nightmares and was afraid. As she talked, I traced the spasm down her neck to her shoulders. She relaxed and together we developed a plan to tell her mother, who was waiting outside. I moved down the side of the table to touch the sigmoidal dam: "Yes," Rosaria said, and reported that she had had *estrenemiento* (constipation) for a few weeks. In Ayurvedic medicine, the neck and colon are related, considered to be of the same element: earth. Fear often grabs hold of and loosens the colon as it stiffens the neck. In order to release one, the other must also be released. As I touched bowels moving in a gentle clockwise direction of peristaltic rhythm, feeling for the pockets that held several days' food, my view charted the swollen river out the window to the east, where it met the ocean and the sand spit. When Rosaria relaxed, I moved to the right side of her body to gently touch the ileocecal gate with my left hand and applied pressure with my right hand to the corresponding point called *He Gu* (meaning Union Valley), a large intestine point in Chinese medicine, found in the web of the thumb. My fingers sank with their own sight, and as I continued to work, Rosaria fell into sleep and I went into a light trance, letting my eyes rise above the bamboo walls that framed the trunk of the ironwood tree on my neighbors' land next door. These neighbors were Alicia and Marcos. Alicia was a good friend who had taught me about herbs, but there were also times when she hid out in my little *palapa*, avoiding Marcos when he had been drinking.

My thoughts traveled to a time a few years earlier when Marcos was be-witched by an owl that lived in the tree next to my treatment house. Early one morning, Marcos came out and shot the owl, against the silent advice of Alicia. He then axed the *Papelillo* (*Bursera simaruba*) tree in half, taking with it all the burnt red bark that had always filtered the glow of the setting sun while I worked. For a long time after that incident, when I heard a noise late at night, just to make sure Marcos wasn't now seeking crazed absolution from an arma-dillo on his property, I'd pop down from the *topanco* where I slept and flash my light, only to illuminate two wire-framed, disembodied red eyes that traded stares back from the horned tangle that only a hungry cow could create. From that day on, only my sagging barbed-wire fence separated Marcos and his be-liefs about the owl from my property.

When Rosaria awoke she went to the bathroom and could now move her neck easily, though it would still take a few days to feel the full effects. Then we shared with her mother the story she had long kept to herself. A few days after her treatment, Rosaria's brother Angel carried a *raicimo* of over a hundred ripening bananas to my home. Later in the afternoon, I went to the *tienda*, where Rosaria laughingly refused to weigh the chayote I wanted to buy; she said her neck was much better. She told me about the huge black manta ray that had been caught up in Victor-the-pedophile's boat line that morning and had pulled him out to sea while he held onto both sides of the *panga*, rocking and sliding, while everyone gathered on the beach to watch and howl with laughter.

When I develop a contract to work with an individual by integrating talk and touch, I use the term *body psychotherapy* or *somatic psychotherapy*. This refers to the integration of bodywork with psychotherapy. The United States Association for Body Psychotherapy (2009) defines body psychotherapy as recognizing

> the continuity and the deep connections that all psycho-corporal processes contribute, in equal fashion, to the organization of the whole person. There is no hierarchical relationship between mind and body, between psyche and soma. They are both functioning and interactive aspects of the whole. (Definition of body psychotherapy, para. 3)

Because complex trauma occurs "at the hands" of other human beings, I believe at some juncture healing must be rooted in reestablishing somatopsy-chic resonance with another. Touch is the curative language of the body and is a mode of healing uniquely suited for treatment of people with posttraumatic stress. Thus the agents of psychic and somatic disaster, the hands, may hold metarestorative value as a method that fosters human connection.

In this chapter I shall discuss

- an overview and definitions of touch therapies for the treatment of post-traumatic stress

- indications and contraindications for body psychotherapy
- research on biofields and touch
- a brief history of touch and the taboo of touch in psychotherapy
- the concept of somatic empathy
- the role of animal companions in restoring the capacity to touch and be touched

TOUCH AND ATTACHMENT

Life forms in symbiotic connection to another human and grows with the development of love for other human beings and animal life. Attachment begins first as somatic attachment to the uterine wall, with the fetus floating in the osmotic sea and tethered to the umbilical cord. Properly nourished, the child grows to express the spectrum of affective mutuality and cognitive exchange. The healthy development of an infant is dependent upon a secure base from which to explore the world. As the analyst Erik Erikson suggested in his work on human development, trust, the first task of development, is the foundation upon which life is built. Trust develops only if there is a solid, tactile, physical, trustworthy object of attachment. Trauma calls that trust into question—trust in oneself, in others, in nature, and in God.

Touch is the first language—a maternal, preverbal language. The language of touch continues to survive in a culture that gave rise to therapeutic worship of the paternal and blame of the maternal. Mother, *mater*, and matter are etymologically related, with their common root from the Sanskrit word *ma* meaning to balance or measure. *Meter* is the Greek word for mother, hence Demeter (mother of Persephone). The Egyptian goddess of truth and justice, *Mut* or *Maat*, was born of the marriage between chaos (matter) and the wind (breath). The essential sound of meditation is called *ma*ntra, and sacred the chant contains the vocalization ma; *om mane padme om*. Thus touch and mother are bound together in our ancient language of balance, regulation, and healing.

The historical, secular (Freudian) and Judeo-Christian dichotomies have traditionally associated the rational with mind, with verbal language and paternity and privileged rationality in contrast to matter, maternity, the preverbal language of the body (touch), and nature. Touch is the language of trust and attachment. Trauma causes a crisis of attachment. Complex traumatic stress disrupts the capacity to trust. Trauma adversely affects the capacity to develop and maintain healthy interpersonal relationships. Not surprisingly, research suggests that the lack or loss of a safe, caring person affects the somatic functioning of humans and animals alike. When children are separated from their caregivers, they become agitated and experience distress similar to the freeze, flight, fight, or fright response.

Beginning in the 1950s, Harry Harlow focused on the effects of isolating monkeys from their mothers. These filmed experiments show how primates cling to mother "surrogates," made of wire, choosing their "touch" over food, so great was their need for affection (Harlow, 1961). Infants in orphanages who receive no touch fail to thrive, and indeed many die (Berman, 1989). In her research with the Yequana Indian tribe of Venezuela, Liedloff (1986) observed that infants are held nearly continuously from birth for the first 2 years of life. As a result, Liedloff asserts, they do not experience the psychological dysfunction, the intrapersonal and interpersonal alienation, that is endemic in low-level-tactile societies.

The capacity to provide psychological and physical safety is called psychobiological attunement (Field, 1985) or affect attunement. Reite and Capitanio (1985) suggest that attachment "represents a neurobiological based and mediated biobehavioral system one of whose major functions is to promote the development and regulation (or modulation) of psychobiological synchrony between organisms" (p. 475). Attachment behaviors are shared with parents, caregivers, friends, family members, and companion animals.

Attachment behaviors can be appropriately cultivated in the context of therapy without cultivating dependency. Touch, the original language, accesses the psychobiological template of attachment and is the cynosure of healing for people who were not touched adequately or appropriately as children. On the other hand, psychoanalytic theories of neutrality, withholding, and distancing reflect the antithesis of psychobiological attachment. Psychoanalysis and many of the verbal psychotherapies are constructs of patriarchy in their privileging of verbal communication. About this Hunter (1985) writes, "Our sense of ourselves as separate beings, as 'subjects,' is bound up with our entry into the order of language, in which speech becomes a substitute for bodily connection." She continues, "In patriarchal socialization, the power to formulate sentences coincides developmentally with recognition of the power of the father" (p. 99).

Indeed, the "grist" of psychoanalysis is predicated on the anxiety arising from withholding gratification. It is thus no surprise that feminist analysts developed the cultural-relational model of treatment with a focus on mutuality and shared connection. Ending this tug-of-war between (false) attachment and the fear of separation is one of the challenges of working with people who are trying to leave abusive relationships. Their ambivalence around the physical and emotional attachment often has its roots in a palpable, somatopsychic programming by the abuser. This is especially evident in mind control, which is often reinforced or manipulated through the sensory body—often with sex, drugs, or sound. This points to the need for deprogramming that incorporates somatic detachment.

Understanding further the complex role of oxytocin as a neurohormonal mediator of attachment may illuminate strategies for helping abused people physically separate from their abusers. Oxytocin, also called the "love hormone," is released in response to both stress and touch and may play a role in the reward system of addictive sexual behaviors. How close is the line between love, addiction, and abuse, and how does the body tell the difference when the mind cannot? How then might therapeutic modes of touch offer an alternative

to address neurobiological and psychophysiological basis for "negative attachment" that occurs in domestic violence, among cult members, and clients of
abusive practitioners? The protective presence of a caring person, both during
and after exposure to trauma, may explain why some people survive as well
or as poorly as they do. Decades of research demonstrate how the loss of a care-
giver negatively influences the capacity to regulate arousal and self-soothing
when experiencing distress (Reite & Capitanio, 1985).

One of the greatest challenges clinicians face is to sensitively empathize
with a client who has experienced what is often horrific and unimaginable interpersonal trauma. Cultural-relational clinicians emphasize the importance of
empathy and mutuality in the therapeutic relationship and understand both the
strengths and vulnerabilities of complex trauma survivors. If successful, the
clinician helps the individual to tell the story of the trauma, restore the capacity for autonomic balance, and empathize with and care for herself or himself.
When this is accomplished, the survivor is free to empathize and share "affect
attunement" with others. Empathy and attunement clearly occurs at a psycho-
bioenergetic level; yet as psychotherapists we rarely consciously engage acknowledge or cultivate this state of consciousness. Synchrony of physiological
rhythms such as electroencephalography (EEG), cardiac ultradian rhythms, and
movement has been reported between partners, friends, and client/practitioner
(Field, 1985; McCraty et al., 2004; Rossi, 1986), and nursing students report
increased levels of anomalous cognition (telepathic "attunement") both within
the treatment setting and in everyday life as a result of practicing therapeutic
touch (Krieger, Peper, & Ancoli, 1979). The experience of thinking exactly
what one's client is thinking at the same moment, known as anomalous cognition, is common among most practitioners at one time or another if they have
become attuned to their clients. Traditionally, this is understood as part of the
cognitive-affective "transference" experience. Anomalous cognition can also
manifest as the simultaneous crossing of a leg or scratching of the nose—a sign
of (hypnotic) suggestion.

However, there are psychophysioenergetic mechanisms that may possibly
be explained by a number of theories that facilitate this transfer of information.
I believe that anomalous cognition is rooted in the same interpersonal synchrony that fosters attachment and healing and that it can be cultivated and enhanced. This concept is not new: the world's healing traditions speak of love,
compassion, and empathy as the foundations for healing. This type of interpersonal synchrony draws on psychology, biology, physiology, and bioenergetic
exchange. Levenson and Ruef (1992) define empathy as "the ability to detect
accurately the emotional information being transmitted by another person"
(p. 234). They demonstrated physiological linkage in their studies of psychotherapy and psychodiagnosis, which they interpreted as a component of empathy
between two people. Furthermore, synchrony involves the matching of physiological rhythms between individuals. The brain alpha wave rhythm (10 cycles
per second) has been shown to be the underlying rhythm of communication
(Field, 1985). However, communication is not limited to that which takes place

during alpha rhythm. EEG research mapping brainwave synchrony between healer and client suggests that different forms of communication result in a variety of synchronic, interhemispheric frequencies and locations (Fahrion, Walters, Coyne, & Allen, 1992). Becker (1991) suggests that the "magnetic fields generated by an internal direct current system are detected by the same system of another organism" (p. 86)—that they derive from the glial cells in the brain and spinal cord and the schwann cells surrounding the peripheral nerves. The geneticist Mae-Wan Ho (1999) suggests that body consciousness is a complex web of communication and memory mediated via the connective tissues; the skin, bones, tendons, ligaments, and membranes made of mostly collagen and form a liquid crystalline continuum with electromagnetic properties far beyond what we normally consider as just structural "skin and bones."

What in psychology we call transference and the unconscious is mediated through both a palpable and a nonlocal psychophysioenergetic transfer of energy and information. This involves the conscious entrainment of a number of psychophysioenergetic rhythms, resulting in a shared state between practitioner and client. I propose that touch can be a therapeutic ritual that facilitates an overarching state of consciousness called somatic empathy (Korn, 1996). I suggest that in energetic bodywork therapies we are extending the therapeutic range of interpersonal synchrony that can occur through talk by cultivating intentional somatic empathy. This is a form of consciously shared psychophysioenergetic interpersonal attunement that is cultivated and directed for the purpose of helping the client to heal. By functioning as the psychophysioenergetic baseline of empathic consciousness, somatic empathy improves a traumatized person's capacity for bonding and attachment, balances autonomic and affective self-regulation, and restores dynamic oscillation and rhythm to psychobiological processes.

Somatic empathy is enhanced by the therapeutic intention to care. When the practitioner cultivates compassion, it leads to psychobiological attunement. Therapeutic forms of touch use various methods to activate, transfer, and balance the subtle energies between practitioner and client in order to affect mutual parasympathetic dominance. This state-specific treatment has some aspects in common with mutual hypnosis, in which two (or more) people enter into a mutual hypnotic state (Gleason, 1992) and thereby enhance empathy and communication. In somatic empathy, mutuality refers to the reciprocal entrainment of psychophysiology for the sole benefit of the client. That the practitioner may "benefit" from being in an integrated parasympathetic state is neither the focus nor the goal but rather the state of consciousness required for effective treatment. Treatment remains focused on the client's needs. Clearly this approach is not limited to touch; as previously stated, attunement occurs in mutual hypnosis, practitioner trance states, some forms of shamanism, and group meditation; it is thus a viable therapeutic approach for practitioners who do not touch their clients.

In the context of Western psychotherapeutic practice, hypnosis facilitates the transduction of information from the semantic to the somatic. This means that words are used to access body states. Touch, on the other hand, proceeds from the somatic to the semantic. In other words, it involves accessing body awareness as the primary language to bridge cognitive and affective expression and integration. This distinction is important for making choices about stage-appropriate treatment for a survivor of trauma.

Somatic empathy includes and extends beyond the concepts of psychological empathy and transference to the energetic transference of psychophysical and nonphysical subtle energies. Bioelectromagnetics and subtle energy medicine are two disciplines that explore information transfer between organisms. These exchanges occur as both local and nonlocal effects. E. Green (1990) writes, "The physical, physiological, psychological and parapsychological phenomena, without exception, depend on the transmission of *energy* of some kind, and that the concept of transmitting information without expenditure of energy is a non sequitur" (p. 6). E. Green's (1990) experiments at the voluntary controls program explored the range of these effects, finding that some healers experience body potential shifts of more than 80 V, leading Green to hypothesize an electric charge oscillation in the body. E. Green (1990) also reported considerable delta band activity among healers during healing sessions, which supported the idea of an unusual awareness of normally unconscious processes, leading him to hypothesize that by providing delta feedback in the 4-Hz region to nonhealers, they would be enabled to experience increased awareness of deeply buried psychological processes.

The contemporary multidisciplinary fields of biofeedback, bioelectromagnetics, and applied psychophysiology provide a conceptual bridge between modern and ancient healing arts and sciences. The effects of external fields—whether generated by human beings, the earth, or technology—are believed to impact the human being through electrical systems within the body. Significant research on bioelectromagnetics during the last century points to a range of electromagnetic radiation encompassing both adverse and beneficial effects (Evans, 1986; Levine, 1993). Adverse effects were first noted in epidemiological studies that raised questions about the increased incidence of childhood leukemia as a result of long-term exposure to low-frequency electromagnetic fields in the range of 60 Hz, such as those emitted by electric poles, electric blankets, microwaves, heating pads, and heated waterbeds. Their emissions have been associated with increased rates of cancer, miscarriage, and decreased melatonin production by the pineal gland (Levine, 1993). The physician who pioneered the use of electric currents for healing nonunion bone fractures, Robert Becker, suggests that DC electrical currents flow throughout the body, regulating function; he therefore postulates that acupuncture points and meridians serve as input channels for the total DC system, conveying information about peripheral injury (Becker & Selden, 1985) Acupuncture points are related to the nervous system, linking muscle and bone areas with spinal nerves, and are directly connected with the autonomic chains (Evans, 1986). Acupuncture has a long history of efficacy with humans and animals. Becker (1991) postulates that the meridian field could be detected outside the body, and that this might indicate the operational state of the internal DC system, which would be sensitive to external magnetic fields such as the geomagnetic field. Dubrov theorizes that the "meridian system is part of the magnetic structure and polarization through which the geomagnetic field acts on the body" (as cited in Evans, 1986, p. 146). Becker suggests that interorganism communication is based upon these magnetic fields. In Chapter 1, I presented evidence for the effects of geomagnetic fields on human fields, in particular referring to the pineal gland as transducer of these field waves. Persinger correlates geomagnetic activity and the incidence of bereavement hallucinations (Levine, 1993). It has also been pointed out that there is an increase in anomalous cognition (AC) in response to exposure to low magnetic fields (Braud & Dennis, 1989).

Before discussing further the role of touch and energy medicine in the treatment of PTSD, I will explore some of the basis for the taboo on touch in psychotherapy and medicine and the professional obscurity surrounding energy medicine in general.

THE TABOO

In spite of a renewal and revisioning of ancient practices of energy medicine as currently seen, for example, in eye movement desensitization and reprocessing (EMDR) and energy psychology, controversy prevails, and psychology and medicine generally relegate practices associated with energy biofields and touch therapies to "religion" and often quackery. This resistance also occurs on the context of the taboos on touch, the unseen and the historical relationships between female patients and male doctors. This confluence of history and healing appears during similar reenactments in the 18th, 19th and 20th centuries, beginning with the work of Franz Anton Mesmer who practiced in the years leading up to the French Revolution.

Mesmer (whose legacy endures today with the ambiguous word derived from his name, *mesmerize*, meaning to bewitch or spellbind) used his hands or iron magnets to place "hysterical" women into a trance via his "magnetic passes," believing that he was the "living conductor of cosmic energies" (Stafford, 1993, p. 454). Mesmer believed that animal magnetism was a "physically grounded, ethereal fluid coursing through the cosmos possessed of the capacity, when properly funneled through the afflicted, to relieve illness-causing obstructions that if channeled properly could heal illness" (Rousseau, 1993, p. 184). Mesmer was destined for disrepute, since in his cosmology,

> The eroticism of finer masculine energies was embodied in telepathic rays searching out intimate emotions lodged within the tender female bosom. Nothing could be more explicit than the attractive *deshabille* and vulnerable swan of the young patient. The seductiveness of the conjurer was tied up with a nonphysical yet sensual contact made under the intense scrutiny of male voyeurs. (Stafford, 1993, p. 454)

Thus it was not just his theories of animal magnetism and energy transfer that were so distasteful to Benjamin Franklin and his cohort at the Academy of Science but also the grandiosity and seductiveness toward women enshrouding Mesmer's technique that led to the well-founded charges of charlatanism and his subsequent fall from grace.

While Mesmer's ideas today appear antiquated (and spoiled by seduction), many of his basic theories have some clinical and scientific merit and are certainly repeated in many of the healing traditions (*sans* seduction); his work marshaled the modern era of interest in dissociation, healing, and trance states. It was not until Martin Charcot waved his own hypnotic wand, nearly a hundred years later, that some mainstream physicians entered into the serious study of altered states of consciousness. Charcot considered hypnotic states an "appendage" of the women he treated at the Salpêtrière, the French insane asylum (Crabtree, 1993). Unlike Hippolyte Bernheim, who distinguished the hypnotic state as a psychological one that resulted from suggestion, Charcot, like Mesmer, believed that hypnosis was physiologically based. In the light of current knowledge of the interrelationship between interpersonal synchrony, energy transfer, and state-dependent memory, both theories are correct. Psychological states of consciousness change physiology, and physiology changes states of consciousness. During his work at the Salpêtrière, Charcot treated women hysterics and identified regions of pain in the front and back of the female torso that he called hysterogenic zones. He developed a machine called the "ovary compressor" to apply pressure to the ovarian region. The metal harness was buckled around the belly and the screw placed to apply pressure directly over the ovary (Goetz, Bonduelle, & Gelfand, 1995; see Figure 5.1).

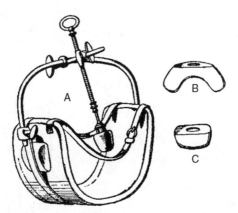

Figure 5.1 Ovary compressor. "The ovarian compressor belt, used to prevent hysteric attacks in ovarian patients. The compressor was directed at the hysterogenic point and then tightened. (From *Iconographie Photographique de la Salpêtrière*, 2:165, 1878)."

He observed that applying pressure to these areas would either avert or bring on a hysterical attack of convulsions and paralysis. Ostensibly designed to avert hysterical paralysis, the ovary compressor just as often brought it on.

I propose that hysterogenic points are musculoskeletal sites of state-dependent memories and are what we call today fibromyalgia points. They are also linked to the 12 alarm points in acupuncture, called *Mu*, located on the trunk of the body designating *Qi* collection points that signify disharmony (and increased electrodermal skin resistance) when sensitive (see Figures 5.2 and 5.3).

In 2011, amid much controversy, the American College of Rheumatology eliminated the fibromyalgia painful points criterion as a diagnostic requisite. These areas are often more sensitive in people with fibromyalgia syndrome:

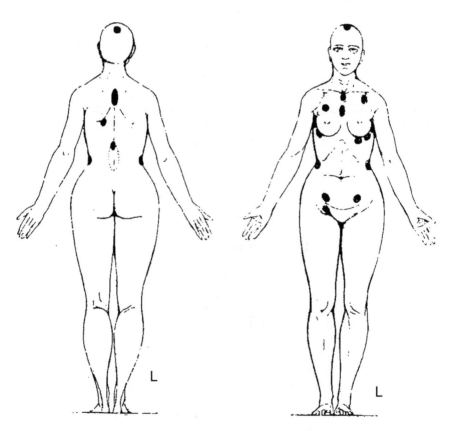

Figure 5.2 Hysterogenic points. (From *Iconographie Photographique de la Salpêtrière*, 2:182, 1878).

Source: Adapted from *Charcot, the Clinician: The Tuesday Lessons,* by J.M. Charcot and C.G. Goetz (Trans.), 1987, p. 119. © 1987 by Raven Press.

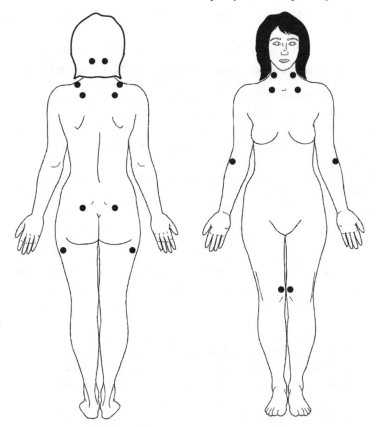

Figure 5.3 Fibromyalgia diagnostic points. Of 18 points, 11 are required to be painful for a diagnosis of fibromyalgia, according to the American College of
Rheumatology, c. 1990–2001.

Source: Adapted by Fatima Moras.

- 1 and 2: occiput—on both sides (bilateral), at the suboccipital muscle
  insertions
- 3 and 4: low cervical—bilateral, at the anterior aspects of the intertrans-
  verse spaces
- 5 and 6: lateral epicondyle—bilateral, 2 cm distal to the epicondyles
- 7 and 8: knee—bilateral, at the medial fat pad proximal to the joint line
- 9 and 10: second rib—bilateral, at the second costochondral junction, just
  lateral to the junctions on the upper surfaces
- 11 and 12: trapezius—bilateral, at the midpoint of the upper border of the muscle
- 13 and 14: supraspinatus—bilateral, at origins, above the spine of the
  scapula (shoulder blade) near the medial border
- 15 and 16: gluteal—bilateral, in upper outer quadrants of buttocks in anterior fold of muscle
- 17 and 18: greater trochanter—bilateral, posterior to the trochanteric
  prominence

When touched, these points may either decondition or trigger autonomic arousal.

Charcot was considered to be one of the greatest neurologists of his time; thus his theories on hypnosis were accepted by the same Academy of Sciences that had condemned Mesmer a hundred years earlier (Showalter, 1993). However, like Mesmer, Charcot saw his work subsequently fall into disrepute due to accusations of charlatanism. Of central importance to our discussion of taboo is that, as in the case of Mesmer, these doctors were (considered or actually) "Svengalis" who controlled their (female) patients and their production of hysterical symptoms (Porter, 1993).

By the late 19th century investigators had identified psychological phenomena called *hypnoidal* states of consciousness or what is now called dissociation. Long ignored in the practice of psychology, dissociation (and the use of hypnotherapy) were again resurrected in the late 20th century after nearly a hundred years of somnolence, in large part in response to feminist calls for renewed attention to traumatic stress and sexual abuse of women and children. Thus, at the end of each of these last three centuries, there was both flourish and controversy, with the convergence of hysteria, healing, dissociation, and women's bodies. Mesmer and his concept of "animal magnetism" influenced not only the development of modern theories of hypnosis and dissociative phenomena but also represented investigations into the realm of psychophysics, the study of the effects of matter on mind and mind on matter, with psychophysiology seen as a special type of psychophysics referring to self-regulation, the effects of the mind on internal phenomena. This last is one of the main foci of clinical intervention today for the treatment of PTSD. As a scientific discipline, psychophysics has been largely ignored by mainstream medicine (E. Green, 1990). The investigations by Mesmer and Charcot and their subsequent collapse reflect the reigning paradigm shifts of the day. Newtonian laws still dominated their epoch and, until recently, and the same reliance on Newton accounted for the dearth of research into subtle energy and electromagnetic healing. By postmodern standards, the milieu of these early "scientific investigations" appears preposterous. But I suggest that these "modes of healing" reflected a more global state-dependent restriction, the consensus trance of patriarchy in which women, suffering from the effects of oppression itself (hysteria), served as spectacles on the platform of medical science. The "spectacular" ethos surrounding these therapies is rarely addressed in the context of its negative influence on current attitudes regarding bioenergies, "magnetic" healing, and the therapeutic value of physical and nonphysical touch and healing.

THE TABOO OF TOUCH IN PSYCHOLOGY

The relegation of magnetic healing and hypnosis to quackery intersects with the taboo on touch and the conflation of touch with sex. While there have been important gains in the practice of mind/body medicine in the early 21st century, there remains a great deal of fear of touch, especially when used with trauma-tized and suicidal patients. The taboo on touch and taboo of the body signifies social dissociation from life in the body, *leibhaft*, "in the flesh," which is evi-dent at all strata of society. Destructive touch—rape, occurs in domestic pris-ons as well as in state prisons, on the street, in the home, in schools by teachers and coaches, and in doctors' offices, often under sedation and in general right before our eyes. But how is it that touch as therapy is taboo? In his *Studies on Hysteria*, Freud (1955) wrote,

> I decided to start from the assumption that my patients knew everything that was of any pathogenic significance and that it was only a question of obliging them to communicate it. Thus when I reached a point at which, after asking some question such as, "How long have you had this symp-tom?" or "What was its origin?" I was met with the answer "I really don't know." I proceeded as follows. I placed my hand on the patient's forehead or took her head between my hands and said, "You will think of it under the pressure of my hand. At the moment when I relax my pressure you will see something in front of you or something will come into your head. Catch hold of it. It will be what we are looking for." (p. 110)

When Freud placed his hand on the forehead of Elizabeth Von R., self-disclosures flowed from his touch, as images and associations rose through the archaic floor, caught light, and formed a narrative that another patient, Anna "O," called the "talking cure." For Freud, though, touch was just a tributary of his technique, which of necessity he abandoned early. Mintz (1969) points out that Freud turned to touch only when he became disappointed in the paucity of associations resulting from his hypnotic technique. But more importantly, with his increasing awareness of the role that transference played in the psy-choanalytic process, he believed the correct therapeutic relationship required neutrality and nonintervention (Mintz, 1969). It is useful to place Freud's work and the psychoanalytic codification of the taboo on touch within a historical context. It was Freud who first peeked under the wimple of sexual prudery that blanketed Vienna and the Western world in the early 20th century. Touch was then spirited out the back door, for it was fraught with "suggestion" in a new science where sexuality was the great theme awaiting discovery. Freud was not alone in his anxiety to separate the treatment of mind from that of body. Western science was embedded in the Cartesian schism between subject and object, a philosophical legacy that religiously renewed the mythic dictum of eternal separation: separation of man from Eden, female from man, and mind from body. It was also a time of internecine struggle. Psychiatry was becoming medicalized (Freud was a neurologist by training), and all of medicine sought to dissociate itself from the influences of magic and religion.

It was during the fin de siècle that empirical medical practices fought with the newly powerful American Medical Association and midwives lost ground to medicalized births. In the United States, the taboo on touch, reflecting the

Puritan ethic of the 17th century (Dossey, Keegan, Kolkmeier, & Guzzetta, 1989), was enfolded into the psyche of Western healers. Remember that psychoanalysis developed out of the major neurologic preoccupation of the day: Hysteria and burgeoning industrialization as well as the intensification of repression during the Victorian era resulted in a dramatic increase in "hysterical" women (Bernheimer & Kahane, 1985).

And if sex was the secret Freud discovered in stirring in the Victorian cauldron of unconscious passion and guilt called *Mind*, then *Body*, that alchemical repository, had a "dirty" job to do—name itself as "Enemy" (no one else would touch "It") and transmute the unthinkable into hysterical corporeality. Freud called this "somatic compliance." Bernheimer and Kahane (1985) suggest that hysteria was "the bedrock of psychoanalysis" (p. 3) and that "hysteria was born in complicity with a moral condemnation of its victims" (p. 5).

It is from this historical juncture of hysteria and psychoanalysis that many of our therapeutic attitudes and values about touch are derived. Hunter (1985) suggests that "Psychoanalysis entered the history of consciousness in dialogue with the subjectivity of women" (p. 114). Our sensibilities about touch are inextricably linked to our consciousness about the body as a source of knowledge and power. Eve is cast as the temptress in taking Adam's hand, and her punishment is the pain of childbirth. As God decrees in the Old Testament, "I will greatly multiply your pain in childbearing and in pain you shall bring forth children." Touch is a sense-lessly maligned gesture; a therapeutic act that has been decried precisely because it is the first language, an essentially maternal language, the sine qua non of sentient mutuality. To frame touch as a therapeutic method that is inherently a precursor to sexual arousal or erotic transference is to remain "out of touch." Touch is thus embossed with images of the female and sin and with pleasure and pain, and it is out of this matrix of (m)other that the taboo is derived.

The current signs of this taboo in the United States and much of Europe is the polarization of touch, both inappropriate touch (sexual abuse, rape, physical violence) and the dearth of appropriate touch (medicine as technology). Even as therapeutic massage and forms of manual medicine and healing become increasingly integrated into the mainstream therapies and are covered for some by insurance, healing touch remains a stepchild method, adoptable only by the wealthy. Popular culture reflects the current preoccupation (obsession) with these issues, proceeding from child sexual abuse; sexual harassment of women; sexual abuse of female and male clients and parishioners by practitioners, doctors, and clergy; spousal abuse; and murder. However, revelations and prosecutions of widespread abuse have, in turn, fueled a backlash that is a reenactment of historical (professional) denial. The taboo on touch in U.S. society is a calcification of the natural, rhythmic fluidity inherent in a continuum of different modes of perception and experience. While (human-mediated) trauma cannot be reduced to a simple cause, I suggest that it is this social-somatic dissociation that has led to (human-mediated) trauma in the first place. Paradoxically, like a self-fulfilling prophecy, the fear of touch has led to its abuse.

The full flowering of touch as a therapeutic modality in Western culture cannot occur until a clear delineation of when to touch and when not to touch is observed in all aspects of social, familial, and therapeutic interaction.

TOUCH AS THERAPEUTIC

Touch is the oldest form of healing. It is associated with the transmission of life force between people and across cultures dating back to prehistory. Evidence of its ancient origins is found throughout old Europe, in cave paintings dating back 15,000 years, where the hands of the goddess symbolize her touch and life energy (Gimbutas, 1989). Massage has been an organized method of healing in Egypt, India, and China for over 5,000 years. It was prescribed as a treatment for hysteria in ancient Greece and was one of the treatments offered at the Aesculapian temples. Homer, writing around 700 BCE, described how soldiers returning from battle were rubbed and kneaded (Dossey et al., 1989). Plutarch, writing some 700 years later, described Julius Caesar's treatment for epilepsy as consisting of being pinched over his entire body every day (Dossey et al., 1989).

TOUCH THERAPIES AND TRAUMA

The field of touch therapy and its integration with psychotherapy for the treatment of trauma has broad application. The body is the locus of traumatic experience; the embodiment of pain that presents a tangible, tactile text, a moving memory that requires a witness who will listen and respond. People with PTSD present for treatment with spastic perineal muscles, torticollis, chronic back pain, and temporomandibular joint pain. They also seek treatment for migraines and tension headaches, muscular spasms, chronic stomach pain, hyperventilation, sexual dysfunction, chronic fatigue, depression, multiple sclerosis, and more.

There are many modalities of touch applied by a variety of practitioners in the United States and internationally with survivors of torture, sexual and physical abuse, veterans and their families, and victims of disasters as well as with people with diagnoses of dissociative identity disorder, borderline personality, prenatal and perinatal trauma, and those who are suicidal and self-harming. Massage therapists, energy medicine practitioners, healers, *curanderas*, physical therapists, osteopaths, chiropractors, and naturopathic physicians are among the professionals who treat children and adults with PTSD and complex trauma histories using touch and manual therapies. Increasingly, psychotherapists are working with individuals who are receiving different forms of bodywork, massage, and somatic therapies or are training in and integrating these methods. Clinicians require a rationale and model for appropriate practice. In presenting this material, I do not suggest that psychotherapists practice touch with their clients. Indeed, there are some professional disciplines whose codes of ethics prohibit touching. Practitioners should either receive comprehensive training in therapeutic methods of touch or refer people to trained practitioners with whom they collaborate as a team. I do not address here issues of casual or spontaneous touch—the holding of a hand, a hug, or a pat on the back—all of which I am less inclined to recommend for trauma survivors any more than one might chat about the weather or a movie. To be effective, touch, like talk, must be rooted in ritual, method, and purpose. My focus here is on the therapeutic contract to engage in prescribed disciplines and rituals of touch for the purpose of healing from trauma.

People of all ages are candidates for touch during all stages of their recovery and different techniques of touch therapies facilitate specific responses at different stages with a variety of methods that are isomorphic for each individual.

HOW DOES TOUCH HEAL?

- Touch arouses, desensitizes, and transduces state-dependent memory; it also facilitates consciousness states associated with alpha, beta, theta, and delta brainwaves.
- Touch can induce trance and simultaneously provide the grounding rod to gain control over dissociative processes.
- Touch is anxiolytic and soporific; it also stimulates circulatory, lymphatic, and immune responses and regulates the primary respiratory mechanism (the cranial-sacral rhythm).
- Touch activates assorted neurohormonal responses, including the release of beta-endorphins, oxytocin, and serotonin; it improves cortisol levels and stimulates the endocannabinoid system.
- Touch provides a nonverbal form of biofeedback, allowing for the simultaneous retrieval of somatosensory memory, body sensations, articulation of associative feelings, and cognitive reframing.
- Touch changes body image and improves body concept, including the exploration of kinesthetic and proprioceptive boundaries as it reduces autonomic hyperactivity.
- Touch reduces lactic acid, thereby reducing the chemistry feedback loop of anxiety.
- Touch facilitates somatic empathy, a psychobiological attunement that is a prerequisite for attachment and bonding.
- Touch alters favorably the subtle human biofields that are the foundation of healthy functioning of the human organism.

Massage is used extensively along with psychotherapy for the treatment of torture victims at rehabilitation centers around the world; it often comprises a special massage of the galea, a band of muscle around the head, for relief of the headaches common to nearly all torture victims (Bloch, 1988). Complementary forms of touch physiotherapy are practiced at rehabilitation centers throughout Europe with a focus on specific physical injuries; it includes body awareness methods that help the torture victim to accept his or her body again (Ortmann, Genefke, Jakobsen, & Lunde, 1987). A number of studies have demonstrated that massage and bodywork decrease depression and anxiety; they were used in children with PTSD following Hurricane Andrew (Field, Seligman, Scafidi, & Schanberg, 1996), in female survivors of sexual abuse (Field et al., 1997; Price, 2005, 2007), and in dementia caregivers with a history of trauma (Korn et al., 2009). Several studies and metastudies have demonstrated efficacy for massage and bodywork for the treatment of fibromyalgia (Cao, Liu, & Lewith, 2010; Kalichman, 2010; Sunshine et al., 1996).

During the 1960s, the early pioneering work of biologist Bernard Grad, a student of the body-oriented psychoanalyst Wilhelm Reich, measured changes in the growth of plants and bacteria in response to the "laying on of hands." Since then, numerous studies have measured functional alterations in brainwaves, heart rhythm, and hormone levels in response to direct touch or nonlocal "touch" or intention within healer and "healee." Among the biofield touch therapies are methods called therapeutic touch, Reiki, healing touch, and the light touch of polarity therapy. They all appear to reduce sympathetic activity (Cox & Hayes, 1999; Gehlhaart, 2000; Rowlands, 1984) by stimulating vagal response. Biofield therapies also lead to a reduction in pain (Sansone & Schmitt, 2000), anxiety (Gagne & Toye, 1994), cancer-related fatigue (Roscoe, Matteson, Mustian, Padmanaban, & Morrow, 2005), quality of life (Metz, 1992), and depression (Field, 2000; Rowlands, 1984; Wardell & Engebretson, 2001). These therapies have, furthermore, been found to increase energy (Lee et al., 2001) and mood and improve sleep (Smith, Stallings, Mariner, & Burrall, 1999).

POLARITY THERAPY

The therapeutic rituals of energetic touch I practice, polarity therapy, derives from the integration of the healing traditions of China and India and 20th-century cranial osteopathy developed in the United States. These traditions posit the existence of a life force that underlies all forms of psychophysioenergetic function. The Chinese refer to this energy as *Qi,* and the Hindus call it *prana.* Many healing methods focus on balancing the *Qi* or *prana*, and techniques are designed to increase it or direct it through various parts of the body. *Qi* is subject to the internal and external forces of yin and yang. These biphasic, oscillating rhythms of life force, discussed in Chapter 1, provide an empirical foundation for reregulating the disrupted rhythms of autonomically "live wires." The varieties of touch in these traditions focus on the stimulation of life force either through touch, like acupressure, cranial-sacral therapy, nonlocal touch, called *Qigong Qiping*, which means roughly, "using the breath energy to heal," and polarity therapy. These traditions of healing are found across all cultures.

These energetic practices are also part of a larger repertoire of bodywork methods that focus on structure and balance, muscle and tendon, blood and lymph, and benefit the client without any attention to or theory of "energy." In speaking about bodywork methods, I believe the analogy to psychotherapeutic methods is apt; in counseling there are methods that focus on short-term solutions, that engage cognitive and behavioral aspects, or that focus on family systems or intrapsychic conflicts. Whatever the theory and method, they all rely on being congruent with a client's belief system and a "good fit" with the empathic, caring practitioner. Bodywork therapies run a similar gamut of theories and methods. I have practiced many types of massage therapy—deep tissue, abdominal/visceral, and lymphatic—along with polarity therapy, and like many clinicians, I work eclectically, attuning the method to the needs of the client.

Polarity therapy is derived from the integration of manual therapeutic traditions that evolved during the early 20th century in the United States, including cranial-sacral osteopathy, chiropractic, and visceral manipulation techniques with Ayurvedic healing traditions that evolved from the Indus-Sarasvati culture of northern India (3500–1700 BCE) and became codified during the classical period of Ayurveda (1700 BCE–700 CE) (Frawley, Ranade, & Lele, 2003). Polarity therapy was developed by Dr. Randolph Stone, an Austrian émigré to the United States who spent much of his career attending to the "incurables" in India. Polarity therapy integrates methods of touch yoga, nutrition, attitudinal healing, and meditation to help the individual achieve balance. A major tenet of polarity therapy is that health and healing are attributes of energy that flows in its natural and unobstructed state (American Polarity Therapy Association, 1996). Artful touch, focused attention, and intention—empathy and love—are the foundations of the practice.

Stone (1986) delineated concepts of energetic, myofascial, and structural manipulation based on what he referred to as "wireless energy currents," a concept that is linked to field theory explicated by physicist David Bohm (Korn, 1987). Stone began his work as a cranial osteopath, which informed his integration of subtle touch by working with the movement of cerebrospinal fluid from the cranium to the sacrum through the spinal cord in order to improve central nervous system function. In this form of touch, light contact is made with the cranial sutures of the skull, along with the spine and sacrum, to induce the release of restrictions in the fascia, nerves, and flow of cerebrospinal fluid. It is useful for almost all imbalances and especially to treat chronic pain, migraines, traumatic brain injury (TBI), stress, temporomandibular joint (TMJ) syndrome, back pain, PTSD, and birth trauma. Bodywork like polarity therapy and cranial-sacral therapies, works at many levels, from the gross myofascial to the subtle energetic. An experimental study on the mechanism of action of polarity therapy demonstrated statistically significant fluctuations in gamma radiation during treatment, leading the authors to hypothesize that radiation hormesis, the beneficial physiological effects derived from low-dose linear-energy-transfer radiation might underlie mechanism of action in polarity therapy (Benford, Talnagi, Doss, Boosey, and Arnold, 1999).

One goal of polarity therapy is to trace (by palpation) and release (by skilled touch) those energy blockages that manifest as pain or dysfunction. To do this, the practitioner applies three depths of touch depending on whether the energy blockage reflects a hyperactive, hypoactive, or neutral state of activity. This application of the continuum of touch pressure (from very light to very deep) makes polarity therapy unique among all the systems of biofield therapies currently employed. These touch techniques range from very light palpation (5 to 10 grams of pressure)—similar to cranial-sacral therapy, healing touch, Reiki, and therapeutic touch—to a moderate moving toward a much deeper pressure. The pressure of moderate touch is where pressure meets tissue resistance, where it may be tender but still feel good. Deep pressure incorporates manipulation through the myofascia, similar to some of the techniques of Rolfing, myofascial release, and of the (neo)-Reichian practitioners following in the tradition of Wilhelm Reich. This deep form of touch appears to resolve stagnation, crystalline deposits, and scar tissue and adhesions. Pressure on energy points, rocking, bone manipulation, stretching, and rotation of joints are some of the methods used to help the patient achieve deep relaxation, improve digestive function, gain greater self-awareness of behavioral and cognitive impacts on health, and take an increasingly responsible role in creating a healthier lifestyle. The full range and parameters of the mechanisms by which mind influences matter and, in turn, matter influences mind are not yet understood. However, the touch of the hands (and intentionality), using either direct touch or nonlocal (mind) touch, is the subject of ongoing research.

Like other forms of biofield/touch therapies, polarity therapy appears to facilitate responses associated with a reduction in sympathetic activity by stimulating vagal response. Direct contact of the vagal nerve occurs while contacting areas on the ear, neck and on the diaphragm. Pressure points on the concha of the ear provide direct access to vagal nerve fibers (Tiller, 1997). At least a moderate pressure is required to stimulate vagal activity and induce parasympathetic response (Field, Diego, & Hernandez-Reif, 2010). Polarity therapy facilitates a reduction in pain, anxiety, and depression (Korn et al., 2009) as well as therapist-patient psychophysiological entrainment (Korn, 1996; Oschman, 2000). Entrainment, a quality of somatic empathy, describes a state in which two or more of the body's oscillatory systems, such as respiration and heart rhythm patterns, become synchronous and operate at the same frequency (McCraty, Atkinson, & Tomasino, 2001). Entrainment occurs intraorganism and interorganism, as between therapist and patient and between individuals, groups, and cosmic rhythms. As I note below, entrainment also occurs between dogs and people during therapeutic connection.

One of the most important methods of polarity therapy is called the perineal technique, which begins with placement of the palm on the lower back over the sacrum (sacred bone) and the other hand in contact with the 10th cranial nerve in the neck and rocking for deep relaxation and sleep. This method may then advance toward gentle contact underneath the coccyx and along the pelvic floor muscles that proceed along the inferior rami of the pubis, ischial tuberosity, and the sacrotuberous ligament. These gentle contacts are often vital for the treatment of trauma-related chronic pain and dysfunction such as chronic pelvic pain, bladder pain syndromes, and chronic noninflammatory nonbacterial prostatitis, which occur at high rates associated with survivors of abuse (Meltzer-Brody et al., 2007). Some trauma-trained orthopedic physical therapists (not massage therapists) specialize in working therapeutically internally in the pelvis with both men and women to help release chronic myofascial restrictions (Pastore, personal communication, January 16, 2011).

Ethel came for bodywork therapy because of chronic pain in her abdominal and pelvic region. She described a dull, belly-filling pain that was internal but that she couldn't "touch." It went deep into her belly and pelvis, sending shooting pains into her buttocks, down her thighs, and the vaginal and anal regions. I sat to her right side and placed my left hand gently on her belly and my right hand directly underneath her lower back, palm up, on her sacrum to establish a warming, felt connection between the areas of pain she described as being the most intense. We breathed together for several minutes in silence, which broke with her sobs and memories of the trauma of an abortion and her desire to have children. At the next session we continued and I began providing gentle pressure points along the inner thighs and buttocks where the pain radiated, and she revealed how during puberty she was taunted and fondled by her grandfather. After this session I suggested that for the third session we focus on an area of her body where there was no pain and where we could focus on her deep relaxation and not "memory work." She wanted to press through the memories; however, I felt that she needed time to integrate her memories and feelings and not have them overwhelm her and thus affect her ability to carry on with daily life activities. At the next session we focused on her head, neck, and shoulders; the occipital and cervical vertebrae all have reflexes to the pelvic region, and I suggested that we focus on the physical for this session only. Once memories come and some pain relief is in sight, individuals can become both exhilarated by the release, but they can also become counterphobic, pushing ahead in spite of the threat to their stability. Our job is to gently set therapeutic boundaries. At the following session Ethel said she wanted again to focus on her legs and feet, and we integrated working with the imagined body and breath so that she could breathe and move the pain down through her legs and out through the soles of the feet. In this technique of combining touch and visualization, the client engages in and focuses on areas where they experience pain or feel "stuck." Ethel continued to use breath and visualization at home between sessions. We worked together for seven sessions and she reported that her pain was reduced by 80%; she was aware of it but it no longer bothered her. This comment also reflected the nature of the trauma she experienced; she would never forget it but it no longer ruled her life. Like many survivors, she checked in a few times a year for a session or two and remained virtually pain-free. In addition to the body scan exercise (see Online Exercise 6.2), I taught the Resting Butterfly exercise to Ethel.

EXERCISE 5.1: THE RESTING BUTTERFLY (ONLINE EXERCISE)

The Resting Butterfly is appropriate for pelvic pain, menstrual cramps, endometriosis, and hip pain.

Polarity practitioners also touch *marmas*, special energy centers, to induce both functional and structural balance. *Marmas* are like the acupuncture points but include larger areas of the body, such as the abdomen or heart region. The *marmas* are areas linked to the chakras and reveal pathologies via oscillations in temperature and other qualities and sensations palpable to the skilled practitioner. Like meditation, polarity therapy (Korn, 1987) focuses attention, interoception, and sensory processing and provides the opportunity to reframe experience and interpretation of one's experience. This type of touch entrains rhythms between the client and the practitioner. The reestablishment of interhemispheric coherence and heart/brain coherence mediated by the nervous system is central to recovery from trauma and has a special import for people with traumatic brain injury (TBI). This suggests an explanation as to why people with TBI respond so well to cranial work, neurofeedback, and sound therapies, which I discuss in Chapter 7.

Traumatized people are often particularly sensitive to shifts in sensory perceptions and benefit from the opportunity to track them and understand them in a therapeutic context. Recipients of touch therapies including massage, polarity therapy, and both cranial-sacral and cranial osteopathy will report feelings of deep relaxation, floating, and a sense of well-being and integration associated with a preponderance of alpha and theta waves. This state of deep relaxation often leads to sleep during the session and improved sleep at night. Though generally believed to be an effect of bodywork in reducing sympathetic tone resulting in relaxation, it may involve even more.

Deep rest and sleep that occur in response to polarity therapy and cranial osteopathy may result from one of the most important methods of touch in bodywork: the gentle compression of the fourth cerebral ventricle. This gentle hold requires the practitioner to sit at the head of the treatment table and contact the client's occiput (lateral to the external occipital protuberances but medial to the occipitomastoid suture) with his or her thenar eminences (Cutler, Holland, Stupski, Gamber, & Smith, 2005). This manual hold is also called the "cradle" in polarity therapy, since one is cradling the head, which leads to deeply comforting sensations and often sleep. In response to the compression on the fourth ventricle, the cerebrospinal fluid (CSF) pauses briefly in its flow, which increases pressure within the ventricles where the CSF fluid is momentarily at rest (in a hydrostatic state), creating what is called "the still point" as the flow of the CSF stops. With release of the flow and a gentle flush of CSF throughout the system, a stretching of the membrane brings about a release of restriction and a self-correcting balance to the tides of the nervous system. In clinical practice this hold leads to deep relaxation and often sleep during the treatment and also decreases the time it takes the patient to fall asleep subsequently (Cutler et al., 2005).

Researchers speculate that this ventricular "stretch and flush" following the still point triggers a release of endocannabinoids, including serum anandamide, the "ananda" or bliss chemicals that fill the CSF and contribute to the relaxed "high" (McPartland et al., 2005) of this treatment. Clearly the endocannabinoids as well as the phytocannabinoids, like cannabis, influence consciousness. A deficit of endocannabinoids is implicated in pain and depression (Russo, 2004); conversely, supplementation with cannabis appears to reduce depression, pain, and anxiety and to aid sleep while also playing a role in memory extinction in trauma survivors.

The recent discovery of the endocannabinoids—and the application of many 21st-century consciousness-altering methods—provide a modern language for what was empirically well known to our ancestors. Chinese Taoists understood that meditation changed the mind and the brain, and while the alchemists were occupied in their laboratories during the day with the transformation of base metals into gold, they delved after hours into their real work—the "inner" alchemy, concerned with the transmutation of spiritual energies. This Hermetic (Hermes/Mercury) alchemical opus is depicted in Figure 5.4, attributed to the

Figure 5.4 Alchemical representation of the ventricular system. The lateral and fourth ventricles are represented by the contesting swordsmen. Mercury (center) represents the third ventricle in equilibrium between them.

Source: Adapted from *Man: Grand Symbol of the Mysteries—Thoughts in Occult Anatomy*, by M. P. Hall, 1972, p. 145. © 1972 by The Philosophical Research Society, Inc. Public Domain.

alchemist and Benedictine monk Basil Valentine, one of the founders of analytic chemistry. In the image, Mercury/Hermes represents the third ventricle of the brain, mediating between the fourth and lateral ventricles. In esoteric science, the third ventricle is the location of the handshake between spirit and matter, where spirit imprints information to guide ("in-form") matter via the fluid medium, the CSF, which then is conveyed quickly to all the cells of the brain and body through the spinal canal and exits at each nerve sleeve pair (Chitty, personal communication, December 3, 2011).

Recalling that Mercury is the "messenger of the gods," whose staff, the caduceus (the nervous system) helps him guide the traumatized Persephone through the dark passage of the underworld in a journey leading from the unconscious to awareness, we find similarities reflected in the consciousness-raising (and CSF-enriching) practices of bodywork, yoga, meditation, entheogens, and psychotherapies we use today. As the fluid "stuff" of consciousness, the CSF circulates to the bottom of the spine through the sacred (sacrum) bone where the she-serpent, the Kundalini or psychic vitality, sleeps. In yogic and alchemical practices one meditates (controls the nervous system) and wakes the sleeping Kundalini so that she rises up through the endocrine energy centers (chakras) to the crown chakra, which is the pineal gland attached to the posterior end of the roof of the third ventricle. Anatomically, fibers from the hypothalamus descend to the spinal cord and ultimately project to the superior cervical ganglia, from which postganglionic neurons ascend back to the pineal gland when influenced by the cervical manipulation in bodywork. The pineal provides melatonin, our sleep/wake chemical, and also tryptamines, the "spirit molecules" that "awaken" us by lifting the mood or causing "spiritual" visions. (The role of endogenous tryptamines in the production of psychotic visions remains inconclusive).

The disruption of endocrine (and chakra) function by traumatic events must be transformed for healing to occur. Sleeping and waking up are both literal and metaphorical in their meaning here. Hence the journey through trauma recovery involves awakening from victimization (loss of control) into the vivification of self-awareness. The nervous system and emotions make possible self-regulation and exerting control over one's choices in life. People receiving bodywork experience a harmonizing of their rhythms; they then carry home this state of well-being, where it lasts for a while. There are additional methods to induce sleep and reduce anxiety that can be practiced by friends and family at home during the days between bodywork sessions. I began my practice rocking children with autism; they had been brought to my clinic in Mexico for a combination of nature adventure therapy and bodywork. Distressed children often rock themselves in an effort to self-soothe. I did my first internship on a psychogeriatric ward in a public health hospital in Boston. The staff were interested in whether we could avoid giving benzodiazepines to the aging bedridden women who were diagnosed with paranoid schizophrenia. I offered to rock them while they lay on their sides to see if that could help to decrease their agitation. Most went to sleep when rocked. Despite its efficacy, rocking an individual is more labor-intensive than a pill, and it may be that what we have come to accept as effective is really just more efficient. Nevertheless, rocking is something I teach couples, partners, or friends as well as bodyworkers; it can be used to help military veterans who cannot calm down in the evening; for rape survivors who cannot sleep; and for children and adults of all ages to reduce anxiety, panic, and pain; and to induce sleep. The benefits of rocking derive from the simple principle that we rock babies to sleep; we pat the sacrum at the bottom of the spine in a soothing rhythmic way with one hand as we hold and cradle the brachial plexus at the lower neck (or holding the head) with the other. The baby may be placed on its stomach or in a hammock to sleep or held by an adult relaxing in a rocking chair. Rocking is a universal behavior; it synchronizes the brain and accelerates and improves the quality of sleep (Bayer et al., 2011). Rocking increases sleep spindles, which are associated with being able to sleep through environmental noise (Bayer et al., 2011). Rocking engages the template of touch and the inner infant. We don't grow out of the need for this kind of soothing; we just don't generally receive it or give it as adults.

EXERCISE 5.2: TWO-PERSON EXERCISE: BODY ROCKING

This can be done with clothes on or off. To begin, have the person receiving the treatment lie on his or her right side (if that feels comfortable). The right side activates the rest cycle of the right brain hemisphere and this position will induce sleep more quickly. Place a pillow under the person's neck. Some people also feel comfortable hugging a pillow to the belly. The person giving the treatment will sit behind the one receiving it. Then the "giver" will take his or her left palm, fingers placed upward (toward the sky), and place it directly over the sacrum. The left palm should be covering the sacrum, so that the outer edge of the little finger is just above the intergluteal cleft before the buttocks (the hand will not be in contact with the buttocks), and the thumb is around the sacroiliac line. The right hand can be placed right on the neck on the cervical vertebrae, and the hand will cup very naturally around the neck. The quality of touch is very light, with no pressure. Very gently begin rocking the sacrum by pushing with the left palm. You don't need to get a lot of movement for this to work, and your movement should be adjusted for the comfort of your partner. Do this for a minimum of 10 minutes, with gentle suggestion for breathing, up to 20 minutes until your partner falls asleep or is sufficiently relaxed.

Polarity therapy also is associated with reverie and healing imagery. Commonly during sessions one hovers in the state of reverie associated with the theta state of just before sleep. During our randomized study of polarity therapy with depressed dementia caregivers (90% of whom had significant histories of trauma) (Korn et al., 2009), 65% of the women reported several experiences of visual imagery during treatment that they associated with integrative and healing states of consciousness. One woman described her experience this way:

As you were slowly taking away the stress and then I felt it was being replaced by energy. My eyes closed, and the negative energy went up to the ceiling. I could see it. It looked like waves of steam coming out. Not in the shape of smoke, but more like fireworks disappearing in the ceiling. Then, it was replaced by positive energy and I saw white lilies. I've never seen that. And the light off of the lilies had halos around them and I could smell fresh linen. I saw a dove walking on the shore. His feet were really red, and body was really white. And the tide was coming in, and I distinctly remember his little red feet. I don't know if it was the same dove. And then I saw a dove under a waterfall and it was picking something out of its foot. I was with it behind a waterfall. Then I saw a portrait of an angel on a balcony from the side profile with arms in front, extending out its hands. And a dove was sitting in the hands about to take off. I don't know if the angel was male or female and the angel's face was beautiful. It was relaxing. Overall, it's been the most positive experience I have had in months. I feel an extra sense of relief and release. I've been holding this stress for years. I've never dreamt of lilies before.

While the passivity a client may experience by the use of touch may be contraindicated for some people or appears to contradict efforts to help the individual remain in control of the treatment, there is value in helping the trauma victim feel safe enough to assume a state of psychophysical receptivity. Treatment may be undertaken in either a seated or a prone position, depending on the individual's comfort level. The touch practitioner tunes in to the individual and uses her or his own capacity for autonomic self-regulation. This general state of consciousness helps the individual tune in to this rhythm as well. By consistently "turning down" the hyperarousal, the organism can learn to reset itself.

As I have mentioned, this type of touch is akin to interpersonal biofeedback, but it is replete with a range of affective meanings and responses that are lost in traditional biofeedback machinery. This kind of feedback also helps to clarify and define body boundaries. A distorted sense of body image and boundaries is common among survivors of sexual and physical trauma and among those with eating disorders. Touch helps bring tactile reality to the body and bridges the difference between image and reality. It also helps to clarify both the connection and separation between client and practitioner. There are many forms of touch: many types of massage, manipulative techniques, postural integration, and connective tissue therapies that may be explored, just as psychotherapeutic counseling techniques are matched to the client's needs and stage of recovery.

Elana, a 60-year old Brazilian woman, complained of a recurring painful spasm in her shoulder. As her muscles relaxed under the pressure of my fingers, she recalled for the first time that the nuns who taught in her convent school had berated her for curling her shoulders and placed a broomstick behind her back, passing it between her elbows to enforce her improved posture. She sat like that for 3 hours. Over 50 years had passed since this trauma occurred, and touching her pain touched the past, helping her remember and tell her story until her spasm subsided.

Disordered breathing almost always co-occurs with traumatic stress and is also associated with asthma, representing a profound inflammatory breathing disorder. In addition to manual therapy and the application of pressure along the transverse processes of the upper thoracic vertebra, hydrotherapy, in particular the placement of ice directly along the spine between the shoulder blades, will drive blood deep into the spinal cord (Stone, 1986). While I was living near waterfalls in Mexico, I could accomplish the same effect by placing people with chronic asthma or in the middle of an attack under the rushing cold water in contact with the spine. Whether one is using ice packs or cold sprays from showers or waterfalls, the effects are very positive and will often stop an attack. Polarity therapy is used effectively to enhance respiration in people with asthma by releasing constriction of the scalenes, the sternocleidomastoid muscles, and diaphragm and by deep pressure on the thoracic vertebrae coupled with hydrotherapy consisting of ice applied to the thoracic vertebrae on a self-care basis. One of the common areas of complaint centers on the diaphragm, including inhibited respiration, hyperventilation, and pain, constriction, or numbing in the diaphragm. The diaphragm is the main and lower muscle governing respiration. Chronic constriction in this area inhibits respiration and emotional expression. This area, also called the celiac plexus, popularly referred to as the solar plexus, thus named by 18th-century anatomists because of the raylike appearance of the nerve fibers (Scarborough, 1992). Also called the "brain of the stomach," it is regarded by kabbalists as the "light of the underworld" (Hall, 1972, p. 199) and considered by occultists as a "receiving organ." Hall (1972) traces the etymology of celiac to *koilos*, meaning "hollow" or "heavens." This region was considered the lowest heaven, ruled by Hades, the lord of the underworld. Occultists consider the solar plexus the organ of mediumship, for it acts like a mirror to the ethers (Hall, 1972). It is this region where one cannot "stomach the thought" and the "undigested" trauma sits. Ancients believed the sun or heat energy was generated and transmuted through this center, which accords with the physicist Tiller's concept of the role of chakras as energy transducers for the physical endocrine glands (see Figure 5.5).

Ayurvedic medicine ascribes the emotions of anger and fear to the liver and stomach in this region, which they associate with the fire element. Cultural descriptions for the somatic sensations in this central area are filled with images of (Promethean) fires, "butterflies," and associated with the Yiddish term *spilkes*, for nervousness, the burning of gastric acids, and the bitter, bilious rage (Latin: *bilis* meaning "anger" or "displeasure") (Scarborough, 1992). Binge eating engorges the stomach and puts pressure on the diaphragm, producing a "full" feeling, which staves off the emptiness felt by many victims of trauma. The contraction and heaving motion of the diaphragm stimulates the vagus nerve and releases the chronic muscular contraction of the diaphragm. Purging is anxiolytic in effect. *Phren* is the Greek word meaning both diaphragm and mind, suggesting the ancient understanding of the important

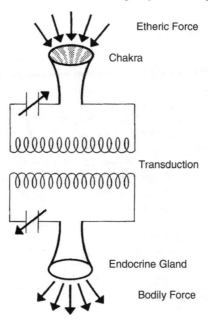

Figure 5.5 Chakras as energy transducers for the endocrine glands.
Source: Adapted from *Science and Human Transformation: Subtle Energies, Intentionality and Consciousness*, by W. Tiller, 1997, p. 123. © 1997 by Pavior Publishing. Reprinted with permission.

EXERCISE 5.3: THE GRIEF POINT

Begin this exercise by either lying down or standing. Make sure you remove a bra or any restrictive clothing. Place the middle finger of your dominant hand on your breastbone (sternum), in the area between your breasts. Gently apply pressure, moving down to the end of the breastbone. You will notice that it becomes a little softer and more sensitive as you reach the tip; this is the xyphoid process, also called an "alarm point" in Chinese medicine, denoting a vital diagnostic area. Once you reach the xyphoid process, continue to move your fingers along the underside of the ribcage. Begin to gently press under the ribs and against the bone, feeling the diaphragm, again noting areas of sensitivity or tension. Allow yourself to breathe and relax as you release any tension or discomfort. This region is often tense due to anxiety and armoring; it may also be sensitive due to poor digestion. Do this first on the right side and then the left side. This gentle exercise is a way to check in with yourself, to decrease anxiety, and to improve respiration and digestion as you prepare to release the grief point.

Next, place the palm of your less dominant hand on your belly, allowing the warmth from your hand to guide the rhythm of your breath. Next take the middle finger of your dominant hand and palpate back to the tip of the sternum; slowly, point by point, move up the sternum, applying pressure as you go, noting any sensations you feel. Some points will be more sensitive than others. When you reach the middle of the sternum, perhaps between the breasts or a little higher, you may feel a point that is especially tender. This is called the heart-grief point.

Close your eyes and, as you continue to apply pressure, breathe into this region. You may note that your breath is a bit more fluid as a result of the gentle touch you just applied under your ribs. Allow yourself to breathe in awareness of love and compassion for yourself; as you breathe out acknowledge the losses you have experienced. You may notice some resistance, fear, anger, or sadness, or you may notice that one particular memory dominates. Continue breathing and allow yourself to enter more deeply into your heart, opening to the compassion and love as well as the grief that is there. Tears, memories or unpleasant feelings may emerge. Allow the process to unfold, staying focused on compassion for yourself and for the hurts you have experienced. Note in what ways it is easier to experience love for yourself and the areas where you may not forgive yourself. Know that you can return to this exercise to continue to process these feelings and deepen your awareness and compassion each time. At the conclusion of this process you may wish to reach out to friends, family, or a counselor to further process your experience, or you may wish to do something especially loving for yourself, such as buy flowers, walk to a favorite spot, or take a nap.

relationship between the two (Scarborough, 1992). Gentle manipulation of the diaphragm (like the techniques of polarity therapy and visceral manipulation) and surrounding digestive viscera releases muscular contraction and stimulates vagal activity and parasympathetic response, providing relief and relaxation.

In my experience, people often undergo an immediate reduction and gradual elimination of behaviors—including binge-purge, cutting, and suicidal cycles—in response to this form of therapeutic touch. I believe that these responses result from an integrative response that includes deep relaxation, increased respiration, increased endogenous endorphin and serotonin levels, and rhythmic entrainment occurring in the context of a developing a new connection to oneself and therapeutic attachment with another person. Touch not only helps one to relax but invariably arouses the hypervigilance common to the survivor of sexual assault. Like many methods that involve deconditioning, touch is a powerful, inexact, and often treacherous journey, requiring more art than science.

Some of the practitioners of various forms of bodywork that I have personally observed are too directive (and often brutal), emphasizing pain and catharsis, which is not an appropriate choice for individuals vulnerable to hyperarousal and flashbacks. Whether it is the body-oriented therapies themselves that are rooted in harsh attitudes or the practitioners themselves, it seems

Mark was a young man referred to me by his psychiatrist because he thought a somatic approach might help him clarify memories that he "just couldn't accept." He had been abused by his mother and I thought it likely that touch would arouse those memories. I discussed my concerns with both him and the practitioner, and we agreed that it was worth exploring. While he lay on the table and I cradled his head, he experienced profound kinesthetic, visual, and aural memories of his mother abusing him and became very frightened; he asked me to stop, which I did. We talked about his experience, and when the session was over he said that he wasn't going to continue but that he had received a confirmation of his memories that he could no longer deny.

This was a valuable experience for Mark, his practitioner, and me. I first discussed with Mark and his therapist how he felt about working with someone of the same sex as his abuser. This treatment became a form of a powerful exposure technique, made possible by the ability of both his practitioners to support his request and help him contain his fear by not being fearful themselves. One of the major stumbling blocks to using touch as treatment for sexual or physical abuse survivors is that the referring practitioner (or physician) is fearful of her or his own body's voice.

as though they often go together to recreate the authoritative domination inherent in the original traumatic experiences. I agree with the approach elucidated by Bloch (1988), who works with torture survivors, that

> Our clients have experienced so much pain and suffering, we seek to inflict no pain, or as little as possible. Gentle massage is applied to make the individual relax and to create a situation in which a relationship of trust can be built to help the client overcome his/her defensiveness. (p. 27)

For somatic approaches to be effective in traumatic stress, they must emerge from the primal, subtle nurturance and gentleness characterized by early attachment and bonding behaviors. This is not the same as fostering regression but an adult recognition of the rhythmic template, which still pulses.

Milton came for a series of treatments, referred by his surgeon. He tried to detoxify from the pain medication he had been on since falling from a truck several years earlier. As we worked through the pain, located in the lumbar and sacral regions of his spine, he talked about the accident. As we moved deeper, he began to have memories, images, and then the feelings as he recalled being beaten bloody on his back by his drunken stepfather, as his sister and mother stood by, helpless to act. We worked together intensively for 3 months. In this time he stopped taking medication and began a program of rehabilitation that centered on touch, exercises, and expressing the rage and then grief over the theft of his childhood. When he returned home, he was pain-free and drug-free.

Working in the diaphragm (and every area) requires a gentle approach. Both client and practitioner must be prepared for the activation of state-bound memories. One way in which I introduce the individual to the sensations of the diaphragm is through an ancient yoga exercise called *Uddiyana* ("flying up") *Bandha* ("internal seal" or "lock").

EXERCISE 5.4: UDDIYANA BANDHA

Bandhas regulate the flow of *prana*. This *bandha* is designed to move the energy up toward the head. Stand with the feet a foot apart and bend over slightly, knee slightly bent, placing hands on the thighs. Lower the head between the collarbone and the breastbone, and let it rest there in that notch. Inhale deeply and exhale quickly, forcing all the air to exit the lungs. Immediately after the exhale, hold the breath, pull the abdominal region back toward the spine, contract and lift the diaphragm toward the breastbone, putting your weight on the hands on the thighs. Hold and then release. When you have mastered this motion, then repeat and instead of holding, exert a pumping action, pushing out and pulling in, all the while maintaining this pose and holding your breath.

This exercise (which can be demonstrated in person or seen on video) can be taught to clients for home use when the urge to purge arises; it serves to desensitize somatic sensations in the "solar plexus" and to quiet affective fires by reducing tension. Yogic practice prescribes this exercise to improve digestive function and cleanse the spirit. Because chronic dissociation among individuals interferes with experiencing body-based perceptions, these exercises foster new sensory awareness in a titrated manner. Making sounds, singing, chanting, toning, and yogic (polarity) voice exercises like the polarity "HA" breath vibrate the diaphragm, releasing tension and often lead to laughter, the polarity of the tears held there for so long.

EXERCISE 5.5: THERAPIST EXERCISE: DIAPHRAGM BODYWORK TECHNIQUE

During the bodywork session, sit to the right side of the client, placing your right hand on her belly and holding the trapezius muscle with your left hand. Ask the client to begin breathing by expanding the belly so that it is pushing your right hand up with the expansion. At first this may be difficult because it is the opposite of how she usually breathes. The tendency will be to complete the breath by filling the lungs up to the neck. This is to be avoided. After a few minutes of breathing from the belly, the next step is to place your right hand on the left side of her lower ribs at the diaphragm region and bring your left hand and place it on the ribs at the right side. Now you can ask her to bring the breath up only as high as the lower ribs, visualizing and expanding the ribs *to the side*. This will feel unusual and be difficult to master. Your hands will feel whether or not she is doing this correctly and during this time provide verbal feedback on whether and how well the ribs are expanding. Keep guiding her and giving response to when she is bringing the breath too high into the chest and keep her breathing rhythmically so the breath expands the ribs. While she is breathing you are making sure that she does not breathe high into her upper lungs or her neck. Having your hands on her ribs will help her feel kinesthetically the different areas for breathing and help her breathe lower in her body. Every few minutes ask her to make a loud "HA" sound, contracting the abdominal muscles as she exhales. This breathing exercise can be practiced at home and during subsequent bodywork sessions.

At the following session, place your right hand on the client's belly and the left hand on the neck with the thumb applying gentle but firm pressure in the scalenes while the other fingers in back of the neck contact the upper vertebrae. Rhythmic motion with light pressure should be applied to the scalenes upon each exhalation.

Hyperventilation is an unconscious process, and the process outlined above begins bringing awareness and retraining to the unconscious patterns. As the breath is retrained, memories may emerge, because the breath is often "lost" at the moment of trauma and the natural rhythm of breathing is held with the dissociated memory. Restoring the breath brings one back into the body, along with the memories and feelings. These may be processed slowly and gently.

EXERCISE 5.6: CLIENT EXERCISE: BREATHING FROM THE ABDOMEN

The client places her hands behind her head and bends her knees with her feet flat on the bed (or table). The client breathes gently, feeling the rising and falling of the diaphragm and the abdomen. The second phase is the client can place her hands on her belly to make sure the belly rises first, then the upper chest. A fan may be used during risk situations that might trigger a panic attack or hyperventilation. The sensation of moving air over the trigeminal nerve outlet (along the jaw line and cheeks) on each side of the face helps deepen and calm respiration (Chaitow et al., 2002).

Comparatively, touching the diaphragm is often used during later stages, when the sense of trust is more secure and when it is safer to touch in soft tissue and viscera unprotected by bone. By contrast, gentle manipulation of the occipital ridge and condyles is often the first stage of touch, as touching the bony protuberances at the back of the skull and cradling the head, either in a prone or seated position, tend to feel less threatening. There are always exceptions and ongoing assessment can indicate what is appropriate and when. Something apparently as innocuous as applying pressure to the toes of someone whose feet were abusively "tickled" can be traumatic, so the known meaning of each region can be discussed in advance or will be discovered during treatment. Applying pressure to the occipital ridge and palpating the cranial-sacral rhythm are effective for chronic muscle tension, eyestrain, jaw pain, frontal headaches and migraines, common in trauma and dissociation. Holding the back of the skull may feel safe enough and lead to deep relaxation and trance and by holding the head, one can move to touching the neck muscles and the jawbone. Tracing the muscular tension down the neck can release state-dependent memories of a car accident or of unwanted kissing or oral rape. Once these memories are accessed and processed, touching the neck becomes less "charged" until the "exposure" no longer activates a response and the chronic pain and tension are released.

One winter in Mexico, an older gentleman with a soft German accent typical on the border between the Czech Republic and Germany arrived at my *palapa* with an acute flare-up of a chronically "frozen" (adhesive capsulitis) right shoulder. Nothing had provided sustained relief over the years. Robert had used pain medication, Valium, anti-inflammatories, physical therapy, psychoanalysis, and ultrasound. He lay on his side and, as his scapula spread like a wing under my hands, he told me the story of his escape from Germany, carrying his ill sister (on his right side) to safety just minutes before the Nazis swept through the Sudetenland in 1939. As we worked, he drifted and relaxed and said he felt "like a baby." During the course of the four treatments, he talked about his traumatic experiences as I rigorously rotated the glenohumoral joint to break up adhesions and crystalline deposits to pain tolerance and release areas of state-dependent pain. He cried. His symptoms disappeared. We stayed in touch over the years and his pain never returned. This was one of the most dramatic responses to accessing and releasing state-dependent memory I have ever witnessed.

THE TOUCH OF ANIMAL COMPANIONS

One of the ways in which I introduce touch and affection into the therapeutic setting, whether I am working in my capacity as a psychotherapist or as a body psychotherapy practitioner, is to integrate an animal copractitioner. My animal companion, a Golden Retriever named Bodhi Sattva, accompanied me to work for 11 years. *Bodhi* (pronounced with a long "o") is a Sanskrit word meaning "compassion" and "love." The Bo tree was a wild fig tree under which the Buddha was sitting when he attained enlightenment. *Bodhi Sattva* is the Buddhist appellation given to any being who, though she or he attains nirvana (liberation), remains on earth to help others achieve enlightenment—a rather lofty assignment for a dog, yet one that others throughout history and across cultures have considered suitable for such an animal.

Many of my clients have experienced little appropriate touch or attachment to others in their lives. Bodhi's contribution to their lives has proved integral and immeasurable. They regard him as an essential assistant, worthy of massages, confidences, tears, and bones. With the exception of a few clients who are oblivious to his presence, most actively engage in a relationship with him and to differing degrees become attached, receiving and giving love through him.

Much of what is known about human development has come from the study of dogs. There are two periods in their growth as puppies during which they are especially vulnerable to traumatic experiences: during the 12th and 16th weeks. In spite of my careful watch, several potentially traumatic events happened to Bodhi during these two periods of growth—a tumble down a flight of stairs and a ferocious dog-bully, neither of which seemed to leave a lasting impression, whether due to his innate hardiness or to my care and massages. In fact, his great charm for my clients is his trusting, goofy nature.

As Bodhi grew, I socialized him extensively in order to prepare him for a "public" life. In addition to private practice, he joined me in meetings with the police and district attorneys during testimony by crime victims. Early in his life, I gave him daily massages, rubbed his gums and belly to promote bonding and to help him grow into a relaxed dog who was comfortable with being touched and not fearful of anyone. I also included methods of titrating abrupt experiences, including grabbing him from behind, as an unknowing toddler might; exposing him to sudden loud sounds; being bumped by a wheelchair; and keeping a hand in the food bowl while he munched, so he wouldn't become aggressive around his food. As an adolescent, he trained and passed tests, including registration as a Canine Good Citizen and as a Therapy Dog International.

Much has been said about the loyalty, affection, intelligence, optimism, and unconditional love shown by dogs, especially Golden Retrievers. Bodhi nurtured the oft-submerged, latent, or distressed capacities for attachment common to victims of chronic childhood violence. This is how Bodhi became a healer. However, I also discovered that the interpersonal affinities between human and dog took on an important rhythm. Bodhi had his own bed, on which he invariably stayed when not actively engaged with a client; yet whenever a client lay down on the treatment table, he would move to lie underneath it. I soon noticed that the rhythm of clients' respirations often became entrained to his (or his to the client's), leading to a relaxation in both their rates and depth of respiration. This was first apparent to me when during the course of the hour, several sighs would occur in both dog and client simultaneously. Dogs generally breathe 10 to 30 times a minute, while humans normally breathe 12 to 16 times, depending on gender, age, and health. People with chronic anxiety states often have a pattern of sighing up to once a minute, holding the breath for 8 to 15 seconds at a time and breathing 18 times a minute (Fried & Grimaldi, 1993).

Sometimes a client would notice the respiratory entrainment and remark on it. Intimate interaction, such as talking and touching with companion animals, reduces levels of arousal, such as blood pressure; relaxed facial characteristics and speech patterns are characteristic of the dialogue between parents and young infants (Katcher & Beck, 1987). There is a reciprocal effect of facial expression on emotional experience; for example, various qualities of contraction and relaxation of the facial muscles are directly associated with certain emotions. Take a moment to hold a smile and observe how fast positive feelings increase. Indeed, this is a positive psychology exercise, somatic-style. For survivors who are in great pain and find no reason to smile, the smile or laugh elicited by an animal can begin to reactivate the neuromuscular pattern of pleasure.

Susan, aged 30, had made several suicide attempts by wrist cutting and had been in and out of hospitals as a result of severe abuse by several family members during her childhood. She came for treatment while she was still in the hospital. She reported, "I have no touch in life, not even hugs. I'm afraid of it." After discussing the parameters of the touch I proposed, I asked if she would like to first touch Bodhi. I then demonstrated on his paws how I would touch her hands. After she touched Bodhi, we discussed her preference for seating position and I began by holding one hand in both of mine, contacting *He Gu*, an acupuncture point in the web of the thumb. Susan's first responses included an almost overwhelming mixture of pleasure and disgust, and we adjusted the amount of time we worked according to her tolerance. After the second session, I suggested that she might want to massage her hands and that she purchase some skin oil. I showed her how by demonstrating on myself. She came in the following week excited about having massaged her hands and was now doing it for a few minutes every night before bed. Her suicidal ideation diminished and she was released from the hospital. In the early sessions, we did touch therapy for 5 minutes. Other days Susan preferred only to talk about how she felt and to discuss plans for the next session. Each time Susan came in, we began our ritual with touching Bodhi. This provided a reliable structure and the chance for Susan to experiment with her own "technique" of touch. She was experiencing her own sensations but also becoming cognizant of the effect of her touch on the dog. Bodhi's joy and receptivity, apparent when he rolled over and dog-cooed, reinforced her own deepening sense of connection and capacity to soothe. This opened the opportunity for Susan to reminisce fondly about her family dog. Until this time, she had been unable to recall any fond memories of her early life.

One week Susan came in and said that she had allowed a friend to give her a hug, although she struggled with allowing herself that pleasure. The next week she came in exclaiming, "I can feel my hands, I can feel my hands, now I want to feel my arms!"

Our work progressed steadily. Her tolerance for pleasure increased. Hugs with friends became routine and she exchanged shoulder massages with friends. Six months later, she was no longer harming herself and there were no further hospitalizations.

During one of Susan's final visits, she asked if she could lie down on her stomach on the treatment table and asked me to work on her upper back. As she did, she began to get scared and to dissociate until we "talked her back into her body." She called Bodhi close to her, and he sat near her head. At the close of the session, she said, "I could come back in my body because Bodhi is here and I trust him." Soon after, Susan decided to terminate, saying that she had accomplished what she had set out to do. Two years later, her psychologist reported that she had remained free of self-harming behaviors and was working part-time.

Bodhi meant many things to my clients. My relationship with him presented a model for caring interaction that was external to the client-practitioner relationship. As "my child," or a dependent, he may serve as an object of identification for my client. How I talk to him and treat him gives important clues to traumatized clients who live with the dread that I will eventually betray them.

When clients want to bring him a biscuit, they can give freely. When they want to question me about my approaches to dog-rearing, we can discuss some themes that are a subtext for a future exchange about how I feel about them and they about me. We often talk about Bodhi's vulnerability and dependence, for he reflects the open, generous, and eager state of the (inner) child my client and I try to reach and reassure, whose memories are often subsumed with pain and fear.

Lucy was a survivor of childhood rape who was crying deeply and shaking over the losses she had endured. Bodhi got up out of a sound sleep and grabbed her coat off the couch between his teeth and brought it to her. She was amazed by his response, talking about it for months afterward, for it signified to her the level to which Bodhi (and I, in ways I could not otherwise sufficiently convey) was attuned to her pain and suffering. This experience allowed her to begin to receive care and empathy from others and began a new level of care for herself.

When a particular memory or story engenders too much shame to share with me, my client, with gentle encouragement, can tell Bodhi first and make it safe to tell me. Conversely, I can catch the wrath of the abandoned person. For if Bodhi has rolled in something (that is perfume only to him) during his morning run and he has to stay at home until he has a bath, I'll be advised by everyone that day that *both* practitioners better be there next time. However, this unexpected and temporary loss often proves fruitful as well, for old memories of loss and death, of childhood animals, and of people create an opportunity to explore grief, loss, and trust, often for the first time.

There is a long cross-cultural history of the use of dogs as agents of healing. Contemporary renewal of interest in clinical applications and research with dogs started after World War II. For the Sumerian goddess Gula, the "Great Physician," and of the Babylonian and Chaldean god of healing Marduk, the dog was the sacred emblem of healing. In ancient Greece, dogs were considered "emissaries of the gods" (Serpell, 1986), and along with the sacred snakes of the temples licked the people while they slept as part of the healing ritual. Hermes' son Pan was a woodland deity associated with animals (Sansonese, 1994). Aesculapius, the Greek god of healing, was guarded by a dog as a child and is often shown pictured with a dog by his side. In Greek cosmology, the serpents ruled in the valley and the dogs ruled in the mountains, they were considered two sides of the same essence. The dog also represents transition in many cultures. Quetzelcoatl, the Nahuatl deity, was accompanied by a dog (who was his twin) on descent to the underworld, and the dog also travels with Hekate, midwife and goddess of the gates in the underworld. Thus the dog passes between light and dark, death and life, representing "the turn for the better at the brink of the underworld" (Kerényi, 1959, p. 32). In the late 18th century in England, animals were used at a country retreat for the mentally ill (Ruckert, 1987). The first recorded use of animals for therapy in the United States was during World War II, with veterans recovering from traumatic stress at the Pawling Army Air Corps Convalescent Hospital in New York. In the 1950s, Levinson (1984) introduced his dog into the treatment of children and elders. During the 1970s, the Corsons (Ruckert, 1987; Serpell, 1986) published their research on pet-facilitated therapy in which they brought dogs onto psychiatric wards to work with nonverbal patients.

In their role as modern-day healers, dogs continue to serve: to lick the wounds and to guide the traumatized individual back from the underworld of despair and detachment. Animal-assisted therapy works with almost every type of animal. Dogs, cats, horses, rabbits, birds, fish, and even dolphins are increasingly integrated into the treatment of PTSD in private and public settings. Fine (2010) has written a comprehensive handbook that provides a guide to integrating animals into treatment, and Chandler (2011) provides a counseling-specific approach that includes training and methods for treating specific emotional and psychiatric issues using animal assisted counseling techniques. The Delta Society sponsors the Pet Partners training program for people and their dogs who wish to undertake animal-assisted therapy.

Psychiatric Service Dogs

Clients with PTSD may benefit from living and working with emotional support dogs or psychiatric service dogs. The Psychiatric Service Dog Society is a resource that provides advocacy and educational services. Psychiatric service dogs require training in basic obedience, public access skills, and disability-related assistance. A professional should do temperament testing if a dog is going to be adopted for service. Psychiatric service dogs have all the rights of public access as service dogs. Psychiatric service dogs might undertake the following services for symptoms of PTSD: they can be alerted to the presence of other people or check a room to address hypervigilance or fear; they can turn on lights or awaken their companions in response to a nightmare; they provide tactile stimulation and hugging for anxiety and grief; they can wake up clients who may be sleeping due to depression and cause them to have to leave the house for walks; and they can assist in memory loss by performing daily routines and finding lost objects.

Emotional Support Dogs

Emotional support dogs provide therapeutic support to someone with a disability by providing companionship, nonjudgmental positive regard, and affection. If a licensed clinician determines that the client is disabled by PTSD and would benefit from an emotional support animal, the clinician writes letters to support a request by the client to keep the animal in "no pets" housing or to travel with the animal in the cabin of an aircraft. The dogs must be trained to be obedient. A minimal level of obedience training will include Canine Good

Citizen training. In addition to dogs, other animals, most notably horses and dolphins, participate in organized assisted therapy programs.

SUMMARY

As with all therapeutic interventions, the efficacy of touch depends on its isomorphic utility and also on the ineffable—an amalgam of the known and unknown, of visible and invisible forces that stir the soul to heal as they transmute the pain of suffering through somatic awareness and discovery. Our professional attitudes about touch are culturally and historically determined and should be understood in the context of present-day taboos and resistance. Animal companions play an important role as copractitioners in animal-assisted therapy for trauma treatment; they can facilitate safe touch and trust, and they help to restore attachment behaviors.

6   Integrative Assessment

"What's the use of their having names," the Gnat said, "if they won't answer
to them?" "No use to them," said Alice, "but it's useful to the people that name
them, I suppose."

—Lewis Carroll

Traumatic stress syndromes can be divided into four distinct yet interrelated
diagnostic categories: posttraumatic stress disorder (PTSD) (acute, chronic, or
delayed onset), complex posttraumatic stress disorder (CPTSD), acute stress
disorder (ASD), and developmental trauma disorder (DTD). Early and correct differential diagnosis, based on compassionate methods of assessment,
will help the practitioner to begin the process of establishing trust and initiate effective treatment strategies. The assessment and diagnosis of traumatic
stress must give special attention to assessment for the integration of mind/
body interventions.

In this chapter I shall

- define 4 trauma disorders
- review philosophy, methods, and tools of assessment
- provide assessment questions that include complementary and alternative
  medicine (CAM) and nutrition
- explore the diversity of culture and assessment

My approach to assessment flows from a feminist, somatic, integrative
posttrauma, culture-centric viewpoint. A posttrauma lens posits that trauma
is the central cause of the individual's presenting symptoms, whether they
include anxiety, depression, physical illness, dissociation, self-harm, or substance abuse. This means that when people present with any of the sequelae
associated with trauma, one identifies any traumatic events in the individual's
life and makes the connection between these events and the current level
of function. Our theoretical lens determines how we listen to our clients,
and this in turn determines our assessment, diagnosis, and treatment. An

improved understanding of trauma as a central cause of psychological and physical disease requires an integrative approach to assessment. A somatic approach to assessment engages the myriad ways in which the body communicates the story of trauma and seeks to understand the language of the body in its own voice, not as the "handmaiden" to the mind. A culture-centric assessment elevates one's understanding of the cultural and ethnic heritage(s) of the individual and explores the diversity among cultures and the myriad ways in which people express pain and discomfort. This perspective requires that practitioners examine their own cultural value systems and how they affect treatment. A feminist model of posttrauma assessment brings to treatment an analysis of how gender relations contribute to complex trauma—the abuse and misuses of power that manifest as power over individuals in contrast to sharing power. This model of assessment is not static but requires ongoing evaluation of the sociopolitical underpinnings of trauma in specific cultural contexts. An integrative posttrauma model of assessment is a comprehensive approach to the physical, emotional, mental, and spiritual aspects of the individual and how trauma has affected those parts of the self. Finally, since I believe complex and developmental trauma is a social disease, assessment must also be rooted in an understanding of social oppression. The task of assessment is to

- provide a safe climate for the client to tell the trauma story
- elicit the client's history
- identify the traumatic antecedent(s)
- assess current (intensity of) symptoms and level of functioning
- establish empathy and reassure the client about the causative role the trauma has played in presenting symptoms
- identify the complex relationships between physical, mental, emotional, and spiritual function

The ordering of the physical, mental, emotional, and spiritual functions of assessment will be unique to each client. Since clients do not always present for treatment and name trauma or abuse as the central focus, asking trauma questions first is not advisable. Conversely, clients often give hints about trauma during the initial interview; sometimes they are testing (consciously or not) to see if the clinician can read between the lines, will tolerate the topic, or can "hear" what the client is saying. Power is a central issue in treatment and assessment. Because issues of power are central (Herman, 1992) to the experience of victimization, acknowledging the power differential inherent in the practitioner/client relationship and not accentuating these differentials contributes to healing. The practitioner has implicit power by virtue of the professional position, of availability for help because of payment for services, and because the practitioner is not the victim. While different forms of therapy may have more of a power differential, all therapy, regardless of how "egalitarian" or mutual it tries to be, contains a power dynamic that favors the practitioner. Because of this, all efforts must be directed toward the empowerment of the client. Empowerment is the antithesis of trauma. Therefore the assessment process must begin to help the client regain control over her or his life through telling his or her story and then, through treatment, defining that story. Control of assessment is in the hands of the client. The client determines the content, the amount of what she wants to discuss, and the pace. However, the therapist must also manage the session, making sure that it is a safe process. Empathy, which involves nonjudgmental, heartfelt receptivity to the client's story, is essential to the process. I do not push but wait or inquire gently, gauging by the response how far to proceed. When the therapist has empathically acknowledged the pain and terror of what the client has survived and has agreed to begin the process of a therapeutic partnership based on the rhythm of recovery, healing can begin. Appropriate methods of evaluation may include open-ended questions; structured interviews and self-reports based on verbal dialogue; written response to questionnaires; nonverbal expressive methods such as art or somatic therapy; or affective responses to bodywork methods. Clients may share journal entries or write parts of the story that she or he cannot yet speak out loud. Initial discussion should include an evaluation of current mental health status including suicidality, degree of substance use, and danger of self-harm.

ASSESSMENT SCALES

Assessment scales and tools can assist the evaluation process. The purpose and meaning of an assessment instrument can be discussed with the client, who should have the choice and access to the results of the instruments used. A client may appreciate a structured interview or forms to fill out or he or she may find this cold and distancing. The utility of these tools is to illuminate information for the practitioner as well as for the client in a focused and structured format. Good assessment instruments should focus as heavily on the actual trauma as on other symptoms.

Structured interviews are especially useful (and often required) in forensic, workers' compensation, or disability assessments. Other reasons for using a structured interview include cases that may involve filing malpractice complaints, where the clinician is serving as a consultant in another case, or to clarify puzzling questions about a diagnosis. As a rule, I begin assessments with open-ended interviews and use interview tools when I am trying to otherwise quantify or elaborate various symptoms. I also use assessment tools if they will serve a psychoeducational purpose; the client may feel that it will enhance my knowledge, or the structure may make her or him feel safer. The clinician must titrate the pace of assessment to the client's capacity to tolerate affect and story, and the clinician should disclose the limits of confidentiality, including a handout detailing policies about fees, cancellation, and phone calls.

Specific testing identifying nutritional status or neurotransmitter and adrenal function may also be included in cooperation with other providers. The point is to arrive at a working conception or diagnosis that can guide treatment.

LISTENING TO THE LANGUAGE OF SUFFERING

Assessment is an interactive communication process. It sets the stage for enunciating a language of suffering, of finding a language in which to express what cannot be named—the often speechless terror of trauma. The clenched-jaw pain, teeth-grinding, frontal headaches, and temporomandibular joint (TMJ) syndrome common to survivors result from this tension of the "unspeakable." During the initial assessment period, the victim is also assessing—appraising whether or not the clinician has the empathy and the capacity to tolerate listening to the words and tears and often rage that will emerge. Much of this evaluative communication takes place at a level commonly called "chemistry," which flows in both directions. Though the anxious speech of the acutely traumatized person reflects a *hyperaroused*, untrusting nervous system (which does not respond well to the clinician's verbal reassurances of trustworthiness), the body with a "mind of its own" can kinesthetically perceive the clinician's quieting, empathic rhythm.

These responses to extreme trauma are not surprising given the assault on the self experienced in complex trauma. The right to need, to ask, and to demand is nonexistent in complex traumatic events. Therapy, then, must involve relearning or perhaps learning for the first time how to feel, to sense what one needs and define these needs, to ask, and finally to take care of those needs and protect oneself.

DEFINITIONS OF FOUR MAJOR STRESS SYNDROMES

Diagnostic criteria change and evolve, and are often culture-specific. The assessment of distress in response to trauma is especially subject to variations in culture and in ethnic, and gender values. The disciplines of cross-cultural psychology, transcultural psychiatry, and medical anthropology can all contribute to clinical assessments. Ultimately we listen to and learn from our clients about what they experience and how we might be of service to them.

Posttraumatic Stress

Posttraumatic stress occurs in response to stressful events that overwhelm the individual's capacity to cope. These events, called stressors, may include actual or threatened death, serious injury, or a threat of injury to self or others. They would distress virtually anyone, causing intense fear, horror, or helplessness

(Davidson & Foa, 1993; Koopman, Classen, Cardena, & Spiegel, 1995). B. Green (1990; p. 135) has outlined eight generic dimensions of trauma: threat to life and limb, severe physical harm or injury, receipt of intentional injury/ harm, exposure to the grotesque, violent/sudden loss of a loved one, witnessing or learning of violence to a loved one, learning of exposure to a noxious agent, and causing death or severe harm to another.

In response to one or more of these stressors, a person experiences a sense of victimization. This includes bereavement, loss of safety and a way of life, loss of family or friends, and loss of physical and emotional well-being. The individual also feels betrayed; whether by a person, by nature, by God, or by his or her own faith in the goodness and justice of life. In addition to the responses to the mind/body trauma I discussed in Chapter 3, individuals may experience negative intimacy, struggles with meaning, loss of faith and hope, and death imagery (Lifton, 1979; Ochberg, 1988).

PTSD Assessment Scales

The Clinician-Administered PTSD Scale (CAPS), a 30-item structured inter-view that corresponds to the DSM-IV-TR criteria for PTSD, is the gold stan-dard in PTSD assessment. It can be used to make a current (past month) or lifetime diagnosis of PTSD or to assess symptoms over the past week (Blake et al., 2000).

The Trauma and Attachment Belief Scale (TABS) was designed for use with individuals who have experienced traumatic events and to assess the effects of vicarious traumatization. It assesses beliefs/cognitive schema in five areas that may be affected by traumatic experiences: (1) safety, (2) trust, (3) esteem, (4) intimacy, and (5) control (Pearlman, 2003).

The Traumatic Screening Questionnaire (TSQ) (Brewin et al., 2002) is a 5-minute 10-item symptom screen designed for use with survivors of all types of traumatic stress.

The Trauma Symptom Inventory is a 20-minute 100-item questionnaire used in the detection and measurement of posttraumatic states (Briere, 1995).

Complex Posttraumatic Stress

In the early 1990s, a definition of trauma that more accurately encompassed the effects of chronic, extreme stress on personality development was described by Herman (1992), who called it complex posttraumatic stress disorder (CPTSD). As clinicians listened ever more closely to accounts of the horrors of war and sexual trauma, they reached beneath the surface of the often misapplied diag-noses to discover that the factor common to up to 70% of such patients was their prolonged exposure to traumatic events (Herman, 1990).

People who have been subject to prolonged physical or emotional captivity—as occurs in cases of domestic violence, long-term abuse, and in individuals who have been prisoners of war or held in concentration camps—are among those likely to experience complex changes in their physical, emotional, mental, and spiritual functioning.

In such instances, alterations in affect regulation may include

- persistent dysphoria
- chronic suicidal preoccupation
- self-injury
- explosive or extremely inhibited anger (may alternate)
- compulsive or extremely inhibited sexuality (may alternate)

Alterations in consciousness may include

- amnesia or hyperamnesia for traumatic events
- transient dissociative episodes
- depersonalization/derealization
- reliving experiences, either in the form of intrusive PTSD symptoms or as a ruminative preoccupation

Alterations in self-perception may include

- a sense of helplessness or paralysis of initiative
- shame, guilt, and self-blame
- a sense of defilement or stigma
- a sense of complete difference from others (may include a feeling of specialness, utter aloneness, belief that no other person can understand, or the belief that one has a nonhuman identity)

Alterations in perception of perpetrator may include

- preoccupation with relationship with the perpetrator (includes preoccupation with revenge)
- unrealistic attribution of total power to the perpetrator (caution: the victim's assessment of power realities may be more realistic than the clinician's)
- idealization of paradoxical gratitude
- sense of a special or supernatural relationship
- acceptance of belief system or rationalizations of perpetrator

Alterations in relations with others may include

- isolation and withdrawal
- disruption in intimate relationships

- repeated search for rescuer (may alternate with isolation and withdrawal)
- persistent distrust
- repeated failures of self-protection

Alterations in systems of meaning may include

- loss of sustaining faith
- a sense of hopelessness and despair (Herman, 1992, p. 121)

The experience of self-blame is intrinsic to victimization, more so when one is objectified and degraded by another human.

John came into treatment depressed about his relationship with his girlfriend, who would physically strike out at him when they argued. He was a talented writer who had trouble staying at jobs and was a compulsive spender and gambler. He described a history of chronic digestive problems, including bulimia. There were large gaps in his memory about his childhood, though he expressed discomfort (without knowing why) when he talked about his aunt and uncle, who had lived with his family for a period of time. During our work together, John tentatively revealed a history of being physically assaulted by his girlfriends, beginning when he was 17. As we explored these experiences, John felt tremendous shame even while he expressed relief that he was being taken seriously. When he had tried to talk about the abuses with his friends, they just laughed at him, he said. John and I focused on stabilizing his finances, his work life, and nutrition, and then we slowly explored his relationships with women. After 12 months, he took a 2-year break, during which he continued to successfully create the life he wanted. He returned to therapy when he began to experience nightmares about his childhood and we began exploring the violent relationship between his parents and his aunt and uncle.

Complex Trauma Assessment Scale

Assessing CPTSD requires time to do a comprehensive history. This can occur during the initial sessions or it may occur over time, as the victim's story emerges. Most people with CPTSD fulfill the criteria for PTSD and, as I have argued throughout this book, many, particularly those diagnosed with borderline personality disorder, will best respond to treatment when diagnosed and treated for trauma.

Two instruments may be used to help organize the interviews. The clinician administers one and the other is a self-report. They are (1) the Structured Interview for Disorders of Extreme Stress (SIDES) (Pelcovitz, van der Kolk, Roth, Mandel, Kaplan, & Resick, 1997) and (2) the Self-Report Instrument for Disorders of Extreme Stress (SIDES-SR).

Acute Stress Disorder

Acute stress disorder (ASD) occurs in response to the same kinds of stressors that precipitate PTSD (Brett, 1993), including accidents, death of a loved one, and natural or technological disasters. Symptoms include: dissociative and anxiety symptoms reexperiencing the traumatic event and avoidance behaviors that interfere with social, task-oriented, and occupational functioning.

The episode must last for at least 2 days and occur within 4 weeks of the trauma to warrant this diagnosis (Davidson & Foa, 1993). Assessment and treatment must begin immediately following exposure so as to maximize benefit. If symptoms last beyond a month following the traumatic event, PTSD may ensue and continue for months or even years after the precipitating event. (Koopman et al., 1995). The important diagnostic difference between ASD and PTSD is that ASD is time-limited, occurring within a month after the event and lasting not more than 4 weeks (Koopman et al., 1995). Following a traumatic event, there is an increased risk of suicide.

Roger came to treatment with his partner, Bob, after they were assaulted coming out of a restaurant late one night. During the attack they were called gay and epithets were hurled at them; they were kicked and beaten and threatened with death if they went to the police. One week later, Roger was not getting out of bed. He reported panic attacks, nightmares, feeling in a fog and not wanting to go to work or see friends: "It's bad enough getting beaten up, but then the police acted like I deserved it, and my landlord suggested that if we didn't "look" gay we wouldn't have had any trouble. I don't feel safe anymore and I don't want to go out.

Acute stress can be complicated not only by earlier traumas but also by the additional stressors of social bigotry. Bigotry against homosexuality resulting in "gay bashing" is one trauma. However, nonviolent bigotry also extends the impact of trauma and limits the capacity to access social supports for recovery. Roger's acute stress was prolonged by the homophobia of the health and legal professionals in his small rural community. His fear was exacerbated by his concern that police reports would reveal his victimization for being homosexual and word would reach his family and colleagues, jeopardizing his job and social network.

Secondary Trauma ExpTeriences

Catherall (1989) differentiates between the primary and secondary trauma. The original traumatic event and the subsequent physical and affective storms are part of the primary trauma. The secondary trauma occurs with the ruptures in the survivor's sense of connection with her personal and work relationships. This concept of the secondary trauma intersects with Herman's observation that trauma is contagious (Herman, 1992). The intense pain the victim experiences leads him to isolate himself from his social circle, but it may also create an intense need that can overwhelm family and friends, leading to a tremendous strain on social relationships and often causing them to wither under the pressure.

The Disaster Syndrome

The disaster syndrome is another form of acute stress that affects direct victims and rescue workers alike. The bombing of the federal building in Oklahoma in 1995; the attacks on the Twin Towers in 2001 in New York City; the Indonesian tsunami in 2004; Hurricane Katrina in the southeastern United States in 2005; and the 2011 earthquake off the Pacific coast of Tohoku, Japan, which resulted in a Tsunami and nuclear meltdown of the Fukushima I Nuclear Power Plant all caused acute trauma to victims and survivors, their friends and families, the rescue workers, and the community at large.

Often an acute stressor activates a powerful response that appears to be multilayered, with qualities that lead the clinician to suspect unresolved traumatic experiences from the past. In this case, acute stress is differentiated from the acute activation of (delayed) PTSD, where traumatic stress has been treated but subsequent life (traumatic) stressors restimulate the symptoms. In these cases it is wise to proceed with establishing safety and addressing the current concerns. The past traumatic events can be addressed after the client has stabilized.

Acute Stress Disorder Scale and Measures

The Acute Stress Disorder Interview (ASDI) (Bryant, Harvey, Dang, & Sackville, 1998) is a structured clinical interview that has been validated against DSM-IV criteria for ASD. The Acute Stress Disorder Scale (Bryant, Moulds, & Guthrie, 2000) is a self-report measure of ASD symptoms that correlates highly with symptom clusters on the ASDI. These scales may be found in Bryant and Harvey's (2000) text on ASD.

Developmental Trauma Disorder

Developmental trauma disorder (DTD) is a new clinical concept that addresses the need to identify, assess, and treat in children the effects of interpersonal trauma including neglect, assault, betrayal, and witnessing during childhood.

Current categories of PTSD do not adequately address the responses children experience to trauma, including intense affect, avoidance and numbing, dissociation, trauma reenactment, and somatic distress. All too often children are misdiagnosed with oppositional defiance disorder, ADD/ADHD, bipolar disorder and separation, anxiety reactive attachment disorder, and obesity (Burke, et al., 2011; van der Kolk et al., 2009). DTD is similar to the construct of complex trauma, adjusted to and reflective of early stages of development in children.

THE STAGES OF PRESENTATION

People present for assessment at all stages of discovery, ranging from having vague or fragmented memories to suffering from long-standing chronic physical symptoms exacerbated by current life stressors that have triggered powerful emotional connections to being acutely suicidal following rape. The constellation of neglect and trauma—with the associated symptom cluster of depression, anxiety, chronic pain, interpersonal difficulties, somatic complaints, substance abuse, and eating disorders—provides clues to a traumatic history.

> Lisa, an active college student, came to treatment expressing suicidal thoughts after she was raped on a date. In addition to suffering in the aftermath of the rape, the rape caused memories of childhood abuse to emerge: "I had always remembered some things had happened to me, but I told myself it was no big deal. It was as though I had stored memories in one place, the feelings in another and the knowledge of it in yet another and had kept them all separate. When I was raped, all the walls came down."

Though a full trauma history is always indicated, the client must not be pushed to discuss the details but rather allowed to follow natural rhythms. The practitioner must express interest and concern but without overinvolvement or pressure to reveal the trauma stories. It is not the role of the clinician to tell the client that one may suspect a history of trauma based on the presentation of symptoms but rather to let the client's story unfold. A client may discuss experiences that are traumatic without acknowledging or naming them as such. This may be due to minimization, dissociation, or the effects of self-blame and self-hatred. When this occurs the clinician can gently reframe for the client how she sees these experiences of victimization: as traumatizing to anyone, not the client's fault, and the likely cause of her present problems, which will improve with treatment.

A client may hesitate to discuss the details of her experience, being fearful of generating painful feelings. There may be a temporary increase in symptoms such as intrusive memories, nightmares, distress, substance abuse, avoidance, or self-harming behaviors. Assessment may also have a positive impact; people often feel relief and validation. People rarely present with dissociative symptoms as a complaint and often do not know that they dissociate. It is difficult to identify dissociative features when one is first sitting with someone, though over time both client and clinician will be able to identify dissociative patterns. Therefore it is advisable to conduct an assessment for dissociative symptoms.

TRAUMA STORY

The process of assessment should invite the client to tell the story of her or his life covering history of the traumatic events, including

- the intensity, duration, and features of the actual events
- the ages and developmental stages during the events—what occurred
- what role the victim and the other people played; how the victim functioned prior to the traumatic events
- past and current coping styles, current self-care behaviors
- resiliency and strengths
- the current meaning of the events
- the current environment and social supports
- the work/school environment
- the role of the family and their attitudes about the traumatic events, past and current practitioners, and treatments

Asking about previous and current treatments allows for the exploration of both positive and negative experiences so as to gain insight into what the client felt to be helpful and not helpful. A client may share information about discomfort with a practitioner's interpersonal style or about behaviors that suggest boundary violations. I will ask for more detail, including questions such as whether or not any professionals have crossed boundaries with the client or if he or she has ever felt uncomfortable in a relationship with a practitioner. During history taking it is essential to ask about previous therapy experiences in addition to experiences with authorities such as clergy, teachers, supervisors, and employers. Asking about previous experiences with people in authority will also provide insight into the potential challenges of therapy and the relationship. People do not always offer these experiences unless asked directly and in several ways; they may be reluctant to reveal previous negative experiences, or they may be confused or in denial about the nature of the previous treatment/clergy relationships. Survivors are often abused or mistreated many times by many people before they arrive at therapy. During the assessment the clinician will integrate knowledge about all relationships where there are or were power imbalances or abuse and begin to develop a picture of short- and long-term needs for treatment.

The intersection of patriarchy and culture is observed in all areas of trauma and no less so in "white collar" crime. White-collar rapists are people who, under the guise of their professional garb, prey on the vulnerabilities of people they are supposed to care for and protect. Among these are teachers, coaches, clergy, lawyers, clinical practitioners, physicians, and therapists of all kinds. A large nationwide study found that 9.6% of students reported sexual misconduct by an educator (U.S. Department of Education, 2004). Sexual boundary violations increase at the university level. One study reported that 17% of female psychology graduate students had been sexually involved with their professors and 30% more had been harassed (Rutter, 1991). Estimates of prevalence of sexual assault by practitioners and other professionals range from 7% to 10% in studies based on self-reports (Gartrell, Herman, Olarte, Feldstein, & Localio, 1986). A survey of psychiatrists revealed that 88% of the sexual contacts occurred between male psychiatrists and female patients (Gartrell et al., 1986), and each perpetrator averaged abusing eight patients. The sequelae of professional exploitation or practitioner-client sex may include feelings of loss, ambivalence, emptiness, and isolation; a sense of guilt; sexual confusion; impaired ability to trust; identity, boundary, and role confusion; emotional lability; suppressed rage; increased suicidal risk; and cognitive dysfunction. These sequelae manifest especially in the areas of attention and concentration and frequently involve flashbacks, nightmares, intrusive thoughts, and unbidden images (Pope, 1988). The abuse of power by a practitioner is devastating to the life of the victim. Many victims never return to treatment, but if they do, the new practitioner must be prepared to deal with the distrust and traumatic transference engendered by the abusive therapist.

During the course of treatment clients may reveal somatic phobias or discuss their inability to undergo routine examinations or treatment by dentists or gynecologists or other clinicians. Women who were orally raped may have anxiety about seeking dental care. Women with histories of violent trauma are far less likely to obtain mammograms (Farley, Minkoff, & Barkan, 2001).

The aftermath of treatment abuse requires that the subsequent therapist sensitively support the client as she makes choices about her next steps, for boundary violation trauma often causes the victim to "second guess" many of the decisions she will now make in her life. Whether these choices involve legal action or a search for treatment with other practitioners—or simply where to go shopping or what food to eat—the clinician must exercise patience during this phase of recovery.

Although most victims of treatment abuse never pursue their assailants legally, if a complaint is filed, the victim must contend with a legal and administrative relief system that is often unbelieving, in denial, or hostile to the victim (Bisbing, Jorgenson, & Sutherland, 1995). In cases where therapy abuse victims initiated court proceedings, it required an average of 10 years following the end of abuse for such a complaint to be filed. The practitioner who is counseling a victim of such abuse should be well versed in both the symptoms and treatment approaches (group treatment in such instances may be more efficacious than individual therapy), and also be able to provide referrals for additional support services, when necessary, to any number of advocacy and support groups, including victim advocacy, peer support, legal, and forensic services.

Professionals who abuse may also include clergy, spiritual and meditation gurus, esoteric practice groups, and cult leaders. These sexual predators often use the ideology they espouse, via mind control, to confuse and control individuals who are then left confused, depressed, and often suicidal. Revelations of clergy abuse have followed from the awareness of therapy abuse. Victims, who are often the most vulnerable members of religious congregations, experience similar feelings of loss, grief, and betrayal as those who are abused by therapists, with the additional component that their experience often leads to their loss of faith and loss of belief in God (Disch & Avery, 2001).

Donna presented for treatment when she decided to leave a religious cult. She was raised by a Christian fundamentalist mother who sexually abused her. Early in therapy, Donna said, "God gave me this experience because I was meant to suffer . . . this is what momma always said before she'd abuse me. I must have done something wrong in a past life. Maybe I abused someone. If I suffer enough, it will make me strong. It is my duty to serve others." During the course of treatment, this theme of self-blame tied to religious retribution emerged repeatedly. Her abuse was woven with the religious beliefs of her abuser. Her current belief system was based on the cult's distortion of the Buddhist concept called the law of karma, which she used as the reason for her sexual abuse. Our difficult task was to help her define her own religious beliefs in contrast to what she had been programmed to believe first by her mother and then by the cult.

We discussed her ideas about God, faith, and the meaning of life. Over time, mindful of her past experience of indoctrination, I also shared a range of possible interpretations that would help to reframe her beliefs in the context of releasing her from self-blame and guilt. During the course of therapy, she was able to give spiritual and religious meaning to her experiences and at the same time sort out where the responsibility lay. She was also able to understand how her early life experiences made her vulnerable to the cult experience.

TREATMENT BOUNDARIES AND SELF-DISCLOSURE

Following initial discussions about individuals who victimized their clients, the therapist has an opportunity to explore and set boundaries and identify the safety of the therapy at this stage of the interview. It is an opportunity to take a break from asking the client questions and to ask her if she has any questions for you.

It is essential to provide the prospective client with an opportunity to ask questions about your theoretical orientation, training, experience, and general approach to treatment. More personal questions may ensue. There is debate, for example, about the efficacy of disclosing one's own history of trauma (Courtois, 1988), and there is an increasing move toward more self-disclosure in the counseling field. Often a client asks, "How do you know what you are talking about?" in order to ascertain whether the practitioner can empathize with her or his experience or to convey the unspoken question about a practitioner's history. The response remains a personal choice based on one's personal feelings and clinical perspective.

Maintaining appropriate boundaries, which is de rigueur and includes limits on self-disclosure, should not be mistaken for neutrality and emotional inaccessibility. The details of a practitioner's own history are not as relevant as the model of hope and recovery she or he can offer. In conventional psychodynamic theory, a client's questions about a therapist's personal history serve as a basis for exploring the meaning of the question (and potential answer) with the client. Complex trauma is a form of suffering due to the effects of power over behavior; I caution against the use of interpretation for this purpose. However, interpersonal trauma is always about the perpetrator getting his or her needs met at the expense of the victim. In spite of increasing movement in the counseling field to disclose personal information, my theoretical approach remains one of less disclosure, all the more so when there has been no request for information. The decision to disclose information is usually a function of the type of information requested, the dyadic relationship, and what will be best for the client. Limiting self-disclosure, I think, is also advised when doing therapies that involve touch. Less talk by and about the therapist balances out the fact that the therapist is touching the body, so there is no mistaking the safety of the moment.

While we often work on boundaries with our clients, it's useful to check in on our own boundaries for the ethics of client care and self-care. Disch (n.d.) has written a questionnaire entitled: "Are You in Trouble with a Client?" that has also been adapted for use by bodyworkers and coaches (see Online Assessment 6.1).

CULTURE AND IDENTITY

> To provide meaning is to restore power. But to tell people what they mean is to usurp power.

> —Robin Lakoff

When I was working in a community hospital in Boston, Señora Lupita Martinez was referred to me after extensive physical workups had found "nothing wrong," in spite of her insistence that she had terrible pain. Lupita's pain brought her repeatedly to the emergency ward, where she said she was having a stroke. She was referred to psychiatry, which she experienced as an affront: *No hay ningún problema con mi mente. El problema está en mi cuerpo! No me entienden!* (There is no problem with my mind! It's my body! They don't understand me!). I went to see Lupita at her home and entered a tiny apartment steamy with beef *caldo* and brightened by dozens of neon *Virgenes* and a baby *Christos*. She was seated at a small window overlooking a train track, and I asked her to tell me about her symptoms, explaining that I was from the clinic and did *masajes* (massages) and used *hierbas* (herbs). She sat with her back to me and I touched the areas she identified as painful in her shoulders and chest. Within a few moments, out came a flood of tears: she spoke of the pain of relocation from rural Santo Domingo, the loss of her husband, the new life her children had made, and the life that was going on without her. The loss and grief she felt poured out over the several weeks during which we worked together.

By speaking her language, verbally and somatically, we formed a bridge. She felt understood and I believed that I understood her. Our work spanned 3 months, during which her pain and distress resolved. Together, we developed ways for her to stay connected with the past and her family and yet to also move forward in her present. We were able to bridge our cultural differences and find the rhythm of a "third culture," which held her healing.

Definition of Culture

There are many definitions of culture; at its root, the words *cult* and *ure* mean worship (of the) earth (Korn & Rÿser, 2006). Culture is thus defined in terms of the connections between people to their land and to their "'shared creativities,' which include values, art, language, and other symbols of collective life" (Comas-Diaz & Griffith, 1988). Everyone has at least one cultural heritage, and several identities often influence us, reaching back into many generations. A common mistake among many therapists who derive from European immigration is to think that they do not have an ethnic identity; I have heard counselors say: "Oh I am Heinz 57," referring to a blend of many cultures into catsup. Another mistake is to regard one's own culture as the "norm" or dominant culture and another's culture as a minority or "other." Yet another misconception reduces behaviors to their cultural influence, and this may include the idealization or denigration of culture-specific behaviors. These include such ideas as that American Indians don't like to look you in the eye, or Latinos like physical affection, or African American men aren't good fathers . . . and on and on the stereotypes go. Thus a practitioner must first clarify her or his own belief systems and also identify his or her own positive and negative cultural legacies. This process decreases the ethnocentric impact on assessment, facilitating empathic regard.

Ethnocultural Assessment

As we consider culture and the conduct of an ethnocultural assessment, we ask

- How is the experience of trauma the same or different among cultures?
- What symptoms may be universal or relative to the culture, including so-called culture-bound symptoms?
- Are assessment tools and methods appropriate to the sociocultural background of the client?
- Even if they have been translated into the correct language, what are the potential communication issues?
- How might a translator be of assistance?
- What is the interaction between culture and trauma? This includes the experiences arising out of social, political, and economic oppression as well as traumatic refugee and immigrant experiences affecting first, second, and future generations. It also includes the strengths and social supports derived from culture-specific or culture-intact attachments and ceremonies.
- What are cultural attitudes about victimization, somatization, help seeking, medications, and traditional healing?
- What are the skills, biases, or blind spots the clinician brings to the evaluation process?

The five stages of ethnocultural assessment include the following:

1. Obtaining information about ethnocultural heritage, including cultures of origin for maternal and paternal families and their identified heritage.
2. The circumstances of translocation(s) and the events leading to the transitions from the culture(s) of origin.
3. The client's perception of the family's "niche" in the host society since translocation. This includes stability of the family, financial situation barriers, and obstacles as well as successes.
4. The client's perception of her own adjustment as separate from other family members.
5. The practitioner's examination of her or his own ethnocultural heritage as it affects treatment (Jacobsen, 1988, p. 137).

The depth of awareness and knowledge we bring to our clients' diverse cultural backgrounds is dependent on our own knowledge of the ways in which we have been shaped and conditioned by our own heritage(s), culture, and religious influences. Just as trauma is passed down intergenerationally, so are cultural values, practices, and mores, which will affect, consciously or unconsciously, the assessment and treatment of clients. By going through a process of exploration, the clinician is better equipped to work with a client to make meaning and incorporate culture, religion, and other values that may have positive or negative effects. Brown (2008) suggests that cultural competency for the treatment of trauma extends beyond ethnicity but must also embrace an understanding of the role of sexual orientation, age, and class/socioeconomic status of both the clinician and the client.

Knowing one's own historical roots complements knowing the history of cultural or ethnic groups. To know another person's culture, you must first know and embrace your own. Therapists of European heritage can undertake a process of exploring and uncovering their indigenous roots and family migration history.

Cultural Barriers to Seeking Help

The individual's personal appraisal of events is affected by both implicit and explicit cultural expectations and assumptions about victimization. Examining the symbolism and meaning of sickness, intrapersonally (within the individual), interpersonally (between individual and practitioner/healer), and intraculturally (between individual and culture) provides a solid foundation for understanding the effects of trauma as well as the paths to recovery. For example, Shalhoub-Kevorkian's (1999) work with rape victims in Palestinian society revealed that an oppressive patriarchal ideology about rape was an obstacle to treatment, suggesting that increasing awareness of oppressive cultural values and the meaning that the patient assigns to them can reduce the perpetuation of victimizing ideologies.

Trauma victims experience significant barriers to seeking help and cultural barriers amplify these concerns. Obstacles to seeking help may be rooted in culturally traditional conceptions that are negative toward certain types of practitioners. Limited accessibility to resources—for example, lack of money, living in a rural area, lack of transportation, and concerns about the language capacities of the practitioners—can also contribute as obstacles. In addition, trauma victims may be using traditional medicine and have concerns about whether this fact will be discovered or negated by the practitioner. There may be legal concerns about immigration status and the possibility of relocation. Recent epidemiological research from urban Mexico, for example, suggests that a lifetime prevalence of exposure to traumatic events was 76% and the prevalence of PTSD 11.2% (Norris, 2002). Many of these individuals travel between locations north and south. Rates of trauma are high among migrating and undocumented women. Severely traumatized refugees have special needs and factors important in assessment, including war background, escape experience, location and conditions of the refugee camp, time spent there, and the extent of family fragmentation (Comas-Diaz & Griffith, 1988).

Psychological assessment is often based on Western concepts and diagnoses. A common misunderstanding in assessing individuals is to lump people who may speak a common language together—an example of which is the term *Hispanic*. This will miss the distinctions among diverse individuals and communities: between a Mayan refugee from war in Guatemala who speaks two languages, *Ixil* and Spanish or a middle-class business owner from the border of Chihuahua, Mexico, who left the drug war behind. Learning about body language and cultural values within a specific culture or ethnic group or subgroup is a good start. I always use this knowledge as a basis for asking the individual or family what is important to them and whether these values are the ones that they embrace. Cultural values are also determined by socioeconomic status, religion, and often whether one lives in an urban or rural area. Demonstrating some initial knowledge shows respect and interest, and in some communities such as many American Indian communities, it is common to share knowledge of one's own background and family heritage and where one comes from as a way to demonstrate respect and value the important foundation of cultural identity. It is also useful to demonstrate respect for the traditional medicine; this will open the path for communication about healing and the opportunity to collaborate as a team member. Adjusting to the varied needs of indigenous peoples, especially when one is working in small rural communities, may challenge some concepts of boundaries and self-disclosure, especially when one is asked to play multiple roles, including that of advocate.

Culture and Traditional Medicine

Exploring the role of the traditional healer and the traditional medicine used by clients is essential to the healing process. Openness, acceptance, and encouragement are validating and trust-building. Traditional healing and traditional explanatory models of illness must be understood in their own context.

> When I work in rural Mexico, it is very common for people to come in from villages complaining of stress-related problems for which, I know, they have their own cultural explanations but which they also feel hesitant about sharing. One day a caballero, Epiphanio, and his daughter, Lucinda, arrived from a distant village. She was very distraught, crying and unable to sleep. The lack of sleep had caused psychotic symptoms, which is what the physicians in the city observed when they prescribed antipsychotic drugs. Alisia, our clinic coordinator and herbalist, and I sat down with them. Epiphanio had been to several doctors in the city and they had not been helpful. I began asking both the daughter and father to tell me their story from the beginning and also to share with me what the other doctors had said, and, importantly, why they felt or believed that those doctors had not helped them. I also asked them to tell me what they felt the problem was. As they both shared their stories and perspectives, they were describing what I knew to be *mal de ojo*, without

using those exact words. In *curanderismo*, the syncretic healing tradition of Mexico, *mal de ojo* (evil eye) is a type of soul loss that can result from the effects of another person's feelings of jealousy or envy. The jealousy can lead to one giving the other the "evil eye." When I asked if they felt that perhaps Lucinda was experiencing the *mal de ojo*, they both relaxed and became very animated; they began telling in more detail a story about how Lucinda was the object of jealousy of a distant cousin. They told me that they had gone to a *curandera* but the treatment had not worked, so they decided to try *medicos* (physicians) but had not had success there either. I sensed that this family was living between two worlds. Lucinda had gone to the city for her education and had recently returned to the country to be with her father, a traditional Indian rancher. On the one hand she had an illness that they named and understood but that the doctors did not recognize, but on the other hand she was feeling conflicted about where the treatment would come from because the "city" treatment was congruent with her new values of her city education. Likewise Epiphanio, while he believed in *curanderas*, also had worked hard to send his daughter to the city and believed in the power of doctors. Alisia and I conferred; we felt that validating and integrating a treatment that combined both traditional beliefs and other psychological and physical methods might address their needs as a daughter/father dyad in this healing process together. We suggested to them that we felt a combination of treatment would be most effective. As a "doctor" I understood *mal de ojo* as well as conventional approaches, and as an herbalist Alisia also reinforced the power of herbs. Because Alisia and I both understood each other's approaches, we also represented healing and could reinforce and validate one another in front of them, which reflected the inner divide they felt. Alisia suggested that she perform a healing ceremony for *mal de ojo* and that I would provide a prescription of herbs, vitamins, and minerals for Lucinda to take for several days following the healing, along with some cranial sacral treatment that focused on the upper cervical and the lower lumbar regions to help her relax and sleep. She slept on the table during the treatment. It proved to be a good combination, as the next week the pair returned and Lucinda reported that she was now sleeping and felt that she was doing much better and on the road to recovery. I believe that the treatment began when we were able to recognize their reality, understand and interpret their language of distress, and discuss the meaning they assigned to their dilemma, including identifying where the daughter and father diverged. Working together, Alisia and I were also able to mirror the multiple realities they navigated by providing a spectrum of services that they understood and accepted.

Culture and the Meaning of Trauma

The meaning of the traumatic experience is central to the development of PTSD. Two factors, social support systems and the meaning of the trauma, significantly affect the development and intensity of PTSD. The ameliorative effects of social supports and the (cultural) meaning of the trauma for individuals and the community can be compared by reviewing two divergent disaster experiences: the bombing of the Oklahoma City Federal Building in 1995 and the volcanic eruption of Mt. St. Helen's in 1980. The bombing in Oklahoma was an unexpected human-made catastrophe that took lives (including those of children), maimed people, and brought heightened awareness of terrorist activities in the United States. In a survey of survivors of the direct blast who experienced the bombing, 35% developed PTSD (North et al., 1999). The eruption of Mt. St. Helen's in Washington State in 1978 was an act of nature with some warning. Of those exposed to extreme stress during the eruption, 40% reported major psychological disturbance 3 to 4 years following the disaster (Keane, 1990).

However, the Yakima, Tietnapum, Wanapums, and Klikitat Indians, who live near Mt. St. Helen's and in the path of the wind, reported few incidents of traumatic sequelae in response to the eruption. For these people, stories about the mountain blowing open had been shared for as long as they could remember. The "old ones" had predicted its rising and believed that the ashes would renew the earth (Rÿser, personal communication, August 14, 1995). It may be that the elements of group meaning making through story and social supports were protective against the development of stress disorders when the mountain did blow. Conversely, whereas both Alaska Natives and European Americans experienced social disruption resulting from the *Exxon Valdez* oil spill in 1989, Alaska Natives experienced higher levels of PTSD associated with low family support, participation in spill cleanup activities, and a decline in subsistence activities, in contrast to the European American sample (Palinkas, Petterson, Russell, & Downs, 2004). The definition of PTSD in this example must serve as a starting point only for a diagnosis, considering that ethnocultural studies of trauma demonstrate the potential contribution of social conflict and isolation following disasters. For example, among Alaska Natives, the loss of subsistence and involvement in cleanup may have had more cultural meaning related to social integrity than it did for European Americans. The cultural variation of response to both the volcanic eruption and the oil spill emphasizes the primacy of social and cultural context and meaning making in the development of PTSD and its sequelae.

EXERCISE 6.1: CLINICIAN EXERCISE: CULTURAL HERITAGE

Trauma occurs in both a culture-specific as well as in a universal context. The assessment of traumatized individuals must consider the content and meaning of experiences in both these contexts. To gain cultural competency in assessment and treatment, a clinician should assess her or his own cultural heritage(s), which may include a multilayered genogram of family history, migration experiences, intergenerational trauma, ethnic/ cultural identities, sexual identities, and beliefs about gender.

On a piece of paper, make three columns: In the first column, write what you know about your cultural heritage(s); in column two, write what you don't know; and in column three, write what you have discovered. A family genogram can be superimposed on a cultural genogram.

Intergenerational Transmission of Trauma

The United States is a country of immigrant populations, reflecting wide cultural diversities. Effective assessment and treatment depends upon an understanding of the complex relationship between culture and trauma, including the intergenerational transmission of trauma. This refers to the transmission of victimization, traumatic exposures, and traumatic meaning-making systems from one generation to another. The term also refers to how whole cultures pass this information along.

Traumatic experiences have affected every cultural group in the United States today. Before the 17th-century arrival of religious refugees escaping persecution in England, the Spaniards arrived in Mexico, Puerto Rico, and California. The effect on the lives of indigenous peoples on the continent was often traumatic. Between the 16th and 19th centuries, Chinese, Philippine, and African people arrived under traumatic conditions, often as slaves. The arrival of the Europeans had a varied effect on the more than 500 tribes of indigenous peoples populating every corner of the continent. Popular (stereotyped) notions about the current lives of American Indians illustrate the complex role of trauma and culture and the tendency toward cultural reductionism. Attempts to classify people by their blood quantum or their "color" perpetuate oppressive stereotypes. The tribes of North America all had varied experiences with the Europeans, ranging from productive relationships to situations marked by various degrees and types of trauma and genocide (Mann, 2011).

Currents of the traumatic past remain strong today, especially where government and social policies reinforce them. Among non-Indian populations, American Indians are often an "invisible people" (Rÿser, 2001)—or, if visible, they are usually seen through the lens of stereotyped notions of "drums and feathers," powwows, casinos, or rates of alcoholism. Stereotypes limit the analysis to the negative social issues confronting Indian country and ignore its creative resiliency. Approximately 50% of the American Indian population resides in urban settings. Charting the specific types and kinds of traumatic exposures and successful coping strategies reservation and off-reservation peoples employ to resist discrimination and genocide counteracts the tendency toward cultural reductionism.

Historical Trauma and Postcolonial Stress Syndrome

Historical trauma and unresolved grief arising from the legacy of colonization have implications for therapeutic interventions and community healing with American Indians (Brave Heart & DeBruyn, 1998; Whitbeck et al., 2004), Alaska Natives (Korn, 2002), and Mexican Indians (Korn & Rÿser, 2006). Within the therapeutic community, there is a "culture of denial" about the ongoing nature of the colonization of tribal communities (Weingarten, 2004). Colonization of the land, some suggest, has led to colonization of the mind (Martin-Baro, 1994), leading to dissociation, depression, substance abuse, and suicide, all part of a nexus called postcolonial stress disorder. This disorder is linked conceptually to posttraumatic stress and community trauma (Duran & Duran, 1995; Korn, 2002). Depression, somatization, substance abuse, and trauma are comorbid at high rates among aboriginal populations (Kirmayer & Valaskakis, 2009). Colonization and its ongoing effects on American Indians and Alaska Natives are diverse and affect the individual family and community differently. Assessment of historical trauma and intergenerational trauma should begin with telling the story and identifying meaning. I begin this discussion by asking about tribal or community identity and affiliation and about family relationships and experiences. I also ask about grandmothers and great grandparents, back into generations and the role they played.

Historical Trauma Scales

The Historical Loss Scale

The HLS is a 12-item measure developed to measure how often thoughts pertaining to historical loss occur. Some examples of the types of historical losses included in this instrument are loss of land, language, culture, and traditional spiritual ways as well as loss of family/family ties (Whitbeck et al., 2004).

The Historical Loss Associated Symptoms Scale

The HLASS is a 17-item measure of the frequency with which certain emotions are experienced in thinking about or being reminded of historical losses of Indian people and culture (Whitbeck et al., 2004).

COPING SKILLS, RESILIENCY, AND POSTTRAUMATIC GROWTH

Survival requires a range of personal skills, talents, and sheer bravery. Assessment should provide time to acknowledge and explore all these capacities that allow one to survive. Often a client will not have acknowledged to herself the strengths and resiliency she has drawn on. Therapy includes telling the story as well as bolstering the innate resiliency of the survivor and helping her identify ways to acknowledge strengths as well as to develop new skills. This includes focusing on what is working and productive and a source of joy and pleasure, what has been and what she imagines it could be.

Who is resilient? Much of the literature points to protective factors, including a good relationship with a dependable, loving adult, whether a family member or teacher and a strong internal locus of control (Grossman & Moore, 1994). The strengthening of an internal locus of control, which includes both personal control and situation-specific skills, is one of four stress management strategies elaborated by Flannery (1987, p. 222). The other strategies are

- Task involvement, including general competence; this signifies becoming absorbed in the task and being guided by what the task demands.
- Lifestyle choices.
- Social supports.

Finally, resiliency refers to meaning-making capacities: to make something good come out of a terrible experience. Meaning making forms the basis for exploring spirituality and the role of the self in relation to others and the cosmos.

Identifying the strengths and resilience that the individual has and supporting those throughout the process is key throughout treatment. Research has traditionally focused on factors that lead to the development of PTSD. Less understood are the factors that are either protective against the development of PTSD or contribute to the triumph over tremendous odds.

Resiliency is defined as the capacity to continue to function in the world despite a history of abuse, to demonstrate adaptive characteristics, to convert defensive strategies into unusual strengths, to transform relationships from abusive to rewarding, and to make meaning out of the experiences in a way that benefits or has meaning for other people.

To be resilient means to meet the developmental challenges appropriate to the stages of life. These include intimacy, work, self-care, and meaning making (Grossman & Moore, 1994). Evaluating areas of resiliency is essential to assessment. Because resiliency, like self-esteem, is a fluid force, increasing and decreasing with the vagaries (and traumas) of life, it has to be evaluated both in the present and as part of an overall history.

The Stress-Related Growth Scale

The Stress-Related Growth Scale (SRGS) measures stress-related positive outcomes (Park, Cohen, & Murch, 1996).

SPIRITUAL/RELIGIOUS/PARANORMAL
OR ANOMALOUS EXPERIENCES

Questions about spiritual or religious practice will flow naturally at any point in the assessment, from discussions of resiliency and coping methods, self-care, culture and traditional medicine, or if there is a disclosure of clergy abuse. In my disclosure forms for new clients I mention my interest in working with issues of religion and spirituality so that clients will feel comfortable discussing these issues. Questions may include the following:

Do you have a spiritual or religious practice? If so, can you tell me about it? Do you see yourself as a spiritual or religious person? From there one can explore the client's practices and the role of religion and spirituality in coping with stress. The client may also discuss anomalous experiences such as alien encounters, altered states, or religious visions they have experienced. Depending upon the earlier history and trauma story, one may conduct a spiritual history, ecomap, ecogram, or genogram (Hodge & Limb, 2011). An ecogram combines a genogram with an ecomap to depict both family and whole ecological systems at play in an individual's life. A spiritual genogram is useful to explore intergenerational relationships regarding religion and spirituality and can be added to a family genogram (Meichenbaum, n.d.). If the trauma is associated with or results from a religious experience or affiliation, like clergy abuse or abuse by a guru, that provides a new dimension to explore. While often people either lose faith or become hyperreligious in the face of trauma, the loss of faith may occur as a direct result of religion.

Because a victim's capacity to trust has often been shattered by trauma, the trustworthiness of the clinician will emerge among the first important themes during assessment. A successful assessment depends on establishing the appropriate rhythm of discovery. Limit setting can provide assurance to the client that the practitioner can be relied upon to set appropriate boundaries and to help the individual care for herself or himself. Furthermore, the client can see that the practitioner has no vested interest or vicarious need to hear memories.

Louis came for therapy because his recurring nightmares and somatic memories of being sexually abused by his mother had become overwhelming. He had been in and out of therapy in the past and each time explored memories and feeling at new and deeper levels. He arrived for the first session feeling unsafe and suicidal. Two days later he called and wanted to come in sooner than his regular appointment. When he arrived, he wanted to continue to discuss his memories, asking that I "probe" him with questions.

I suggested to him that we first help him establish a sense of safety and some control over his environment and to make plans to connect with his social supports prior to going deeper into the memories and feelings. When he objected,

I assured him that we would have time to explore the memories and that we needed to identify ways to help him live "in his body" and create a life as best as he could, so that he had a foundation. I assured him that my intent was to keep the assessment process a safe experience for him and that the memories and knowledge would come when he was ready and that there was preparatory work to do first.

PHYSICAL HEALTH HISTORY

When we sit with clients, we receive a lot of information about how they're doing based on their posture and how they look. We can learn a lot by paying attention to how someone is sitting, if a client is hunched forward and the shoulders are rolled in, there may be compression on the respiratory muscles, and that may alert us to look for disordered breathing. When people are depressed, their shoulders roll in and the chest is compressed, as if the weight of the world were upon their shoulders and it was too much to bear. Puffiness under the eyes suggests water retention and adrenal stress, darkness on the eyelids denotes adrenal stress, and redness suggests liver and gallbladder congestion. A dull gaze may suggest dissociation. Listen to the sound of the voice. What does the voice tell you about the person? Is it constricted, deep and mellifluous, screechy, contracted, or childish? Allow yourself to receive the vibration of the voice and compare it with the content of the words being spoken. Is there congruence?

Ask the client about the age of onset, duration, and associated memories of physical complaints and illnesses as well as past and current pain, accidents, hospitalizations, eating disorders, substance abuse, self-harm, all surgeries, and the current level of somatic complaints. Include history and current attitudes about activities like athletics, exercise, and complementary/alternative methods such as meditation, massage/touch, and bodywork nutrition.

PSYCHOACTIVE SUBSTANCE USE/ABUSE ASSESSMENT

Abuse of alcohol and drugs is common among survivors of trauma. I reviewed the self-medication model of addictions and discussed the relationship between self-harm and dissociation in Chapter 3. Among Vietnam War veterans, current and lifetime prevalence rates for alcoholism are 23% and 75% respectively, while rates for current and lifetime drug abuse/dependency are 6% and 23% respectively. Rates for alcohol or drug dependency among Vietnam veterans with PTSD who seek treatment with PTSD are 60% to 80% (Kulka et al., 1990; Solomon, Mikulincer, & Flum, 1988). One study revealed that 74% to 77% of chemically dependent inpatient women reported a history of sexual abuse, while 11% to 18% of inpatient teenage boys disclosed sexual abuse (Trotter, 1992). The interface of culture, trauma, and substance abuse is common. The rates of alcoholism rose among American Indians after World War II, in association with war trauma and the trauma of the termination and relocation movement of the 1950s and 1960s, which separated children from their families and took away land and aboriginal rights from tribes (LaDue, 1994).

Asking about the role of all forms of substances, drugs licit and illict, medications, alcohol, food, and sex provides insight into self-medication history and illuminates the current needs of the body, mind, and spirit and the ways in which the individual requires support in making healthier choices. It is useful to ask about family history of use and the cultural context of use. I assure my clients that am not judging anything they have used or are using and begin by telling them that by knowing what they have used, how they have responded, and why they felt they used certain things we can better understand what the body/mind needs. I also explain the concept of self-medicating behavior at this point.

The concept of abstinence, while it works for some, is not successful for everyone. Use of substances serves many purposes. Understanding the substance of choice and its biological effects provides a basis for finding effective substitutes. Educating the client about the effects of trauma and the effects of substance use helps them understand why they behave in certain ways and builds collaboration on identifying what substances can be useful for addressing psychobiological needs. This provides the background for a deeper exploration of nutrition as well as the use of botanicals and entheogens. I also inquire about spirituality and psychoactive plant use. There is a spectrum of use from self-medication and suppression of unpleasant symptoms to recreational exploration and then spiritual experiences facilitated by substances. Understanding the spectrum of meaning and behavior provides a foundation from which to develop treatment. The assessment of substance use and abuse includes an exploration of the history and current use of drugs and alcohol, medications and other substances; the role played by alcohol and drugs in the abuse experience(s); and the identification of use patterns such as "triggers." I also ask about periods of abstinence and current attitudes about use. It is common to work with people who are using and who have PTSD. I decide on a case basis whether the individual needs to stop using before addressing trauma or whether addressing trauma should occur first. There is considerable debate and controversy about this "chicken and egg" dilemma and which to treat first, trauma or substance abuse; as a result, it is often resolved ideologically rather than on behalf of the client. The resolution depends on the clients—what they are using, the effect on their lives, and their capacity to enter into recovery. Stopping substance use triggers memories and feelings regarding the trauma that underlies most substance abuse. The integration of nutritional interventions into treatment is an effective choice for managing the transition.

Joan, an attractive, soft-spoken, accomplished musician 25 years of age, came for an assessment, complaining of fatigue and depression. She said she had not "felt right" since her parents divorced 2 years earlier and she could not motivate herself to play music. She discussed a history of bulimia and current substance abuse, including alcohol and opiates.

Joan reported a happy childhood and denied any memories of trauma. However, she reported a currently distant relationship with both her parents, though she was close to her two sisters. She revealed chronic headaches, digestive problems, and dysmenorrhea as well as reproductive problems. She had had three romantic relationships since she was 19, each lasting less than a year, and was currently involved, unhappily, with her partner of a year.

We proceeded with treatment by addressing the issues that she chose for discussion, focusing on her substance abuse, relationships, and depression. The clinical picture of depression, anxiety, chronic pain, substance abuse, dissociation, amnesia for past events, and health issues, alongside her insistence about a rosy childhood, suggested to me that she might have a history of physical and sexual abuse. One year into treatment, Joan stopped her use of opiates and reduced her use of alcohol. Joan then received word that her father had been arrested for abusing his daughters, Joan's younger sisters. The guards of her memories came crashing down and she was flooded with feelings and memories of her own abuse by her father from the ages of 9 to 12.

PAIN SCALES AND QUESTIONNAIRES

There are several ways to describe and measure pain that are useful in assessing pain perception and experience. The results can contribute to choosing and measuring change in response to specific mind/body interventions.

Pain Diary

Patients may be advised to record their experiences of pain in a dairy as follows:

Maintain a pain diary for a minimum of 7 to 14 days. You may also use these scales to rate your pain and record your experience from day to day, week to week, and month to month. This record keeping is called a pain diary. A pain diary can be useful in determining whether treatments are working and whether lifestyle changes or other pain management strategies are helping. Keeping a pain diary is important because it will help you remember details about your pain that you may want to discuss with your health care provider, and it may demonstrate patterns in your pain that are not obvious from day to day. For example, pain may be worse at certain times during your menstrual cycle or when you are at work or after you eat something in particular—a pain diary will make these associations much easier to see.

Body/Pain/Visual Analog Scale

This online pain assessment (see Online Assessment 6.2) provides two scales in one. The first is an image of the body, front and back where the client can locate and define areas of the body and qualities of pain or discomfort. The Visual Analogue Scale (VAS) is a simple visual image that measures pain across a continuum ranging from values from no pain to severe pain. Both these measures may be used at the first session and reintroduced to measure change over time.

SLEEP HISTORY, PAST AND CURRENT

Understanding the rhythm of sleep is important to both mental and physical well-being. In the assessment it is important to ask specifically about sleep behaviors.

- When did your sleep problems begin? Did they precede current problems (depression, PTSD, etc.)?
- How long does it take to fall asleep?
- How long after you fall asleep do you awaken?
- How often do you wake up during the night and for how long are you awake?
- What time do you awake in the morning?
- What are you dreams like? If you have nightmares, what are they like?
- Do you have sleep apnea?
- Does pain affect your ability to sleep?
- Describe your sleep environment (partner, child, animals, light/dark/noise etc.).

The Pittsburgh Sleep Quality Index (PSQI-A) is a valid instrument for PTSD applicable to both clinical and research settings. Specifically, disruptive nocturnal behaviors may represent PTSD-specific sleep disturbances.

HYPERVENTILATION AND ANXIETY

I undertake a three-part evaluation of anxiety. In addition to anxiety scales, I incorporate the Nijmegen Scale (see Online Assessment 3.1). A score above 23 suggests hyperventilation disorder, though a score below 23 may still signify disordered breathing. I also include an evaluation for a biochemical basis for anxiety, including hyperventilation, hypoglycemia, sugar handling, preservatives or toxins in the diet, food allergies, low levels of essential fatty acids, use of statin drugs, low cholesterol, and low hydrochloric acid.

EXERCISE 6.2: BODY SCAN (ONLINE EXERCISE)

Assessment of body image may be done verbally by asking the client how she feels about her body, what she likes and doesn't like, or by asking the client to draw a picture of herself. A more in-depth assessment may include guiding her through the body scan and stopping at each new body area to ask her to describe what she sees in her mind's eye and how she feels about this body area. This process may also illuminate dissociativity issues and may be used as a periodic posttreatment assessment tool for the treatment of pain or discomfort.

ALEXITHYMIA

When I am working with a client who has complex chronic health problems, and he or she has a difficult time identifying or describing feelings and are unable to think symbolically or work with imagery, I will assess for alexithymia (Brett, 1993; Krystal, 1988). Alexithymia is characterized by difficulties in the capacity to verbalize affect and maladaptive self-regulation. These difficulties are observed in severely traumatized individuals and often involve paucity of dreams or images, which may lead to using the body to express distress. Alexithymia is associated with early-life neglect, PTSD, substance abuse, and Asperger's syndrome as well as with heightened physiological arousal. Primary alexithymia is considered a personality trait, and these individuals will be less responsive to psychotherapy; secondary alexithymia may reflect a more transitory state that is more responsive to therapy. People who experience somatic symptoms, have PTSD, are unable to express emotions, or are unable to undertake an imaginal exercise are candidates for assessment. If they have secondary alexthymia, they will benefit from treatment that incorporates both the somatic and imaginal approaches—nonverbal and preverbal approaches that restore or enhance interhemispheric brain synchrony through a variety of methods such as meditation (de la Fuente Arias, Franco Justo, & Salvador Granado, 2010), neurofeedback, and body-oriented therapies.

EXERCISE 6.3: CLIENT EXERCISE: ANNIVERSARY DIARY

The body remembers the seasons, months, and days when the traumatic events occurred. When these days roll around, somatic or emotional distress may arise. There could be any number of associations linked in time and space. When someone, for example, is going on a substance abuse binge or has a stomachache for a week or is sobbing without an apparent trigger or cause, it's very useful to work with him or her to make a trauma anniversary calendar. The calendar is a way to conceptualize and think through the distressing events that have occurred in a person's life and link them to a time of year. By reviewing this calendar and having it on hand, you can bring into awareness the relationship between events and feeling states that may have been previously submerged, and it also enables one to plan and prepare and recognize the difficult period of time coming up and how to increase self-nurturing activities.

DIET, NUTRITION, AND MEDICATIONS

I ask my clients to provide me with a list of current medications (prescription, over-the-counter, supplements, etc.) and their dosages. When this cannot be done, I ask them to bring in everything they are taking and we make a record together. It is important to know what clients are taking, why and who is the prescribing clinician, or whether these agents are self-prescribed. This also provides an opportunity to open the discussion about what clients feel that they need and what is effective but to also discuss if there are interactions of medications that are contraindicated. Below I define questions and assessments designed to complement Chapter 8 on nutrition. Tests identified below may be obtained by working with a variety of holistic medicine practitioners. In designing a nutritional program for the treatment of PTSD, anxiety, depression, and insomnia, the following questions should be included.

- What is the intake of packaged, frozen, and refined foods, including low-quality fats, white flour/rice, and sugar?
- What are the daily eating patterns—for example, what are the hours, types of food, and food quantities? How does mood correlate with these patterns?
- Is the client eating according to her or his metabolic type? For example, is the client eating as a vegetarian or vegan when he or she is really a carnivore? Is the client eating too much meat or purine-rich foods and fats when more fruits, vegetables, and grains are needed?
- Are there food allergies, especially to glutens, dairy, soy, or eggs?
- What are the cortisol/DHEA levels and their ratio and is there hypo- or hyperfunction?
- Is there a history of use of antacids for heartburn or reflux?
- Is there a thiamine deficiency?
- Is there hypothyroidism?
- Is there lack of exposure to sunlight?
- What are the vitamin D levels?
- Is there use of caffeine or other stimulants?

Metabolic Analysis

Metabolic analysis may be evaluated using a variety of approaches ranging from self-questionnaires to a 4-hour specialized glucose tolerance test conducted in the office. To begin, the simplest method is to identify what combination of foods enhance energy or cause fatigue, using a comprehensive diet-behavior questionnaire (Kristal & Haig, 2002).

Tissue (Hair) Mineral Analysis

Tissue (hair) mineral analysis can also be conducted by a laboratory, which will provide information on mineral ratio status by measuring levels of various minerals excreted in the hair. This analysis reveals endocrine gland function, metabolic type, and heavy metals (see Online Resources). The rates of endocrine gland function (for example, whether the thyroid or adrenal glands function fast or slow) lead to various excretion patterns and ratios of certain minerals. Two intersecting factors influence function. One is genetics: the constitution one is born with. The second is environment, such as stress, illness, and food choices. The goal of tissue analysis is to identify current function and suggest strategies (food and supplements/herbs) that bring mineral ratios into balance. I explore this in more detail in Chapter 8.

Glucose Tolerance Test

A thorough 4-hour specialized glucose tolerance test may be administered to determine metabolic rates (Kristal & Haig, 2004). Start by asking your clients what types of foods make them feel best; you may recommend that they use a food diary (see Online Assessment 6.3) to document physical and mood responses to foods. Because many survivors are dissociated from how they feel, what they need, or how they respond to certain foods, helping them focus on their observations and experiences and reinforcing their knowledge can be an important first step. All change is a process of increasing self-awareness; people who smoke or drink too much or eat a lot of salt and sugar are often unable to discern the effects of food on mood. Identifying motivation and resistance by using motivational interviewing methods can be very successful when applied to nutritional and dietary changes, and the creation of step-by-step goals will be essential to success. Of course, testing is important at a certain stage especially if positive results to dietary change remain elusive. There are metabolic analysis practitioners who can conduct these specialized tests that provide exact ratios of foods that will be optimal for the individual's "engine."

Essential Fatty Acid

Essential fatty acid status influences mood and can be measured easily in the office by obtaining salivary pH levels on litmus paper. The measure should reach at least a 7 or 7.2. This test is limited by its lack of specificity, but it can serve as a first step. However, a blood test such as the Omega 3 Index can provide even greater accuracy (see Online Resources).

The Barnes Thyroid Temperature Test

This test may be conducted at home every morning for 5 days using a thermometer (see Online Assessment 6.4). It will measure functional hypothyroidism, which is not always identified by blood tests.

Adrenal Assessment

Symptoms may include premenstrual syndrome as well as cravings for sweets and carbohydrates, headaches, indigestion, postural hypotension, insomnia, irritability, inability to concentrate, fatigue and depression, chemical sensitivities, food allergies, airborne allergies, hay fever, asthma, hives, dermatitis, rheumatoid arthritis, low body temperature, hypothyroidism and dry skin, all of which are commonly associated with adrenal insufficiency. Low back pain, especially in the sacroiliac region, and ligament laxity are also common in response to adrenal stress.

There are several in-office tests that can be used to identify signs and symptoms of adrenal dysfunction; these include the pupilary response test and the Raglands postural hypotension test (see Online Assessment 6.5).

The adrenal stress hormones salivary test is a 24-hour cortisol/DHEA salivary laboratory test that calls for the collection of saliva at four specific times daily to assess hyper- or hypoadrenia; the results can contribute to choices for botanical or nutritional interventions (see Online Resources).

Neurotransmitter (NT) Analysis

Neurotransmitter (NT) analysis involves a morning collection of urine to measures neurotransmitter metabolites and their ratios.

Gastrointestinal Analysis

Gastrointestinal analysis is a noninvasive approach that analyzes saliva and stool samples to measure a variety of parameters such as pancreatic digestive enzyme output, immune function, food allergies, yeast/candida, parasites, and bacteria levels.

DETOXIFICATION

Like all behaviors, detoxification can be a healthy response for healing or be linked to maladaptive self-regulation strategies and addictions, such as bulimia.

Assessment for the role of detoxification in a client's life will inform methods that will not trigger old behaviors but can incorporate new strategies that derive from healthy self-care. Assessment should include a history of purging and cleansing in individuals with bulimia and can include a discussion of what people may be interested in exploring for their health. Some questions may include the following:

• Have you engaged in detoxification methods? If so, which ones?
• Have you engaged in purging methods? If so, which ones?
• What is your history of fasting?
• Do you have a history of acne, psoriasis, skin problems, or food allergies?
• Do you have gallstones?

FROM ASSESSMENT TO TREATMENT

The initial assessment may require several hours, span several consecutive appointments, or occur over several months or years of treatment for complex cases. At the end of the initial assessment phase, in discussing my assessment, answering client questions, and making a contract to work together if appropriate, I will often utilize a story or metaphor that is congruent to the client's belief system in order to broaden and contextualize the perspective of our work. In order to help my clients understand metaphorically the confusion of consciousness they experience as a result of the traumatic experience, I often use the image of a house to represent consciousness and the path of healing. A house has many rooms of different sizes and locations that serve both discrete functions and purposes that are by nature flexible in use and importance. Ordinarily, multiple passageways connecting all the rooms permit free access, under the control and decision-making power of the occupant. However, traumatic experiences can erect doorways of impenetrable steel or that are locked, apparently without key. Trauma can also tear doors down where they have been or should be. Or sometimes passing through the door will lead to a precipitous drop, leaving the occupant feeling stranded or hanging on for dear life. I suggest that the function of assessment and treatment is to explore the house and make choices about what doors to open, what to unlock (which may include casting the key), where to hang a hammock for rest and repose, and where to do some remodeling. Because trauma makes a person feel as if they were crazy or going crazy, I assure them that they are not and that we will inspect the foundation of the house and make whatever repairs are required by using the strengths the clients already have, as well as by building new skills. The metaphor of the house can be referred to repeatedly over the course of the treatment process. It is a way of helping the clients to locate themselves when they are having a difficult time and a way to rejoice when some "remodeling" has been successful or elicits a sense of peace or joy. By following and returning to the metaphor over time, the practitioner helps create continuity and a history of treatment progress.

This metaphor (or another of the client's choosing) can also serve as an image for use during visualization or hypnotherapy to create an image for self-soothing.

SUMMARY

Assessment is the start of the treatment process. It requires that the therapist sensitively engage the client, create a safe space to tell the story of her or his life at his or her own pace, and to explore the memories and meanings of the traumatic events. An integrative assessment requires gathering information about the individual's physical, mental, emotional, and spiritual domains of function. Just like putting together the pieces of a puzzle, a posttrauma lens views the intricate relationships among the current domains of function and the traumatic events in the context of culture and gender, giving special attention to the developmental stage of the event(s) and their type and duration. Treatment requires ongoing assessment. Periodic use of scales and measures and simple dialogue provide a variety of ways to measure the effectiveness of mind/body interventions. Adrenal Assessment

7   Transmutation of Trauma

> [H]ealing must be sought in the blood of the wound itself. It is another of the old alchemical truths that no solution should be made except in its own blood.
>
> —Nor Hall

Integrative posttrauma therapy combines methods that concentrate on the physical, emotional, mental, and spiritual needs of the individual. Integrative posttrauma therapy is transformational, working with individuals to help them not to just return to a previous level of function but to transform the traumatic experience into a new state of personal well-being—a condition greater than was thought possible. The role of "story" and clinician facility in the various mind/body methods or "languages" through which to help the client tell the trauma story is central to the success of therapy. Clinicians often want to incorporate innovative mind/body methods, spiritual healing, and traditional (indigenous) medicine into their work and question how these methods fit in with their theoretical orientation, their training, or the demands for evidence requested by their agencies or clients. I examine these approaches here by exploring the use of complementary/alternative medicine (CAM) and traditional medicine strategies for self-regulation and the role of ritual, spirituality and posttraumatic growth in healing and recovery.

In this chapter I shall discuss

- the basic tenets of integrative posttrauma therapy
- CAM methods
- traditional medicine (indigenous systems) methods
- treatment innovations that complement existing psychotherapeutic interventions

CAM practices include health techniques that complement conventional medicine practices or can be employed as an alternative to those practices. Almost any method can be considered complementary or alternative depending on whether it is used with or instead of conventional medicine practices.

Over time this term of reference will likely change as the boundaries across methods dissolve. Other terms of reference that refer to similar approaches to holistic health include *integrative medicine, naturopathic medicine, functional medicine,* and *traditional (indigenous) medicine.* There is considerable overlap between traditional methods, complementary, and alternative methods. For example, acupuncture is traditional Chinese medicine, though it is often used to complement conventional medicine. This synthesized approach to health recognizes the wisdom and knowledge of both traditional and conventional methods. Integrative medicine combines aspects from conventional medicine that are compatible with holistic healing methods.

BACKGROUND

Evidence from a growing number of studies suggests that 33% to 38% of adults living in the United States use CAM therapies (Department of Health and Human Services [DHHS], 2011), yet less than half of those respondents spoke to their primary physician about using CAM. Twenty-two percent of the U.S. population, according to these studies, had used massage therapy, chiropractic, or other bodywork in the previous year (DHHS, 2011). Among American women, the most commonly used forms of CAM are spiritual healing and herbal medicine (Upchurch & Chyu, 2005). CAM is widely employed for the treatment of mental health issues, including PTSD, depression, and anxiety.

Cultural competence is essential for the mind/body clinician serving specific culturally distinct subgroups that may be living in various geographic regions. The use of CAM, traditional medicine, or indigenous healing systems can be considered essential in the treatment of individuals from such groups. For example, American Indian veterans may practice peyote ceremonies in the Native American Church, and others, in the Pacific Northwest, may turn to canoe journeys, while Mexican *curanderos* treat PTSD in Hispanic women and men using *limpias* (spiritual cleansings). To be added to this list are the Hmong refugees living in California, Minnesota, Wisconsin, and North Carolina whose spiritual practices include shamanic rituals and beliefs about illness; then there is also African American folk healing. CAM use is practiced in all ethnic groups and frequently by parents for their children.

Integrative posttrauma therapy emphasizes a comprehensive perspective of whole human development and functioning, including body/mind/spirit and gender and culture-specific issues, multiple styles of communication, active engagement and empathic expression, activism and advocacy, individually designed treatment plans rather than plans resulting from a prescriptive hierarchy, and the transformational potential of trauma.

In earlier chapters I explained that traumatic stress is characterized by a reduced capacity to balance or self-regulate one's "rhythms." The mind/body and spiritual methods I discuss here are approaches that I have used success-fully with my clients. These approaches can be incorporated into counseling and other therapies. While most of these methods are commonly used to treat people with PTSD, some of them are as yet less widely known, understood, or practiced.

Rather than providing a prescriptive model, an integrative posttrauma lens illuminates the connections that link every aspect of the individual, including social relationships to others and relationships to the environment. This lens remains flexibly responsive to the physical, mental, emotional, and spiritual concerns of the individual, acknowledging each as equally important while rec-ognizing that trauma is the central factor contributing to the client's symptoms. Healing involves engaging and activating the individual's innate capacities for transformation and transmutation. An integrative approach acknowledges the client's innate capacity to heal and grow beyond the trauma and recognizes the strengths he or she has used and will continue to develop. The clinician may serve as catalyst, a guide to "jump start" and support the client's capacities throughout the healing process. The transformation of trauma and its physi-cal, mental, emotional, and spiritual effects is the goal of treatment. This most often involves helping clients to tell the story of their experiences, accessing and integrating memories and feelings, and making meaning of these experi-ences. As individuals gain functional control over their psychophysiological extremes, they also reconstruct their agendas and choose a life course. From the ancient past to the present, "story" arising from personal experience has had the effect of revealing the influences that transform us.

RHYTHMS OF RECOVERY

How did ancient peoples, bathed in the geomagnetic aura of the earth, cultivate their spinal columns, enliven their neuronal antennae through rituals of yoga and meditation, and position themselves as divining rods in order to resonate with both earthly and heavenly bodies? What meaning do these traditions have for us today?

Before the domination of male gods over female ones in the Eurasian re-gion, ancient stories tell us that Persephone, daughter of the Greek god Zeus, was in her earlier form a pre-Greek goddess, the Sumerian Ereshkigal, queen of the underworld. Persephone's trauma, her rape and abduction, do not ap-pear in the stories until the era of Hesiod and Homer, coincident with the rise of patriarchy. During this era, the gods and goddesses traveled the roads be-tween Egypt and Greece, stopping to rest by the hermai—square stone pillars each crowned with a head and having a phallus—that were erected in honor of Hermes, the wing-footed messenger of the gods. Hermes protected the borders of earth and hell, where, as a psychopomp, he transported the souls of the dead to Hades and in return received the cloak of invisibility. It is the "invisible" Hermes, caduceus in hand, who guides the stolen maiden Persephone back from the underworld to reunite with Demeter, her mother self. Hermes is the "messenger" who represents consciousness; he is invisible but transformative. Historically, Hermes was believed to have traveled to Egypt, where he united with Thoth, the Egyptian God of medicine, reflecting the merger of Greek and Egyptian science, which led to alchemy, the ancient science of the transmutation of consciousness. The ancient Egyptian hermetic alchemical concept of transformation of base metals into gold tells the story of the early science of chemistry. Its esoteric meaning lies in the process of transmuting (un)consciousness into the elixir of conscious awareness. Healing trauma involves a similar ineffable, alchemical transmutation during which the therapist is the client's guide on a path of restoration and return to the self.

Ancient Egyptian rituals of initiation as well as Ayurvedic and yogic practices, the Kaballah, Chinese Taoism, Christian mysticism, and the Sufi practices of Islam all describe methods that are today called meditation, prayer, intention and nonlocal healing, imagery, visualization and hypnotherapy, ritual dance and chants, and self-regulation through breath control. All of these practices focus on mobilizing energy currents (the caduceus) to accomplish control over autonomic processes and thus to extend optimal capacities in the service of health and become "awake and aware."

Many of the yoga, meditation, and shamanistic rituals I describe below are increasingly integrated into conventional treatments, though denuded of their religious or spiritual origins. This approach has allowed these methods to become more fully integrated into secular practice, as they should be. Yet many clients may not want to separate self-regulation methods from the spiritual experiences to which they often lead. The integrative therapist can support this deeper yearning for spiritual growth out of trauma. On the other hand, there are many individuals who would not engage in these practices if they were associated with spiritual or religious concepts or concepts that seem alien to their own religious precepts. Thus many approaches have been "secularized" for application in the West. For example, biofeedback is a modern form of meditation and will appeal to many who will not want to meditate. However, while these methods have intrinsic value as psychophysiological techniques and are effective for introducing people to their capacities for self-regulation, they are also drawn from universal rituals, replete with elaborate enactments that bond individuals with their families, communities, and spiritual life. The introduction of these techniques—whether breathing, meditating, or applying biofeedback—can be offered and taught in a variety of ways to match the client's belief system.

STORY AS THERAPY

The word *therapy* is derived from the ancient Greek word *therapeuticos*, meaning, "to attend" and "to worship." Two thousand years ago, *therapeutae* were attending priest/healers of ancient Greece who interpreted the dreams of people who came to the Aesculapian temples, named after Aesculapius, the Greek god of medicine. These temples offered quiet beauty, music, massage, and restful sleep, during which sacred snakes and dogs roamed the temple grounds and licked the wounds of those seeking healing. The provision of therapy is sacred work; our work with clients often requires walking with them along the precipice of pain as we listen to their stories, explore with them the meaning of the story, and then help them to create a new life, much as a pruned limb sprouts new growth. I make the case throughout this volume that the body has a story to tell as well as the mind—indeed they are one and the same story. Our first task as *therapeutae* is to create a sacred space for storytelling in all the forms in which a story emerges.

The tradition of storytelling is age-old. Stories and myths commonly convey universal experiences of trauma and are typically expressed across all cultures and traditions. Myths and their images carry archetypal and cultural messages of meaning. Stories drawn from the universal myths of the journeys of heroes are relevant to the challenges confronted by the individual. These stories often involve images of descent and the triumph of rebirth. They may call on metaphors of being lost in a maze or tell of the descent of Inanna, the abduction of Persephone, St. John of the Cross's dark night of the soul, Homer's story of Achilles (Houston, 1987; Shay, 1994), or the Athabascan legend of betrayal and forgiveness called "Two Old Women." Such stories may be drawn from science fiction, detective fiction, or fantasy. Stories need not take the form of ancient myths but may focus on contemporary tales of political and personal heroism, recalling the bravery of women and men who speak out about their victimization in the face of great social or personal odds. McGrath (2011)— in working with a mourning survivor who, longing for her "idealized" past, struggles between the need to restore and the need to transform—draws on Jewish narratives that find meaning in exile.

One way in which I engage clients at this level is to ask them what their favorite myth or fairy tale is and how it has meaning for them. As adults they may remember important stories from their childhood that helped them to survive. These stories can then form a theme that will provide images and metaphors throughout the healing process. Knowing clients' religious beliefs and history also provides clues to the images and figures with whom they may identify and from whom they may draw strength. They may not remember stories, so exploring, reading, or listening to stories is another option. The book *Women Who Run with the Wolves* (Pinkola-Estes, 1996) is a book of transcendent stories and myths that many women enjoy, along with listening to *Seeing in the Dark: Myths and Stories to Reclaim the Buried, Knowing Woman* (Pinkola-Estes, 2010). Both offer inspiration during a client's healing. One of my clients fell asleep each night listening to audiobooks, both story and soothing voice lulled her to sleep, something she missed as a child. Many of my Christian clients draw inspiration from the Bible. Clients benefit from writing their own stories as myths or heroic journeys. To begin the mythic story process I may share with a female client who has been raped or assaulted and who faces a journey of recovery the story of Persephone and Demeter. I will relate the universal myth of abduction, rape, and rebirth. Shay (1994) explores the similarities between Homer's *Iliad* and the stories of Vietnam War veterans.

Calling upon the sacred out loud in therapy may not be appropriate for everyone, or it may be left for the final phases of treatment. Certainly in the United States there is a growth of religion in counseling as well as other types of spiritual counseling and healing.

A competent trauma clinician will be able to work with the individual to explore her or his spiritual needs during recovery while remaining open to the meaning and processes that will support personal growth. This approach provides an anchor—a larger vision toward which healing and recovery can move.

THE STAGES OF TREATMENT

Trauma treatment is stage-oriented. Healing proceeds in stages, often throughout the course of a person's life. The outcome of an assessment will determine the emphasis of treatment. Initially planning for treatment involves assessing the length of treatment and identifying the client's stage of recovery. The duration of treatment depends upon the degree to which trauma has affected the individual's developmental processes as well as how it affects his or her current quality of life. Acute stress is less likely than complex trauma to require long-term intervention. Rather than focus on the diagnosis or the stressor itself, one focuses on the unique requirements of the individual (McCann & Pearlman, 1990). The concept of stages is a fluid one, with passage through each stage resembling the movement of a spiral.

Herman (1992, p. 155) has defined the central tasks of three main stages of treatment: establishment of safety, remembrance and mourning, and reconnection with ordinary life. Here are some mind/body methods in the context of these stages, which overlap; also, the needs of each client will differ.

The First Stage

The first stage is safety and stabilization. During the early period of treatment, the client will be anxious about finding solid earth on which to stand; it is then too early to "find meaning" or make sense of the client's trauma. The first steps toward safety often involve simple day-to-day activities of maintaining bodily functions. Many methods are linked to both cognitive behavioral therapy (CBT) and the sacred. These include breathing meditation, visualization, and relaxation strategies. Religious faith is rooted in beliefs that interface with cognitive beliefs about the world. The breath and breathing methods are the most basic physiological rhythm of life and their practice underlies all of the world's spiritual traditions.

It is essential that clients engage in self-care activities that provide daily support for effective, self-soothing mechanisms (in contrast to self-medicating behaviors). Self-care strengthens one's control in daily living. It helps one to manage feelings and controls the overwhelming affective "roller coaster" while also strengthening social supports. Every new memory and new level of memory integration, experience, and feeling disrupts the fragile stability that was hard won during the first stage of stabilization. Helping clients to define their needs and fulfill them by relying on themselves and asking others for help is an ongoing requirement. Clients may be directly encouraged to pay attention to their somatosensory ("gut") reactions during therapy, to define their needs and expectations from the therapy, and to ask questions of the therapist. The needs of complex trauma victims have been neglected or manipulated, and such victims will benefit from the "practice" they get in therapy in defining their needs.

One of the distinguishing features of any therapy is how language is used (Lakoff & Coyne, 1993). The efficacy of treatment rests with the capacity of clinician and client to find a common language of communication. When a practitioner understands a client's behavioral and metaphorical languages, she or he can offer an empathic response. The most common breakdown in treatment occurs because of a break in empathic attunement (Wilson, Lindy, & Raphael, 1994). If the practitioner uses the theme of rhythm and the innate dynamic of polarizing forces in communication, it is possible to more accurately temper empathic statements.

EXERCISE 7.1: THERAPIST EXERCISE: POSTURAL/EMOTIONAL EMPATHY

Do this 2- to 5-minute exercise in the privacy of your office after hours following work with a client with whom you are having difficulty empathizing, establishing a connection, or "reading." Enter into his or her kinesthetic world by recreating your client's physical posture in order to better understand how he or she feels. This includes walking into the office, sitting down, and copying postural changes that stand out during the session. Inhabit the client's space kinesthetically and within a minute you will begin to sense and feel how he or she feels. Then find the pitch and range of the client's voice, even his or her sighs as you put yourself in the client's shoes. This is a useful exercise to do after some initial meetings with a client or whenever it feels as if a connection has been lost. Following the exercise, make sure to undo the kinesthetic connection; shake out, stretch, run your hands under cold water, and consciously reclaim your complete sense of self. Observe your rapport and empathy with the client the next time you meet.

Understanding your client at this level will enhance your capacity to connect and make recommendations for somatic therapies.

The Second Stage

The second stage of recovery focuses on telling the story of the trauma (Herman, 1990). Uncovering occurs in small steps and leads to a process of grieving and mourning of the losses endured as a result of the trauma. During this stage one also begins decreasing dissociation by integrating affect, memory, and cognition as new meaning is created. In traditional verbal therapy, meaning making includes the use of words to construct a coherent narrative that, as it is told and retold, takes a new and fuller shape than the earlier story, which is often marked by a "wordless" or speechless disjunctive quality.

Lethargy, helplessness, depression, loss of faith, and their psychophysical substrates are formidable hurdles occurring cyclically to undermine the client's capacity to assume full responsibility and take action on his or her own behalf. These issues persist or return throughout different stages of treatment and should be regarded as part of the normal rhythm of healing. I find it useful to work with these feeling states and their biobehavioral symptoms from a rhythm-sensitive approach as part of the dynamic swings of trauma. By actively naming and acknowledging the ebb and flow of despair, we educate and remind the client (and ourselves) of the cyclical nature of trauma and healing. This includes discussing how the affective tides that the individual feels are a result the natural balance of basic biological functions gone awry and experienced as the oscillating symptoms of traumatic stress. If behaviors are understood as conscious or unconscious efforts to balance the extremes, sharing this perspective with clients helps to ameliorate the intense shame that they feel at being out of control.

The Third Stage

Herman (1990) describes the third stage of recovery involving "reconnection." This includes decreasing isolation and shame, developing mutual peer relationships with the possibility of reestablishing and renegotiating relationships with families and friends, and embarking on a new stage of life that includes the option to incorporate social action and what has been called the survivor mission (Herman, 1990) or the mission of the wounded healer. The group rituals described below and many of the energy medicine and somatic therapies are often useful at this stage when memories have been delinked from arousal.

THERAPEUTIC METHODS

Physical Exercise

One of the most essential ways to reestablish rhythm and manage anxiety and stress is through physical exercise. Regardless of the treatment modality being used, moving the body (unless this is not possible due to injuries) is central to a successful recovery. Movement and exercise are central to the first stage of recovery, safety, and self-care. Exercise can provide a positive alternative to addictive behaviors, and commonly people "transfer" addiction to substances to addiction to exercise. As a temporary transition, this often works well. There are many reasons why clients will not or cannot exercise; the clinician's challenge is to identify methods that will encourage and support physical movement. There have been clients for whom it was appropriate for me to walk with them as an introduction to movement. Some clients do well working with a coach, a class, or a friend they can commit to. There is some evidence that motivational interviewing about exercise, including reminder phone calls, is effective (Ang, Kesavalu, Lydon, Lane, & Bigatti, 2007).

Below I explore a variety of methods reflecting the spectrum of physical movement that are beneficial for the trauma survivor.

Night Walking

One of the things I loved most about living in the jungle of Mexico before electricity arrived was walking at night along narrow dirt paths, jumping over rocks, twisting around streams, avoiding cow turds and toads—both of which were squishy when I didn't manage to avoid them. My pace would pick up as I raced against the setting sun, anticipating the rising moon. The local people didn't need flashlights since they had walked the paths at night from an early age and now were able to navigate the black paths with ease. No matter how much I practiced, I always stubbed my toes and got really rigid in my gait after a few minutes of walking blind. While I most often required a flashlight or candle to see my way, there were many times when my candle blew out or the batteries died midway home and I had to use my other senses (and faith) as I leapt into the night. One day, Don José and Flip, my black Labrador Retriever, and I went on a 9-hour hike into the mountains to see José's land and waterfalls. José was 65 years old and I had a hard time keeping up with him. It did not occur to him that we had to get back before dark (nor had it occurred to me to bring a flashlight), so we were still an hour away from home when the sun set. Man and dog were soon in the flow and, after several stubbed toes, I finally caught on, and it was exhilarating.

When I read about night walking, it occurred to me that Zink and Parks (1991) had identified much about what made my experience of walking along the dark jungle path that night so exhilarating and life-altering, defining some of the reasons and benefits that apply to the treatment of traumatic stress. Night walking is an activity that includes walking over remote terrain in the dark of night as a way of developing second sight, also called peripheral vision, or insight. This ancient method of walking meditation is a tradition of the Tibetans, Japanese, and Chinese and likely occurs as a matter of daily life for those who live in rural and remote areas of the world.

Night walking can be done by individuals but is best done in pairs or small groups; the experience leads to deep relaxation, heightened senses, improved balance, and elimination of fear, anxiety, and physical pain, all seemingly associated with focused vision (Zink & Parks, 1991). The "not looking but seeing" that night walking engages helps redirect hypervigilance and autonomic arousal. Night walking is a way to consciously "scan" the environment and reclaim peripheral vision among those for whom scanning is a daily unbidden imperative. Trauma victims "lose authority" (Shay, 1994) over physical and mental functions and often "second guess" or doubt their perceptions. Night walking provides an opportunity to test and restore those perceptions, wedding the physical and perceptual. When a person is exhausted by a constant state of alertness, the surveying for hidden dangers, paradoxically, narrows the focus. This narrow focusing of sight that can occur as a result of trauma in turn occludes a more far-reaching peripheral capacity to envision the possible. Night walking restores peripheral vision and thereby returns it to the seer's authority. Suffering from more than a metaphorical myopia, the survivor of trauma obtains insight during the process of trying to "see in the dark."

Night walking will not be for everyone, but there are many options for movement and exercise to meet a client's needs at every stage of recovery. There are innumerable benefits to exercise, and it should be an essential part of a recovery program. Yoga, Pilates, and aerobic exercise reduce anxiety, depression, and panic. Exercise must be carried out at appropriate levels in order to be effective. The factors to be considered include intensity, duration, and frequency. As with any intervention, identifying a tailored approach to each stage is most effective. There are four interrelated kinds of physical exercise that are useful for trauma victims. They include aerobic exercise, anaerobic exercise, stretching, and energetic exercises.

Aerobic Exercise

Aerobic exercise is effective for alleviating anxiety, depression, and dissociation as well as for improving body image and self-esteem. It increases norepinephrine production, which is assumed to be low in people with depression (Feuerstein, Labbe, & Kuczmierczyk, 1988). It also stimulates endorphin production. Running and walking are cost-effective; they increase cardiovascular endurance and respiratory efficiency by improving muscle tone, digestion, and blood volume, promote fat loss, increase energy, and improve sleep (Sachs & Buffone, 1984). Aerobic exercise levels should be maintained at the *perceived level of exertion*, where breathing is heavy and sustained but where one can still carry on a conversation or whistle comfortably. Interval training, involving short bursts of intense activity for 1 minute or more, is also effective. This is a good approach for building endurance by using a machine such as the treadmill or elliptical, or alternating walking with running, for 15 minutes or more. A minimum schedule would comprise 20 minutes of exercise, gradually increasing to 60 minutes, three to six times a week.

Anaerobic exercise includes resistance and weight training; it increases strength, improves body image, and decreases dissociation. It is complementary to aerobic exercise, though it may also be a place to start, depending on the individual. Because it builds muscle strength, it is effective with men and women who have been victimized. Anaerobic exercise builds lean body mass, and increases metabolism and energy so it is effective when people are fatigued or want to lose weight. It is best conducted under the guidance of a trainer. One of the benefits of anaerobic exercise is that the results accrue quickly. For the greatest benefits, individuals should eat protein immediately after an anaerobic workout. For individuals who feel hopeless or out of control, such an exercise program can help to counteract these negative feelings.

Physical exercise also increases levels of a protein called brain-derived neurotrophic factor (BDNF), which improves cognitive function and is neuro-protective of brain regions affected by PTSD (Russo-Neustadt, Beard, Huang, & Cotman, 2000). Interestingly, curcumin, the main ingredient in curry, which is a powerful anti-inflammatory and reduces muscle soreness postexercise, has also been shown to increase BDNF levels as well (Xu et al., 2006).

Energetic Exercise

The energetic exercises that are most commonly practiced in the United States derive from the health systems of India and China; they include yoga, tai chi chuan (tai ji kuan), chi kung, and the martial arts.

Yoga

There are many types of yoga, ranging from gentle yoga (also called yin yoga, designed for gentle restorative movement and relaxation) to power yoga, the fitness-based approach of *Vinyasa* yoga, which means "breath-synchronized movement." Yoga has broad appeal and continues to grow in application. Its practice in the United States ranges from formal Hindu-based traditions influenced by different yogis and yoginis from India, to a secular approach to exercise and meditation, to Christian yoga classes, which remove references to Hinduism and incorporate Christian imagery for health and purification. There are also chair yoga classes for people who are in wheelchairs or are obese, and trauma-based yoga. Hatha yoga combines postures (*asanas*) and breathing (*pranayama*) to decrease muscle tension and eliminate lactic acid, reduce anxiety, facilitate parasympathetic dominance, and improve balance and mental equilibrium. Yoga increases levels of gamma-aminobutyric acid in the brain (Streeter et al., 2010). It is used extensively in Mexico by urban women to promote well-being and reduce pain, and it is also practiced by Latina women with PTSD in the United States (Kirlin, 2010). Yoga helped to manage feelings of sadness in flood survivors after severe flooding in northern India (Telles, Singh, Joshi, & Balkrishna, 2010).

Yoga is often combined with mindfulness for use with children and increasingly incorporated into schools by teachers and counselors as an exercise to support the self-regulation of mood, stress, and resilience (Khalsa, Hickey-Schultz, Cohen, Steiner, & Cope, 2012). Finally, there is doga—yoga for dogs and their people—which may be done at home or at special doga classes (Brilliant & Berloni, 2003).

Yoga Exercises

EXERCISE 7.2: THE LION POSE (SIMHASANA) (ONLINE EXERCISE)

The lion exercise can be a fun way to release emotional stress and tension that is held in the face. This exercise is relaxing, induces parasympathetic dominance, and helps release feelings of emotional intensity. It is one of the few exercises that releases the platysma, which, when tight, causes jaw pain and disordered breathing. It is easy to teach in the office; it releases inhibitions and children and adolescents especially enjoy it. People with TMJ dysfunction or who are having trouble finding their voice or are angry or anxious all benefit from this simple exercise, which may be done anywhere. It's also effective for clinicians after a long day at work.

EXERCISE 7.3: HA BREATH/WOODCHOPPER (ONLINE EXERCISE)

The HA breath/woodchopper is an effective exercise that combines a forceful breath/sound and a yoga movement to release tension. By releasing tension in the diaphragm, one can release anger and other negative emotions and decrease dissociation. It can easily be taught to individuals and I also teach it in my mind/body recovery groups, where it often becomes to source of great laughter and release. I also use it with children and adolescents to release emotion. Once this high-intensity exercise is finished, people are often ready to move into the stage of repose.

EXERCISE 7.4: QIGONG WALKING EXERCISE (ONLINE EXERCISE)

Qigong (pronounced chee-gong) is a gentle therapy that uses movement and intention to strengthen vitality. It can involve specific moving exercises or still meditation. One study found that walking qigong contributes to a client's feeling happier, healthier, stronger, and being able to walk with ease, perform difficult tasks with ease, sleep well, and feel less hungry or thirsty (Jinfu & Xinha, 2008). Qigong walking is even more beneficial because it is gentler on the body and thus better for older patients or those with heart problems, where raising the pulse or rapid breathing is contraindicated.

Taiji or Tai Chi

Tai chi is similar to qigong; it incorporates gentle movement. It is a martial art that involves slow movement. One story about the development of tai chi suggests that the movement is like that of a snake on the ground, moving slowly out of the way of the predatory hawk watching from above. Tai chi provides a variety of benefits at all stages; in recovery it is a simple way to begin movement again; it is also easy on the joints. Qigong and tai chi have been used with torture survivors (Grodin, Piwowarczyk, Fulker, Bazazi, & Saper, 2008) and have improved well-being and the quality of life in people with fibromyalgia (Wang et al., 2010). In my experience tai chi has proved to be an effective exercise for decreasing anxiety during the later stages of recovery, improving body image and body boundaries, and decreasing dissociation.

Expressive Therapies

Movement therapies are also part of the discipline of expressive therapies, which include art, dance, movement, music, and psychodrama, all of which can be used as primary or adjunctive approaches. Journals, art, movement, or voice therapies provide ways to find one's voice, express one's feelings, and tell one's story. Expressive therapies provide a variety of ways in which to tell the story and also to explore creative expression. Their utility for the treatment of trauma lies in the variety of creative languages they give victims for expressing feelings and images, accessing memories, and clarifying experiences. Movement therapy is the somatic imaging form of what art is to visual creation. In movement therapy, a client may express somatically through movement or dance the "wordless" feelings held within. Group movement therapy has been demonstrated to be effective in working with clients with dissociative identity disorder. Expressive therapist Baum (1991) suggests that efficacy results from establishing trust through kinesthetic empathy, negotiating social interaction, eliciting expressive movement and traumatic material, and integrating a more coherent sense of self. Voice movement therapy is both creative and therapeutic in that it provides an approach to explore oneself and one's issues by using voice and movement to tell one's personal story.

Art therapy is one example from the field of expressive therapies that can be easily integrated into conventional psychotherapy. Art is a universal language that transcends verbal constructs. Because of the centrality of imagery in traumatic stress, art provides an isomorphic approach to treatment at all stages of recovery. In trauma, imagery oscillates from intrusive, in the form of flashbacks and nightmares, to inaccessible or absent, as in alexithymia. Therapy is then designed with the specific goals of the individual in mind. Art therapy has been used to help veterans create and transform traumatic symbolization (Howard, 1990) and in cross-cultural settings with Cambodian victims of war trauma (Wadeson, Durkin, & Perach, 1989). Malchiodi (2008) explores trauma informed art therapy, which may be used with children or adults with specific activities geared toward the developmental needs of the individual. Art therapy can be integrated at various stages of therapy. During the assessment process, art can be used to bridge verbal, concrete, and kinesthetic modes of communication. If telling the trauma story in words is too painful, or if shame engenders silence (Marks & Thayer, 1989), the patient can discuss a picture of a feeling instead of the feeling itself (Howard, 1990).

Laughter

After years of practice during which I was listening to stories of trauma all day and supervising interns at night who were also sharing the painful stories of their clients, I realized that I wasn't laughing a whole lot. So when I discovered laughter yoga clubs, started by Dr. Madan Katariat, I began to use laughter yoga with my clients; as a result, I—and my interns—found ourselves feeling much happier and filled with more gratitude. It is no surprise that smiling and laughing is a hard-wired physical response that triggers a concomitant emotional reaction. We also learn a lot about ourselves and our clients—how easily we can let go, how embarrassed or silly we might feel—and this also provides insight into how restricted we might have become. During this exercise people often remember early life experiences of being told to be quiet or that laughter was not allowed, and they often also remember happier times. One begins just by laughing and experimenting with all types of laughter sounds. Laughter can be done in the office, with family, and in groups, and "laugh clubs" have sprouted up all over the world. Like all methods, it must be used at the right stage. In general, it is best applied during the later stages of healing. Like forgiveness, neither laughter nor gratitude should be rushed, and there are some people for whom it will never be a good "fit."

There are some effective apps for smart phones that support positive thoughts, gratitude, and happiness that are a useful adjunct for use between sessions. They include "Live Happy" and "Gratitude Stream" by Signal Patterns.

Body Image

In Chapter 5 I discuss the role of touch therapies to help the body tell the story of the trauma in order to transform dissociation, pain, eating disorders, and depersonalization. Working with the body need not always involve touch, and these symptoms can also be addressed integratively as cognitive distortions of body image. Cognitive-behavioral therapy (CBT) is effective for changing body image because body-image problems are associated with cognitive distortions about the body more than with the objective reality of the body itself. In addition to CBT, I use the arts and imagery.

When the body is locus of the abuse, restoring one's relationship with the body by exploring body image is central to recovery from abuse. This affects men as well as women. An integrative posttrauma model includes a feminist analysis of body image distortions, since they are closely tied to social conditioning and values about female and male stereotypes. Freedman (1990) asserts that women who live in societies that value a variety of women's shapes and sizes have lower rates of eating disorders. Thus body image is not only a personal struggle of overcoming objectification of the body but also a challenge that exists within the context of family, social, and cultural values.

Janoff-Bulman and Frieze (1987) discuss gender schemas such as conceptions of physical differences, reproductive functions, division of labor, and personality attributes that are culturally defined as male or female. Thus men are typically viewed as aggressive, competitive, and independent, whereas women are typically regarded as passive, emotional, and dependent. When they do not fit the dominant gender schema, men are often subject to bullying as children and adolescents. Lisak (1995) proposes that psychotherapy with male survivors should include an exploration of both personal and gender socialization as part of the process of recovery. Exploring socialization in the context of the body, whether male, female, or transgender, supports the goals of recovery, which include restoring the capacity for pleasure, increasing self-esteem through acceptance of one's body, engaging in physical activities, and reducing distortions of image and capabilities.

Because body image distortions are common to complex trauma victims, exercises that are easily incorporated into a daily routine and combine both cognitive and somatic approaches, such as visualization and physical movement, are most effective. Body image issues are often tied to dissociative processes, and body dysmorphic disorder is linked to sexual abuse and neglect. Therefore it is essential to incorporate exercises that are acceptable to the client and easily incorporated for use both in the office and at home. Testing these exercises in the office together with the client will reinforce their use at home.

I use the following exercises to address body image, body dysmorphic disorder, pain, and dissociation: drawing the body, body scan (see Online Exercise 6.2), and perceptual retraining.

EXERCISE 7.5: CLIENT EXERCISE: DRAWING THE BODY

During assessment I provide the client with an outline of the body (see Online Assessment 6.2) in order to identify areas of the body that are painful or problematic or otherwise important. This assessment serves as the basis for a more amplified drawing using colored pens or other art supplies that track or envision change over time. The client may draw her body when she experiences different moods in order to illuminate nonverbally the connection between mood, pain, and body image. Using the arts to represent the body provides a "moving picture" to record important insights, changes in self-perception, and goals for change. Body image is best explored by integrating a developmental, psychodynamic, cognitive-behavioral, somatopsychic (touch and movement therapies), and cultural lens.

EXERCISE 7.6: CLIENT EXERCISE: PERCEPTUAL RETRAINING

Phillips (2009) describes a process called perceptual retraining. People who experience body dysmorphic disorder constantly check themselves in the mirror and make a negative self-assessment each time they do. Perceptual retraining encourages the individual to stand at more of a distance, look in the mirror, and observe the whole body image nonjudgmentally without focusing on the details.

Movement and Exposure Techniques

During the second or third stages of recovery, clients may benefit from a method that integrates the body via specific martial arts training and the movement, imagery, and the flooding method associated with exposure techniques of cognitive-behavioral therapies. Exposure techniques access and reframe state-dependent memory learning and behavior described in Chapter 3. They focus on the stimulus or antecedent conditions to change behavior (Sheikh & Sheikh, 1989) and are intended to activate and modify fear reactions (Olasov-Rothbaum & Foa, 1992). Flooding is an exposure technique that involves the use of highly feared stimuli to activate high levels of anxiety (Olasov-Rothbaum & Foa, 1992; Sheikh & Sheikh, 1989). It can be invoked either through imagination or in reality until anxiety reduction occurs (Olasov-Rothbaum & Foa, 1992). Examples of the use of flooding include exposing veterans to visual and auditory replications (movies, audio recordings, or photographs) that are evocative of the traumatic images that haunt their lives.

Sarah's abuse throughout childhood was associated with being led up several flights of stairs. When the elevator in my office was broken one day, her climb up several flights constituted a trigger that precipitated a panic attack. By the employment of techniques of flooding and systematic desensitization that focused on climbing the stairs (at first with me and then alone), Sarah's fears were reduced. As therapy progressed, she often chose to climb the stairs, exultant about her progress.

Purpose, preparation, timing, and meaning determine the appropriate use of intentional flooding, which is a powerful person- and stage-specific treatment.

However, to some degree exposure and flooding often occur spontaneously in the context of therapy. Flooding can also constitute one aspect of somatic therapies that employ the use of touch for survivors of sexual and physical abuse, including torture. Because flooding can be destabilizing, its use in the first stage of treatment is rarely indicated. While flooding is not usually a reason to use touch therapies, if touch is used to decondition state-dependent reactivity via "exposure," it is best applied to intractable symptoms toward the later stage of recovery, when good client-practitioner rapport and strong self-care and social supports are in place. Even at this stage, touch or flooding can activate sensory-based memory, however, the reaction may be more easily integrated. Systematic desensitization involves the reduction of fear by the teaching of responses that cannot simultaneously exist with anxiety. These may include deep muscle relaxation, breathing, and imagery. Meichenbaum and Cameron developed stress-inoculation training (SIT) as a self-instructional method for coping with stress (Feuerstein et al., 1988). Treatment includes education about how anxiety functions, followed by the learning of deep muscle relaxation and breath control. SIT can be used to teach anger management. During the cognitive phase, the individual learns about the functions of anger and his or her personal styles of anger while also learning cognitive skills that provide alternatives to understanding the provocative events and modifying the importance attached to the events (Feuerstein et al., 1988).

Model Mugging

An experiential seminar that combines martial arts, body awareness, and both flooding and desensitization is called model mugging and is conducted with homogeneous groups of women, men, or teenagers. It is designed to build personal safety skills and also decondition hyperarousal and hypervigilance. The course offers the opportunity to simulate scenarios of physical and sexual assault scenes for survivors in order to overcome the "freeze" response that contributes to a sense of helplessness. While the past cannot be changed, the survivor can choose to recreate the scene of the assault and emerge victorious after learning cognitive, affective, and physical skills that overcome the freeze response. Integrating cognition, physical reeducation, and musculoskeletal deconditioning results in a new sense of empowerment and resolution and provides one of the best outlets for rage and the freeze state that I know. I have observed significant long-term reductions in nightmares and flashbacks among women and men who have completed this seminar. I also recommend this class for children who experience many benefits, including trauma prevention through the development of self-protective skills and body boundaries. Children who are already experiencing developmental trauma gain the opportunity to integrate body and emotion in constructive ways.

Meditation

Meditation is the intentional regulation of attention from moment to moment. There are two types of meditation: one is attention-based, such as mantra meditation or chanting, and the other, such as mindfulness, involves nonreactive monitoring of the content of experience (Lutz, Slagter, Dunne, & Davidson, 2008). Meditation promotes self-awareness and improves concentration, attention, and relaxation. The practice can quiet intense affective states and internal dialogue and increase awareness of muscle tension. The use of meditation during the first stages of recovery is not necessarily the first choice as a method of relaxation, for it is very difficult for acutely traumatized individuals to relax and sit still. Instead, hard aerobic exercise has been shown to be a more effective means of relaxation than meditation (Flannery, 1987).

The Buddhist tradition of Vipassana meditation, also called mindfulness or insight meditation, encourages focusing attention on the rhythm of the breath, allowing thoughts that pass through the mind to be observed without judgment or any effort to change them. It is an approach to developing detached self-observation of the processes of the mind rather than focusing and identifying on the content. Though mindfulness derives from Buddhist psychology, it is often taught as a secular approach to meditation in the United States. It can be done while sitting, talking, or running. Mindfulness meditation may be the focus of counseling, or it can easily be integrated with psychotherapy, yoga, and physical exercise. When it is combined with yoga, mindfulness is effective for the treatment of chronic pain. The practice of mindfulness by novice meditators is associated with changes in the volume of gray matter in brain regions related to learning, memory, the regulation of emotion, self-referential processing, and perspective taking (Hölzel et al., 2011). Mindfulness has wide application for the treatment of PTSD and improves the effects of exposure therapies (Treanor, 2011). Its utility with survivors, many of whom struggle with feelings of self-hate, is that it encourages a nonjudgmental attitude and loving-kindness toward oneself. Mindfulness is a central strategy in dialectical behavioral therapy, used for self-regulation with trauma survivors, and also integrated successfully with people incarcerated in prisons.

There are many meditation teachers, psychologists, and healers who use mindfulness with individuals undergoing trauma treatment. Kornfield and Hall (1988a, 1988b) have used mindfulness meditation with male and female survivors of sexual abuse, and Thich Nhat Hanh, a monk who survived the Vietnam War, has worked extensively with trauma survivors and Vietnam veterans using mindfulness. Thich Nhat Hanh (1990) has recorded an audio series on the practice of mindfulness in psychotherapy. Salzberg (2011) provides an accessible introductory program called "Real Happiness."

There are many innovative methods that integrate mindfulness into treatment programs, such as mindfulness-based cognitive therapy for the prevention of relapse of depression and substance abuse. Equine-assisted mindfulness programs using mindfulness with horses as therapists, some of whom may themselves be traumatized, are used to assist veterans with PTSD in their recovery. Mindfulness is integrated into culturally relevant models of relapse prevention. For example, the traditional canoe journey among American Indians of the Pacific Northwest is used as a metaphor for a journey that urban adolescents undertake as they develop bicultural life skills and learn behaviors to prevent substance abuse (Marlatt et al., 2003). The canoe journey is an active annual cultural event that enacts traditional values and lifeways for cultural healing and healing from trauma and the addictions; in general, it celebrates tribal culture. Over 5,000 indigenous people of the Pacific Northwest participate in the canoe journey, traveling in giant hand-hewn canoes across ancient sea routes of trade and exchange. These cultural-specific community rituals restore the health of communities as part of the healing process in response to postcolonial trauma.

For clients who begin a program of meditation and breathing, there are also free computer applications that can be used to support a daily practice. One application I have found helpful is "Breathe2Relax," which is a free, portable stress-management application created by The National Center for Telehealth.

Heart and Mind

Stress dramatically affects the function of the autonomic nervous system; this contributes to high rates of cardiovascular disease, anxiety, and depression among people with PTSD. Positive emotion with a focus on gratitude and concentration on positive feelings is increasingly linked to both emotional and physiological benefits. Methods that attune the heart with brain and mind restore psychophysiological coherence. In Chapter 3 I discussed of the effects of trauma on heart rate variability (HRV), which is a conventionally accepted measure of autonomic stress indicating a loss of flexibility in the normal beat-to-beat variations evident in health.

HRV biofeedback focuses on the creation of coherence between the brain and heart via forms of meditation or biofeedback technology. Coherence building is a concept that links to somatic empathy, discussed in Chapter 5. The HeartMath Institute employs the use of brain-heart meditation and positive emotion along with heart rhythm biofeedback. Practitioners can generate "a coherent pattern" in the subtle electromagnetic environment to which patients are exposed. HRV biofeedback is designed to build physiological coherence and demonstrates a significant increase in HRV in a variety of populations with stress-related low HRV, including police (McCraty, Tomasino, Atkinson, & Sundram, 1999) and veterans (Tan, Dao, Farmer, Sutherland, & Gevirtz, 2011)

A study measuring the heart rates of therapists and patients showed that at moments when the therapist's empathy was high, there was often a synchronization of the therapist's heart rate with the patient's (Rosch & Markov, 2004). While somatic empathy derives from energy-based bodywork, HRV coherence provides a nontouch alternative. The HeartMath Institute provides comprehensive training for therapists and has developed an interactive computer-based tool called "Heart Rhythm Coherence Feedback Training," which helps users to measure changes in their HRV in response to positive emotions, and meditations. Portable and desktop "emWave" devices are easy to use. I keep some machines in my office for clients to use. The "Wild Divine" is a more complex HRV-biofeedback software program designed for use at home or in the office. The "story" is an animated journey of spiritual discovery; as one relaxes and regulates the breath and heart, the "doors" to the next stage open and one progresses in the program and in HRV coherence and relaxation. This program helps people with PTSD, depression, anxiety, and attention deficit disorder; it can be used by children and teens as well as adults for whom computer games are more appealing than meditation.

Biofeedback and Neurofeedback

Biofeedback is a powerful and effective approach for the treatment of PTSD and traumatic brain injury. It is an ideal intervention to use with individuals with symptoms refractory to psychotherapy or for people for whom "talk therapy" is not an option. There are many types of biofeedback, including electroencephalographic (EEG) neurofeedback (NFB). Biofeedback is a process that enables an individual to learn how to change physiological activity for the purposes of improving health and performance. Precise instruments measure physiological activity such as brainwaves, heart function, breathing, muscle activity, and skin temperature. These instruments rapidly and accurately "feed back" information to the user. The presentation of this information—often in conjunction with changes in thinking, emotions, and behavior—supports desired physiological changes. Over time, these changes can endure without continued use of an instrument. For example, in targeting the frontal region with EEG neurofeedback, one develops the ability to regulate the frontotemporal limbic system. Individuals can learn to regulate amygdala reactions (Zotev et al., 2011) and thus gain control over emotional lability. Peniston pioneered "Alpha Theta" neurofeedback with war veterans for the treatment of PTSD and substance abuse (Peniston & Kulkosky, 1992; Peniston, Marrinan, Deming, & Kulkosky, 1993). NFB is effective for the treatment for pain, psychological symptoms, and impaired quality of life associated with fibromyalgia (Kayıran, Dursun, Dursun, Ermutlu, & Karamürsel, 2010). A combination of NFB methods can be tailored to the needs of clients to help accelerate their recovery. Some of these NFB applications use software programs that include imagery and sound as well as protocols that include emotionally distressing videos to increase autonomic arousal, thus teaching the client to self-regulate the responses of the brain and autonomic nervous system (Jose Vasquez, personal communication, October 16, 2011). Passive infrared and near infrared hemoencephalography

(HEG pIR and nIR) are used to measure cerebral blood flow or the amount of heat, respectively, generated by the neuronal assembly in the brain region targeted by the clinician. HEG nIR monitors and encourages the increase of blood flow, oxygen, and glucose to all parts of the brain. This NFB modality is effective for increasing cerebral blood flow and is commonly used in the treatment of traumatic brain injury (TBI) or for enhancing frontal lobe and executive function. The nIR HEG headband is noninvasive and placed around the skull to assess the color of brain tissue changes upon increased oxygenation in response to increase demand of NFB. NFB may be used at any stage of treatment and may have different applications throughout a course of recovery, ranging from relaxing muscle tension or headaches to improving memory and cognitive function or addressing pelvic pain or bladder control. NFB is especially effective in increasing concentration and reducing depression and mood lability in PTSD, attention deficit disorder (ADD) and attention deficit hyperactivity disorder (ADHD).

"Lumosity" is one of several scientifically validated web-based games developed to train five core areas of cognitive function, including processing speed, attention, memory, flexibility, and problem solving. It has special modules designed for PTSD, TBI, and ADHD to address emotional regulation. It is smart, fun, dynamic, and appropriate for all ages. The first sessions are free and subsequent sessions are low in cost. "T2 Mood Tracker" is a mobile application that allows users to self-monitor, track, and reference their emotional experience over a period of days, weeks, and months using a visual analog rating scale. Users can self-monitor emotional experiences associated with common deployment-related behavioral health issues such as posttraumatic stress, brain injury, life stress, depression, and anxiety. Additional ratings can also be added. With each self-rating, notes on environmental influences on emotional experiences can be added. Self-monitoring results can be a self-help tool or results can be shared with a therapist or health care professional, providing a record of the patient's emotional experience over a selected time frame.

Hypnotherapy

Hypnotherapy is often combined with other trauma therapies and may be used during all stages of recovery, with specific methods geared toward safety, uncovering, or integration. Hypnotherapy can be an effective tool to engage the body and to explore imagery about the body before actually incorporating movement or touch. There are simple approaches to hypnotherapy that practitioners can incorporate as well as comprehensive training and certification programs and professional societies.

Hypnotherapy is defined as a patterned use of communication designed to elicit an altered state of consciousness (Gleason, 1992) characterized by cognitive, perceptual, and sensory changes (Brown & Fromm, 1987). Also referred to as ideodynamic healing, it is based on the relationship that words and ideas have with dynamic physiological function (Rossi & Cheek, 1988). Forms of ideodynamic healing date back to 1500 BCE (Rossi, 1986). Hypnotherapy has broad application for integrative posttrauma therapy in areas of body image, pain, and health. Hypnotherapy provides an important conceptual link between the mind, body, dissociation, and trance states. People with dissociative symptoms are often capable of an unusual degree of psychological control over various somatic functions (Spiegel, 1994) making them good candidates for hypnotherapy. As a method of trance induction for clients, hypnotherapy is isomorphic, facilitating a dissociative-like (hypnoidal) consciousness familiar to victims of abuse. However, the difference is that the locus of control is with the client. Thus hypnotherapy can help a client utilize this control for his or her benefit. In Chapter 5 I explored briefly the interlocking currents of politics, gender, class, and race in the development of hypnosis and psychoanalysis and how the modern practice of psychodynamic psychotherapy has its roots in the exploration of trance and the symptoms of hysteria.

Hypnotherapy bridges the use of words with visual imagery and engages the ultradian rhythm to help reestablish systemic equilibrium and integrate cognitive-affective-somatic changes. Hypnotherapy that is nondirective and nonsuggestive uses the natural trance of the 90-minute ultradian rhythm as a psychotherapeutic tool.

EXERCISE 7.7: CLINICIAN EXERCISE: CREATING A HYPNOTHERAPEUTIC RECORDING (ONLINE EXERCISE)

Utilization of the ultradian rhythm, both in therapy and through methods for home use, helps to access the mind/body's innate capacity to self-regulate the autonomic nervous system. Creating a hypnotherapeutic recording is an effective method to help a client reduce pain, fear, and anxiety or to reduce body image distortions.

During the treatment process a client may hear about age regression hypnotherapy and become eager to uncover early life memories; he or she may ask about, or even insist on, doing hypnotherapy. An experienced hypnotherapist should do this type of therapy. In evaluating the variety of options for supporting self-regulation strategies with clients, I consider the portal—that is, does one enter via the body, the mind, or spiritual or energetic methods? They all lead to the same place. However, much like the house with several entries, so do the strategies or technologies become more effective when they are linked to the specific needs of the individual and her stage of recovery.

Energy Medicine

Energy medicine includes a variety of therapies that use energy in its various forms to support self-regulation and balance the human energy field. For example, light and sound are forms of energy, as are ultrasound and laser, which are technologies used to treat pain and inflammation. Energy currents can be generated by the hands, as in polarity or Reiki, which are used to balance meridians, or by needles, as in acupuncture, or by technologies such as cranial electrical stimulation and low-energy neurofeedback (LENS) machines. Energy psychology is a discipline that integrates energy medicine practices such as meridian therapies with CBT and EMDR and is practiced by counselors, psychologists, and energy medicine practitioners and their clients. Among these effective methods are the emotional freedom technique and thought field therapy. As I explained in Chapter 5, the integration of touch, in particular energy-based touch, with emotional processing engages the whole self and works to decondition state-dependent memories and behaviors. These methods also include instructions for use at home by clients, making them an effective approach to self-care.

Sometimes people are skeptical about or afraid of the concept of energy because of their religious fears or beliefs. Often people experience a taboo because of (early) life experiences of sexual abuse or boundary violations. In Indian country, healing methods or spiritual practices were outlawed by the U.S. government as part of the strategy to control Indian lives and ways; the legacy of that trauma persists and continues to affect attitudes about touch, energy, and spirit healing. Immigrants with traditional practices may feel that they have to practice in secret, assimilate, or just not share their approaches with disbelieving medical professionals. Some sects of Christianity practice energy medicine while others reject it. However, in spite of these obstacles, a renaissance that reclaims and revisions these methods is under way. The methods I discuss below are cost-effective (insurance will often pay for these treatments or technology), they can be learned and practiced by professionals and lay people alike, and they are generally noninvasive. Finally, there is good research and empirical evidence that supports efficacy for our clients.

Cranial Electrical Stimulation

Cranial electrical stimulation (CES), an effective energy medicine, is a non-pharmacological intervention for the treatment of chronic pain (Kulkarni & Smith, 2001), depression (Tan et al., 2003), anxiety (Novakovic et al., 2011), addictions, and sleep disturbances (Shealy & Thomlinson, 2008). It provides a simple, cost-effective approach to managing many of the symptoms of PTSD. CES is a noninvasive form of microcurrent stimulation that uses the application of a high-frequency low-level pulsed current that is conducted through the skin and into the cranium. CES units are class II A, type BF medical devices generating microcurrent pulses that reach the hypothalamus (Ferdjallah, Bostick, & Barr, 1996) directly via earlobe or wrist stimulation. The CES device is easy to use as the electrodes are typically clipped onto the earlobes or applied behind the ears with patches. They may also be applied to the left wrist, where the vagal nerve is also contacted. The small electrical pulses generated by the CES unit can stimulate neuron regeneration and repair (Kirsch & Smith, 2004), and CES can be a very effective treatment for fibromyalgia. Positive effects of CES also include enhanced ability to think, likely due to neurotransmitter synthesis. It is approved by the U.S. Food and Drug Administration for the treatment of anxiety, depression, insomnia, and addiction withdrawal symptoms. It is hypothesized that the low voltage administered by the CES increases neurotransmitters by converting the amino acid glutamine into gamma aminobutyric acid and tryptophan into serotonin and promoting the conversion of choline to acetylcholine and increased serotonin levels over a 2-week period (Shealy et al., 1989). CES has been found to decrease cortisol levels and increase levels of norepinephrine, dopamine (Rosch & Markov, 2004), CSF serotonin, DHEA (Liss & Liss, 1996), and endorphins (Southworth, 1999). Schmitt, Capo, Frazier, and Boren (1984) found CES to be effective in controlling anxiety in recovering alcoholics. CES can improve the effects of vascular and analgesic medications. It appears to stimulate the hypothalamus and increase rapid-eye-movement (REM) sleep and can therefore stimulate dreams. Most clients will benefit from CES. Contraindications include pregnancy or lactation and the presence of a pacemaker or other implanted bioelectric equipment. However, an assessment of its utility for each individual is advised. I sometimes loan a home unit to a client for 2 weeks and recommend a protocol of use twice a day from 30 to 60 minutes each time. When I instruct my clients on the use of the CES, I analogize it to drinking a glass of water to quench thirst. Drink until you are no longer thirsty; the client may also follow his or her intuition. It should be used at home, not while driving or working due to its soporofic effects. If the client experiences benefits after 2 weeks, a home model may be purchased.

Light Therapy

Widely used for the treatment of seasonal affective disorder (SAD), light therapy decreases carbohydrate cravings while also relieving depression, pain, premenstrual syndrome, and sleep problems. The light/dark cycle of nature regulates the circadian rhythm of the brain and therefore regulates sleep, adrenal function, and glucose levels. Ideally one should wake with the light and sleep in the dark; however, this is rarely possible. Light therapy is available outdoors or from 10,000-lux light boxes. Full-spectrum light bulbs may be installed at home and at the office. I recommend light therapy delivered for 20 to 30 minutes between 7 AM and 10 AM and supplement with 1 to 2 mcg of sublingual methylcobalamin (vitamin B12). After a month, 0.5 to 1 mg of melatonin can be added 1 hour before bed. Fibromyalgia may also be treated with this protocol. If there is a light box in the office or lunchroom, it may be used by many people during the course of the day. I always have one available for use in my waiting room. Some light boxes include a blue-spectrum light, which stimulates serotonin production and is especially beneficial for mood and pain. There are no contraindications to light box use. However, excessive use can be too stimulating, and people with a diagnosis of bipolar disorder or with migraines should start out with 5 minutes of exposure and increase it incrementally according to comfort. During the summertime, obtaining 20 minutes of sunlight at midday is also advisable or can be done in place of the light box. (Sun glasses should be not be worn as a rule). Light therapy is often covered by many insurance plans upon a diagnosis of sleep disorder or major depression.

Blue Light–Blocking Glasses

Glasses that block the blue wave of the light spectrum have been demonstrated to support sleep. The blue light suppresses melatonin, which is why watching television, reading late, or working on the computer is stimulating and contributes to insomnia. It is also why one is exposed to blue light during the morning to regulate the wake cycle but should block it at night. There are special inexpensive blue light–blocking glasses that are very effective (see Online Resources). I recommend wearing them for at least an hour or more before bed.

Music and Sound Therapies

Music has profound integrative effects on the mind/body and spiritual healing. Listening to music as well as singing or chanting is central to reestablishing a sense of rhythm within. Many ancient spiritual and healing traditions have long employed music to achieve states of consciousness that support healing, access creativity, and expand the sense of the divine. These methods include traditions of chanting among Gregorian, Tibetan, and Buddhist monks as well as among the Lakota, Hopi, and Pueblos peoples of the Americas. One common link among all these chants and among many religious and spiritual healing rituals, in fact, are the tones and harmonics that synchronize the function of the right and left hemispheres of the brain. Specialized rhythms "entrain" the brain to function coherently. It may be argued that synchronized functioning of the brain is a psychophysiological substrate of healing. Listening to gongs, singing bowls from Tibet, and singing in choirs are all methods that synchronize individuals with the group. Tuning forks are often combined with acupuncture and bodywork therapies like polarity therapy. The use of tuning forks deepens relaxation and increases the release of nitrous oxide, enodocannabinoids, and endogenous opiates (Salamon, Kim, Beaulieu, & Stefano, 2003).

Binaural Sound Technology

Robert Monroe, an engineer and composer, developed the technology he called "Hemi Sync," which delivers two different tones into each ear simultaneously. When the brain receives a different frequency from each ear, it responds by "creating" a third frequency, the difference between the two incoming frequencies. Binaural sound impulses alter EEG brainwave patterns and cause both brain hemispheres to come into coherence. Binaural sound technology is effective, easy to use, and facilitates a sense of peace and relaxation. It is useful for sleep problems, acute and chronic pain, substance abuse recovery, and pre- and postoperatively to stabilize mood and speed recovery. Monroe coined the term *out-of-body experience* in response to his experimentation during the early days of research into sound-facilitated "sleep-learning." Brainwave synchronization may also be achieved with variable-frequency photostimulation and is effective for relaxation and the treatment of chronic pain and stress illnesses, anxiety, insomnia, and depression (Cox, Shealy, Cady, & Liss, 1996; Picker, 1993).

Toning

Toning is a form of singing that focuses on making sounds, often using vowels as extended notes. Toning does not require the ability to sing but does involve making sounds that create vibrations, which can be directed toward pain or discomfort or unpleasant emotions in areas of the body. Chanting is the saying or singing of sounds or songs individually or in a group and is most often associated with spiritual or religious devotion. Repetitive sounds and singing

EXERCISE 7.8: TONING

Toning involves making sounds based on the vowels. First one inhales and then on the exhale makes a vowel sound for the length of the breath; with just a pause to inhale, one exhales again, repeating the sound. This may be repeated several times. You can experiment with different sounds and vowels. Toning sounds include Ohhhhhh . . . Ahhhhhhh . . . Eeeeeee . . . Iiiiiiiiiiii, and Uuuuuuuuuu. When I work with clients who have pain or physical discomfort, I ask them to place their hand on the area and to send the sound vibration to the area they want to relax and release. If I am doing bodywork I will place my hand on the area of pain. When both the therapist and client tone together, an overtone often occurs.

are gateways to altered consciousness, and sound can transform mood. Many religions and cultures use chants, including Gregorian, Mongolian, Buddhist, and Hebrew chants. Many cultures do harmonic overtone singing for health and joy.

> Cindy, age 25, was deaf and blind in one eye because of a malignant tumor. She was dying and she came for bodywork because she was anxious. As I cradled her head, we toned together. I followed her lead, matching the sounds that she made, and within a minute or so I was listening to a chorus of sound as though there were others there singing and harmonizing with us. I was transported and a bit perplexed, wondering what she had experienced. We finished the session and while saying good-bye she said, "Did you experience what I did? I heard all of this sound. It was like a chorus of angels singing with us as we toned. I don't feel afraid anymore."

SPIRITUALITY AND TRANSPERSONAL PSYCHOLOGY

Spirituality is an integral part of integrative posttrauma therapy. Spirituality and religion contribute to personal and community beliefs about the trauma and to the potential for making meaning. The role of spirituality and religion in a client's life should be assessed early so that the clinician can find ways to integrate it at each stage of recovery. The spiritual self is often occluded by the experience of trauma. Engaging spirituality in posttrauma therapy requires assessing and understanding pretrauma beliefs and practices as well as the effects of the trauma on spirituality. Spirituality and religion will have different definitions for people, and understanding what people mean by these terms is an important starting point. This information can be obtained during the initial assessment or during the early stages of treatment in exploring strategies for self-care and social supports.

There is a growing integration of spirituality and religion in the healing process and a diminution of the taboo of incorporating spirituality in psychotherapy. Transpersonal (beyond the personal) psychology attends to the psychospiritual needs of the trauma victim regardless of organized religious practice by addressing the loss of hope and meaning she or he experiences and through the process of identifying what elements enact the sacred. When traumatic experience is human-mediated, it often leads to the exploration of questions of good and evil, karma, fate and predestination and other religious and philosophical ideas.

When victims have been abused by a spiritual leader, guru, or clergy member who has introduced them to prayer or meditation, they will experience ambivalence about religion and spirituality, especially if religious doctrine or spiritual methods were used as a form of mind control (Galanter, 1989). This type of trauma is also called betrayal trauma (Freyd, 1996).

Recovery then necessitates a reconstruction of beliefs and values that are the client's as separate from the trauma so that he or she may choose what feels right.

Debbie entered therapy because she was depressed and had debilitating headaches for which no organic cause had been established. During the second interview, I asked her if she had ever prayed or meditated, and she responded that she was no longer able to pray. She began to tell her story of abuse by her pastor, who told her that they had to pray together in order for her to heal from cancer. He insisted that she take her clothes off and let him fondle her while she prayed, for it would "strengthen her message to God." Now, 10 years later, she entered therapy, confused about this experience and not wanting to "talk to God." The first step was to affirm that what had happened was inappropriate and abusive and could very possibly be causing her depression and headaches. We explored relaxation techniques that did not remind her of prayer or meditation and I referred her for cranial-sacral therapy, which provided effective, gentle hands-on treatment for her headaches. During our work together, which spanned 5 years, Debbie processed the memories of her experience and the ways in which the pastor had "stolen her spirit" from her. This included her loss of innocence and her trust in the church and in God, her resulting difficulties with sexuality, and a debilitating depression that had prevented her from achieving the career goals she held in her heart. She grieved over many losses and, toward the end of our work, decided to experiment with some new forms of prayer and meditation and started a secular group comprising people interested in spirituality.

Mind/Body Group Therapy

Trauma isolates the victim. Group therapy may be the treatment of choice for trauma victims after the initial crisis (Harvey, 1990). In her work with survivors of the Nazi Holocaust and their children, Danieli (1988) found that group work counteracted the profound sense of alienation that occurs after exposure to extraordinary events. This beneficial effect of groups provides an opportunity to listen to and be heard by peers. Groups also tend to reduce the power differential between practitioner and client. The sense that no one else can understand, the sense of being singled out and the proverbial question "why me?" are all cradled within the context of a group that provides support and insight. In recovery, one often loses family members or old friends; one gives up drugs, or leaves abuse, and some friends cannot tolerate the grief they observe. There are many reasons why a group also serves as a transitional "family," especially during the early and middle stages of recovery. Even the interpersonal challenges that arise in a group provide a safe place to explore and practice new communication skills and risks. Groups may be designed in short- or long-term "renewable" modules as some people graduate, some remain, and others join. The success of groups with trauma victims depends on carefully matching the stage of recovery; assessing the individuals' support systems and their capacity to tolerate listening to the painful stories of others; and matching activities focus, gender, and often, the type of traumatic exposures.

Stress management groups may emphasize psychoeducational and cognitive-behavioral methods and address specialized needs such as managing anxiety or panic. These groups often support individual treatment. Short- and long-term models for victims of treatment or clergy abuse are effective because the group diffuses the trust issues that may arise in individual therapy.

Psychoeducational and process-oriented group for mid- and late-stage recovery can evolve into mind/body or somatic therapies groups that include activities that address body image, sensory experiences such as of touch, relaxation using visualization and imagery, sexuality, nutrition, and exercise. They also provide support and holistic education for relapse prevention. These group experiences may provide the client's first experience of somatic therapies and they may feel safer in a group than with an individual practitioner. The size of the group varies from between six and nine, with meetings once a week or bimonthly for 12 sessions. I conduct an initial interview with prospective members to understand what their goals are, what their current supports are, how they are functioning, and where they feel they are in the recovery process. At the start of the group, people introduce themselves, ground rules for safety are established, and we discuss the kinds of topics and activities that people want to explore as well as what their fears may be. A tentative schedule is developed with a balance of structure and flexibility maintained from week to week. Participants are asked to keep a journal of their feelings and experiences throughout the week and are welcome to share this with the group. It also serves to help support them between sessions. During the weeks we incorporate mindfulness and visualizations including the body scan exercise, process work, and self-massage and we explore obstacles to deepening self-care at home. I incorporate many of the exercises discussed in this book and adapt them to the needs of the members. If the group is held in a large space, movement and yoga is possible for part of the time, after which people can discuss what they experienced and how they felt. During the 10th session, we begin to discuss the final group meeting, during which we have a ritual created and orchestrated by the members of the group. The ritual often involves people reading poetry or parts of their journals, bringing in an item, preferably something they have made or found in nature, or sharing letters. One ritual involves each individual acting out or dancing out through movement the story of her life and recovery, followed by a shared meal. Each person has the opportunity to define and express creatively what has been meaningful and what being a member of the group has meant.

From Group Therapy to Group Ritual

The perceptual skills and biochemical substrates required to survive the traumas of prehistory developed hand-in-hand with rituals of healing. Where external nature could not be tamed, ancient peoples learned to use natural forces to control the wild forces within themselves. The ancient (and contemporary) requirement to survive and flourish by identifying with nature (including animals) was achieved by rituals that resonated with reverence. In response, nature's gifts were revealed. Rituals became a way to cradle illness and ignite medicine, thereby balancing the nerves, altering mental states, and aligning humans with the sacred. The practice of healing becomes a ritual when the sacred is embraced and *therapeuticos*, the act of worship, is enacted. Ritual behavior is patterned, repetitive and rhythmic (D'Aquili & Laughlin, 1975). Group ritual engages the whole being and synchronizes the rhythms within the individual, entraining her to the community's nervous system; together they then align with the cosmic pulse bringing coherence, meaning, and healing for the seekers.

Cultural healing activities, undertaken in the context of a safe group ritual at appropriate stages, promote the healing process. Group cohesion supports the individual's renewed capacity for social bonds. Therapeutic rituals are intentionally designed to enhance self-esteem; provide specific times for spontaneous, individual actions, or comments by members; and allow for greater arousal of the disturbing situation and therefore for greater emotional catharsis. Ceremonies should allow for the expression of distressing emotions within a safely contained structure; help to recontextualize the experience of trauma victims; engage the patient in utilizing social defenses; promote the experiencing of emotions within a communal ritual; encourage identification and attachment with the group; and alleviate pressure on the individual (Johnson, Feldman, Lubin, & Southwick, 1995).

In the context of psychotherapy, an individual might create a solitary ritual or enact one with a practitioner or with family and friends to celebrate a positive change, mourn a present or past loss, or transmute an emotional state such as anger or grief. During middle or later stages of healing, people may benefit from a group ritual. War veterans and their families, have cocreated rituals within family psychotherapy (Johnson et al., 1995). Rituals help the client to decondition hyperarousal and state-dependent memory. They restore clients' capacity for healthy attachment, helping them to gain control over altered states of consciousness, including dissociation. Rituals also stimulate endogenous brain chemicals and reconnect to spiritual perspectives. Group therapy rituals facilitate a sense of belonging, which brings the future into focus and leads to a vision that includes new possibilities. Making rituals explicit, codesigning healing rituals with clients, and developing rituals for group process provides healing opportunities that draw on the power of the group to support and regulate the body, mind, and spirit.

In order to develop and integrate rituals for healing, a therapist should explore his or her own attitudes about ritual. As we give more attention to ritual as a self-regulation strategy, we find creative approaches with which to help our clients.

Psychotherapy is a verbal therapeutic ritual arising out of Western psychological culture. Psychoanalysis, psychodynamic interpretation, hypnotherapy,

EXERCISE 7.9: THERAPIST EXERCISE: EXPLORING THE ROLE OF RITUAL IN YOUR LIFE

Consider the role of ritual in your life. Did you grow up with rituals? Do you have pleasant, neutral, or negative memories? How did those early experiences inform your current attitudes and feelings? Do you currently have rituals that you engage in individually or within a group setting? What types of rituals can you imagine might be helpful for your clients? What rituals might you not conduct yourself but refer to another facilitator to conduct? What rituals would make you uncomfortable?

EMDR, 12-step programs, and biofeedback are all rituals of healing that contain structure, format, and rhythms of communication. Rituals—like prayer, meditation, and visualization—may emphasize faith and balance and psychophysiological function by helping people to explore different states of consciousness and to reconnect to their bodies.

How can ancient rituals complement the process of psychotherapy today? There is a resurgence of group cultural practices that facilitate trance states for healing. These methods focus on deconditioning from hyperaroused states and activating parasympathetic response and endogenous opioid and cannabinoid production. Importantly, they include group activities that foster interpersonal connection and mutuality. Wilderness retreats conducted for veterans and abuse survivors by trained "adventure" practitioners, or companies such as Outward Bound, incorporate a reunion with nature through the healthy challenge of risk taking and organized cooperation with others to experience competency, achieve altered states and decondition from stress. Activities such as exposure to extreme temperatures, prolonged running and dancing, and drumming all directly affect the hypothalamic-pituitary-adrenal axis and limbic-hypothalamic system and produce parasympathetic dominance and slow-wave/theta activity (Wilson, 1989).

The Lakota sweat lodge is a culture-specific traditional healing ritual that is used by American Indians and non-Indians alike. The Lakota sweat lodge ceremony offers a traditional medicine approach to healing where the group participates cooperatively to build a sweat lodge, including construction and gathering the stones for the fire. During the prolonged exposure (several hours) to intense heat, prayers are offered to the earth and the ancestors for self-purification and healing. Afterwards, a meal is prepared and shared (Wilson, 1989). Sweats are most often gender-specific. The Veterans Administration and the Indian Health Service organize such rituals, as do women's healing groups. One can also gain benefits from sweating in a sauna. However, when one is participating in a complex ritual ceremony such as a sweat lodge, one must seek out trained practitioners or guides who understand the preparation required before, during, and after the ceremony.

Neoshamanic Rituals

The transition from group work and group rituals into healing that consciously facilitates altering states of consciousness often involves shamanic healing traditions and what Winkelman (1990) refers to as neurotheology. Neurotheology is the study of the neurological bases of spiritual experiences with a special focus on shamanic practices (Winkelman, 2011). *Shaman* is a specific term that derives from the word *saman* from central Asia, but it has been applied more generally to refer to practices that involve techniques of ecstasy (Eliade, 1972). These techniques are as ancient as are the first people who picked entheogenic mushrooms. There are many practices referred to as neoshamanism used for the treatment of trauma and the addictions. These practices provide techniques, carried out in dyads or in groups that offer methods of altering consciousness. Many trauma survivors are attracted to the shamanic path because they are already experiencing dissociation, which is a common shamanic technique.

In the context of visionary experiences, the shamanistic altered state of consciousness involves the reexperiencing of powerful memories and symbols representing emotionally important material for abreaction, insight, catharsis, and release (Winkelman, 1990). Shamanic healing is a form of neurobiologically mediated attachment that leads to psychobiological synchrony among the ritual participants (Frecska & Kulcsar, 1989).

The success of any approach or technique depends on the sensitive matching of the victim's personal beliefs and inclinations with the appropriate model. Often, a victim may explore a variety of options for healing within and outside of psychotherapy. The clinician can better help a client who undertakes the practices of "soul retrieval" or the "vision quest" by exploring the meaning and its benefits in the context of the whole self. The practitioner can also provide education, assist in planning and goal setting, serve as a liaison, and provide support for the client's essentially solitary journey toward self-knowledge.

Winkelman (2003, 2007) uses the term *psychointegrators* in referring to drug-based forms of altered states of consciousness that include the use of entheogens. When used for religious and therapeutic purposes, they stimulate areas of the brain that process emotions, memories, and attachments leading to the integration of information and consciousness. Shamans enter states of consciousness (with or without entheogens) to retrieve parts of the soul of their initiate lost to trauma. As I explore in Chapter 11, people use entheogens to explore and integrate parts of the psyche that hold healing wisdom for transmuting traumatic events.

Today neoshamanism is practiced throughout industrialized societies and represents a renewal of practices that are often syncretic, often drawing from ancient traditions of worship and integrated with modern methods. Trauma survivors engage in these practices for many reasons, including transformation of the traumatic events or symptoms within a group context or with a "shamanic guide." These practices are widespread and varied, ranging from undertaking pilgrimages to work with shamans to working with shamans from various indigenous communities from around the world. The shaman is the wounded healer and provides a model for the transmutation of suffering through a journey of self-discovery. Counseling and psychotherapy is our modern shamanic practice that seeks to reestablish the rhythm and connection to self and the cosmos. Core shamanism or neoshamanism involve activities that actively alter consciousness in order to cross into the liminal realm as they prepare to retrieve a lost aspect of self (or soul) and to restructure identity.

Activities may include soul retrieval, trance dance, drumming ceremonies, fire walking, vision quests, and entheogenic-facilitated experiences. Shamanic practices reflect the reclamation of the capacity and need of the individual and group to experience direct contact with the divine; these rituals also stimulate serotonin and opioid neurotransmitters (Winkelman, 2010) and endocannabinoids to promote healing.

There are important concerns about cultural property rights and appropriation of spiritual or religious practices by nonindigenous or nonlocal participants. Many indigenous peoples feel that the current use of tribal rituals performed out of context or by untrained people, or involving commercialization, constitutes yet another theft of cultural heritage (LaDue, 1994). Other tribal members argue that similar rites and rituals exist within most cultural and religious traditions and that individuals should first explore the rituals of their own heritage (Rudolph Rÿser, personal communication, March 24, 2010). For many people, however, ritual traditions such as religious ceremonies that derived from their family of origin are nonexistent, meaningless, or filled with traumatic memories. Rituals of another culture offer renewed opportunities to join with others in the universal rites of worshipping the earth. Still others explore the integration of psychotherapy with Amazonian shamanism, using a combination of techniques that resonates with Latino immigrants to the United States (Dobkin de Rios, 2002). As I have discussed, the ancient Eleusian mysteries of Greece and the journey of Persephone reflect a shamanic journey of trauma resolution, and the shamanic practices—whether through asceticism, hedonism, music, or entheogens—are an important path for many who seek to realign their rhythms with the cosmic breath. Their own journey of discovery often leads them to become the next "wounded healer."

Posttraumatic Growth

Whether or not a survivor embarks upon a "mission" to use her or his own experiences in service to others or chooses otherwise to contribute to social change, one of the outcomes of healing often includes posttraumatic growth (PTG). PTG refers to the ways in which we grow in response to adverse or traumatic events. While a discussion of PTG can be incorporated into treatment at any stage, it often involves an ongoing exploration during the later stages of recovery, following a full discussion of the memories, pain, and losses.

Therapy facilitates the understanding of how one has grown as a result of having dealt with trauma. PTG is a type of spirituality, concerned with the ultimate questions about life's meaning as it relates to the transcendent (McGrath, 2011). Evidence suggests that trauma survivors who rely on spiritual or religious beliefs for coping may show a greater ability for PTG (Wiechman Askay & Magyar-Russell, 2009). Shaw, Joseph, and Linley (2005) conducted a systematic review of studies showing that religion and spirituality are beneficial to people in dealing with traumatic events and that these events often deepen one's spirituality. McGrath (2011) found that PTG burn survivors reported that spiritual or religious beliefs played an important part in their recovery and that they wished health care providers were comfortable talking about these issues. This need among many trauma survivors suggests new avenues for therapist growth. There are many roads to PTG; a greater appreciation of life often leads to changes in one's priorities, closer relationships with others, a greater sense of personal strength, and a new sense of the path for one's life and spiritual development (Tedeschi & Calhoun, 2004). When traumatized individuals no longer define themselves solely or primarily through the darkened lens of misfortune, they have entered the final phase of the journey that will still, for many, last a lifetime.

SUMMARY

There are many paths to healing and many ways to tell the story of trauma. Our role as integrative trauma practitioners is to draw on methods that speak the language of our clients, help them to tell their story or find balance through a variety of expressive modes and help them to reestablish their physical, emotional, mental, and spiritual rhythms. When used for healing from trauma, rituals employ activities that focus attention, create symbolic activities of change, and provide a means for people to join together, share a common experience, and achieve altered states for spiritual inspiration. Participants create rituals that have meaning for them and signify their process of healing. This, in turn, may nourish a new ontological perspective that mobilizes fortitude and frees the faith they need to cope with the pains of the past and engage with the challenges of the present, while a vision for the future is restored.

8   Nutrition

Big Mac + Zantac = Prozac.

—Alan Gaby, MD

INTRODUCTION

I first learned about the use of foods and plants for healing when I lived in the jungle where there were no doctors. I relied on the women of the village to help me navigate the numerous subtropical diseases I encountered, along with the accidents, bites, and the many maladies no one could name. My apprenticeship with the women in the village began very naturally. I learned from trial and error and I served as my own laboratory. It was only later as I sat with my grandmother as she entered her ninth decade that I learned that I came from a long line of Dacian Jewish women who used their hands for healing. These women healed with herbs, foods, and glass cups or wine glasses, to which a little alcohol was added and ignited and then placed flush against their patient's skin. The combustion of the alcohol and evacuation of the oxygen produced a vacuum that would pull up on the skin, creating a suction, which in turn brought blood and oxygen to the surface, dispersing the pain and stagnation in the tissue. This was believed to rid the body of poisons. The Yiddish saying: *Es vet helfen vi a toiten bahnkes* (It will help like applying cups to a dead person) (Seicol, 1997), points to the centrality and importance of cupping in the healing repertoire of 19th-century eastern European Jewish women. "Cupping" is also widely practiced throughout the Middle East, Europe, and by indigenous peoples of the Americas who used a variety of animal horns like buffalo in the old days. Cupping was widely practiced by illustrious Boston physicians through the mid-19th century and it remains an integral method of traditional Chinese medicine, practiced by acupuncturists and massage therapists today. My great-grandmother brought these traditions with her, along with her borscht, brisket, and the *bris* (ritual male circumcision) when she left the old world, but as she and her neighbors settled into their new lives in Boston, cupping and herbs went into the cupboards and they now took their troubles to the *mein tsores* (my troubles) hospital (the Massachusetts General

Hospital), where the new medicine was now concerned more with the inside of the body and how chemistry could cure. Like most immigrants, their diets changed in the new culture along with their physical activity and diseases, setting the stage for intergenerational epigenetic changes that we continue to see among all immigrants (and native peoples) today.

While I learned traditional healing and herbal medicine in the indigenous village in Mexico, I also observed over a period of 30 years changes in health and food practices due to what I call *nutrition trauma* (Korn & Rÿser, 2006). Nutrition trauma is defined as the disruption in access to endemic, natural food resources due to overwhelming forces that make inaccessible foods that are bioculturally and biochemically suited to healthy digestion and nutrient utilization. Nutrition trauma occurs when introduced foods overwhelm the capacity of the local indigenous peoples to digest and metabolize these new foods, which often cause conditions that were unknown or rare before the colonial process. While this definition evolved in response to my work with indigenous populations, nutrition trauma is applicable to all people whether by choice, addiction, or conditions that overwhelm their capacity to digest, thus resulting in chronic illness. Why is this concept relevant to our exploration of nutrition and traumatic stress? My answer is: food is either medicine or it is poison, and people who experience traumatic stress require food that is medicine; food that is poison exacerbates the effects of trauma on the mind and body. One of the approaches we developed to counteract nutrition trauma at the clinic in Mexico was to restore the use of traditional, indigenous foods that had been used for hundreds, even thousands of years, but were increasingly being replaced by refined foods. Many of these traditional foods like *capomo* (*Brosimum alicastrum*), *chaya* (*Cnidoscolus aconitifolius*), and *chilacayote* (*Cucurbita ficifolia*) were being pushed aside under pressure from progress or the ease that cans brought, and because the new foods grabbed the taste buds and didn't let go. So the women (and some young men) gathered together, and we collected food along the paths and in the mountains, shared stories, cooked, and ate together, experimenting with the traditional foods and using them in old and new ways. Over many years I was witnessing and treating the effects of nutrition trauma in the clinic I also had the honor of sharing local foods at community dinners and participating in acts to restore, revive, and even restore these foods to their rightful place. Following many years of sharing in "culinary pedagogy," I both led and continue to learn from similar efforts among American Indians of the Pacific Northwest and among First Nations Peoples in British Columbia and in Eastern Canada. The study of the nutrition patterns of indigenous cultures and the study of modern natural medicine science informs the approaches I suggest below.

In this chapter I shall discuss

- the concept and application of biochemical individuality and culture specific nutrition
- protocols for treatment of PTSD sequelae

- nutritional program design and protocols for treatment
- nutritional alternatives to psychotropic medication
- food and diet for mental health

Chapters 8, 9, 10, and 11 are designed to be used together to improve physical health and well-being and to serve as a complement to the psychological and spiritual healing of trauma. None of the recommendations in these chapters should be construed as directives for individual actions designed to replace pharmaceuticals; those decisions must be undertaken with an educated health provider. Yet, while it is absolutely possible to eliminate pharmaceutical use, the paradigm that allows for this must be holistic in scope; thus a holistic paradigm informs choices; where drugs might target one or two particular functions, for example, selective serotonin reuptake inhibitors (SSRIs) pool serotonin (5-hydroxytryptamine) at the synapse; this is an allopathic approach. A holistic or naturopathic approach, on the other hand, aims at improving all levels of brain function. This includes increasing amino acid precursors to neurotransmitters via the diet, amino acid supplementation, and improving digestion to make more neurotransmitters in the gut. Improving gallbladder function will help emulsify the essential fatty acids (EFAs) and thus improve communication between synaptic clefts. Identifying and reducing allergens or heavy metals like copper or mercury and aluminum that are neurotoxic to brain function will improve mood and energy. The three major mistakes people tend to make when self-treating with natural medicine include (1) using nutrients or botanicals "allopathically," that is to target only symptoms; (2) underdosing the type and variety of nutrients; and (3) expecting change to occur quickly.

By virtue of this reality one must shift one's understanding of how psychobiological change occurs. Without the mind/body approach, the use of nutrition or psychoactive plants will necessarily fail or only meet with a little success.

My approach is rooted in the following principles:

- Mental health interventions are very limited unless biochemical changes via nutrition are implemented.
- Parents pass down their nutritional deficits to their offspring; the best way to ensure mental health is for the parents to eat good quality food.
- Most of our physical and mental health problems are more lifestyle related and in United States society the pressures to assimilate include the relinquishing of dietary traditions that served our elders quite well for millennia.
- With rare exceptions, most people can eliminate or replace pharmaceuticals with specific (mega) nutritional interventions.

Even when people have other options, they often for complex reasons cannot resolve some or all of the first three issues. This is important to understand about your client because knowing what they are able to do helps you work with them to plan achievable change over time. It also suggests that the clinician who wishes to promote nutritional therapies must also improve her diet just as a clinician undertakes therapy when in training and supervision when in practice.

Why do people use psychotropic pharmaceuticals?

- They are told to by physicians/psychiatrists.
- They are less time-consuming and less expensive to use.
- People don't usually know of any other options.
- Like clinicians, people are conditioned to believe that pharmaceuticals are the best or most effective approach.

Even when people know other options, they often for many reasons cannot resolve some or all of the first three issues. This is important to understand about your clients, because knowing what they are able to do will help you work with them to plan achievable change over time. It also helps if the clinician who wishes to promote nutritional therapies also knows how to improve her or his own diet.

Most of the clients with PTSD with whom I have worked have experienced depression, anxiety, sleep problems, pain, and digestive problems. Many of them also show symptoms of dissociation as well as eating disorders, the addictions, seasonal affective disorder (SAD), premenstrual syndrome (PMS), and menopausal or andropausal symptoms. PTSD ages with the individual; what may be PMS experienced in the thirties can become severe menopause in the fifties; what is depression in the forties is exacerbated when estrogen drops in the fifties; what is fitful sleep in the forties is chronic insomnia by the sixties, when melatonin reserves are low. Treatment thus becomes both preventive and preparatory for aging with PTSD.

Stress and trauma affect all aspects of physical function: blood glucose levels, brain metabolism, energy, and alteration of brain structures where neurons misfire or fail to communicate. Stress disrupts the autonomic functions which normally signal digestive enzyme release, and stress dysregulates hormones—all of which affect mood, cognition, sleep, and immune function. PTSD and its sequelae of depression, anxiety, insomnia, eating disorders, self-harm, and addictive behaviors can be treated effectively using diet, nutrients, and botanicals. Every person can benefit from a holistic approach to restore mental health without the use of pharmaceuticals. The question the clinician must answer is: Who will choose to or be able to benefit from this approach? Not everyone is willing or able to afford what is required. Quality foods and nutrients are often expensive, and the time required for food preparation and detoxification can be demanding. Only a small percentage of people will be able to make the sustained commitment required intensively over several years and then for lifetime maintenance. But the rewards are worth it and they promise good health.

People with depression, anxiety, and PTSD have often had unsatisfactory results with pharmaceutical use to manage symptoms or have experienced intolerable side effects. Often they look to their therapist or physician for information about alternatives. Often they are self-prescribing, or the therapist may need to liaise effectively with other providers. Nutrition and self-medication pose special challenges for treatment. The client may feel that he or she must withhold information about her activities from other practitioners because she may know or suspect their biases. Possessing scientific knowledge about the efficacy of alternative approaches supports the client who wants to avoid, reduce, or eliminate pharmaceutical use. The therapist is often called upon to:

- support a client's desire to find alternatives to pharmaceuticals by having working knowledge of the options for treatment;
- discuss the range of alternatives to pharmaceuticals where either the side effects or low efficacy warrant a change;
- provide referrals to a competent nutritional therapist or botanical consultant if the client is self-prescribing and requires professional analysis.

PRINCIPLES OF EFFECTIVE TREATMENT

- Treatment must be isomorphic to the client's capacity at each stage of change.
- Diet must be based on the biochemical individuality of each client.
- Integrate proactive behaviors first, then slowly eliminate negative behaviors.
- Cocreate compliance strategies, which are adjusted every 6 weeks.
- Address habituation reaction when change occurs.
- Identify current self-medication behaviors and develop new strategies based on biochemical needs.
- Regulate the sleep/wake cycle.

BASIC PRINCIPLES

Principle: There Is No One Diet for Everyone

In psychotherapy, we treat the individual, not the illness. In nutrition, individuals have unique needs and require different nutrients and foods to address specific requirements. The term *biochemical individuality* was coined by Williams (1998) to explain the biochemical and metabolic differences among people and the wide variation in response to nutrition. The three major principles of biochemical individuality are as follows: (1) there is no one diet for everyone, (2) dietary needs can change throughout the life cycle, and, (3) nutrition must focus on the *individual*, not the disease.

Metabolic analysis is a method of assessing biochemical individuality based on the Krebs cycle, the speed of glucose oxidation (Kristal & Haig,

2004). Oxygen alkalinizes the blood, while carbon dioxide, which is produced as a by-product of the oxidation process, is acid-forming. The optimal ratio between them is intimately connected with maintaining the optimal blood pH of 7.46. At this pH level, all of the systems of the body function harmoniously. If there is an excess of oxygen, the blood becomes overly alkalinized, with the converse, acidification, occurring from an excess of carbon dioxide (Kristal & Haig, 2004). People who oxidize carbohydrates fast require more protein and fats to slow the glucose combustion process. People who burn them more slowly require more glucose (carbohydrates) to fan the flames. This determines whether one will function best physically and mentally as a carnivore, omnivore, or closer to the vegetarian end of the spectrum since foods like vegetables and fruits alkalanize and animal proteins acidify. Methods of metabolic analysis are provided in Chapter 6, on assessment.

Biochemical individuality is rooted in the intersection of genetics, environment, and cultural/ethnic heritage. For example, the traditional diets of the Inuit of the circumpolar region are rich in fat and blubber from fish and sea mammals supplemented with seaweeds and small amounts of fruit in the form of summer berries. This diet has sustained the Inuit for centuries without adverse health effects and evolved as a function of people and place. Not until colonization and 20th-century development brought refined flours, sugars, and soy protein as substitutes for their traditional diets did the Inuit suffer suicide, depression, and heart disease. While not as rich in fat and seafood as the diet of the Inuit, the daily intake of the American Indians of the Pacific Northwest also depended historically upon huge stores of fresh, dried, and smoked salmon and oolichan (smelt) along with the meat of deer and elk, huckleberries, and starchy roots. So central was the oolichan to the lives of the native peoples that the name *Oregon* derives from this little powerhouse of a fish.

Before 1493, wheat, beef from cattle, milk, and pork did not exist in the western hemisphere; therefore these foods may not be the most beneficial to peoples indigenous to this region. By contrast, peoples in India evolved in a warmer climate with subtropical foods and an emphasis on more vegetables and carbohydrates. The tropical peoples of Mesoamerica, Africa, and India have accessed fats from nuts, plants, ducks, insects, and turkeys, and they have depended upon many more vegetables, fruits, and grains endemic to their regions. Weston Price, in the course of his global travels in traditional societies, asked the question: "Who is the healthiest among peoples on the planet?" In looking for an answer, he found that they all consumed moderate amounts of animal fats, suggesting that our modern fears of saturated fats are among the paradigmatic myths of modern medicine.

Peter D'Adamo's (2001) "blood type diet" is a popular, simple subcategory of metabolic analysis that focuses on the role of specific sensitivities to lectins in determining dietary needs and reactions. Lectins are specific proteins present in large quantities in certain beans, grains, potatoes, and nuts. D'Adamo asserts that the different blood types benefit from certain foods and are especially sensitive to foods with specific lectins. The role of these lectins is to adversely affect the delicate lining of the intestinal tract. D'Adamo (2001) suggests that people with type O blood have lower levels of the enzyme monoaminoxidase (MAO) inhibitor, which may explain why many such people react poorly to St. John's wort (an MAO inhibitor) or have disturbing dreams. He also suggests that people with type A blood respond to stress with higher levels of cortisol than the other blood types. The blood type diet is a good first-step approach with clients undergoing dietary changes. Over time they can continue to integrate additional aspects to metabolic analysis.

Principle: Natural Medicines Do What Pharmaceuticals Can Do, and Most Often Without Side Effects

The use of foods and plants as medicine is as ancient as trauma itself. Indigenous science provides ample records of thousands of years of empirical testing of a variety of plant and animal substances native to all regions of the world. Biomedical science has identified many "active substances" from plants and in turn synthesized them for pharmaceutical delivery or herbal medicine patents. Yet active chemicals alone do not guarantee efficacy. Plants work best when several parts are used; the leaf produces different effects than the root or might moderate the power of the root. Foods also provide the greatest nourishment when used closest to their natural state. This principle of nature reinforces the whole approach rather than the parts. This philosophy may be found in a worldwide movement to revive local and indigenous foods and traditional and culture-based methods of food production and preparation, called *slow food*.

Nutritional therapies bring about systemic functional and biochemical balance and work in conjunction with other therapies. By contrast, pharmaceuticals target a specific set of neurotransmitters or other chemicals, often lead to systemic imbalances, and do not address root causes. Generally, natural products are gentler and have few or no side effects. However, in using nature one works to restore the whole person using natural products. Most natural approaches work more slowly, but since the results are designed to create lasting change rather than just to manage or suppress symptoms, they tend to be longer-lasting and have fewer side effects than synthetic products. While specific treatment suggestions are provided, the caveat is that biochemical individuality will militate against rigid rules. Both the suffering inherent in PTSD and the pressures to produce "quick results" may result in impatience. It is important to educate clients about the benefits and limitations of natural approaches so that they may make informed decisions. With clients who are impatient for results, I offer the imagery of a growing tree, which grows slowly and steadily, often imperceptibly, planting its roots deeply to draw nourishment from the groundwater as it also extends its branches and leaves to catch water from the sky. This slow growth ensures its stability and strength and that it will not be toppled over easily. The same concept can be applied to the growth and healing that is possible for those suffering from PTSD.

Yet often the gentle nature of botanicals or nutrients may not be powerful enough to manage acute symptoms, and pharmaceuticals may be required for limited periods. For clients whose symptoms require immediate relief or who have been on drugs for a while, a review of options with a prescribing practitioner who understands alternatives and is amenable to offering short-term treatment transitioning to supplements may also be an avenue to explore.

Natural products potentiate natural healing responses and, like pharmaceuticals, do not always work or work well enough. While it is possible to use nutrients and herbs to suppress physical or psychic pain and provide relief immediately, most nutrient and botanical approaches work best over time when used in conjunction with a whole health program to restore balance.

Many nutrients can substantially alter consciousness, and this may or may not be desirable in people following the 12-step or other addiction recovery programs. For example, kava, a potent anxiolytic, can in sufficient doses induce a substantial high (and low), while at lower doses it reduces anxiety and induces sleep. Individuals in addiction recovery may eschew this product so as not to alter consciousness. Like the benzodiazepines, kava binds to the gamma-aminobutyric acid (GABA) receptors and is a safer option for people who might otherwise choose the extremely addictive benzodiazepine class of drugs. I explore kava further in Chapter 9. An alternative, however, is another nutrient reviewed below, biopeptides derived from milk casein, which are anxiolytic in action but do not cause a "high."

Where some nutrients do not produce results, others may be tried. Product quality is essential to achieving results. As a general rule, products obtained at large discount stores are of lesser quality, while health food stores provide a moderate alternative. The highest-quality nutrients are most often standardized, pharmaceutical-grade supplements.

Principle: Food Should Be Fresh, Nutrient-Dense, and Combine Raw and Cooked Options Chosen From All the Colors of the Rainbow

Eating like one's ancestors did will restore health. For most people this will mean a diet rich in whole foods such as wild and grass-fed, humanely raised animals that have not been given antibiotics or hormones; seafood, including sea vegetables; raw and cooked vegetables and fruits; cold-processed (virgin) fats from nuts and seeds that are stored in dark-colored glass containers; legumes; and for those who are not allergic, dairy foods and grains. Discovering one's ancestral nutrition is a key to health.

Most people will do well with a combination of raw and cooked foods. It is easy to ensure a range of nutrients from foods if one selects foods from the whole color spectrum. The yellows and oranges of sweet potatoes and carrots ensure beta carotene, which converts to vitamin A to protect the immune system, and they also provide a natural sweet alternative to sugar. The reds and purples of berries, figs, and grapes provide antioxidants called anthocyanins, which reduce brain inflammation. The red peppers and tomatoes have vitamin C, and greens provide chlorophyll, the "blood of plants." Chlorophyll is similar to hemin—the constituent of hemoglobin that transports oxygen; the only difference is that it has a magnesium molecule (instead of the iron found in hemoglobin), making it a potent source of energy and detoxification for blood cells. Both raw and lightly cooked dark greens are essential to health. Garlic and onions are high in sulfur, which is anti-inflammatory, antibacterial, and antifungal. Prior to the introduction of penicillin in the 1920s, people used garlic and onions along with oregano oil to treat infections.

Principle: Preparation Methods Must Retain and Enhance Food Nutrients

Most of one's daily food intake should comprise organic whole foods that are nutrient-dense and freshly prepared. Some proportion of this daily food should include both raw and cooked foods and some should include wild foods. Canned and packaged foods should be minimized. The least amount of processing ensures the maximal nutrition of most foods, including vegetables, fish, fruits, and meats. Raw foods contain the richest source of enzymes required for digestion. However raw foods should be introduced slowly and in small amounts if they are new to a client's diet.

Slow cooking in water, boiling, salting, broiling, pickling, roasting, baking, drying, steaming, fermenting, and smoking are the essential processing methods that ensure maximum nutrition. Frying should be limited to special occasions. By preparing fresh foods, one can control the preparation, including the amounts of salt and fat used, in order to maintain optimal nutritional value. Fresh foods are also free of harmful preservatives, though care should be taken to soak nonorganic produce and wash it with soap to eliminate pesticide residues.

Principle: Eliminate Functional Hypoglycemia

Without reducing the intake of refined carbohydrates such as sugar, balancing mood will remain out of reach for the mood-disordered, and one may never know why. Hypoglycemia refers to low blood glucose, which is often associated with poor adrenal function. People under stress are vulnerable to reactive hypoglycemia because stress negatively affects the regulation of blood glucose. Most patients who do not eat a healthy diet and binge on carbohydrates have hypoglycemia and do not know it. Many vegetarians experience it, since they do not consume enough proteins to stabilize their blood sugar. This syndrome causes mood lability and inattention, which is often misidentified as the rapid cycling of bipolar disorder or ADHD. Recently, bipolar disease has become the diagnosis du jour, but without eliminating hypoglycemia as a cause of mood cycling, an accurate diagnosis cannot be made. I have treated many children and adults with severe mood swings and irritability, which is diminished or eliminated when the hypoglycemia and carbohydrate addiction are addressed. Other symptoms include irritability (due to hunger) and orthostatic hypotension, which occurs when one rises from a supine position to standing and becomes light-headed. This reflects adrenal fatigue, hypoglycemia, and often low blood sugar, which can be addressed by adding a thiamine-rich B-vitamin complex. Sugar derives from the sugar cane plant, a grass indigenous to the western hemisphere. Like many foods, the original whole food form is healthy, tasty, and rich in vitamins and minerals. It does not significantly raise blood glucose. Like many other indigenous plants with mood-altering qualities (coca, tobacco, cocoa, and others), sugar cane is medicinal and nutritional when used traditionally or as a treat (such as sucking on a four-inch piece of fibrous stalk in the midafternoon). However, when the constituent parts of the plant are extracted and refined into cane sugar, the refined product we know as white (or brown) sugar, it becomes detrimental to human health. (This principle of the dangers of extraction and refinement can be applied to many medicinal plants.) Sugar depletes B vitamins and immune support minerals, such as zinc, and also reduces the body's capacity to digest and absorb glucose. Refined sugar is also highly inflammatory; it exacerbates pain and raises triglycerides and cholesterol levels. Its use is a major cause of the worldwide epidemic of type-2 diabetes. Sugar is a food of trauma. Its trade derives from colonization, which turned sugar into a commodified drug by introducing the extraction and refining process and giving impetus to the slave trade.

There are several good alternatives to sugar and sweeteners that do not have the side effects of artificial sweeteners, such as aspartame. Individuals with mood disorders are particularly sensitive to aspartame, and aspartame makes depression worse (Walton, Hudak, & Green-Waite, 1993). Stevia is a plant indigenous to South America; it is a hundred times sweeter than sugar and has been shown to reduce blood sugar (Curi et al., 1986). It is available both as a liquid and as a powder. While the powdered form of stevia can tend to leave a bitter aftertaste, the liquid form does not. Either form can be used in drinks or food preparation. Xylitol is another sweetener without side effects. It was first extracted from birch trees and provides a healthy sweet taste that does not raise blood glucose levels or negatively affect dental health.

Principle: Strategies for Adherence to a Program and Methods of Nutrient Delivery Must Be Tailored to the Needs of the Client and Adjusted Regularly

Adherence to a program is required for success. Knowing if a client will only take one pill a day or will organize to take 20 pills a day or if they have difficulty swallowing pills, if they prefer liquids or whether they require help organizing their protocol and thus an aide is enlisted all helps in the tailoring of a program. Some clients may elect to use pharmaceuticals because it is generally a simpler process. During the nutritional therapy assessment of clients I use motivational interviewing (Rollnick, Miller, & Butler, 2007) and explore in-depth attitudes, phobias, and willingness to swallow pills, capsules, and liquids, what times of day they eat and any other behaviors that may pose obstacles to success or that will enhance adherence. Motivational interviewing is a semidirective approach to identifying ambivalence to change that engages the client in resolving obstacles that may prevent changes in behavior. Alternatives to swallowing pills or capsules include powdered or liquid forms of many supplements, capsules that can be opened, or pills, which can be ground into powder using a small herb or coffee grinder. Liquid fruit smoothies are a good choice for all ages for powders, and liquid fish, borage, or hemp oils can be added. One of the best forms of delivery of herbal medicine is in extracts. Herbal extracts are made by macerating the herbal material in alcohol so that the active chemicals and qualities are made available in the solution. Extracts are administred by taking drops or teaspoons of the liquid. Still other herbs are available in nonalcoholic glycerites. Alcohol may be contraindicated for people in recovery from alcohol, and glycerites, teas, or capsules provide an alternative. In my opinion extracts and capsules are the best mode of delivery. Teas may be used but can be less potent.

Making simple additions to one's daily self-care regimen is a good way to start a nutritional program and can make a significant difference, serving as a first step. For example, drinking a tea made from boiled fresh ginger root quells nausea, aids digestion, and is anti-inflammatory. Mint and chamomile teas quiet the belly and reduce anxiety. Start with simple, "feel good" measures that promise success.

Principle: It Is Best to Incorporate Healthy Behaviors While Slowly Eliminating Unhealthy Choices

The first step in dietary change is to begin incorporating healthy fats and fresh foods cooked appropriately. People who do not cook need to start doing so; a slow cooker offers an easy way to prepare healthy food with a minimum of time and effort. Taking a cooking class is also a good way to start learning about cooking, or inviting a friend or family member to teach you how to make a favorite recipe. Eliminate foods that contribute to depression, anxiety, and inflammation and replace them with foods that treat those three symptoms. Replace all trans fatty acids, sugar, and white flour with healthy alternatives. Replace table salt with unrefined sea salt, which contains rich amounts of minerals that support adrenal function. Eliminate coffee and colas (see Online Resources for a list of coffee substitutes) as well as hard liquor and reduce fermented alcohol to three glasses a week.

Principle: Changing Dietary Intake Alone Is Not Enough; Actively Improving Digestion Is Also Required

Each phase of digestion and thus each organ of digestion must be working well to make use of the nutrients ingested. Digestion is always disrupted in PTSD because digestion is governed by parasympathetic activity. In the sympathetic arousal of traumatic stress, the head hurts, the stomach aches, and the intestines are too active or immobilized by fear, leading to diarrhea or constipation. Digestion begins in the mouth and ends with elimination—this provides a simple guideline for introducing treatment. Simple steps can be taken, such as chewing food until it is liquid and replacing antacids (acid reflux is due to excessive carbohydrate use and low levels of hydrochloric acid) with digestive enzymes.

DIGESTION

Where there is depression and anxiety, panic, and PTSD, there is always impaired nutrition. Digestion starts in the mouth with the breakdown of starches by chewing and mixing food with salivary enzymes and finishes in the colon with the excretion of waste. Under stress, one eats too rapidly and swallows food whole; under stress, the acids and enzymes required to break down food cannot do their job. With food undigested in the belly, pains and gases develop, nutrients are malabsorbed, and organs including the brain are malnourished. Eating food slowly allows for the initial breakdown of starches, and enhancing gallbladder function with taurine, betaine, detoxification, and foods like beets and bitter greens enables the emulsification of essential fatty acids (EFAs). The use of digestive enzymes helps to break down foods.

There are many reasons why people do not receive the nourishment their minds/bodies need. Many experience chronic poverty or injury-related economic loss that precludes access to high-quality food. Some don't know what good nutrition is and are vulnerable to advertisements or medical myths. A multitude of people are not nursed at birth, leading to both nutritional and attachment deficits. Or people may suffer deficits in self-care, leading to poor nutrition; or they may have been hospitalized for extended periods during which they have been fed poor-quality food. Still others who are addicted to substances such as alcohol, cocaine, or methamphetamines do not eat well or even enough at all, and what they do eat is not metabolized properly. Additionally, pharmaceutical medications, alcohol, and many drugs deplete important nutrients. Finally, the standard American diet of refined carbohydrates and trans fatty acids leads to chronic inflammatory states and sets the stage for neurotransmitter imbalances.

EXERCISE 8.1: EATING MINDFULLY

Observe yourself chewing, pay attention to the texture and flavors of the food, the smells, and the position of the food on the plate. Embrace the whole of the sensory experience: the creation of saliva breaking down the food tends to heighten the experience of texture and flavors on different parts of the tongue. Chew every bite until it is liquid in the mouth, allowing the food to travel down the throat and into the belly.

PTSD, BRAIN FUNCTION, AND NUTRITION

Trauma affects all aspects of physical and mental well-being, including endo-crine and immune system function, and there is significant evidence that brain structure is altered as a result of exposure to trauma. The brain can change, both structurally and functionally, for many reasons, and it can be positively and negatively affected by the nourishment it receives. All substances, toxic and nutritious, change brain function and structure. Alcohol and methedrine, when viewed in single-photon emission computed tomography scans, darken and light up the brain, respectively. There is some evidence that SSRIs increase hippocampal volume but also cause deleterious effects. Children who have not received enough EFAs in utero and after birth via fat-rich breast milk are more likely to have learning problems by 10 years of age.

Brain injury is common as a result of domestic violence, accidents, and war. With stress comes the release of high levels of the stress hormone corti-sol. Cortisol is called "the death hormone" because neurons bathed in cortisol die. Hippocampal volume is reduced in people with PTSD, and it is unclear whether a smaller hippocampal volume makes one vulnerable to PTSD or if trauma reduces brain volume. Chronic high exposure to cortisol levels also contributes to decreased cognitive function and dementia. Male war veterans with PTSD have a doubled risk of developing dementia (Yaffe et al., 2010). It is certainly possible that we will find a correlation between chronic high stress and trauma in our industrialized societies and increasing epidemics of demen-tia and Alzheimer's disease. The continuous release of cortisol in response to stress is like a car with its gas pedal always depressed; first the engine revs at a high rate, but it eventually runs out of gas and the engine burns out. When this happens to people, the revving stage is called hypercortisolemia, which leads to hypocortisolism, also called biological or adrenal exhaustion. This is the final stage of stress identified by Selye. This overproduction of cortisol results in a lack of responsiveness (Yehuda et al., 2005) to the normal function of the HPA axis. Gunnar and Vazquez (2001) found that repeated early-life stress also led to hypocortisolism, and this becomes part of the psychobiological complex that turns children into ill adults.

The exhaustion (and depression) that people feel when they awaken in the morning is reflected in below normal cortisol levels upon awakening, just when they should be the highest, delivering the "get up and go" the body is designed to feel when the sun rises. This is the region of the brain associated with learn-ing and memory. Stress and cortisol overproduction is significantly influenced by refined sugar intake, suggesting that there is an interactive synergy between chronic stress and the inhibition of glucose regulation. People drink coffee and sugar in the morning to address the fatigue, but they receive only temporary relief. The rise and fall of energy during the day often coincides with ingesting copious amounts of coffee, sugar, or other drugs to regulate energy. This up and down variation continues throughout the day and night; it may be difficult to fall asleep, or once asleep, the body wakes up when blood sugar drops. When people awaken a few hours after they fall asleep it is often due to a drop in their blood sugar, which may be preventable by eating some protein and carbohydrate before bed. Cortisol depletion also reduces the capacity of this natural steroid to quench inflammation in the body. Under normal conditions the level of cortisol is high in the morning and slowly drops throughout the day, so that as one prepares for sleep, there is no hormonal stimulation to keep one on alert. Yet the opposite diurnal rhythm of low cortisol in the morning and high cortisol at night has been observed in PTSD, early childhood loss, chronic fatigue syndrome, chronic pelvic pain, fibromyalgia, irritable bowel syndrome, asthma, low back pain, and atypical depression. This symptom picture is seen in those who sleep late and cannot get going in the morning, yet toward the end of the day they feel wired and then can't get to sleep at night. This is the psychobiological picture of depression, and restoring a normal circadian rhythm in such individuals should be a priority. Fortunately this diurnal dysregulation is very responsive to a combination of nutritional and botanical interventions and light therapies.

Poor adrenal function contributes to chronic pain because the naturally anti-inflammatory adrenal steroids are often suppressed and ligaments that should be mineralized and strengthened by the adrenals become lax and unable to support the skeletal structure. This makes the individual subject to more sprain and strain and accounts in part for the common low back pain associated with stress. This pattern occurs both with and without specific accidental or occupational antecedents and certainly many survivors have experienced the trauma of physical abuse whose memories persist in soft tissue. This is the body's story of breaking under the burden of trauma. This type of individual does not generally improve in response to drugs or surgery. Massage, physical therapy, or chiropractic can help, but without nutritional support for adrenal function the ligaments cannot hold their structure in place. With the adrenals exhausted, excessive amounts of potassium are excreted, causing the retention of excess sodium, which leads to (mild) edema, manifesting as swollen ankles or puffiness under the eyes. People who experience chronic stress and exhaustion have darkness on their eyelids and repeatedly sigh, which is a sign of hyperventilation and respiratory fatigue. They grit their teeth while they sleep, have jaw pain during the day, and often cannot open their mouths fully. Sensitive to sunlight, these individuals often wear sunglasses, which is also a sign of adrenal exhaustion (it can also be a sign of serotonin poisoning). Clients should be encouraged to gradually take off their sunglasses in the light so that the light can pass through the eyes to stimulate the neurohormones that govern mood and health in general.

DIGESTION AND DEPRESSION

Mood is labile in PTSD, depression, and anxiety, and improving digestion is important to managing stress and stabilizing mood. Mood also responds to blood sugar levels. I have no doubt that many people are incorrectly diagnosed with bipolar disorder due to the steep rise and precipitous falls of blood glucose called hypoglycemia. When blood glucose is balanced, mood is also balanced and the emotional ups and downs of the day even out. Because glucose regulation is carried out by the HPA axis, in particular adrenal function, it is no wonder that dysregulation occurs in PTSD and mood is labile. It is no surprise that people with PTSD are more vulnerable to the development of type-2 diabetes, which is always preceded by hypoglycemia.

Digestion and intestinal health are also important to mood because many of the neurotransmitters that support mood, such as serotonin, are made in the small intestine, where food is digested. Neurotransmitters (NTs) are brain chemicals that communicate information throughout our brain and body. They relay signals between neurons and affect mood, sleep, concentration, weight, carbohydrate cravings, pleasure, pain, and the addictions. NT imbalances contribute to depression, pain, anxiety, and insomnia. Most antidepressants and neuropathy medications work by increasing the availability of specific neurotransmitters; sometimes they work, but they often have side effects, leading to an imbalance, or they become less effective over time. Among the side effects are weight gain and loss of libido. Because they are often used for stimulation during the day, one often requires sleep medication at night, and thus the cycle continues. The use of amino acid therapies serves as an alternative to pharmaceutical antidepressants or anxiolytics. These pharmaceutical-grade amino acids may be compounded according to the specific biochemical needs of the individual to provide the building blocks that support specific NT production.

INTESTINAL HEALTH

Gershon's (1998) research on the enteric nervous system has illuminated the importance of intestinal function to mental health. He aptly named the gut the "second brain" because of the discovery of an abundance of NTs secreted into the wall of the intestinal mucosa, where they regulate a variety of activities. The importance of digestive function to mental health is rooted in part in this important function of the second brain. This may explain many nagging digestive complaints in addition to those that result from the increased permeability of the small intestine caused by exogenous toxins or food allergens. When toxins pass from the intestine into the bloodstream, they contribute to a host of allergies and sensitivities, pain, and fatigue that are often misdiagnosed as somatization. Without teasing out these specific contributions to mental illness, psychotherapeutic interventions remain only partially effective. For this reason, identifying food sensitivities or allergens is crucial. I have previously addressed the hypersensitivity to foods and chemicals that occurs in response to PTSD.

Colon Health: The Rhythm of Peristalsis

Humbaba, the "sevenfold terror" whose "breath is death," represents the bowels (colon) in ancient Mesopotamian mythology (see Figure 8.1).

I suspect that the ancients knew what we know today—that a "breath of death" is a sign of a fermenting colon. The lower belly (the underworld) is where "waste" (traumatic memory) is filtered, stored, and then forgotten unless it is transformed and eliminated. The rhythmic tides of affective arousal disrupt peristalsis; the normal undulations of colon movement that move waste toward elimination may be too fast or too slow.

Colitis and irritable bowel syndrome (IBS) are inflammatory responses that are often part of the somatization diagnosis and comorbid with PTSD and chronic stress. Traumatized individuals may have significant negative associations and experiences associated with bowel function, including anal penetration, forced enemas, harsh toilet training experiences, or other fears or concerns about fecal matter. These experiences can all influence the elimination process. In my clinical experience, many women and men who were raped have very negative experiences with their elimination; they may experience chronic spasms in the rectal sphincter, alternating constipation and diarrhea, and may be resistant to undertaking colonics or healing enemas even though these may be clinically indicated. People with chronic bowel problems (inflammatory bowel syndrome and colitis) respond well to SSRI supplementation (Gershon, 1998). The natural serotonin/melatonin-enhancing amino acid that may be substituted is 5-hydroxytryptophan (5-HTP). Begin with 25 mg at

Figure 8.1 Humbaba, god of the fortress of intestines.
Source: Adapted from *Hamlet's Mill: An Essay Investigating the Origins of Human Knowledge and Its Transmission Through Myth*, by G. De Santillana and H. Von Dechend, 1969, p. 291. © 1969 by David R. Godine, Publisher, Inc. Public Domain.

night and increase it by 5 mg a week, increasing up to 150 mg until a response is felt. Beginning with a lower dose at night ameliorates the nausea that can occur during the first weeks of use, as a result of increased NT production in the gut.

Some studies have identified a causal chain linking childhood abuse, dissociation, and somatization with irritable bowel syndrome (IBS) (Salmon, Skaife, & Rhodes, 2003). Somatization is conventionally described as symptoms that cannot be fully explained or impairments due to somatic symptoms that are more severe than generally expected. What is called somatization is more likely a complex neuroimmunomodulatory communication system between the gut and the brain that contributes to low mood and chronic pain. The sum total of life's assaults—psychological, physical, and biochemical— wears down resilience. Once nutritional status has improved, it is possible to tease out the various contributions to the mood disorder. The symptom picture becomes even more complex because depression, chronic pain, and digestive problems can occur as part of a systemic cycle of inflammation, all the more so as people age. Trauma and stress lower immune function. The immune system produces inflammatory cells called cytokines that affect the brain, causing depression and anxiety (Gershon, 1998). It thus becomes clear that there is a bidirectional dynamic between intestinal illness, chronic pain, and depression and anxiety. Also, living with chronic pain is depressing and depression results from inflammation. There are many causes of inflammation, many linked with food, alcohol, and drugs. One of the most common causes of inflammation is the use of refined foods such as wheat and sugar.

Colon Health, Gluten Intolerance, and Sugar

Gluten is the protein in grains, most notably wheat, barley, and rye. Gliadin antibodies are proteins in the blood that are components of gluten. Approximately 1 in 250 people have celiac disease, a severe allergy to gluten (Nelson, 2002), and many more have lesser sensitivities to gluten that still result in profound mood and digestive problems. It is the antigliadin antibody that is tested for via saliva to reveal sensitivity, leading to the recommendation to eliminate gluten products from the diet. People with celiac disease are often vitamin D– deficient, which exacerbates depression and pain. In addition to grains, many gluten by-products are used in foods, so gluten-sensitive people must read labels. Even mild gluten sensitivities can contribute to depression, chronic diarrhea, and autoimmune disease. Wheat and other gluten-containing foods are a major cause of bowel problems such as IBS, Crohn's disease, chronic diarrhea, and gas in gluten-sensitive people.

The association between gluten, depression, and addiction has long been observed. People who crave wheat and grains experience mood elevation upon eating these foods. This response often co-occurs with a phase-delayed circadian rhythm and may also include waking late, early-morning depression, premenstrual syndrome, carbohydrate-binging, and seasonal affective disorder. Binging associated with bulimia is linked with addiction to gluten, which releases opioid peptides and may account for addiction to carbohydrates in these individuals. A gluten-free diet, 5-HTP, and light therapy will generally eliminate or reduce cravings and reset the circadian rhythm. Most carbohydrate cravers will tell you that abstinence, as with many drugs, is the only way to stop binging. The quickest way to test this response is to eliminate glutens for 2 weeks and eat only protein and root vegetables instead. Within a week, such cravings will usually stop.

Clinicians should assess for gluten sensitivity or celiac disease in mood and attention disorders. Questions about the history of celiac disease or gluten sensitivity in maternal or paternal family members can be incorporated into the food history, and there are also saliva tests for gluten sensitivity. D'Adamo (2001) contends that people with type O blood are intolerant of gluten, based on the evidence that type O blood evolved as the first blood type among humans, prior to the widespread use of agriculture and the cultivation and eating of grains. Type O is the most common blood type and also most often found among native peoples of the western hemisphere, which may account for the many gluten/sugar complex–related illnesses, such as diabetes and alcoholism, among peoples of this region (Korn & Rÿser, 2009). There are also high rates of gluten sensitivity among people diagnosed with schizophrenia (Cascella et al., 2011).

The use of refined wheat and sugar products should be avoided except on rare occasions. If the diet is good, most people can tolerate an occasional birthday cake with white flour and frosting; but a steady diet of white flour, sugar, and soft drinks inflames the gut lumen, where serotonin is stored.

Fermented Foods and Colon Health

Fermented foods are among the best foods for the colon. Their value is renowned among traditional cultures everywhere, as they are used to restore and maintain the bowel "garden," where the bacterial flora grow. Where fermented foods are not available, they can be made easily and inexpensively, or probiotic supplements may be used.

Probiotics (*pro* = "for," *biotic* = "life") are important supplements required for good colon health. The colon garden is filled with both healthy and unhealthy bacteria and yeasts, each with a job to do. The health benefits of yogurt and kefir, among other fermented foods, derive from their beneficial bacteria. For example, supplementing with *Bifidobacterium* reduces pain, suggesting an anti-inflammatory effect (Spiller & Shanahan, 2009). Bravo et al. (2011) suggest that probiotics regulate GABA via the vagus nerve, which reduces anxiety and depression. Evidence suggests an overactive HPA axis and inflammatory cytokines are present in IBS (Dinan et al., 2006). Neufeld, Kang, Bienenstock, and Foster (2011) have identified that gut bacteria regulate the set point for the

HPA axis. There are also new approaches to probiotics involving "soil-based organisms," which are effective in reducing the symptoms of IBS (Bittner, Croffut, & Stranahan, 2005).

There are two main ways to increase probiotics and good intestinal bacteria; one is through food and the other is with high-dose probiotic supplementation. I recommend doing both regularly. All indigenous societies developed fermented foods and drinks for health. Among these foods are *tepache*, a fermented juice made from pineapple skins in Mexico; kimchee, made from cabbage or other fermented vegetables dating from 3,000 years ago in Korea; sauerkraut in Germany, which is made from cabbage; *kombucha*, a Russian-derived fermented tea; salmon stink eggs, which are buried by Alaska Natives and Pacific Northwest American Indians until they "stink" with healthy bacteria; apple cider and rice vinegar; miso and natto; pickles; *chicha* from Peru; fermented mustard greens from Vietnam; and yogurt and kefir, commonly eaten in the Caucasus and believed to account for the longevity of its people. These are just some of the varieties of fermented foods that enhance bacteria in the gut and improve overall immunity and mental well-being.

Constipation

People with digestive problems often experience constipation; whether due to lack of fiber in the diet, for emotional reasons, or because of the constipating effects of drugs like benzodiapines or zolpidem (Ambien). In addition to adding probiotics into the diet for colon and mood health, foods containing prebiotics are also essential. Prebiotics provide insoluble fiber, improve intestinal peristalsis, and are the "soil" in the intestines into which probiotics sink in order to do their job. Among the prebiotics are fructo-oligosaccharide (FOS) supplements, oats, garlic, onions, bananas, and ground chia, flax, and psyllium seeds. In addition to vegetables, fruits, and grains, fiber may be added daily by mixing one tablespoon of psyllium powder in water in the morning and/ or at night before bed. Psyllium also reduces the rate of glucose absorption into the bloodstream and is useful for sugar metabolism problems like hypoglycemia and diabetes. Chia (*Salvia hispanica*) seeds, indigenous to Mexico and known to support the energy needed by the Rarámuri and Desert Indians for long-distance running, are also mucilaginous and soothing to the intestinal walls, which may be inflamed by gluten allergies. They are also an inexpensive source of fiber and EFAs. Chia (one tablespoon) may be soaked in a glass of water overnight and then drunk in the morning before breakfast. In Mexico and the southwestern United States, the Nopale cactus is used for food, for its soothing mucilaginous effects on the colon, and for its ability to slow the uptake of glucose following a meal. Still others use aloe vera (*Aloe barbadensis*) to soothe the intestines, though because of its purgative qualities only small amounts should be used. So revered is *sabila* (aloe vera) in Mexico, it is called *varita de los cielos*, the "wand of heaven," and placed at the front door of every home and business, as it is thought to bring protection and good luck.

EXERCISES 8.2: AND 8.3 BELLY MASSAGE AND THE SQUAT (ONLINE EXERCISES)

Exercises augment the effects of nutrition. I routinely teach two simple exercises to my clients to improve digestion and elimination; one is a "belly self-massage" used to release pain and gas or ease constipation and allow one simply to "get in touch" with the "garbage disposal," which is often how the lower abdomen is treated. "The squat" is a yoga posture that is the natural position of defecation as well as a traditional position of childbirth.

LIVER AND GALLBLADDER HEALTH

Efficient digestion of carbohydrates begins in the mouth, and foods must be broken down by the liver, gallbladder, and stomach before they reach the intestines for assimilation. Stress and depression are exacerbated by poor liver and gallbladder function. Poor-quality foods, especially trans fats and fried foods, lead to a liver and a gallbladder that are unable to process the fats, leading to sluggishness and stones or gravel. In traditional Chinese medicine, the emotion of anger suggests a congested gallbladder. The symptoms of gallbladder problems include burping, flatulence, a feeling of heaviness after a meal, shoulder pain, or pain under the ribs on the right side or in the back directly behind the diaphragm. Awakening with bloodshot eyes is another sign of gallbladder problems. Good liver and gallbladder function are essential to the prevention and treatment of diabetes. Gallbladder disease is an epidemic among American Indians (Everhart et al., 2002) and other peoples who have lost their traditional food ways. Conventional medical researchers want to assert a genetic cause for gallbladder disease and diabetes in American Indians. But there was very little gallbladder disease among them prior to the modern diet (Price, 2003). Removal of the gallbladder only exacerbates health problems by decreasing the capacity to digest foods. The gallbladder emulsifies the EFAs needed to elevate mood and decrease stress as well as to maintain artery health and low systemic inflammation. If the gallbladder is not functioning well, even something as nutritious as fish or fish oil capsules will be less effective because those nutrients cannot be assimilated properly. Removing a gallbladder is like throwing out the garbage can instead of cleaning out the pail. Surgery should be avoided except when an individual's life is in immediate danger. For those who have had their gallbladder removed, replacement supplements should include natural ox bile. Beets and beet tops, which are rich in betaine, are excellent foods that assists gallbladder function.

A history of junk food use associated with economic stress or self-medication, or simply many years of eating poor-quality refined foods and trans fatty acids, will contribute to chronic gallbladder congestion, low bile output, and gallstones. The brain is made up of mostly fat in the form of docohexaenoic acid, and neurons require fats to function smoothly.

FATS AND ESSENTIAL FATTY ACIDS

Essential fatty acids (EFAs) are a group of fats obtained through foods and nutrients; they are essential to health and recovery. The brain is made up of 60% fat, called docosahexaenoic acid (DHA). Introducing good-quality fats into the diet as both foods and supplements and eliminating poor-quality fats is the way to begin a nutritional program of recovery.

Every traditional culture has a natural source of fats and oils that reflects the foods proffered by nature in the local environment. For example, traditional Inuit people of Alaska and Greenland use animal fat and protein for up to 70% of their diet as a primary source of food. The Inuit showed few signs of mental illness or heart disease prior to the introduction of nonlocal foods to their diet, such as flour, sugar, and soybeans. Fats from coconut and palm have nourished indigenous peoples of the tropics for centuries without ill effect. Indeed, the coconut (*Coco nucifera*) is a nearly perfect food, rich in fats, protein, and a full complement of B vitamins. Coconut oil is one of the healthiest and most medicinal of fats and should be incorporated into daily food preparation. It is a medical myth that saturated fats are dangerous. Saturated fats stimulate prostaglandin 3, which is a pain-reducing anti-inflammatory. Dietary fats exert a protective anti-inflammatory effect mediated via the vagus nerve and cholinergic anti-inflammatory pathways through the activation of cholecystokinin and nicotinic acid receptors (Luyer et al., 2005). All cultures throughout the world have traditional sources of good-quality fats to draw from. As part of a journey of self-discovery, exploring one's cultural genetic heritage may include researching the types of fats and oils used by one's ancestors.

In the Pacific Northwest, the abundance of salmon and oolichan (smelt, *Thaleichthys pacificus*) provided ample fats that nourished the brains and arteries of the Salish peoples and formed the basis for trade along a vast territorial expanse. Indeed, these major trade routes are called the Oolichan Grease Trails because, as families traveled from the Pacific Coast eastward to trade the precious oolichan oil for the roots and medicines of the mountains, drops of the oil fell along the way. The loss of the oolichan and decline of the salmon and other animal fats is without a doubt linked to the epidemic of depression, anxiety, alcoholism, and learning disorders among the indigenous peoples of the Pacific Northwest and Alaska.

A variety of fish oils from krill, sardines, salmon, and cod can easily be integrated into the diet. Many oils are medicinal both internally and externally. The avocado, known as "poor person's butter," is native to Mexico and nourishes the arteries and promotes weight loss as well as moisturizing the skin. Karité or shea butter from the worthy nut in Burkina Faso provides cooking oil and medicine for the skin.

Even the ignominious pig, brought by Hernando DeSoto during colonization and whose fat has developed a terrible reputation for no scientific reason whatsoever, provides a leaf lard that is anti-inflammatory when used on the body. This is in contrast to the solid vegetable fats like Crisco (crystallized cottonseed oil), which should be shunned like the plague. A complement of fats from animals, vegetables, nuts, and seeds extracted via a "cold process" should be integrated into a daily diet for health with all other oils, along with the much-maligned egg, rich in choline, for the brain and memory.

The coconut is increasingly available in supermarkets; it provides an edible seed, water, and oil, and all three serve as a rich source of nutritious food and medicine. The coconut is easily digested, is rich in nutrients and minerals, and is also antibacterial, antifungal, antiviral, antiparasitic, and antioxidant. Coconut lowers blood sugar, protects the liver, and improves immune function (DebMandal & Mandal, 2011), making it a valuable food and medicine for people with PTSD. Traditionally, indigenous peoples of the tropics use coconuts as a source of protein and energy and medicinally for the treatment of infections. Coconut is also fermented into a probiotic-rich wine, called "tuba," in the Philippines and Mexico. The water is used traditionally in rural areas for rehydration or when people are too ill to eat much solid food. Coconuts contain medium-chain fatty acids, which are utilized by the body primarily to produce energy rather than body fat or arterial plaque. They do not slow digestion, as most fats do, nor do they circulate in the bloodstream to the degree that other fats do. As a result they are much less likely to be incorporated into fat cells and do not collect in artery walls or contribute to hardening of the arteries (Felton, Crook, Davies, & Oliver, 1994).

Coconut oil is very heat-stable, so it's an excellent cooking oil. It is slow to oxidize and thus resistant to rancidity. Coconut oil can be used in cooking and baking and can also be applied to the skin. It increases high-density lipoprotein (HDL) levels, and in so doing improves the cholesterol ratio, thus reducing risk of heart disease (Enig, 2000; Norton et al., 2004). Coconut is rich in lauric and caproic acids (Enig, 2000). Lauric acid forms into monolaurin, which is an antiviral and antibacterial monoglyceride that destroys viruses such as human immunodeficiency virus (HIV), herpes, and cytomegalovirus (Enig, 1998). Coconut is protective against high levels of blood lipids and cardiovascular inflammation (Enig, 1998; Fallon & Enig, 1999). Studies of indigenous peoples worldwide who have a diet high in coconut and coconut oil demonstrate normal cholesterol levels and no signs of cardiovascular disease (Enig, 2000). This is similar to the Inuit, who prior to colonization and development ate a diet consisting of mainly saturated fats and yet evidenced no cardiovascular disease. With all of these attributes, coconut oil makes a healthy choice for people in recovery from the physical health effects of PTSD. The lipids scientist Mary Enig (2006) recommends this ideal blend of oils for daily use in cooking:

1 cup of coconut oil, gently melted
1 cup of cold-pressed sesame oil
1 cup of extra-virgin olive oil
Mix all ingredients together in a glass jar, cover tightly, and store at room temperature.

CHOLESTEROL AS HORMONE PRECURSOR

Sufficient cholesterol is essential for mental health. Cholesterol is frequently condemned as a major cause of heart disease, but this is untrue. There is significant evidence that the efforts to reduce cholesterol, the liquid "Band-Aid" that scouts out and repairs arterial inflammation, with diets extremely low in fat and with medications contributes to significant mental distress, including anxiety, muscle pain, and suicide attempts (Perez-Rodriguez et al., 2008). Indeed, low cholesterol may serve as a biological marker of suicidality (Vuksan-Ćusa, Marčinko, Nađ, & Jakovljević, 2009). A recent study of 50,000 individuals in Norway found that women with cholesterol over 200 lived longer than those with lower cholesterol (Petursson, Sigurdsson, Bengtsson, Nilsen, & Getz, 2012).

The body naturally produces cholesterol in the liver and other organs in quantities essential to maintain good health. The body maintains a balance of cholesterol by producing more of the substance when insufficient amounts are available from food, and the total body cholesterol level reduces when quantities greater than needed by the body are consumed (Enig, 2000). Cholesterol is a precursor of hormones, the raw material for producing certain fat-soluble vitamins and the substance that "patches" or repairs lesions in tissues and arteries resulting from inflammation frequently caused by trans fatty acids, stress, manufactured foods, contamination from waste, and environmental toxins. Cholesterol is a precursor to vitamin D, the fat-soluble vitamin. Low levels of vitamin D are implicated in chronic pain, depression, and hypertension (Vasquez, Manso, & Cannell, 2004). Cholesterol is the precursor of glucocorticoids (necessary for blood sugar regulation), mineralcorticoids (essential for mineral balance), ligament strength, blood pressure regulation, and sex hormones. Cholesterol is also the foundation for pregnenolone, which serves as the predecessor to virtually all other steroid hormones (including progesterone, cortisol, aldosterone, and testosterone). Pregnenolone is an endogenous compound synthesized in the central nervous system as well as the adrenal glands. Decreases in pregnenolone are associated with depression, anxiety, and pain in war veterans from Iraq and Afghanistan (Marx, 2009). Pregnenolone is also metabolized to allopregnenolone, an anxiolytic neuroactive steroid that is decreased in veterans with pain (Kilts et al., 2010) and PTSD. It increases acetylcholine release, which is central to memory and focus and enhances the creation of neurons. Lowering cholesterol decreases the capacity to make pregnenolone and thus affects an already diminished endocrine capacity in PTSD. Pregnenolone is an important ingredient of several brain nutrient support compounds required for brain recovery.

THE DANGERS OF TRANS FATTY ACIDS

Changing diets to include healthy fats for brain function is one positive behavior. The second behavior required is to eliminate the use of unhealthy fats or trans fatty acids. The scientific evidence is strong that trans fatty acids consumed in even limited amounts interfere with the delta-6 desaturase enzyme and other enzymes necessary for the conversion of omega-3 and omega-6 EFAs to the forms necessary for cellular and organ health (Enig, 2000).

MOOD, PAIN, AND FAT

Essential fatty acids (EFAs) are polyunsaturated fats that our bodies need but cannot produce—eicosapentaenoic acid (EPA) and docosahexaenoic acid (DHA). EFAs are obtained from fish, especially fatty fish, and from animals and some plants. The ratio of omega-3 fatty acids to omega-6 fatty acids has changed considerably in the last 100 years in the United States, which has contributed in a major way to the rise of chronic inflammatory conditions. These changes have occurred as dietary patterns and food resources have changed from more traditional, nutrient-dense whole foods to synthetic, packaged, and nutrient-deficient foods. The broad effects of these changes cannot be overstated, ranging from heart disease, depression, anxiety, and ADD in children and adults alike. Chronic excessive alcohol consumption depletes brain stores of omega-3 fatty acids, suggesting that people with PTSD and alcoholism are candidates for supplementation. Deficits in omega-3 fatty acids contribute to mood disorders (Parker et al., 2006), and increased fish intake is associated with reduced symptoms of mood disorders (Smith, Beilin, Mori, & Oddy, 2011). Low levels of DHA are associated with increased risk of suicide in veterans (Lewis et al., 2011); in a randomized blinded placebo-controlled trial, supplementation with 2 grams of EFAs (1.2 g EPA; 0.9 g DHA) resulted in a significant reduction in suicidal thinking and depression among patients with recurrent self-harm (Hallahan, Hibbeln, Davis, & Garland, 2007).

Women diagnosed with borderline personality disorder showed a decrease in depression and aggression when they were randomized to a group receiving 1 g of EPA daily for 8 weeks (Zanarini & Frankenburg, 2003). Supplementation with 2 g/day of fish oil improved both depression and heart rate variability in patients with heart disease (Carney et al., 2010). Green-lipped mussel (*Perna canaliculus*) powder from New Zealand (combined with dimethylglycine) has shown significant immunomodulatory and anti-inflammatory effects in humans (Lawson, Belkowski, Whitesides, Davis, & Lawson, 2007).

Fish oils should be balanced with gamma-linolenic acid (GLA), which is rich in certain plant seeds, like borage seeds, evening primrose seeds, and black currant seeds. The GLA percentage of evening primrose oil is 10% (especially good for arthritis), black currant seed oil has 17% (especially good for PMS and cramps), and borage oil has 23%. Hemp oil, green-lipped mussel, and black currant seed oil are a special case of omega-3 fatty acids that contain precursors to both prostaglandin 1 and 3, with hemp oil containing a 1:3 ratio, which is ideal for human nutrition and for inflammatory conditions. In addition to EFA supplements, unsalted butter is an ideal food. One of the reasons butter is so nutritious when put on vegetables is because vitamins A, E, and K are fat-soluble and thus not well absorbed without the fat. In addition to supplementation, foods such as chia (*Salvia hispanica*) seeds and fish, especially wild salmon and tuna, and are rich in EFAs. Supplementing daily with vitamin E (400 IU daily) supplies all eight forms of natural source tocopherols and tocotrienols, providing the antioxidant benefits of the entire family of vitamin E; it should accompany all EFA supplementation. Finally, canola oil should be avoided. It is generally extracted from genetically modified seed and when used for cooking creates very high levels of trans fatty acids.

General Recommendations for the Intake of Fats

- EPA/DHA (fish oils) 2,000 to 6,000 mg daily (divided in equal doses)
- GLA (borage, hemp, evening primrose, black currant seed) 1,000 mg daily
- Natural complete vitamin E 400 international units (IU)
- Cold-pressed (extra virgin) olive or sesame oil (no canola oil)
- Raw, unsalted butter or fresh lard
- No margarine or butter replacements

THE HEALING NOURISHMENT OF ANIMAL GLANDS

Our ancestors ate the organs, glands, and brains of animals they hunted or raised in pastures for their fat, flavor, and ultimately nutritional value. These food consumption practices continue to nourish peoples around the world whether as part of subsistence, small farms, or increasingly as part of gourmet trends. Many epicurean foods today are made from the glands and organs of animals. Such dishes as liver pâtés, sweetbreads (thymus or pancreas), and dried salami are highly regarded for their contribution to health. In traditional indigenous societies, the elders, the honored, or the ill are first offered these nutrient-rich animal organs, and in the case of fish-eating peoples, fish heads, eyes, livers, and hearts. Chicken liver pâté, prepared beef, goat, or lung (in Mexico and Spain this is called *chanfaina*) are prized for their flavor and capacity to rejuvenate. *Menudo* made from tripe or stomach is a prized dish in Mexico, and haggis (sheep stomach stuffed with cooked oats, blood, and organ meat) is still considered a delicacy in Scotland. Blood pudding (called *moronga* in México), kidneys, goat and pork testicles, tongue, heart, pancreas, bone gels, and head cheese (meat gels) all contribute to body health and support recovery from illness. But these traditional foods are increasingly hard to find and their nutritional and ritual value is often forgotten.

Adrenal, liver, brain, pituitary, hypothalamus, and thymus glands from animal sources play an important role in restoring and rebuilding tissue. Despite their healthful benefits, it is often not possible to obtain enough fresh organic organ meats to consume them in the quantities required for medicinal purposes. Most pork, lamb, beef, and sheep glands are available in dehydrated form. Consider the application of dehydrated liver glandular to the recovering alcoholic, or hypothalamus, pituitary, and brain to support the HPA axis and brain function in PTSD and depression, or thymus to support immune function. These glands are referred to as *desiccated* or *lyophilized glandulars*, which help to regulate immune health and stimulate cell regeneration. Good-quality glandulars derived from healthy animal sources are produced in New Zealand because of that country's strict laws governing the raising of animals and the purity of the stock.

For PTSD and its sequelae, and TBI, I recommend the daily use of hypothalamus, brain, pituitary, adrenal, liver, pancreas, and thymus glandulars. Where there is acute or chronic inflammation, a proteolytic enzyme between meals is also advised. The hypothalamus regulates metabolic function and is the master gland of the limbic system, essential to adrenal health and for long-term stress management (this glandular may also stimulate more vivid dreams, which may be problematic for those who experience nightmares). Heart, lung, thyroid, kidney, prostate, ovary, and orchic (made from bovine testicles), parotid, spleen, and trachea can be used as needed for other health needs. Women and men over the age of 35 can benefit from ovary and prostate/orchic support respectively. People with a history of smoking can use lung, while low thyroid function can be supported by thyroid. These regimens often have the effect of decreasing or eliminating the need for synthetic glandulars.

BRAIN CHEMICALS: NEUROTRANSMITTERS AND AMINO ACIDS

Most pharmaceuticals used for PTSD and its sequelae target brain chemicals called neurotransmitters, which require amino acids, the building blocks of protein, and vitamin/mineral cofactors. Physical and mental health depends upon plenty of amino acids, vitamins, minerals, and fats to support the synaptic transmission of neuronal signals. As discussed in earlier chapters, low levels of NTs are found in PTSD, depression, and anxiety; they also result from poor food quality.

Like the instruments in an orchestra, neurotransmitters work best when balanced and harmonizing together. The lack of efficacy and the side effects of pharmaceuticals result from the increase of just one or two NTs, which is like an orchestra full of trumpets but no strings. Increasing serotonin, for example, usually results in a deficit of dopamine, and this can lead to side effects.

SSRIs also inhibit phase one detoxification enzymes in the liver. Many authors have written about the side effects of SSRIs, which is the most common reason people stop their use. Carl Pfeiffer, the physician who was one of the originators of orthomolecular psychiatry, believed that psychological problems occurred in people who were either "over- or undermethylated." Methyl is an important chemical group consisting of one carbon and three hydrogen atoms. Overmethylation results in excessive levels of dopamine, norepinephrine, and serotonin, leading to chemical and food sensitivities, underachievement, and upper body pain. It is also associated with adverse reactions to SSRIs, including St. John's wort and SAMe, and positive responses to folic acid, niacin, and B12. The undermethylated types (who are more prone to obsessive compulsive disorder, oppositional disorder, and seasonal affective disorder) appeared to do better with SAMe, kava, and inositol.

Sufficient sustained good-quality animal protein is essential for mood for most people, explaining why many vegetarians are depressed and fatigued or may just not attain their full potential. The safest and most effective way in which to obtain amino acids that support NT development is from food—animal and vegetable/legume proteins and "free amino acids." The supplement free amino acids provides a good ratio of all the amino acids necessary, and then one can add specific amino acid combinations to boost serotonin or GABA, dopamine, or acetylcholine. There are additional herbs and energy medicine methods, proposed in the next chapters, that synergize the effects of amino acid therapy in order to boost neurotransmitters. The key to success in nutrition and supplementation is diversity, synergy, sufficient dosing, quality of the product, and sustaining treatment over a long enough period to effect change.

DEPRESSION

Mishlove (1993) suggests that the Buddha was sitting under the fig tree (*Ficus religiosa*), known in India as the Bo tree, eating tryptophan-rich figs when he became enlightened. Other foods rich in tryptophan include bananas, plums, chocolate, oats, spirulina, and milk. Tryptophan in foods converts to serotonin, one of the neurotransmitters associated with the biochemistry of PTSD and depression. Low serotonin also lowers the pain threshold, and sufficient serotonin neurons are required for analgesics to work. The combination of low serotonin levels mixed with the abuse of opiates explains partly why people withdrawing from opiates experience pain even more intensely for a long time after withdrawal and why they benefit from treatments that stimulate their natural capacity to increase their own NTs and endogenous opioids. When the brain receives stimulus from the outside, as in the form of drugs, it does not need to make those natural chemicals. Amino acids—along with other nutrients, herbs, cranial electrical stimulation, acupuncture, massage, exercise, and social connections—all nudge neurons awake.

In depression, the brain requires fuel from amino acids like tryptophan, a potent natural B-complex with extra B6, essential fatty acids, and lithium orotate. However serotonin may not be the only low NT and urinary neurotransmitter, and urinary testing of NT levels can be done to analyze all the neurotransmitter levels, especially if one does not obtain results after 2 months of amino acid supplementation. In depression, there are usually nutritional imbalances that include both deficiencies and excesses of certain vitamins and minerals. The deficiencies may include the B vitamins, (biotin, folic acid, B6, B1, and B12), vitamin C, and minerals such as calcium, copper, iron, magnesium, potassium, and zinc. Yet an excess of minerals can also contribute to depression, as can a lack of mineral cofactors. Elevated levels of lead and copper and excess calcium are often found in depression and mood disorders. People who drink well water that is high in copper or water from copper pipes may be vulnerable to copper-induced depression, just as drinking water that is rich in lithium is protective against aggression, violence, and depression. A good quality natural B complex is essential for many functions including neurological health and glucose metabolism. Abram Hoffer (1962) introduced the use of high dose micronutrients and vitamins, in particular niacinamide, ascorbic acid, and riboflavin, for the treatment of psychosis. A thiamine-rich B vitamin is very effective for chronic nerve pain, adrenal fatigue, and anxious depression; a B-complex rich in the minerals chromium and vanadium will be a good choice for depression and anxiety with hypoglycemia.

5-Hydroxytryptophan (50 mg) is a good choice for additional amino acid supplement for depression, insomnia, anxiety, and intestinal problems and is most effective when used with synergistic cofactors including vitamin B6 (10 mg), niacinamide (50 mg), and L-theanine (50 mg). Theanine acts on GABA receptors and provides an anxiolytic effect. One of the reasons green tea is not as stimulating as other beverages with caffeine is because it contains theanine.

In my experience people can receive benefits from lower dosages of 5-HTP than is normally recommended. People can experience serotonin poisoning from supplements as easily as from fluoxetine (indeed, people often do better on subclinical doses [5 to 10 mg] of fluoxetine if supplemented with additional nutrients, though ultimately they should be weaned from fluoxetine whenever possible). Hoffer consistently found low levels of folate and B12 in depressed people and those with a history of alcoholism. He found that they improved with folate/B12 treatment. Vitamin B12 deficiencies—common among pure vegetarians (vegans) and the elderly—are associated with cognitive deficits and depression. Hemat (2009) suggests doses of 30 to 40 mg daily of methylcobalamin (B12 is required to regenerate neurons). A high level of homocysteine is a functional marker of both folate and vitamin B12 deficiency and a risk factor for depression and cognitive decline. Traditional Chinese diets, which are rich in folates, contribute to lower lifetime rates of depression (Coppen & Bolander-Gouaille, 2005). Low folate is also linked with a poor response to SSRIs, suggesting that taking folate might improve efficacy. Oral doses of folic acid range from 800 mcg daily, and vitamin B12 dosing begins at 1 mg daily (Coppen & Bolander-Gouaille, 2005). Hoffer (1962) suggested that much higher levels of folic acid (up to 5 mg/day) may be used safely.

Niacin in the form of niacinimide (B3) stimulates the GABA-benzodiazapine receptors and is used for mood stabilization and the treatment of depression and alcoholism. Roger Williams, the biochemist who named folic acid, identified pantothenic acid, and was the originator of the concept of biochemical individuality believed that alcoholism was a disease primarily caused by vitamin B

204 Rhythms of Recovery

deficiency and could be treated with complex B vitamins and minerals, suggesting a range from 200 to 500 mg of niacinamide daily. For the treatment of psychoses he recommended 1,500 mg three times a day. Picamilon (nicotinyl-y-aminobutyric acid) is a compound developed in the Soviet Union that combines niacin and GABA in order to cross the blood-brain barrier and increase blood flow in the brain for the treatment of depression, alcoholism, migraines, and TBI (Lake, 2007; Silver, McAllister, & Yudofsky, 2011). Like picamilon and gingko biloba, vinpocetine (ethyl-apovincaminate) is a nutrient that is widely used in Europe. It is a vasodilator, improves brain oxygenation, and enhances cerebral metabolism (Hemat, 2009). It is derived from vincamine, a natural alkaloid found in the periwinkle plant (*Vinca minor*). Vinpocetine treatment has been shown to facilitate the long-term signal transmission between two neurons simultaneously, that is necessary to learning and memory (Medin, 2010). It is anti-inflammatory, enhances glucose uptake, increases the synthesis of ATP, reduces oxidative stress, and has been shown to enhance performance on cognitive tests in humans (Medin, 2010). These qualities make it the subject of significant study for the treatment of neurodegenerative disease, in particular vascular dementia, and also for clinical use by patients with PTSD, depression, and TBI. It has no long-term side effects and is often part of a "smart nutrient cocktail" compounded by nutrient companies. Since it is a vasodilator, it should not be combined with other cognition-enhancing "smart drug" vasodilators like gingko biloba or vinpocetine, huperzine A, or dimethylaminoethanol. If you are taking a blood thinner, vinpocetine should be monitored because it is also an anti–platelet aggregation blood thinner. Recommended doses range from 10 to 15 mg three times a day, and it should always be taken with meals.

Williams (1998), Hoffer (1962), Pfeiffer (1988), and Enig (2000) all present strong evidence for a nutrient-deficit model of the addictions. The concept of self-medication, coined by Khantzian (1990), suggests that challenges to self-regulation results in self-medication of painful affective states, which can also be understood as a need to medicate what the brain/body cannot do for itself. Individuals select a particular drug based on its ability to relieve or augment emotions unique to the individual, which he or she cannot achieve or maintain without outside help. Addicts and alcoholics often experiment with all classes of drugs but discover that a particular drug suits them best. Stimulants energize, opiates quell aggression, and alcohol releases inhibition, allowing for the exchange of feelings that might otherwise not be expressed (Khantzian, 1990). Understanding the affective and biochemical needs of the client will inform amino acid choices.

USING AMINO ACIDS FOR WITHDRAWAL FROM SSRIS

Free amino acids may be combined with specific ones like 5-HTP for withdrawing from SSRIs. During the process of withdrawal, the dosage of 5-HTP may be increased, but only under a practitioner's guidance. Nutrients that combine 5-HTP with cofactors including vitamin B6 (as pyridoxal-5-phosphate) niacinamide, and L-theanine, provide a good foundation for SSRI withdrawal.

DOPAMINE PRECURSORS

Dopamine facilitates attention, focus, and the sense of pleasure. The addictions often involve a dopamine imbalance, and too much stimulation can deplete dopamine and thus contribute to a lack of pleasure that often drives the thrill-seeking cycle. Tyrosine increases dopamine both through supplementation and from tyrosine-rich foods. Avocados, bananas, and beets are especially good food sources for the enhancement of dopamine. Beets contain betaine, which, in addition to enhancing mood, helps to relieve menstrual cramps and improve gallbladder function.

Tyrosine synthesizes dopamine, increases energy, and stimulates thyroid hormones. Using DL-phenylalanine to boost dopamine may be useful when depression co-occurs with pain and fatigue, and DL-phenylalanine may be better absorbed than tyrosine, to which it converts. Use 1,000 mg/day for chronic pain and depression. A good thiamine-rich multivitamin/multimineral complex will also be helpful.

LITHIUM OROTATE

I mentioned in Chapter 1 that lithium (not the pharmaceutical carbonate or citrate form), a natural mineral found in water supplies, elevates mood and is neuroprotective; small amounts stabilize mood and improve cognitive function. Lithium orotate crosses the blood-brain barrier, whereas the carbonate form does not; thus lower doses of the former are effective (Lakhan & Vieira, 2008). Almost everyone with PTSD and especially TBI can benefit from 50 to 150 mg a day of lithium orotate combined with 300 mcg of folic acid. Norman Shealy (2006), the neurosurgeon who pioneered energy medicine with the development of the transcutaneous electrical nerve stimulation unit for pain, recommends 45 mg of lithium orotate a day. In one study, 150 mg of lithium was given to 42 patients with alcoholism. Ten of the patients had no relapse for over 3 and up to 10 years, 13 patients remained without relapse for 1 to 3 years, and the remaining 12 that were analyzed had relapses between 6 to 12 months (Sartori, 1986). I have observed excellent effects at microdoses starting at 50 mg.

ANXIETY

Anxiety is both an emotional and biochemical imbalance. Cognitive-behavioral therapy used to treat anxiety becomes even more effective when nutritional status is addressed. Absent the integration of nutritional-biochemical support with counseling, anxiety usually remains the lifelong hallmark of PTSD.

Depression, anxiety, and insomnia often co-occur, and once the excitatory NTs are addressed with 5-HTP, the next step is to support the inhibitory neurotransmitter GABA to enhance relaxation. Low levels of GABA are associated with depression, anxiety, insomnia, and epilepsy. The anxiolytic, muscle relaxant, and sedative effects of the benzodiazepines target the GABA receptors. However, there are many amino acids, nutrients, and herbs that are effective and free of side effects. When mouse pups cry out their distress at maternal separation, anxiolytic pharmaceuticals that act on GABA receptors reduce or eliminate these calls (Fish, Sekinda, Ferrari, Dirks, & Miczek, 1999). When humans cry out in distress from loss and anxiety, they also respond to nutrients that increase GABA, such as milk biopeptides and the herb kava (Sarris et al., 2009). Bioactive milk-derived peptides have been studied for their ability to induce relaxation and anxiety and to promote sleep. Observations that babies become calm after breast-feeding led French researchers to identify and concentrate the casein peptides in milk, which have anxiolytic activity. These bioactive peptides are amino acid chains derived from cow's milk that act on GABA receptors to induce a sedative effect and improve sleep (Clare & Swaisgood, 2000; Delini-Stula & Holsboer-Trachsler, 2009; de Saint-Hilaire, Messaoudi, Desor, & Kobayashi, 2009). Animal and human studies have shown that bioactive milk-derived peptides significantly reduce stress and cortisol levels, induce relaxation, and improve digestion, cardiovascular health, mental function, and social interactions (Kim et al., 2007; Messaoudi, Lefranc-Millot, Desor, Demagny, & Bourdon, 2005). In one double-blind study, milk biopeptides were shown to be significantly more effective than St. John's wort and kava-kava in reducing anxiety when compared to controls. In my clinical practice I have used these milk biopeptide supplements with excellent results as gentle yet potent anxiolytics. It is often effective to take two or three capsules three or four times a day for acute anxiety or insomnia. This natural peptide was also tested for three major side effects generally attributed to benzodiazepines: dependence, memory loss, and tolerance, and none were observed. These peptides are available over the counter in the United States (by prescription in Europe) and are sold by several pharmaceutical-grade nutritional companies.

The standard dose is 150 to 300 mg to reduce anxiety or to relax and 450 to 600 mg for sleep. This nutrient is gentle, effective, and often works better over a few days, in contrast to the herb kava, which acts as an anxiolytic powerfully and immediately. For people in recovery from substance abuse or those who prefer not to alter consciousness, this nutrient is ideal as it relaxes without other effects.

The amino acid supplement GABA is sometimes recommended as an anxiolytic, but it does not cross the blood-brain barrier very efficiently. There are better nutrients or herbs that stimulate GABA effects, including a combination of inositol, magnesium, milk biopeptides, phenibut, and kava. More effective than GABA at penetrating the blood-brain barrier is phenibut (beta-phenyl-gamma-aminobutyric acid hydrochloride), a derivative of GABA acting on both GABA and dopamine receptors (Lapin, 2001). Phenibut is used in Russia and increasingly throughout Europe and the United States to reduce anxiety, improve sleep, and for PTSD (Lapin, 2001).

Let us recall the interrelationship between digestion and neurotransmitters and thus mental well-being. There are numerous GABA receptors in the stomach and esophagus; following 9/11 there were higher rates of gastroesophageal reflux disease (GERD) among people with asthma and/or PTSD (Li et al., 2011), leading the researchers to suggest a possible role for stress-reducing GABA support and supplementation for PTSD-related GERD. Caffeine inhibits the release of GABA, which supports the intuitive knowledge of eliminating caffeine from the diet. Green tea is an effective substitute that contains the anxiolytic amino acid L-theanine (Yokogoshi, Kobayashi, Mochizuki, & Terashima, 1998). Theanine stimulates GABA and serotonin production and offsets the stimulation of caffeine in green tea, thus serving as a relaxing antiinflammatory beverage. Steel-cut oats are a deeply relaxing and nourishing food for the nerves; rich in silicon, phosphorus, and magnesium; when combined with blackstrap molasses, which is rich in iron, copper, magnesium, potassium, and manganese, it is a late night snack that induces sleep.

Anxiety co-occurs with other chronic disease states that have a bidirectional effect on health; asthma often occurs with anxiety and is a potentially deadly illness associated with a history of childhood adverse experiences and PTSD (Spitzer et al., 2011). As I discussed in Chapter 3, anxiety and disordered breathing commonly co-occur. Hyperventilation and anxiety are often associated with a blood pH that is overly alkaline and thus responds to a diet that acidifies blood pH, such as red meats and vinegar, while decreasing foods such as sugar and white flour as well as trans fats. The Bohr effect refers to the way in which an increase in respiration increases alkalinity. This occurs as carbon dioxide decreases, which in turn increases the affinity of hemoglobin for oxygen, resulting in the failure to release oxygen and leading to hypoxia. Hypoxia then triggers an increase in lactic acid, a precipitant of anxiety and panic attacks. In this state, magnesium is lost in an effort to compensate for the resulting alkalosis. For these reasons and more, magnesium is effective in reducing anxiety; it relaxes smooth muscle, which may explain why dosing oral magnesium supplementation to bowel tolerance (generally from 500 to 1,200 mg daily) or providing intravenous doses of magnesium will alleviate both hyperventilation and asthma. Magnesium is very effective for treating anxiety, depression, insomnia, bipolar disorder, and muscle tension. Magnesium aspartate was found to be as effective as lithium in 50% of severely ill rapid-cycling bipolar patients (Chouinard, Beauclair, Geiser, & Etienne, 1990). People with bulimia and anorexia are especially vulnerable to magnesium deficiency if they use diuretics or laxatives. Corticosteroids used for inflammation or asthma, oral antibiotics, and birth control pills also deplete magnesium. Mixing magnesium (oral or topical) with lithium orotate is a basic approach for the treatment of depression, anxiety, and insomnia, and magnesium at night helps to relieve muscle cramps.

Taurine, an amino acid made in the liver from cysteine, also has a calming effect. It is often combined with magnesium for the treatment of anxiety. It also lowers blood pressure, so it is a good choice for treating individuals who have anxiety and high blood pressure. It is good for the gallbladder when combined with betaine or fresh beets or beet juice. Phosphorus (30 to 40 drops of phosphoinositol) on an empty stomach should be taken every morning before breakfast for up to 8 weeks to decrease anxiety and increase energy. It is an effective treatment for asthma and hyperventilation.

Drugs that may cause anxiety include amphetamines, asthma medications, caffeine, antihistamines, and steroids. Statins and red yeast rice can lower cholesterol too much and thus cause anxiety. I treat panic attacks similarly to anxiety and hyperventilation. In addition, Prousky (2006) recommends placing 2 g of the amino acid glycine sublingual (under the tongue) at the start of a panic attack and adding 2 g every few minutes until symptoms abate. Glycine is an antagonist to norepinephrine, which is released under anxiety and panic and thus decreases arousal.

PHOSPHATIDYLSERINE AND PHOSPHATIDYLCHOLINE

Phospholipids are molecules containing both amino and fatty acids. Phospholipids like phosphatidylserine (PS) and phosphatidylcholine (PC) are concentrated in brain cell membranes and support normal cell structure and function. PS aids in neurotransmitter activity, especially dopamine and acetylcholine. It is used to regulate HPA axis function, reduce circulating cortisol, improve memory, prevent cognitive decline, and improve perceived well-being (Jäger, Purpura, & Kingsley, 2007). Evidence suggests that PS and PC concentrations are significantly affected in the first several days following traumatic brain injury (Pasvogel, Miketova, & Moore, 2010).

Choline helps form phosphatidylcholine, the primary phospholipid of cell membranes. Choline is a precursor to acetylcholine, one of the important brain chemicals involved in memory. Liver, legumes, and nuts are rich in choline, but eggs deliver the most; eating two eggs daily is ideal. Human breast milk is also high in choline, one of the many health values of nursing infants. Choline is one of the nutrients recommended by the Institute of Medicine (Erdman, Oria, & Pillsbury, 2011) for the treatment of TBI, along with creatine, omega-3 fatty acids, and zinc. The conservative panel recommended more research on vitamin D antioxidants, polyphenols, and ketogenic (high fat/ protein rich) diets. Dietary intake of choline ranges from 300 to 900 mg a day. Vegans can easily become choline-deficient. A major use of choline in the body is the formation of betaine, an important methyl donor. Choline has been tested in bipolar disorder. When 6 patients on lithium carbonate were given choline, 5 of them had a substantial reduction in manic symptoms (Lyoo, Demopulos, Hirashima, Ahn, & Renshaw, 2003). Choline is also used as an anti-inflammatory and for fatty liver, thus making it an essential supplement in recovery from alcoholism. I recommend taking 1,000 mg/day. People notice having more focus and being more alert. Two different forms of choline are recommended: CDP-choline (cytidine-5'-diphosphate choline [250–600 mg]) or GPC choline (glyceryl phosphorylcholine), both of which have been demonstrated to enhance the concentration of acetylcholine and release of GABA as well as to increase the number of hippocampal neurons (Ricci, Bronzetti, Vega, & Amenta, 1992).

SLEEP AND INSOMNIA

A hallmark of PTSD is the experience of poor sleep quality and nightmares. The treatment of insomnia is similar to anxiety, as they co-occur quite commonly. Even among the general population, a high percentage of people suffer from significant levels of insomnia associated with major depression, anxiety disorder, and alcohol and drug abuse. Insomnia commonly occurs with bipolar disorder during both depressive and manic episodes. Many individuals are misdiagnosed with bipolar disorder when they instead have complex trauma and experience extremes of affect regulation.

Sleep/wakefulness is governed by the HPA axis, which controls cortisol production on a 24-hour circadian rhythm. Hyperarousal prevents sleep and is often associated with high levels of evening cortisol. As I discussed earlier, when clients say they feel "out of sync" or "turned around," indeed their rhythms are. Their cortisol is low in the morning when they are tired; and they are wired at night. This often leads to drinking copious amounts of caffeine, which can have either positive or negative effects. On the one hand, in small doses caffeine improves mood and the ability to focus. But it also interferes with the delta waves of deep, restorative sleep (Landolt, Dijk, Gaus, & Borbely, 1995).

Hyperarousal drives a cycle of depression and exhaustion in which the survivor is fueled by the stress of waking memories and the anticipatory anxiety about the next evening's nightmares, which inevitably disrupt sleep. Setting the stage for sustained sleep by supporting biological function allows the psychic wounds to begin healing. Restoring adrenal strength and increasing vitality is a central goal of sleep-enhancing nutrition. Diet, supplements, and light and energy medicine balance the HPA axis and reset the circadian rhythm and relax the body so the mind can rest. Medications that are used for sleep also affect sleep negatively, and dependence upon pharmaceuticals to sleep further upsets the capacity to restore the natural rhythmic cycles. People may depend upon benzodiazepines or serotonin antagonist reuptake inhibitors (SARIs) like trazodone to help them sleep. Trauma survivors present for treatment most often complaining of sleep problems and often addicted to medications that still may work only nominally. It is common practice to provide zolpidem (Ambien and other hypnotic sedatives) to military troops in training and on the battlefield for sleep as well as amphetamines to stay awake. While benzodiazepines enhance the activity of GABA receptors in the brain, they also lower activity among norepinephrine, dopamine, and serotonin, which are already depleted in patients with PTSD. The benzodiazepines also disrupt slow-wave and rapid-eye-movement sleep. Benzodiazepines are addictive, depressing, and exacerbate nightmares.

Treatment

People require individualized treatment approaches. An individual's personal pattern intersects with the effects of trauma in dysregulating the sleep cycle. There is also a genetic basis for being a "morning person" or "night owl." Exploring pretrauma functioning can identify reasonable goals for improved sleep. As with all nutritional methods, identifying the biological need and filling it with gentler and more natural means by balancing the whole system will be the approach. It is common that survivors who have been exposed to trauma since early childhood have never had a good sleep rhythm; these individuals may require more time to be treated effectively. While sleep professionals often advise against napping, many cultures have traditional napping/resting practices, like the siesta of Spain and Mexico, the *bhat-ghum* in India, and *Mittagspause* in Germany. Recalling Rossi's concept of the ultradian rhythm, taking a 20- to 40-minute rest/nap break in the afternoon is restorative to the brain rhythms.

GABA-acting nutrients, discussed above for anxiety, and herbs provide effective alternatives to benzodiazapines and other sedatives and hypnotics for sleep—in particular, 5-HTP or tryptophan, phenibut, and milk biopeptides. While kava (discussed extensively in Chapter 9) is a powerful anxiolytic, it can both support sleep and also be a stimulant for some people at night. Thus one must test the effects of kava on one's sleep. Dosing several types of nutrients and herbs and managing food works more effectively than relying on one large dose of a specific herb or nutrient.

Lithium orotate lengthens the circadian rhythm and regulates both sleep and mood (150 mcg along with vitamin B6 and 15 mg of folate three times a day). An effective method to balance the circadian rhythm is combining bright-light exposure in the morning with vitamin B12 (methylcobalamin). Methylcobalamin enhances the light sensitivity of the circadian clock at doses ranging from 1,000 to 6,000 mcg daily.

Melatonin is a hormone synthesized as the final metabolite by the tryptophan-serotonin pathway. The use of tryptophan or 5-HTP may eliminate the need for melatonin supplementation directly. It should always be used with caution, starting with a dose of 0.5 mg about 1 hour before bed and may be increased to 1 to 3 mg as needed. Some people do not respond to melatonin and others may experience side effects, such as feeling tired in the morning. Many people with PTSD have high blood pressure, and the alpha- and beta-blocking drugs used for hypertension often disrupt sleep by decreasing melatonin release (Stoschitzky et al., 1999). Since melatonin activates alpha and beta adrenoreceptors, care must be used to assess these drug interactions. For this reason, it is preferable to manage high blood pressure naturally, without medication, by using potassium, magnesium, taurine, CoQ10, garlic, hawthorn extract, and fish oil. This will also improve sleep (see Table 8.1).

The provision of psychobiological nourishment for the brain synergizes other therapies to aid in the restoration of sleep. For these individuals, rather than coffee and sugar throughout the day, it is preferable to provide adrenal support, extra protein, and a snack at bedtime that combines protein and car-bohydrates. For example, nut butter, cheese, or an egg and crackers will often help one to get through the night. Liquid amino acids also help to support sleep through the night. Upon awakening in the middle of the night, another dose of milk biopeptides can be administered. The principle of weaning off sleep medication is similar to that governing all other medications where the nutrient or herb will serve as a replacement. Begin with the replacement dosage while the medication in use is slowly decreased over a period of weeks to months. The more severe the imbalance, the longer one has experienced the illness, and the longer one has used medication are all factors to consider. For many, sleep patterns may never be completely "normal," but they will improve. As a

Table 8.1 Sleep Hygiene

Time Sequence	Activity
12–15 hours before sleep	Use of (blue) light between 6 AM and 11 AM
5–8 hours before sleep	Use CES unit for ± 30 minutes (no sooner than 5 hours before sleep)
1–2 hours before sleep	Use blue light–blocking glasses at night
45 minutes before sleep	Use milk-derived neuropeptides (150–450 mg)
	Take melatonin (0.5–1 mg)
	Use oral micronized bioidentical progesterone (50–150 mg) (women only)
	Take warm bath with magnesium sulfate (Epsom salts)
Just before bed	Take 150 mg calcium (if type 1 insomnia)
	Take 150 mg of magnesium (if type 2 insomnia)
	Have a small protein/carbohydrate (cheese and cracker, for example) snack before bed
	Use a totally dark room for sleeping
In bed	Turn on white noise machine
	Use binaural music or guided visualization using headphones
Middle-of-night awakening	Milk-derived neuropeptides (150 mg)
	Take small protein/carbohydrate snack

Source: Leslie Korn.

general rule one may take 3 months to make the transition from medication to nutrients/herbs and up to a year to regularize sleep patterns.

Myer's Cocktail

When people are very fatigued, ill, or unable to mobilize to undertake a nutritional program in the early stages of recovery, it can be helpful to obtain the (modified) "Myer's cocktail" by working with a functional medicine physician or nurse. The cocktail contains magnesium, calcium, vitamins B12, B6, and C; it is administered intravenously. People describe a very pleasant feeling as the magnesium courses though the body, bringing with it waves of warming relaxation. It has been found to be effective against migraines, fatigue (including chronic fatigue syndrome), fibromyalgia, and acute muscle spasm (Gaby, 2002; Massey, 2007). Receiving this mixture intravenously is an effective start to any recovery program to boost immunity, strength, and vitality.

PAIN

Chronic pain is often part of the PTSD/depression/anxiety/substance abuse/insomnia complex. There are many effective nutritional approaches to reduce inflammation systemically and locally and thus increase physical mobility and decrease depression and pain.

Nonsteroidal anti-inflammatory drugs like aspirin, ibuprofen, and naproxen are dangerous; they contribute to depression (Browning, 1996) and interfere with antidepressant efficacy (Warner-Schmidt, Vanover, Chen, Marshall, & Greengard, 2011), suggesting a negative relationship between SSRI efficacy and NSAID use. However, there are other dangers to NSAIDs (D'Arcy, 2011), including damage and erosion of joint cartilage and gut and kidney damage. Furthermore, NSAIDs do not address the cause of pain and inflammation. The natural approach presented below identifies methods that combine anti-inflammatories and analgesics. With so many alternatives, NSAID use should be discouraged except in an occasional emergency. What occurs in the body occurs in the brain; with inflammation there is depression. Reducing overall systemic inflammation as discussed earlier is the goal for improved mental health.

These methods provide the biochemical changes that can be further synergized with energy medicine and detoxification. I use a combination of approaches in addressing inflammation. Inflammation exists along a spectrum. Like the rust on a car, it often begins without being seen, and it does not always rise to symptom level. Indeed, using certain anti-inflammatories daily can prevent serious inflammatory processes from developing or symptoms from appearing. Cytokines block tryptophan conversion to serotonin and low serotonin is involved in increased sensitivity to pain. EFAs are powerful NF-kappa

B anti-inflammatories and low levels of EFAs make one vulnerable to pain (Singer et al., 2008).

An integrated approach to nutritional pain management includes the use of

- proteolytic enzymes
- amino acids to support analgesia neurotransmitters
- vitamin D3
- natural cyclooxygenase-II enzyme inhibitors (COX-2 inhibitors) and lipoxygenase (LOX-inhibitors)
- natural analgesic herbs
- balanced essential fatty acids

Indigenous peoples of Mexico traditionally slice an unripe papaya and place the papain oozing from the green skin on freshly slaughtered beef to tenderize it. Just as commonly, they apply the sticky white enzyme to infections of all kinds to reduce inflammation. All of these benefits derive from proteolytic enzymes that digest protein. Proteolytic enzymes are absorbed from the gastrointestinal tract and reduce inflammation, stimulate immune function, and scavenge cancer cells (Gonzalez & Issacs, 1999). Bromelain inhibits the cyclooxygenase enzyme and inhibits the synthesis of prostaglandin 2. It also breaks down fibrin and reduces swelling.

For the treatment of musculoskeletal pain, arthritis, autoimmune pain, and fibromyalgia, take a combination of bromelain/papain. The usual dosage is 500 mg on an empty stomach every 4 to 6 hours. There are also enzyme compounds that also include trypsin and alpha chymotrypsin, pancreatin, lipase, and amylase. Depending upon the level of inflammation and the dosage, people may take several capsules or tablets several times a day, always on an empty stomach. These enzymes should form the foundation of anti-inflammatory treatment; they have no negative side effects, though for some they may cause some gas initially. When used with food, they are digestive aids.

DL-phenylalanine (or tyrosine) can be added to a balanced free amino acid formula. DL-phenylalanine and tyrosine appear to stop the degradation of analgesic endorphins by the enzyme carboxypeptidase A (Christianson, Mangani, Shoham, & Lipscomb, 1989; Russell & McCarty, 2000). Oballe recommends 500 mg of DL-phenylalanine every 2 hours for acute pain or 1,000 mg three times a day (Eidenier, 2000).

Vitamin D Deficiency and Musculoskeletal Pain

Most people are deficient in vitamin D, a sufficient amount of which is essential for the treatment of pain and depression. Vitamin D receptors in the brain stimulate serotonin production (Holick, 2003). Plotnikoff and Quigley (2003) report that 100% of a multiethnic population with musculoskeletal pain in their Minnesota-based study had deficient levels of vitamin D. People living in the northern climes are most at risk due to reduced sun exposure, but even people who get sun exposure often wear sunscreen, which inhibits vitamin D production. The dermatologist Michael Holick (2003) suggests obtaining 5 to 15 minutes of midday sun exposure, stating that "There is little evidence that adequate sun exposure will substantially increase the risk of skin cancer; more specifically long-term excessive exposure and repeated sunburns are associated with non melanoma skin cancers." He recommends treating a vitamin D deficiency with an oral dose of 50,000 IU of vitamin D once a week for 8 weeks. Vasquez, Manso, and Cannell (2004) suggest 1,000 to 4,000 IU a day for the prevention of vitamin D deficiency and 4,000 IU a day for a minimum of 5 to 9 months for chronic pain. The emulsified liquid form of vitamin D is absorbed more easily, especially by older people, and comes in doses of 2,000 IU per drop, making it simple to ingest. A serum vitamin D (25-OH vitamin D) test should be performed annually, with the optimal range being from 40 to 65 ng/mL (100 to 160 nmol/L) (Vasquez et al., 2004).

FOOD

Trauma makes people more sensitive; the response to trauma can make one biologically hypervigilant, leading to an overactive immune system that scouts for danger everywhere, leading to allergies and autoimmune diseases. Sensitivity to foods and medications ensues, and the generally poor-quality diet that most Americans eat sets the stage for chronic food sensitivities and allergies.

The elimination diet is an effective and safe way to assess food intolerances. Eliminating a food or food family for 3 weeks while monitoring symptoms allows sufficient time to observe differences. If symptoms improve during this time, the food is reintroduced to see if it causes the symptoms to worsen. If symptoms improve when the food is eliminated and return when the food is reintroduced, the food should be excluded from the diet for at least 6 months. Strict adherence to the diet is necessary for accuracy and sufficient time for inflammation caused by the food to heal. Once an offending food is identified, it is often possible to eat it once in a while without symptoms, but only on special occasions, and this must be assessed individually.

Among the first foods to start eliminating are grains containing gluten (wheat, bulgur, barley, rye, couscous, kamut, semolina, spelt, triticale, and oats), cow's milk (milk and cheese products), and soy. The nightshade foods (potatoes, tomatoes, chilies, eggplant) can cause joint stiffness and arthritis; hence these foods are also worth eliminating for 4 weeks to see if joint stiffness improves. While soy has received a lot of positive press, significant research suggests that it is actually quite harmful and should be avoided (Daniel, 2005). Soy contains very high levels of phytic acid, which suppresses digestive enzymes; it also depresses thyroid function (Fallon & Enig, 1999) and is high in protease inhibitors, which suppress pancreatic enzymes. Soybeans also contain hemagglutinin, which causes red blood cells to clump. Soy should be avoided (Fallon & Enig, 1999) except in the form of fermented soy products such as miso, shoyu, and tempeh, and then only in very small quantities and on rare occasions.

SPECIAL FOODS

There are many wonderful and healthful foods to choose from that are pesticide-free in their natural state, diverse in color, and that provide ample protein, fats, and carbohydrates. Here are a few of my favorites and some unusual ones to try.

Chocolate

So revered was chocolate in ancient Mexico that it was called the food of the gods and served as currency throughout the ancient empires. Unlike today, when its bitterness is masked by sugar, chocolate was drunk ritually and without sweetener. Chocolate is rich in polyphenols, which likely accounts for its neuroprotective effects and for reducing the risk of cardiovascular disease and stroke among those who eat large quantities of it (Buitrago-Lopez et al., 2011). Epicatechin is a flavonol and an antioxidant found in cocoa, tea, and grapes. I recommend the preparation of chocolate without sugar; for example, a hot cocoa drink of pure cocoa using stevia or *agave miel* as a sweetener, neither of which raises blood sugar.

Green Juice

Juices or smoothies that include blue-green algae, wheat grass, or spirulina provide an abundance of peptides and chlorophyll. For those who may not juice, there are excellent sources of "green drinks" available.

Jamaica

Jamaica (Ha-my-ka) (*Hibiscus sabdariffa*), also known as roselle or red sorrel, is a fragrant dried flower available throughout the tropical world. It is believed to have been brought to the western hemisphere in the 1700s by African slaves, likely from Angola—hence the name Jamaica. The calyces of the Jamaica plant are used traditionally as a refreshing beverage called *flor de Jamaica*. It is a delicious and cost-effective source of vitamin C and antioxidants that is easily found in Mexican and Central American markets in the United States. It has high levels of anthocyanins, powerful antioxidants that scavenge inflammatory cell reactions in the body. Anthocyanins typically produce the rich red, blue, or purplish colors of berries and fruits. Jamaica is rich in calcium; it has hypotensive activity (lowers blood pressure) and has been found to be antispasmodic and antibacterial and also to promote weight loss (Alarcon-Aguilar et al., 2007). Drink one or two glasses daily, hot or cold.

Recipe: Boil water and add a handful of calyces. Reduce heat and gently simmer for 10 minutes until richly red. Strain and add a little honey or agave syrup (sweeten lightly and do not add sugar—sugar is a powerful inflammatory food that counteracts the effects of the natural antioxidants and also stimulates mucus production).

Root Vegetables

Roots and rhizomes provide a nutritious, inexpensive alternative to sweets, and they provide minerals that support the nervous system. Sweet potatoes, carrots, parsnips, and beets should be included in at least one serving in the daily diet.

Bitter Greens

Arugula, dandelion greens, purslane, kale, stinging nettle, collards, and plantain are all greens that have a bitter flavor. This bitterness stimulates digestion. The traditional use of "bitters" (alcoholic and nonalcoholic) is a worldwide practice to aid digestion after a meal. Fennel seeds taken after a meal (a common practice with Indian cuisine) stimulate digestion and reduce gas. Black pepper also reduces gas.

Seaweeds

Seaweeds are rich in iodine and other minerals and are thus among the best foods to support thyroid function. They are also rich in alginate, which eliminates toxic metals from the body. Seaweeds vary in taste, and the mildest forms like *hijiki* (*Sargassum fusiforme*) and *arame*, a kelp (*Eisenia bicyclis*) make tasty salads. Of course nori is a favorite wrapping for sushi rolls, and it makes a great snack by itself. Finally, many types of seaweed can be used in soups or with beans instead of salt.

WHEN COST IS A FACTOR

Limited financial resources often call for creative approaches to obtaining the necessary nutrients. This is especially true for financially deprived people, who often need pharmaceutical support but cannot afford commercially prepared medicines; often too, nutrients may not be approved in their pharmacy plans. Nutrients as seeds are generally more cost-effective than the extracted oils. For example flax seeds can be ground and added to food (do not heat). Chia seeds are a rich source of omega-3 and omega-6 essential fatty acids (about 60% of the seed). Chia seeds are not only beneficial for their EFAs but also contain a full complement of amino acids as well as a significant amount of digestible fiber.

It is important, however, to recognize that the beneficial use of some nutrients requires consuming significant amounts; while whole, nutrient-dense foods are an essential nutritional foundation, effective therapeutic value often requires daily doses consistent with the findings of empirical or scientific research. Magnesium is low cost and can be tried first for depression, sleep, and/or muscle pain. A nightly Epsom salt bath may be used in place of oral magnesium. One of the best sources of minerals and neurotransmitter precursors is a bone broth (see Online Resources for the recipe); the cheapest cut of meat is most often the best, and a slow simmer in a slow cooker including bones provides a very good source of amino acids, minerals, and fats. Buying high-quality nutrients in bulk via cooperative purchasing, or tribal clinic purchases reduces the cost, often by as much as 50%.

SUMMARY

The body is the palette of trauma and the palate is an essential route to recovery. Failure to address nutritional and dietary needs limits the potential for recovery. Culturally appropriate nutrition enhances and accelerates recovery; it sustains recovery and must be addressed concurrently with other forms of healing. People with poor nutrition will never recover fully from PTSD and may always be dependent upon pharmaceuticals unless the brain, the autonomic and central nervous systems, and the endocrine system receive specific and sustained nutrient-dense foods to aid in recovery. The challenge of eating well is a community issue, not just an individual or family problem. Traumatic stress is a mind/body/spirit disease and will respond best by addressing all those aspects of the self. Reducing stress and restoring psychobiological rhythm can be accomplished best with nutritional support. Researching one's cultural/genetic heritage as a foundation for nourishment, preparing a mixture of freshly cooked and raw foods, and supplementing with a range of herbs, glandulars, vitamins, and minerals will in most all cases be sufficient to support optimal health and thus avoid or eliminate pharmaceutical medications for the treatment of PTSD, depression, pain, insomnia, and anxiety.

9   Botanical Medicines

E hanai 'awa a ikaika ka makani./Feed with kava so that the spirit may gain strength.

—Hawaiian proverb

Botanical medicines for the treatment of traumatic stress nourish health by building strength and supporting the function of the hypothalamic-pituitary-adrenal (HPA) axis. Botanicals ease the response to stress, aide sleep, reduce anxiety and balance mood. Plant medicines may also support immune function for autoimmune and infectious diseases. Botanicals can be used to ease the pain of withdrawal from addictive substances and to provide health alternatives to altering consciousness. Plant medicines also aid digestion (from ingestion to excretion) and reduce neural pain; they are especially effective as natural anti-inflammatories.

In this chapter I shall discuss

- the use of psychoactive plants as alternatives to or adjuncts to conventional pharmaceuticals
- basic psychopharmacology of plants for PTSD
- selected botanical protocols for stress, anxiety, depression, pain, insomnia, and vitality

Botanicals complement dietary and nutritional supplementation and energy medicine to effect a change in biochemistry. Like nutrients, they may be used in combination with pharmaceuticals or to replace them. **A word of caution:** Botanical medicine must be used with the guidance of an expert on plants/nutrient/pharmaceutical interactions. There are excellent government and private institutional databases on interactions and contraindications that are updated yearly. Most of the problems with combining botanicals, nutrients, and pharmaceuticals derive from "too much or too little of a good thing"— overdosing, underdosing, or synergistic and compounded effects. Combinations might include, for example, taking a selective serotonin reuptake inhibitor

(SSRI), 5-hydroxytryptophan (5-HTP), and *Hypericum*, all of which increase availability of serotonin at the synapse leading to serotonin syndrome, which results from too much serotonin and can cause potentially lethal side effects. However, the use of nutrients and botanicals can reduce the dosage of the SSRI needed or make it more effective. These decisions are most safely made in collaboration with a knowledgeable individual who can guide the process.

Most plant medicines have gentle effects on human biology. Most pharmaceuticals are derived from a plant that nature has modeled for chemists. Herein is the value of plants: they contain combinations of compounds that are designed to work together in ways that many synthetic medicines cannot. Where one chemical is powerful and may cause side effects, another in the same plant provides the balance to cancel or minimize those effects. The effective use of plants requires the same or greater level of expertise as that of a conventional pharmacist. The plant medicines I discuss act synergistically to build health and sometimes alter consciousness. Plants are best used when combined as part of an overall program including nutrition. While you may use plants like substitutes for pills (for example, taking white willow bark for a headache instead of aspirin), most plants will deliver greater benefit when incorporated into the daily diet for extended periods of time. Because the body becomes inured to most substances, I suggest conducting a course of treatment for 3 months and then changing the plant or combination of plants in use. Nature is redundant; for every illness there are many botanicals to try. If one doesn't work, try another, or after using one for 3 months, use another. Clients' bodies differ in their response to plant medicine, so systematic uses of plant medicine can help find the appropriate type and dosage

The plants categories I explore here are *adapatogens, nervines, stimulants,* and *anti-inflammatory/analgesics.* Some special combinations, like polarity tea (see below), serve several purposes—HPA axis support, gastrointestinal health, and allergies. Many of the plants are psychoactive and alter consciousness, like plants described in Chapter 11. I have separated out the plants described here mainly because they are legally available and should be used daily or as needed in combination with the nutritional methods described in the previous chapter. This list is not exhaustive; these are some of the primary botanicals I depend upon in my work with clients. They are well tolerated and have demonstrated efficacy in indigenous traditions, clinical application, and biomedical research.

ADAPTOGENS

Adaptogens help one adapt to stress by restoring the capacity to cope and respond. These plants and their active extracts support adrenal function, build endurance, and reduce fatigue. By supporting adrenal function they also support immune function and resistance. Adaptogens help utilize oxygen and increase cellular respiration. Common adaptogens include Panax ginseng, Eleuthero (also known as Siberian ginseng), and ashwagandha, which has activity like that of gamma-aminobutyric acid (GABA) and has been used in Ayurvedic medicine for more than 2,500 years to enhance vitality and endurance. The three criteria of an adaptogen are that it (1) should be generally free of side effects; (2) be nonspecific—that it should increase resistance to a wide array of physical, chemical, and biological stressors; and finally (3) be able to normalize function and restore homeostatic balance (Brekhman & Dardymov, 1969).

Polarity Tea

Polarity tea is an adaptogenic Ayurvedic medicine containing one part licorice root (*Glycyrrhiza glabra*), one part fennel seed (*Foeniculum vulgare*), one part fenugreek seed (*Trigonella foenum-graecum*), and two parts flax seed (*Linum usitatissimum*). This tea is beneficial to reduce stress, fatigue, liver or gallbladder problems, and allergies; it is also soothing to respiratory and intestinal mucous membranes. It may produce slight laxative effects and is also a mild stimulant. Mix the dry ingredients together, add 1 teaspoon to water, and simmer for 20 minutes, then strain and drink hot or cold.

Licorice (*Glycyrrhiza* spp.) is one of the most important botanicals of both American Indian and Chinese traditional medicine. Of the four ingredients in polarity tea, it provides most of the adaptogenic qualities. The glycyrrhizic acid in licorice inhibits the breakdown of cortisol and increases the amount of cortisol production, making it useful in moderating adrenal fatigue and hypocortisolism. The root is rich in minerals including sodium, potassium, iron, and manganese (Watts, 1995). Licorice may be used in place of steroids and it also prolongs the half-life of steroids. It is also soothing to the mucous membranes of the lungs, making it useful for people who smoke or are quitting. Traditionally used in desert regions for its ability to help cells retain fluids, it is contraindicated for people with hypertension or edema and polarity tea use should be limited to two cups a day. Glycyrrhiza at high doses can result in side effects such as hypertension, edema, headache, and shortness of breath in about 20% of the population. The dose generally needed to cause these side effects is 10 to 14 g of crude plant, but this can vary dramatically from as little as 1 to 2 g in some individuals to as high as 30 g in others.

Fenugreek (*Trigonella foenum-graecum L.*) is from Asia and southern Europe. It is a demulcent, from the Latin word *demulcere*, meaning "to caress." It soothes digestion, reduces gas due to poor digestion, and reduces allergic reactions as it loosens mucus. The seeds contain small amounts of L-tryptophan. It also supports sugar metabolism, making it an effective tea for hypoglycemia.

Fennel (*Foeniculum vulgare*) is endemic to southern Europe. The seeds relieve anxiety-related digestive problems and the essential oil is useful in treating depressed mood. Fennel seed can also be incorporated into cooking or just chewed after eating. Flax is a natural anti-inflammatory and is soothing to digestion.

Flax (*Linum usitatissimum*) is also known as linseed. Its use dates to ancient Egypt. While flax seed oil is used commonly as a source of fatty acids, when used as a seed in a tea it provides mucilage and soothing properties, easing digestion and inflammation. Flax seed is inexpensive, and it is used like Chia seed and psyllium seed husk as a fiber bulking agent. Soak a tablespoon of seeds in 8 oz. of water; let the tea sit overnight and drink it in the morning before breakfast.

Rhodiola

Rhodiola (*Rhodiola rosea*) increases resistance to a variety of chemical, biological, and physical stressors. Rhodiola is a mild antidepressant (Darbinyan et al., 2007) and a stimulant useful for the treatment of anxiety (Bystritsky, Kerwin, & Feusner, 2008). Rhodiola is also an anti-inflammatory. In my experience rhodiola is a very gentle yet potent botanical, making it especially useful for someone who can use only one botanical or who has multiple chemical sensitivities. All of these actions make it an ideal botanical for the treatment of traumatic stress.

Rhodiola increases serotonin in the hypothalamus and midbrain (Brekhman & Dardymov, 1969) as well as opioid peptide levels (Kelly, 2001) and supports serotonin, dopamine, and norepinephrine action at the receptor sites (Hudson, 2011). It has also been shown to reduce adrenaline-induced arrhythmias in animals.

For fatigue associated with stress, a starting dose of 10 drops two or three times a day is gradually increased up to 30 to 40 drops for 1 to 2 months. (Brown, Gerbarg, & Ramazanov, 2002). For memory, concentration, and enhanced cognition, take 100 to 400 mg/day using a standardized extract containing at least 3% rosavin extract or tea from roots (Petkov et al., 1986).

No serious side effects have been reported (Darbinyan et al., 2007), but rhodiola can be stimulating, so it should be used earlier in the day. People who develop mania in response to antidepressants could respond similarly to high doses of rhodiola (Hudson, 2011). Some individuals, particularly those who tend to be anxious, may feel overly activated, jittery, or agitated. If this occurs, a smaller dose with very gradual increases may be needed.

Ashwagandha

Ashwagandha (*Withania somnifera*) has been called Indian ginseng and is considered the preeminent adaptogen from the Ayurvedic medical system used to treat chronic stress and fatigue. Ashwaganda means "the smell and strength of a horse," suggestive of its medicinal power. It contains withanolides, which have steroidal activity in the body. Human studies show that ashwagandha is superior to *Panax ginseng* in its ability to increase endurance and prevent adrenal exhaustion, ulcers, and vitamin C deficiency. Animal studies show that ashwagandha may improve memory (Dhuley, 2001), stabilize mood (Bhattacharya, Bhattacharya, Sairam, & Ghosal, 2000), improve stress toler-ance (Archana & Namasivayam, 1999), decrease anxiety, support the immune system, and prevent morphine dependence. Ashwagandha increases libido (Kuppurajan et al., 1980), reduces inflammation (Rätsch, 1998), and helps to normalize sleep. Ashwagandha is traditionally harvested only in the autumn and dried in the shade. I prefer the liquid extract to capsules, allowing titra-tion of dosages specific to the individual. No side effects have been reported (Rätsch, 1998).

Eleuthero

Eleuthero (*Eleutherococcus senticosus*) is particularly helpful as a support for HPA axis function. It provides a "bottom" where one has fallen, and thus builds basic vitality. Farnsworth, Kinghorn, Soejarto, and Waller (1985) reviewed the results of clinical trials of eleuthero on more than 2,100 healthy human subjects and the data confirmed adaptogenic effects including increased capacity to tol-erate physical and mental stress. It is important to obtain high-quality eleuthero extract; dosage can range from 1/2 to 1 teaspoon a day. There are no serious adverse effects related to the use of eleuthero (Robbers & Tyler, 1999), though frequent use may induce euphoria and sleeplessness (Rätsch, 1998).

NERVINES

Plants that function as nervines are defined by their action on the nervous sys-tem. They may relax and aid in sleep or reduce pain. They may, like chamo-mile, soften digestive distress or lift mood, like St. John's wort. Below are the nervines I find most beneficial and effective. The selection of herbs in this section will answer a range of needs of the nervous system.

Kava

Kava (*Piper methysticum*) is a South Pacific island plant of the pepper fam-ily (Piperaceae) used for both ceremony and medicine. Kava has many folk names, including *agona, ava-ava, kava-kava, kawa pepper, yagona*, and the name *awa* or *kava*, a Polynesian word meaning "bitter" (Rätsch, 1998). It is traditionally used for its relaxing effects, which co-occur with mental alertness.

Kava is one of the most effective botanical anxiolytics and it should be the first choice for people who would otherwise choose a benzodiazepine. Kava contains compounds called kavalactones, or kavapyrones, which are responsible for most of kava's pharmacological effects, including increased GABA transmission, central nervous system depression, and pooling of norepinephrine (Spinella, 2004). Like the benzodiazepines, kava acts on the amygdala reducing fear and anxiety. Kava is a muscle relaxant and improves cognitive performance (Spinella, 2004), and it reduces anxiety and depression associated with menopausal symptoms. Studies using kavapyrones with human subjects confirm that it improves sleep, reduces anxiety, and improves brain function (Rätsch, 1998).

Some individuals can make use of kava for sleep, but since it can also cause mental alertness, it is often contraindicated for this purpose. In working with clients I recommend kava during the day and "the three sisters" (described below) or milk biopeptides for sleep (unless they know that kava helps them sleep). Kava also works well together with St. John's wort for depression and anxiety. Kava is available in an alcohol-based extract or in capsules. The best-quality kava is grown in the islands of the South Pacific. Only the rhizomes and roots are used in the preparation. Doses range from 100 to 400 mg (of a 60% kavalactone capsule) three times daily. I start most people with one 200-mg capsule (60% kavalactone) and increase it to two, if necessary, up to three times daily. People who are sensitive or are shorter in stature may prefer using drops to measure the dose required for effect more specifically. Indigenous peoples of the South Pacific Islands have used kava in ritual for millennia with no apparent adverse reaction. Some deaths have occurred due to hepatic failure associated with combined high-dose kava and heavy alcohol consumption (Fu, Xia, Guo, Yu, & Chan, 2008) in Europe. The aqueous extract of kava has been found to be safe, without serious adverse effects and no clinical hepatotoxicity (Sarris et al., 2009). Kava is now sold with mandatory warnings in the United States and Europe about the potential risk of rare but severe liver injury. These reports have led to advisories that people with hepatic damage should avoid kava. Kava is also contraindicated in people taking benzodiazepines or antipsychotic drugs. It is also contraindicated in patients with Parkinson's disease. Kava should be discontinued at least 24 hours before surgery because of its possible interaction with anesthetics.

The Three Sisters: Hops, Valerian, and Passionflower

The first sister of three, hops (*Humulus lupulus*), is one of the two genera in the Cannabaceae family, along with marijuana (*Cannabis sativa*). Hops buds are used as a bitter in the brewing of beer, a bitter tonic medicine, and a sedative. Hops buds contain the resinous lupulin. They are rich in flavonoids and have been used as an antibiotic, antifungal, and antioxidant as well as a pain reliever. Hops is approved by the Complete German Commission E Monographs to treat anxiety, restlessness, and sleep disturbances (Blumenthal, 1998). Hops (and the B vitamins) found in a good quality dark beer make 4 to 6 ounces of beer an excellent quick remedy for muscle cramps, an anxiety or panic attack, or insomnia due to pain.

Hops and valerian are commonly combined for their beneficial, synergistic effect in the treatment of sleep disorders, acting in a way comparable to the efficacy of the benzodiazepines (Schmitz & Jackel, 1998). A valerian/hops extract was found to neutralize caffeine-induced arousal before sleep (Schellenberg, Sauer, Abourashed, Koetter, & Brattström, 2004).

Many people try using valerian without success; however, its effects are best potentiated by hops and passionflower (*Passiflora incarnata*), both of which also affect levels of gamma-aminobutyric acid (GABA). This three-herb combination reduces overall anxiety and can be used daily without side effects; however, it may not be sufficient for managing very high levels of anxiety or acute panic. For these cases, kava, one of the preeminent anxiolytics of the plant world, is usually more effective. The standard dosage for hops in capsule form is 500 mg one to three times a day (Bratmann & Girman, 2003). It is also available as a liquid extract. The use of hops in large amounts should be monitored for potential estrogenic effects; for the same reason, hops can be useful for menopausal symptoms associated with low estrogen.

Sister two is valerian (*Valeriana officinalis* L.), known for its sedative effects on the nervous system. Valerian is also called *hierba de los gatos* ("The cats' herb") in Mexico because cats react to it as they do to catnip in spite of its repugnant smell to most humans. Traditionally, valerian was an incense used in Europe to protect against evil (Rätsch, 1998). Valerian contains valerenic acid, which binds at the GABA-benzodiazepine receptors (Houghton, 1997). One study examined patients with insomnia who were successfully withdrawing from benzodiazepines by using valerian (Poyares, Guilleminault, Ohayon, & Tufik, 2002). Valerian effectively reduces anxiety and restlessness and promotes sleep (Donath et al., 2000; Muller, Pfeil, & von den Driesch, 2004). It has also been shown to be as effective as benzodiazepines in several studies (Schmitz & Jackel, 1998; Ziegler, Ploch, Miettinen-Baumann, & Collet, 2002). The use of valerian is contraindicated with the use of other central nervous system depressants, such as alcohol (Spinella, 2004).

Passionflower (*Passiflora incarnata* L., *P. coerulea*, and *P. edulis*), the third sister, is a tropical vine plant indigenous to Central and South America. It produces a delicious fruit rich in vitamin C. Passionflower was given its New World name by the Spanish after their arrival in Mexico in the 15th century. They likened the corona to the Christian crown of thorns, the five sepals, and five petals to the 10 apostles, and other parts to the nails and wounds of Christ. Apparently they also experienced at first hand its capacity to alleviate suffering. The leaves are traditionally used as a sedative and anxiolytic. Some species have entheogenic seeds. Studies demonstrate efficacy for generalized anxiety disorder (Spinella, 2004), for sleep, and for reducing anxiety without sedation prior to surgery (Movagegh, Alizadeh, Hajimohamadi, Esfehani, & Nejatfar, 2008.) *Passiflora incarnata* contains chrysin, a natural flavone that has anxiolytic effects equal to those of benzodiazepines (Brown, Hurd, McCall, & Ceremuga, 2007). Master herbalist Ed Smith recommends a combination of equal parts passionflower (*Passiflora incarnate* and *edulis*), valerian (*Valeriana officinalis*), hops (*Humulus lupulus*), chamomile (*Matricaria chamomilla*), and catnip (*Nepeta cataria*) as a sedative for the treatment of nervousness, depression, and insomnia (Smith, 2003).

Skullcap

Skullcap (*Scutellaria lateriflora*) is a member of the mint family (*Lamiaceae*). The name *skullcap* describes the shape of the calyx at the base of the flowers, which resembles a miniature medieval helmet. During the 19th century, the common name used in America was "mad dog" (Joshee, Patrick, Mentreddy, & Yadav, 2002), so named for its treatment of rabies due to "mad dog" bites.

Skullcap acts on benzodiazepine receptors (Medina et al., 1997). It is a gentle and effective anxiolytic and sedative and can be used over a long period of time without concern. It is anti-inflammatory, and it strengthens vitality. Skullcap is beneficial for insomnia, anxiety, and headaches. Skullcap should not be used during pregnancy.

St. John's Wort

St. John's wort (*Hypericum perforatum*) is a herbaceous plant with yellow flowers. It is the leading antidepressant used in Germany (Robbers & Tyler, 1999). The clinical indications for St. John's wort extract listed in the official German Commission E monograph include depression, fear, and nervousness.

A Cochrane Review of 29 studies in 5,489 patients with mild to moderate depression compared treatments of St. John's wort extract with placebo or standard antidepressants. Overall, studies show that St. John's wort extracts are superior to placebo and similarly effective as antidepressants, with fewer side effects (Kasper et al., 2008; Linde, Mulrow, Berner, & Egger, 2005). *Hypericum perforatum* extract at a higher dose (1.2 mL/200 g) but not at lower doses was significantly stronger than clonidine in curbing morphine withdrawal syndrome (Feily & Abbasi, 2009). St. John's wort can be effective during the acute treatment of mild depression. The available evidence suggests that St. John's wort is superior to placebo in patients with major depression, is similarly effective as standard antidepressants, and has fewer side effects than standard antidepressants (Linde, Berner, & Kriston, 2008). St. John's wort extract standardized to contain 0.125% hypericin is dosed at 300 mg three times daily. I prefer to combine St. John's wort with additional botanicals such as skullcap (*Scutellaria lateriflora*) and prickly ash bark (*Xanthoxylum clava-herculis*) (Smith, 2003).

St. John's wort can produce photosensitivity in humans at high dosages. Individuals taking larger amounts of St. John's wort extracts should avoid exposure to strong sunlight. St. John's wort can reduce blood levels of medications metabolized by the cytochrome p450 3A4 (CYP3A4) enzyme. In taking

St. John's wort, avoid foods and medications that are known to negatively interact with MAO-inhibiting drugs as well as cheeses, beer, wine, pickled herring, yeasts, and drugs such as L-dopa. St. John's wort should also be taken with food, as it may cause mild gastric upset in sensitive individuals.

Chamomile

Chamomile (*Matricaria recutita* and *Chamaemelum nobile*) has been used historically, and its flowers are usually made into a tea before bed or for an upset stomach. There is a European variety and a western hemisphere variety. It is called *té de manzanilla* (little apple) in Mexico and Central America because of its fragrance.

Matricaria recutita contains flavonoids and coumarins that act synergistically with the essential oil to produce anti-inflammatory effects (Rätsch, 1998). Flavonoids in chamomile demonstrate anxiolytic and mild sedative effects (Spinella, 2004).

Saffron

In an 8-week pilot double blind randomized trial, the efficacy of *Crocus sativus* was compared with fluoxetine in 40 adult outpatients suffering from depression. Patients were randomly assigned to receive 15 mg twice daily of *C. sativus* or 10 mg twice daily of fluoxetine. At the end of the trial, *C. sativus* was found to be as effective as fluoxetine in the treatment of mild to moderate depression (Akhondzadeh et al., 2007).

Lemon Balm

Studies conducted with lemon balm (*Melissa officinalis* L.) have shown that it promotes sleep and aromatherapy using lemon balm can be effective for dementia-related insomnia. Lemon balm's effects are enhanced when it is combined with valerian (Ulbricht et al., 2005).

STIMULANTS

Stimulants increase energy in the body while adaptogens enhance the endurance of the body (Blake, 2010). For example, coffee is a stimulant and *Eleutherococcus senticosus* is an adaptogen. Stimulants may be used short term for special effect, but over the long term they will lead to exhaustion without the nourishment provided by adaptogens.

Coffee

Coffee is perhaps the most commonly used legal stimulant. Its potent effects exacerbate anxiety in PTSD, but it also acts as an antidepressant. Coffee is a drug, not a beverage; thus it should be used as a therapy. Moderate consumption increases alertness, memory, mood, and physical performance, making it attractive to people with PTSD. However it also increases anxiety and insomnia, and over time one needs more and more to gain the same positive effects. Because of processing methods, espresso is a less anxiety-provoking source than is drip coffee, and espresso can be used to treat asthma. People with anxiety and insomnia should eliminate coffee (or replace it with water-processed decaffeinated coffee). I provide information on coffee detoxification in Chapter 10. Coffee exacerbates premenstrual syndrome (PMS); indeed the more caffeine a woman ingests, the more severe her PMS symptoms are likely to be (Weinberg & Bealer, 2002). Coffee is a diuretic; for every cup of coffee, one should drink two extra glasses of water daily to prevent dehydration.

When I conducted field-based interviews in the jungle of Mexico, a predominance of people complained of insomnia. As I explored the relationship of stress to insomnia and then insomnia to diet, I found that people were drinking cola beverages for breakfast and lunch and to quench thirst during the day; then they drank coffee with *pan dulce* (sweet bread) at night. This excessive use of bottled beverages and coffee is due in part to the historic prohibition against fresh water intake due to poor sanitation in rural areas. With the high rate of coffee consumption, people have become addicted to caffeine. None of the people I spoke with recognized the relationship between their caffeine intake and their insomnia. In the United States, heavily promoted caffeinated energy drinks, marketed especially to teens, are now considered to be a gateway drug to alcohol abuse (Ressig, Strain, & Griffiths, 2009). There are coffee substitutes made from various roasted grains and seeds. A coffee substitute called *Capomo,* also known as *Ramon,* is made from the breadnut (*Brosmium alicastrum*), indigenous to both coasts of Mexico (Korn, 2010), in Guatemala, and as far south as Colombia in South America. It is an important traditional food and beverage commonly used by peoples throughout the east and west coasts of Mexico and is currently being revitalized as part of community healing and reforestation and nutrition strategies. *Café de capomo* is rich in B vitamins (particularly B6), calcium, vitamin C, and trace minerals; it is so rich in amino acids and folate that it lifts the mood and stimulates breast milk in nursing mothers.

Green Tea

Theanine (glutamic acid gamma-ethylamide) is an amino acid uniquely found in tea (*Camellia sinensis*). Green tea is a traditional beverage in Asian societies and is known for its calming effects. Human studies have demonstrated that dietary theanine supplementation increases alpha wave activity (Yokogoshi, et al., 1998) and thus fosters a state of alert relaxation. Theanine stimulates GABA and serotonin production and offsets the stimulation of caffeine in green tea, thus serving as a relaxing anti-inflammatory beverage.

Theanine is often combined in supplements with 5-HTP for the treatment of depression and anxiety. It crosses the blood-brain barrier and has been shown in studies to increase levels of serotonin and dopamine in the brain. Theanine is a glutamate antagonist and suppresses glucocorticoids, which may account for its action as an antidepressant (Paul & Skolnick, 2003).

Green tea is also a powerful antioxidant and is associated with longevity. L-theanine and caffeine in combination appear to significantly improve aspects of memory and attention much more than caffeine alone (Owen, Parnell, De Bruin, & Rycroft, 2008).

Gotu Kola

Gotu kola (*Centella asiatica*), also known as pennywort, is a traditional Ayurvedic and Chinese botanical used as a revitalizing tonic and to treat depression and anxiety. A double-blind, placebo-controlled study of the effects of gotu kola demonstrated a reduction in the acoustic startle response (ASR) (Bradwejn, Zhou, Koszycki, & Shlik, 2000; Wattanathorn et al., 2008), suggesting anxiolytic effects for people with PTSD. Studies demonstrate that high doses of the extract improve working memory and elevate mood (Wattanathorn et al., 2008). Its use is contraindicated in pregnancy.

ANTI-INFLAMMATORY/ANALGESIC HERBAL MEDICINE

Chinese skullcap (*Scutellaria baicalensis*) is a member of the Lamiaceae (mint) family and native to China. This plant contains antioxidants known as flavones—in particular baicalin and baicalein. Combined, the extracts of flavonoids from *Scutellaria baicalensis* and *Acacia catechu* inhibit both of the two pro-inflammatory COX and LOX enzymes to reduce the production of pro-inflammatory eicosanoids (Burnett, Jia, Zhao, & Levy, 2007). *Scutellaria baicalensis* also promotes normal cellular growth (Chi, Lim, Park, & Kim, 2003; Shen, Chiou, Chou, & Chen, 2003). Combined in capsule form, they are effective for pain.

Ginger and turmeric are also COX and LOX inhibitors. They are cost-effective medicinal rhizomes that can easily be integrated into daily tea or food or taken in capsules. Ginger root is especially effective for joint and muscle pain, in part due to *gingerols* (relatives to capsaicin and piperine found in chilies and black peppercorns), which inhibit the COX and LOX inflammatory enzymes. Both of these rhizomes are available in liquid extracts or capsules. A large double-blind study demonstrated that *curcumin* was as effective as the powerful anti-inflammatory drug phenylbutazone in reducing pain, swelling, and stiffness in rheumatoid arthritis patients (Meschino, 2001).

Turmeric is a rhizome that is sold in powdered form and as a fresh root. Both forms can be used for cooking or making a tea. Some people may choose to use capsules or a compounded extract. One way to benefit from the synergistic effects of turmeric and ginger is to obtain both fresh roots (generally found at Indian, Asian, or health food stores) and cut up about 2 inches of each and boil in water for 15 minutes until it's a nice bright orange. Drink 2 cups a day. Piperine, found in black pepper, is required for the optimal absorption of curcumin, and it is often added to curcumin products (Aggarwal et al., 2007) or used in cooking for this reason. In a study of 1,000 elderly Asian subjects, those who consumed curry had significantly better scores on their mini mental status exam than those who never consumed curry (Ng et al., 2006). Cooking with herbs and spices, especially fresh ginger, turmeric, and rosemary, is stimulating to the mood and also anti-inflammatory; but cooking with these herbs alone is not enough. A pharmaceutical-quality dose of these plants is required.

The combination of white willow bark (*Salix alba*), devil's claw root (*Harpagophytum procumbent*), and *Boswellia serrata* provides an effective analgesic. *Boswellia serrata* is a traditional Ayurvedic anti-inflammatory for the treatment of arthritis. It is both anti-inflammatory and analgesic and inhibits the 5-lipoxygenase enzyme in white blood cells (Meschino, 2001). Devil's claw root is also anti-inflammatory, and white willow bark extract contains salicin, which is effective in the treatment of arthritis, back pain, and other joint inflammatory conditions (Meschino, 2001). People who are sensitive to salicylates and should avoid willow bark.

Topical application of capsaicin is very helpful for localized muscular, joint, or scar pain. Capsaicin is the active component of cayenne pepper (*Capsicum frutescens*); it stimulates and then blocks pain. One can obtain a specially compounded gel at a compounding pharmacy.

DIMETHYL SULFOXIDE

Dimethyl sulfoxide (DMSO) is a slight departure from the discussion of plant substances; however, its importance and utility warrant inclusion here. It is a sulfur compound that is a by-product of pulp generated by the tree harvesting industry. It is used topically and intravenously as an anti-inflammatory and analgesic for chronic pain, fibromyalgia, and TBI. It is a powerful membrane penetrant (Jacob & de la Torre, 2009). It is approved by the U.S. Food and Drug Administration for the treatment of bladder pain syndrome. Pharmaceutical-grade DMSO is available for purchase and should be used under the guidance of a practitioner.

HERB-NUTRIENT-DRUG INTERACTIONS

Herb–nutrient–drug interactions often have a synergistic or antagonistic effect. In working with a client or as part of a health care team, it is important that a comprehensive list be compiled for all herbs, nutrients, and drugs being considered and that an analysis of their interactions be conducted. The list should include the types of herbs, nutrients and drugs, their contraindications, and their dosage amounts and frequency. Among the best resources for assessing these interactions is the *PDR for Herbal Medicines*; The Natural Medicines Comprehensive Database; *Herb, Nutrient, and Drug Interactions: Clinical Implications and Therapeutic Strategies* (Stargrove, Treasure, & McKee, 2007; also available as a web guide at http://medicineworks.com/); and a database called the "Interactions Guide," which is a professional resource that looks at the interactions between prescription drugs, herbs, and nutrients. Some of the literature suggests certain interactions that are very rare. For example, there is the suggestion not to combine SSRIs with serotonergic precursors, such as St. John's wort, 5-HTP, or tryptophan out of concern for serotonin syndrome. Yet the use of botanicals or nutrients can decrease the amount of SSRI required and help to withdraw from it. Nevertheless the warning is not to do it alone but with the supervision of someone with a comprehensive understanding of herbal, nutrient, and drug interactions. Such individuals may include herbalists, naturopaths, Chinese herbalists, or traditional herbalists and healers.

SUMMARY

Botanicals are among nature's most important medicines. They may be used alone or in combination, orally or topically to effect changes in physical, mental, and emotional well-being. Plants contain compounds in combinations that are often protective against side effects. Most synthetic pharmaceuticals is an analogue to a plant that exists in nature. Understanding the appropriate harvesting methods, dosages, and delivery systems required for efficacy, along with the potential for side effects, ensures effective application in the treatment of PTSD and the symptoms of depression, fatigue, anxiety, insomnia, inflammation, and pain.

10 Detoxification

Detoxification is a process that occurs at the physical, emotional, mental, and spiritual levels. Cleansing, or purification, transforms the body and spirit and eliminates waste (toxins that impair physical organ function and thus affect mental well-being and cognitive function). Trauma is toxic to the whole person; when fully understood, a toxin goes beyond the metaphor used about "toxic relationships." Stress creates inflammation and metabolic by-products. Many people are exposed to chemical and biological toxins while being traumatized. War, natural disasters, genocide, or the consumption of substances such as alcohol and sugar are all toxic, and these toxins affect brain function. Furthermore, poor nutrition contributes to the buildup of toxins in the body as a natural by-product of daily life, suggesting that everyone can benefit from engaging in detoxification strategies and the activities that support detoxification.

In this chapter I shall discuss

- the role of detoxification in recovery
- the science of detoxification (and the two phases of detoxification in the body)
- detoxification strategies for addictive substances
- specific protocols for restoring brain and digestive function
- indications and contraindications for detoxification methods

Detoxification as a regimen is an essential part of a prevention and treatment program for PTSD and related sequelae. Every culture includes a variety of detoxification methods in its traditional medicine repertoire. Many different indigenous societies use alterative (blood-purifying) plants like burdock, which is also eaten as a vegetable; bitter plants such as dandelion (Asia, Europe, North America, and elsewhere); bitterroot (*Lewisia rediviva*) and its relatives, prized plants among indigenous communities of the plains and the Pacific Northwest; and purslane (*Portulaca oleracea*), the prized *verdolaga* of Mexico, indigenous neighbors, and peoples throughout Europe, Asia, and the Americas. Japanese people use charcoal made from bamboo to purify spaces, and activated charcoal remains the treatment par excellence for accidental poisoning (to be used only under professional guidance). Fibers and barks are also used to absorb and eliminate toxins, and they soothe the sensitive lining of the stomach and intestines. Some, like slippery elm bark (*Ulmas rubra*), are also nutritious. Purge-and-cleanse systems traditionally include the use of clays, plant and animal-derived oils, sweat lodges and saunas, water therapies, induced regurgitation, and enemas that detoxify the body and reestablish metabolic balance.

Detoxification is associated across all cultures with health and spiritual practices. The ancient use of sweats, enemas, and cleansing teas is found throughout the world's cultures. Leeches, segmented worms belonging to the phylum *Annelida*, were used throughout Europe and the Middle East to suck blood impurities and quicken tissue healing. Today surgeons use medical leeches for the same purposes. The use of detoxification techniques for the body is also linked to spiritual purification by religions and cultures, often through ascetic practices such as fasting or limiting the intakes of certain foods. The drinking of urine among the Buddhists, Jains, and early Christians is associated with both health and purification; yoga devotees drink the first urine of the morning (*amaroli*) to enhance meditation. Urine is rich in melatonin and amino acids thought to enhance the circadian rhythm and slow brainwave activity (Mills & Faunce, 1991). Still others prefer carrot juice in the morning, a rich source of carotenoids to cleanse the liver and support immune health. It is common for traumatized people who recover from substance abuse to embark on highly restrictive, often ascetic activities as a way to gain control over their behavior. This may or may not coincide with strict ideological or religious pursuits. Exploring the meaning of behaviors as they relate to a client's belief system is important when discussion options for self-care and detoxification.

In exploring detoxification methods, it may be useful for an individual to identify practices that are rooted in his or her own cultural traditions or religious beliefs. All traditional practices evolve and adapt to the needs of the communities. Many cultural practices are being revitalized for both spiritual and "community" detoxification. Many tribal communities of the Pacific Northwest are restoring traditional practices such as the canoe journey as a ritual that is linked to getting sober and staying sober. The power of the group reinforces the behavior of the individual; in addition, culture-specific attention to the higher purpose or higher power also enables sobriety. The traditional walkabout among indigenous communities of Australia and Papua New Guinea has been reintroduced as a culturally appropriate detoxification method. Wilderness programs, outdoor therapies, and vision quests all provide age-appropriate programs that especially appeal to teens. These programs provide an opportunity to move the body (releasing anxiety-producing lactic acid), withdraw from addictive technologies, and restore rhythms within a community that is sharing both hardships and triumphs. Many of these programs are accredited by the Joint Commission on Accreditation of Healthcare Organizations and provide a modern reenactment of ancient rituals that incorporate detoxification.

Whether one is detoxifying from pharmaceuticals and substances or undertaking detoxification strategies to enhance health, the process is similar. There are two interrelated processes in detoxification. The first is to eliminate and reduce exposure to harmful or toxic substances in food or the environment. The second is to actively engage in specific detoxification activities that support excretion of waste though the many organs of the body. I discussed the elimination of toxic foods in the chapter on nutrition. Eliminating exposure to toxins includes identifying toxic household cleaners or materials in mattresses and carpets that are neurotoxic. By reducing exposure to external (exogenous) toxic foods and substances like pesticides and toxic cleaners, the burden on the liver is reduced and it can function more effectively. The liver and skin are the body's major organs of detoxification. Symptoms of liver and gallbladder congestion include nausea, morning headaches, bloodshot eyes, skin problems, constipation, light-colored or poorly formed stools, and pain in the upper shoulders or under the rib cage. Skin that cannot eliminate waste as fast as it flows may appear dull with boils and infections. Finally, pharmaceuticals have toxic effects on the body. When an individual wants to eliminate their use, detoxification strategies (including a schedule) ease the process and enhance success.

Specific detoxification methods, both internal and external, improve the body's capacity to eliminate toxins. Both activities—reduction of exposure and active methods to stimulate elimination of both endogenous and exogenous toxins—are central to success.

The liver is the human body's largest organ and a primary organ of detoxification. The liver is the center for detoxification in the body and undergoes two interrelated processes, phase 1 and phase 2 detoxification. During phase 1 the liver converts fat-soluble toxins into water-soluble compounds by activating the cytochrome P-450 enzymes. These enzymes attach to toxins and prepare them for phase 2 detoxification, where they are directly excreted by the kidneys and into the duodenum.

Foods are important as both a source of toxins and as supports for their elimination. The cruciferous vegetables—like cabbage, broccoli, and Brussels sprouts—enhance P-450 enzymes, and sulfur-containing onions and garlic, both raw and cooked, are most beneficial when used daily. Seaweeds are a significant detoxifying food (particularly kelp) because they bind toxins in the intestinal tract. Adding seaweed to soups or bean dishes or as a snack is healthy for the thyroid. Alginates from the brown seaweeds bind toxic metals and radioactive isotopes in the digestive tract (Eliaz, Weil, & Wilk, 2007); capsules combining sodium alginate from brown seaweeds and modified citrus pectin can be used every 3 months to reduce heavy metals.

Bread and other yeast-based products can cause toxicity, especially for those sensitive to alcohol. Yeast ferments sugar into alcohol and endogenous alcohol production is elevated after eating foods rich in carbohydrates (Logan & Jones, 2000). Yeast converts the alcohol (ethanol) into acetaldehyde (Nosova, Jousimies-Somer, Jokelainen, Heine, & Salaspuro, 2000), thus changing the levels of gut flora (James, 2006) and leading to chronic candidiasis. The acet-aldehyde toxins can also cause leaky gut (Nosova et al., 2000), which is impli-cated in allergies and autoimmune illnesses.

I encourage all my clients to use detoxification methods for prevention and treatment. The ideal way to approach detoxification is to incorporate daily strategies for detoxification as well as special periods of time for detoxifica-tion, preferably in a safe environment away from daily stressors. Like any treatment, detoxification must be applied appropriately or it can exacerbate problems. Water fasts or citrus juice fasts, for example, are contraindicated in diabetes or anxiety. Indeed, there are many options preferable to water fast-ing such as using fresh vegetable or fruit juices. Carrots, apples, and beets as fresh juices are high in sugar, but together they make a great cleanser for the gallbladder and liver and it is a vitamin-rich drink. Proportions can vary, but I suggest a juice made with approximately 50% carrots, 35% apples, and 15% beets. You can also add celery or parsley, which are excellent as natural diuretics, and cilantro (Chinese parsley) removes heavy metals.

When all members of the family or a close group of friends practice detoxi-fication together, this provides support. It is easiest to first read all the detoxifi-cation strategies and to begin by doing the simple ones or choosing those that you require first.

In addition to starting new behaviors, review the possible sources of exter-nal toxins in your home. Many of these toxins burden the liver and colon. By reducing exposure, you reduce the quantity of waste or toxins that the liver must process.

Many cultures go through rituals to purify living quarters both for envi-ronmental and spiritual purposes. For example, many tribal peoples use the burning of dried sage, also called smudging, to purify the individual and also areas of the home. The use of aromatherapy is a simple and mild approach to improving well-being. In my experience it is an adjunct and serves as one aspect of many approaches to restoring sensory pleasure in people for whom PTSD has decreased the capacity for pleasure.

Essential oils provide therapy via smell, affecting mood, physiology, and behavior (Herz, 2009). Oil of lavender is mildly anxiolytic (Bradley, Brown, Chu, & Lea, 2009). One meta-analysis found that aromatherapy had a mild anxiolytic effect (Cooke & Ernst, 2000). Evidence suggests that oil of laven-der can be useful for helping people with PTSD reduce anxiety and achieve sleep (Cavanagh & Wilkinson, 2002). It is widely used in Germany for the treatment of insomnia. Peppermint has been shown to increase alertness, and ylang-ylang significantly increases calmness (Moss, Hewitt, Moss, & Wesnes, 2008).

The choice of cleansing agents is important so that they don't add to the burden of liver detoxification; it is also part of the ritual process of restor-ing order to a sanctuary in the course of recovery. Allergens and toxins in the home also contribute to the ongoing challenge to the immune system at a time when stress has already diminished its capacity. Mattresses and carpets contain neurotoxins. Look underneath the sink for toxic cleaning supplies and drain cleaners and throw them out. Apple cider vinegar—a powerful antibacterial, antimold, and antifungal cleanser—can address most cleaning needs, and an essential oil can be added to it to enhance the environment. This mixture can be used to clean dishes, counters, floors, toilets, and tubs. Add this to baking soda and salt to make a paste for scrubbing.

Microwaves alter the molecular structure of food and hence its nutritional benefits; therefore microwave ovens should never be used to prepare food. However, the "lazy Susan" plates inside many are ideal for the storage of spice and herb bottles. Similarly numerous artificial compounds are added to foods as preservatives. Artificial sweeteners, dyes, and generally foods that have long shelf lives should be avoided, as should most foods found on supermarket shelves. Many food cooperatives conduct free classes on reading and understanding food labels.

PHARMACEUTICAL WITHDRAWAL

People may choose to detoxify from a variety of substances: selective serotonin reuptake inhibitors (SSRIs), medications for attention deficit disorder (ADD), benzodiazepines, nicotine, coffee, and sugar. Generally the first thing to eliminate is the most harmful pharmaceutical or drug. The principles reviewed below can be adapted to any substance, but the regimen should also be tailored to individual needs. Where one cannot afford to go to a "spa" or detoxification center, one can create a "spa detox" program at home or in a group home with the help of friends and family.

Reducing and eliminating the use of SSRIs requires patience while digestive and brain changes take effect. Everyone will respond individually. However, as a general rule, it is wise to allow 3 to 6 months to withdraw, for it often requires that long for withdrawal to occur. Coming off fluoxetine, for example is managed best by ensuring that all the support therapies are in place. Where available, use liquid preparations (available for both fluoxetine and paroxetine), which allows for reducing the dosage by milligrams (Ashton & Young, 1999). Ashton and Young (1999) describe the "SSRI withdrawal (discontinuation) syndrome," where symptoms appear 1 to 10 days after stopping the medication. Often people ascribe their symptoms to their depression instead of withdrawal. A sufficient detoxification period is required before baseline status is again assessed. Because the neurons have been bathed in excess neurotransmitters, they are now in a kind of "lazy shock" and will take a while to respond. This is the value of nutrition, amino acid therapy, cranial electrical stimulation (CES), acupuncture, massage, exercise, and all of the things that nudge those neurons awake. Reducing stress and having the time and space for detoxification will also help. Using steam baths and saunas, sweats, Korean-style body scrubs, and mineral baths rich in lithium all contribute to the process.

Nutritional strategies to aid in detoxifying include the use of free amino acids combined with 6,000 mg of fish oil (DHA/EPA) and 5-hydroxytryptophan (5-HTP) (25 mg). These should be started 2 weeks before eliminating the SSRI. During the process of reducing the SSRI, the dosage of 5-HTP may be increased, but only under a practitioner's guidance. SSRIs increase blood alkalinity, which exacerbates anxiety and depression (N. Gonzalez, personal communication, June 23, 2002), so this is a good time for eating meat and vinegar-rich foods that help to acidify to body. Products that combine L-5-hydroxytryptophan and cofactors like vitamin B6, niacin, and L-theanine provide effective neuronal support.

NICOTINE WITHDRAWAL

Cigarette smoking has a bidirectional effect in PTSD; PTSD is a risk factor for smoking and smoking is a risk factor for depression and anxiety (Jamal, Does, Penninx, & Cuijpers, 2011). People with PTSD smoke at high rates as a form of self-medication, most likely because it is a euphoriant; it increases cognitive function, it (can appear to) reduce anxiety, and possibly can help to extinguish traumatic memories. However, nicotine has a paradoxical effect depending upon when it is administered: it can either extinguish or strengthen fear memories (Elias, Gulick, Wilkinson, & Gould, 2010). Nicotine can suppress the symptoms of depression and thus cessation can trigger depression.

Approximately 21% of the general U.S. population smoke, but rates of smokers among people with PTSD rise to over 45%. American Indians and African Americans comprise the highest percentage of smokers at 32.8% and 19.1%, respectively, followed by Whites at 17.4%, Hispanics at 14.1%, and Asian/Pacific Islanders at 8.1%.

Nicotine is one of the most difficult drugs to withdraw from, but the process is made easier by using an integrative approach. Among many American Indians, smoking and cessation strategies are culturally linked to sacred uses of tobacco. Understanding the ritual use of tobacco can inform clinical approaches to cessation, especially with American Indian clients. Sacred tobacco is ceremonial tobacco, used in prayer and as offerings; it is central to the spiritual practice of many Indians. In Indian country, the use of sacred tobacco is differentiated from nonsacred, addictive tobacco use. The restoration of ritual using sacred tobacco can be an integral part of cessation methods.

Understanding the role and rituals of tobacco use can enhance the methods used to withdraw, detoxify and eliminate, reduce, or replace nicotine. This protocol is a template that can be used as an approach for withdrawal from any substance.

Withdrawal from nicotine generally begins within 30 minutes of smoking the last cigarette; consequent physical symptoms peak within 3 days and last for at least 4 weeks. An integrative approach includes activities that address physical, mental, emotional, and spiritual needs.

- Preparation begins with diet and balancing blood sugar and oral needs by eating a high-protein meal every 3 to 4 hours. Especially useful are choline-rich foods such as eggs, liver, and fish.
- Sucking on a licorice root stick between meals, when necessary, may be helpful.
- The National Acupuncture Detoxification Association (NADA) acupuncture or acupressure detoxification protocol may be used.
- A CES unit may be used as often as needed throughout the day.
- Binaural beat music technology may also be helpful. Hemi-Sync has created a "Freedom from Smoking" recording that combines both verbal and binaural beat cues that synchronize brain hemispheres.

Botanicals reduce physical and emotional stressors of withdrawal. One of the most important is *Lobelia inflata* L. (Campanulaceae), also known as Indian tobacco or pukeweed. It is native to North America and has traditionally been used to treat upper respiratory conditions such as asthma, coughs, and bronchitis. It contains α-lobeline, an alkaloid that functions as a tobacco substitute because it acts as an antagonist at nicotinic receptors in the brain (Rätsch, 1998). Lobelia is a sedative and a stimulant with psychoactive properties and is often combined with nicotine withdrawal herbal compounds.

Licorice root stick (not the candy, the actual plant root) makes an effective cigarette replacement that can be sucked on for the first 4 weeks. Teas or extracts that combine oat "milky" seed (*Avena sativa*), skullcap (*Scutellaria lateriflora*), St. John's wort (*Hypericum perforatum*), celery (*Apium graveolens*), and lavender (*Lavandula vera*) are also helpful (Smith, 2003) in relaxing the nervous system, easing withdrawal, and boosting mood. Lobelia, licorice root, passionflower extract, and kava also help with anxiety and withdrawal cravings. Vitamins and minerals facilitate detoxification, provide nervous system and blood sugar balance, and help to reduce anxiety. Vitamin B complex, rich in thiamine, supports the nervous system. Two weeks before the quit date and for at least 2 months following, tyrosine may be used (500 mg twice a day building up to 2,000 mg). Taurine has been shown to reverse lung damage and supports cardiovascular health; it can be used following withdrawal. Using adrenal, pituitary, hypothalamus, and lung glandulars will support the function of the HPA axis and reduce stress, cravings, and withdrawal symptoms while also supporting the restoration of lung tissue.

PHYSICAL EXERCISE

Walking and/or climbing or swimming to the point of breathing heavily helps to manage anxiety, decrease dissociation, and satisfy the urge to inhale. Heavy breathing mimics the sensation of inhaling smoke. Sweat in a sauna, steam bath, or ritual group sweat. Place ice packs on the spine between the shoulders to reduce depression and increase lung function.

EXERCISE 10.1: BREATHING EXERCISES: LONG SLOW BREATH AND BREATH OF FIRE (ONLINE EXERCISES)

Two breathing exercises in particular are helpful during and following the withdrawal process. Learn these exercises ahead of time so they may be used upon quitting. These exercises facilitate the changes that occur in inhalation and exhalation associated with smoking and also help restore oxygen to the blood and brain. They are called Long Slow Breath and Breath of Fire. Breath of Fire is part of the Kundalini yoga tradition and is also called Kapalabhati, (Shannahoff-Khalsa, 2006), which means, "skull lightening," presumably because it enhances awareness but also perhaps because it lightens or "loosens the lid." This particular breathing exercise can be used for a minute when one is feeling the urge to smoke. It is energizing and decreases cravings.

ALCOHOL RECOVERY

When people are in recovery from alcohol abuse, they often turn to sugar (after all, alcohol is sugar), carbohydrates, and coffee as part of the withdrawal and maintenance process. However, this practice also taxes the liver considerably and makes one vulnerable to diabetes. Thus alcohol addiction may also be understood as a physiological addiction to sugar. Stress contributes to anxiety and depression and leads to self-medication with drugs, alcohol, and carbohydrates.

STARCHY CARBOHYDRATES AND SUGAR DETOXIFICATION

Carbohydrate addiction is similar to sugar addiction. Dopamine deficiencies are associated with all of the addictions; thus using the amino acid precursors to dopamine—tryptophan and phenylalanine—can be useful. Carbohydrate addiction is highly associated with bulimia and depression. It is likely that much of carbohydrate addiction is either a sugar or gluten addiction; sometimes it can be both. One tends to crave foods to which one is addicted.

The easiest way to withdraw from gluten is to follow a 7-day high-protein diet. Generally the physiological craving for gluten and carbohydrates has diminished significantly after 7 days, but the diet can be continued longer if necessary. A modification of this diet is to incorporate root vegetables such as sweet potatoes, yucca (manioc or cassava), parsnips, carrots, and squash, because these satisfy the need for fiber and for something sweet; unlike other sweets, they raise the blood sugar level slowly and are very nourishing. Sometimes people who are addicted to carbohydrates like the sensation of fullness that these foods bring. This can be replicated not only with root vegetables but also by taking some fiber—for example, a gluten-free source such as psyllium.

There are many gluten-free substitutes using flours such as rice, potato, and tapioca. Because gluten sensitivity is often tied to glucose dysregulation and thus mood lability, it is very effective to eat a hypoglycemic type of diet, ensuring the intake of proteins every 3 to 4 hours. This will generally stabilize mood. It's very helpful during this time, once the client is through the first initial 3 days of withdrawal, to keep a food diary. It takes 3 months, in general, for the intestinal inflammation associated with gluten sensitivity to heal. However, changes in mood, a reduction in joint stiffness, and the lifting of depression will begin sooner. Some argue that oats are not problematic; however, this is controversial. If you are strict about no gluten, make sure you obtain gluten-free oats ground on gluten-free machinery. In severe cases of sensitivity, it's always wise to eliminate all gluten products. In mild cases of carbohydrate addiction, it is possible to reintegrate the use of carbohydrates with gluten on some special occasions without adverse effects. However, as in the case of alcohol addiction, some people do better than others with total abstinence. Total abstinence is better for some, and others appear to manage limited quantities. Often, because carbohydrates and low hydrochloric acid levels are associated with gastroesophageal reflux disease and larygopharyngeal reflux, the elimination of carbohydrates also eliminates or reduces this disease process.

Because glutinous carbohydrates are comfort foods, applying the principle of substituting a less addictive substance for another could be used here—for example, making a non-sugar-based cup of hot cocoa or chocolate. A cup of hot chocolate made with pure dark cocoa to which a natural sweetener such as stevia has been added (use no sugar) can help one through tough times and will raise energy levels and endorphins. The point of any detoxification program is that the client can get through the initial symptoms of withdrawal and then maintain the behaviors consistently, reducing relapse recurrence and ensuring return to healthy behaviors (see Online Exercise 10.2).

COFFEE

Coffee is a drug, not a beverage. Thus it should be used like a drug, sparingly and only for specific purposes. Like many drugs, its beneficial effects can wear off, and prolonged use can cause serious side effects like anxiety, insomnia, and exhaustion. Coffee also enhances mood, stimulates alertness, and improves mental performance. However, it contains hundreds of chemicals, including the powerful and well-known caffeine, an addictive chemical that is known to cause a number of negative health effects. Coffee should therefore be used in moderation if at all. Not only does the coffee bean itself contain naturally occurring chemicals but nonorganic coffee may contain pesticides, herbicides, and other chemicals that can harm your body as well as the environment and the communities where the coffee is grown. Decaffeinated coffee, although nearly caffeine-free, still contains the naturally occurring chemicals as well as harmful chemicals such as methylene chloride used in the decaffeination process. Although there are some proven health benefits to drinking organic coffee, it should be consumed in moderation owing to its addictive qualities and potential for negative effects on health. People with diabetes often use caffeine to combat fatigue. However, over time, coffee taxes the adrenal glands and contributes to adrenal fatigue, a factor in the development of diabetes.

The process of eliminating coffee can be physically accomplished in 4 weeks. Starting with week one, substitute two cups a day with organic de-caffeinated coffee; week two, switch to two cups of organic black tea; week three, use one cup of black tea and one cup of green tea; and week four, drink just green tea. Most people will do well on green tea (*Camellia sinensis*). It is rich in theanine, a natural anxiolytic that counteracts the effects of the caffeine. Tyrosine (100 to 150 mg) on an empty stomach in the morning is effective to counteract fatigue. I encourage clients to observe and accept the real fatigue they feel and become aware of their use of coffee to medicate fatigue and low mood (coffee stimulates dopamine). Some people will be able to use coffee as a drug when needed on special occasions, knowing that this may help them transition from its use as a daily beverage. In these cases adrenal glandulars or herbal adaptogens can also increase energy (see Online Exercise 10.3 for three methods to kick the caffeine habit).

DETOXIFICATION METHODS

There are two types of liver/gallbladder flushes, colon cleansing, the use of clay externally and internally, hydrotherapies (the use of water) as soaks and steam baths, sweats and saunas, castor oil packs, and coffee enemas. Sweats, steam baths, saunas, body scrubs, and mineral baths all contribute to the process of detoxification (see Table 10.1).

Liver and Gallbladder: The Coffee Enema

Indigenous peoples have long used enemas for health or religious purposes, often using animal skins, bladders, or horns to hold the liquid or liquefied plant substances. Substances inserted into the rectum travel into the large intestine, where they are absorbed via the intestinal wall into the bloodstream. Enemas are a direct route for absorbing different substances. Drs. Marshall and Thompson discussed the use of colonic irrigation for "mental conditions" in the *New England Journal of Medicine* (1932). Many types of enemas may be used; however, one of the most effective is the coffee enema. The coffee enema is used primarily for liver/gallbladder detoxification, even though the route is through the intestine. Coffee enemas are a powerful method of detoxification and provide "dialysis of the blood across the gut wall" (Walker, 2001, p. 49). Coffee enemas support liver function; they dilute bile, dilate blood vessels, reduce inflammation of the intestines, and enhance gluthianone S transferase, thus facilitating the phase 2 liver detoxification pathway. While sometimes ridiculed by the uninformed, coffee enemas were until recently included in the *Merck Manual*, the bible of medicine (Gonzalez & Issacs, 1999). Enemas

Table 10.1 Detoxification Methods

Method	Organ	Purpose	How Often	When	Duration
Skin brushing	Lymph	Immune function, decrease dissociation	1–2 times/day	Before bathing	3–5 minutes
Coffee enema	Liver	Phase 2 detoxification, pain relief	1–2 times/day	Before 4 PM	30 minutes
Liver flush	Liver/gallbladder	Gallbladder health/stone removal	Every 3 months	Daily for 5 days	5 days
Ayurvedic liver flush	Liver/gallbladder	Gall bladder health/stone removal	Every 2 months or as needed	First thing in the morning	10 days
Colon cleanser	Colon/bowels	Colon health	Every 3 months	Between meals	5 days
Epsom salt bath soak (magnesium sulfate)	Muscles/nerves	Relaxation, magnesium absorption	4 times/week/for as long as needed	Before bed	20 minutes
Salt and baking soda bath	Skin (whole body)	Whole system detoxification	30 days, twice/year	Before bed	20 minutes
Apple cider vinegar bath	Skin (whole body)	Whole body acidification for fatigue and anxiety due to alkalinity	For 1 week and as needed	In the morning or before lunch	20 minutes
Mustard foot soaks	Circulatory system	Headaches	As needed	For headaches	20 minutes
Castor oil packs	Liver or any of the viscera	Pain or congestion	Every night for 30 days	Before bed	1–2 hours

Source: Leslie Korn, adapted from Nicholas J. Gonzalez.

promote a sense of relaxation, reduce pain significantly, and promote well-being by stimulating the parasympathetic response (N. Gonzalez, personal communication, June 23, 2002). In my practice, people who have been sexually abused, were subjected to abusive toilet training practices as children, have been conditioned to believe that touching the anus should be avoided (anal retentive), or have negative associations with fecal elimination may be resistant to this form of detoxification and need not be pressured but can be reassured. In these cases, following technical instruction, whether to proceed with this method of detoxification must remain a personal decision (See Online Exercise 10.4 for the coffee enema instructions).

LIVER/GALLBLADDER "FLUSHES"

There are two types of liver flushes. One is a simple daily flush that can be used for a 10-day period that is derived from Ayurvedic medicine. I use this flush to introduce the novice to a simple approach; also, someone who is extremely toxic can ease into the flush using this method. (See Online Exercise 10.5 for a detailed description).

The "Western" liver/gallbladder flush is a bit more complex and is designed to improve liver function and flush gallstones and gravel from the gallbladder (see Online Exercise 10.6 for a detailed description). Only in very rare cases of acute infection should surgery be considered. The gallbladder, like the oil filter in your car, requires a flushing of the system, ideally no less than four times a year. Because a well-functioning liver and gallbladder are essential for the emulsification of fats and fats are so crucial to brain function and thus recovery, a healthy liver/gallbladder is essential to recovery from PTSD. Distention, pain (especially pain around the right ribs into the back, shooting up into the right shoulder), and lots of gas may all signify a poorly functioning gallbladder. The orthophosphoric acid works with the malic acid found in apple juice to dissolve and soften gallstones and helps remove calcium and fats from the arteries (N. Gonzalez, personal communication, June 23, 2002) while also normalizing cholesterol metabolism. The magnesium in the Epsom salts relaxes the sphincter of the gallbladder and bile ducts, allowing for easy passage of the softened, shrunken stones. Finally, the cream and the oil cause a strong contraction of the gallbladder and liver, forcing out stored wastes, bile, and stones, which easily pass into the small intestine. These wastes and stones are then excreted. The liver flush is a simple way of removing gallstones without surgery while lowering cholesterol levels and improving liver function.

THE COLON

The colon is like the garden of the body in which both healthy and dangerous bacteria grow. And as in a garden, when the dangerous bacteria begin to overwhelm the healthy bacteria, the conditions for disease exist. Yeast (*Candida albicans*) overgrowth is associated with cognitive and affective dysfunction. The integration of fiber, such as psyllium, improves colon health and bacterial levels as well as glucose metabolism and thus mood (see Online Exercise 10.7).

THE LYMPH SYSTEM AND BODY BOUNDARIES

Skin brushing is very effective for lymphatic health, skin health, and dissociation, depression, and anxiety. It's both pleasurable and grounding, and it's a safe self-care activity that can be done daily as a way to check in and connect with feelings sensations and the boundaries of the body. One of the major benefits is that it stimulates the lymph system. Because chronic stress is associated with lowered immune function, stimulation of the lymphatic system can be very effective at preventing colds and congestion due to allergies. Brushing stimulates the delicate lymph nodes just underneath the skin. It's a simple, cost-effective self-care strategy that is often the first step in a detox program (see Online Exercise 10.8).

HYDROTHERAPY

Water is an ideal medium through which to transfer heat or cold to the body for the release of toxins through the skin and for the treatment of low mood, pain, and inflammation. Along with the use of plants and the hands, the application of water is one of the oldest healing methods, although it has a somewhat bizarre history of use for the treatment of mental illness. I discussed earlier the benefits of soaking in hot springs experienced by indigenous peoples of the Americas and throughout Europe where waters rich in sulfur decrease pain and lithium-rich waters elevate mood.

Water was a central element of the natural medicine repertoire employed by the "eclectic" practitioners of the 19th century who were heavily influenced by American Indian healing traditions. The eclectics were the progenitors of today's medical herbalists and naturopathic physicians, who along with today's fitness trainers, rehabilitation therapists, and physical therapists recognize water as a potent approach to self-care at home. The famed Salpêtrière Hospital where Charcot worked provided elaborate hydrotherapy methods such as baths and water hoses that applied strong pressure to the body. Charcot referred his patients to thermal spas that remain an important part of the European armamentarium. In the late 19th century Simon Baruch opened a hydropathy section in New York's Montefiore hospital and presented on the benefits of hydropathy to the New York Academy of Medicine. His work influenced Emmett Cooper Dent who began applying hydropathy for the "insane." The illustrious psychiatrist Rebekah Wright of McLean Hospital wrote the definitive text on hydrotherapy for the treatment of mental illness in 1932. However until the late

20th century water was also used in the punishment of patients. Cold water in psychiatry was used extensively into the 1950s. The ill were often submerged in ice or wrapped in wet blankets and confined against their will.

The development of psychotropic medicines caused hydrotherapy to wane, in part because administering drugs was less expensive (Weill Medical College, n.d.), but also because in an age of "progress" that elevated the science of psychiatry, hydrotherapy was relegated to the "back waters" of treatment. Hydrotherapy continues to be offered at spas and naturopathic clinics throughout the world, and many types of hydrotherapy may be effectively created at home and are well worth the effort.

There are several types of baths that are effective as part of a pain, fatigue, and mood management program. These include the use of castor oil (see Online Exercise 10.9) to reduce pain. Epsom salts (magnesium sulfate) for relaxation and sleep (see Online Exercise 10.10), mustard foot soaks for headaches (see Online Exercise 10.11), and vinegar baths to increase energy (see Online Exercise 10.12).

SUMMARY

Incorporating detoxification strategies that are congruent with the individual's beliefs and capacities to carry them out is a scientifically demonstrated approach to improving physical health, especially symptoms and illnesses associated with the effects of trauma, such as pain, inflammation, and poor digestion. Each client will benefit from developing a step-by-step plan that is tailored to his or her specific needs at each stage of recovery.

11 Spirit Molecules

> What is sacrificed with the elevation of human consciousness above natural process is not only the idea of the intelligence of nature, but one's experience of being immersed in a larger whole.
>
> —Susan Griffin

Human beings have been exploring and altering consciousness since the first four-legged animals snuffled their way into a mound of mushrooms and shared their discovery with their two-legged companions. It is difficult to say which is older, the experience of trauma or that of religion. The latter, some believe, may have dawned on the earliest hominids after the ingestion of some of nature's psychedelic bounty. Some scholars suggest that the apple of Eden was actually a psychoactive mushroom (*Amanita muscaria*) (Wasson, Kramrisch, Ruck, & Ott, 1988). People have ingested psychoactive plants and mushrooms for millennia to enhance consciousness and as a route to ecstasy, which refers to "the withdrawal of the soul from the body" concurrent with mystical or visionary states.

Frequently peoples of many cultures use plants and mushrooms in group rituals to alter consciousness, to commune with the gods, or to stay alert while engaged in long hunting expeditions. Or they may use such substances individually to stimulate vision quests, sleep, or treat pain and wounds. *Entheogen* refers to 'God within us,' those plant substances that, when ingested, give one a divine experience. In the past, entheogens were commonly called hallucinogens, psychedelics, psychotomimetics (Wasson, Kramrisch, Ruck, & Ott, 1988). Many pharmaceuticals are derived from these plants, whose chemical compounds are now extracted, synthesized, and concentrated in laboratories. In addition to their medicinal uses, psychoactive plants and mushrooms are also used recreationally and ritually. Increasingly they are studied and applied in the clinical setting for the intractable symptoms of PTSD, including depression, hopelessness, anxiety and "loss of spirit."

In this chapter I shall discuss

- definitions and an overview of psychoactive plants for the treatment of PTSD

- the historical and cultural use of entheogens
- the psychopharmacology of entheogens
- clinical studies and application for therapy

ALTERING STATES OF CONSCIOUSNESS

Trauma alters consciousness, and it is no surprise that upwards of 70% of people with PTSD self-medicate to the point of addiction at some point in their lives. Many more use substances but do not become addicted. Substance use intersects both the natural human urge for inner exploration with the need to suppress unpleasant states. Plants/mushrooms and their chemical derivatives are the subject of general empirical science, indigenous sciences, and biomedical clinical trials aimed at identifying their application for the treatment of PTSD, depression, anxiety, addiction, and insomnia and as a catalyst for spiritual and posttraumatic growth. It is at this intersection that a therapeutic approach to understanding psychoactive states can be explored.

Throughout this book I have argued that PTSD disrupts the rhythmic function of consciousness and that we must help our clients find ways to restore their sense of rhythm and balance. We can also teach them methods that they can use at home and under the supervision of therapists, healers, and guides.

Determining which are licit or illicit drugs in the United States and other countries is a matter of political policy, not policies based on therapeutic considerations or dangers to self or society. If this were not the case, nicotine and alcohol would be illegal and cannabis and lysergic acid diethylamide (LSD) would not be. Attitudes about drugs and psychoactive plants/mushrooms change with cultural and epochal mores and in all probability will continue to change. The role of culture and ethos in determining which plants or drugs may be used and which not is highlighted by the suppression of the psychedelics/entheogens during the last 50 years. In the 1950s the hallucinogens were called psychomimetics because they were believed to imitate psychosis. When the Spanish arrived in Mexico, they suppressed not only the sacramental use of the mushroom—called *Teonanacatl* by the Nahua, meaning "flesh of the gods"—but also ritual foods such as amaranth, both of which were safeguarded by indigenous peoples for the future. By all accounts the use of Teonanacatl, alcohol, and other mind-expanding ritual substances was regulated and abuse was uncommon among native peoples everywhere. The suppression of mind-altering drugs that began during the Spanish Inquisition in claimed lands throughout the New World continues today, even as the ability to conduct research is emerging, ever so slowly once again.

During treatment clients explore why they use psychoactive substances. They will benefit from discussing substances without value judgments or shame and by examining the larger context of what it means to be human and to alter one's consciousness. This dialogue can also include a discussion about choosing an altered state for healing in contrast to the helpless states engendered by the trauma they experienced. Finally many people come to treatment, mandated by law enforcement as a result of being charged with driving while intoxicated, domestic violence, prostitution, or possession and sale of drugs. Indeed, there is a profound connection between PTSD, ineffective drug policies, and incarceration. The backdraft of the U.S. government's drug policy filters down to us as clinicians as we are charged with helping people in prison who are there predominantly owing to their skin color and their use of drugs to self-medicate their PTSD. The Global Commission on Drug Policy has announced a call for ending the drug war and ending the criminalization, marginalization, and stigmatization of people who use drugs—individuals who do not harm others (Global Commission on Drug Policy, 2011).

In the practice of conventional medicine and counseling psychology today, there is a "theology of sobriety." While this is therapeutically essential for many people, the orthodoxy of abstinence also prevents an open-minded exploration of the benefits of plant-based drugs and their role in altering consciousness to treat illness without harm or dependence. Too sober an attitude also fails to acknowledge the human yearning and capacity for transcendence, and there is no greater need to transcend than when one is traumatized. Without question the current paradigm of substance abuse treatment, as the orthodox approach exemplifies, is a failure. Treatment efficacy is so poor in inpatient rehabilitation programs and government agencies, like the Indian Health Service, that most agencies will not provide measures or outcome statistics. I have consulted on many cases where I have been deeply saddened for clients addicted to alcohol in revolving 30- or 60-day programs, where they are verbally admonished to "stay clean" while they are being fed a nutritionally deficient diet of mashed potatoes and gravy, fruit cocktail, and three or more medications that make their heads spin. The addicted brain needs physical nourishment, as I explain in the previous chapter, and the brain/mind also needs spiritual nourishment, which derives from transcendent vision and ongoing rituals of connection with others.

Interestingly, the primary pharmacological treatment extant for PTSD and depression involves enhancing the serotonergic and dopaminergic/GABA systems in the brain. Not surprisingly, the hallucinogens and entheogens interact with these same systems. As I elsewhere note, there are many routes to GABA besides benzodiazepines; nature provides an abundance of plants for this purpose. This reality suggests that successful treatment of PTSD may be more about what path we take to arrive at the synapse. As we shall see, the entheogens are serotonergic agonists; more than one client has started on fluoxetine and said: "Gee, it feels like acid!"

The list of plant drugs I discuss below is just a selection of the most often used and the best researched—the ones that I believe hold the best promise for integration into the treatment of PTSD and its sequelae. With this discussion I hope to improve our understanding of the potential for the therapeutic use and abuse of these psychoactive compounds.

Historically, indigenous and traditional societies have used psychoactive plants in the context of a community-based ritual. Under these conditions, the community and the ritual provide the setting to support the process of initiation and healing experienced by the participant user. Industrialized societies have lost many of these rituals and those that remain, even when they are religious, rarely involve the use of plants to commune with God. Such practices were also central to early Christian and pagan worship in Europe.

Many of these traditions continue to evolve, for example, in the Native American peyote ceremony practices in the southwestern United States, among the Wixárikas of central México, the Ayahuasca ceremonies practiced by *Urarina* shaman of the interior Amazon River regions of Peru, the mushroom cults (*Amanita muscaria*) of Siberia and the Mazatec of northwestern Oaxaca, México—who refer to their preferred, trance-inducing mushroom as *nti-si-tho*—and in psychotherapeutic settings where individuals use substances under the guidance of skilled therapists or guides.

The substances explored below are all used by people with PTSD, and most have been or are the subject of ongoing clinical research for the treatment of PTSD or its sequelae. Because the range of the effects of trauma, PTSD, and complex trauma is so great and because these effects often emerge and resolve and reemerge over the life course, the individual so affected will have changing and evolving needs. Symptoms such as hyperarousal, nightmares, and anxiety to chronic pain and spiritual suffering may be helped with the support of the psychoactive medicines described below. For example MDMA (3,4-methylenedioxymethamphetamine) is called both an empathogen, meaning to generate a state of empathy, and an entactogen, meaning to touch within. It shows great promise for helping people with PTSD to reconnect with their inner selves and with others. Empathogens are a subcategory of psychedelic ("mind-manifesting") drugs, such as LSD and psilocybin (Metzner & Adamson, 2001).

One of the key concepts of psychoactive treatment is that of set and setting, first applied to the use of psychedelic drugs but expanded to include the use of all drugs that alter consciousness. *Set* refers to the users' mental and emotional state, hopes, and expectations going into the experience, and "setting" refers to the quality and safety of the environment that will support the initiate on her or his journey. The set and setting help to determine response to the drug.

People with PTSD use all kinds of substances to self-medicate. Understanding the types of drugs that people use can help us understand more specifically their psychological, biological, and spiritual needs and to address the conscious use of psychoactive alternatives. With the exception of tobacco, which I include here because of its historic use as a ritual plant and its problematic use by people with PTSD, all of these substances show promise as allies along the path of healing. Perhaps the most commonly used plant (besides tobacco) for altering consciousness among people with PTSD is cannabis, or marijuana. It demonstrates favorable effects for the treatment of a variety of symptoms associated with PTSD, including depression, anxiety, and pain (see Figure 11.1).

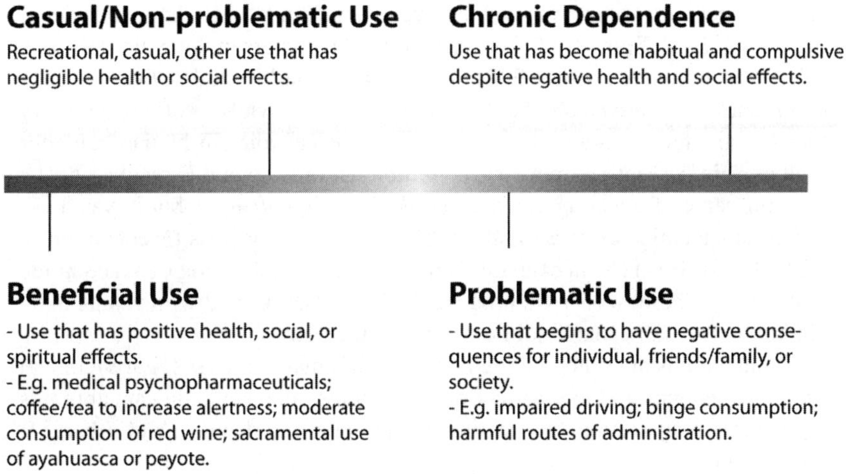

Casual/Non-problematic Use
Recreational, casual, other use that has
negligible health or social effects.

Chronic Dependence
Use that has become habitual and compulsive
despite negative health and social effects.

Beneficial Use
- Use that has positive health, social, or
spiritual effects.
- E.g. medical psychopharmaceuticals;
coffee/tea to increase alertness; moderate
consumption of red wine; sacramental use
of ayahuasca or peyote.

Problematic Use
- Use that begins to have negative consequences for individual, friends/family, or
society.
- E.g. impaired driving; binge consumption;
harmful routes of administration.

Figure 11.1 Rational psychoactive substance use.
Source: Adapted by Fatima Moras. Public Domain.

CANNABIS

As far back as 3000 BCE, shamans of many cultures used *Cannabis sativa, C. indica,* and *C. ruderalis* (Cannabaceae) (also known as marijuana, pot, herb, and ganga) for its psychoactive effects. It is found in the Han Chinese pharmacopeia as early as 2,000 years ago (Spinella, 2001). Archaeological sites in Bavaria reveal pipe bowls made of clay, proving that cannabis was smoked over 3,500 years ago (Rätsch, 1998). Cannabis is mentioned in the Sanskrit Vedas as the "divine nectar" of the god Indra,; and the famed 12th-century silk weavers, the women of Thebes, used it to quell sadness (Spinella, 2001). *Cannabis sativa* L. has been used for treatment of pain and sleep disorders since ancient times (Russo, 2002). In Mexico today, the elder women macerate *mota* (marijuana) in alcohol for 14 days, strain it, and then apply it topically for the relief of *reumas*, or muscle aches and pains. The medical use of cannabis extends back more than 150 years in the United States. It was listed in the U.S. Pharmacopoeia until it was made illegal in 1942 (Hollister, 2001). Cannabis has been the subject of a great deal of media attention. It became a topic of propaganda thanks to the "cult film" *Reefer Madness*, filmed in 1936, which dramatically claimed that smoking cannabis led to murder and madness. In spite of its current status as a federally defined illicit drug in the United States, medical marijuana is as of 2012 legalized in 16 states (with several more pending), and it appears to be on the way to countrywide legalization.

The cannabis plant contains 100 different *cannabinoids*, the most common of which is the psychoactive delta-9-THC (delta-9-tetrahydrocannabinol)

(THC). There are some nonpsychoactive cannabinoids, including *cannabinol* and *cannabidiol* (Spinella, 2001). Cannabinoid receptors in the brain (CB_1 and CB_2) were discovered in the 1990s (McCarberg & Barkin, 2007). *Endocannabinoids* such as *anandamide* and 2-AG (*sn*-2-arachidonylglycerol) are naturally found in the human brain. They play physiological roles in human behavior such as pain perception, memory, cognition, and movement (Spinella, 2001). The full name of *anandamide* is *arachidonoyl ethanolamide*, but it was nicknamed anandamide after *ananda*, the Sanskrit word for bliss (Mechoulam & Fride, 1995). The THC in cannabis is the plant chemical analog of anandamide in the body. These two THCs produce the "high" associated with cannabis by binding to the CB_1 cannabinoid receptors in the brain.

Cannabinoids are potential medications for a many illnesses. Early clinical studies on endocannabinoids, phytocannabinoids, and synthetic cannabinoids show promising results for treating inflammation and pain (McCarberg & Barkin, 2007).

Mental disorders and neurodegenerative diseases are especially likely to be helped by cannabinoids (Fisar, 2009). Studies inquiring into the role of endogenous cannabinoids are revealing important information regarding nerve signal transduction and the role of membrane lipids and fatty acids (Fisar, 2009). The omega-6 pathway elongated arachidonic polyunsaturated acid is the source of endogenous cannabinoids (Fisar, 2009). THC and cannabidiol are neuroprotective antioxidants that inhibit excitotoxicity under conditions of traumatic head injury, stroke, and degenerative brain diseases (Hampson, Grimaldi, Axelrod, & Wink, 1998), suggesting a potential role for cannabis in the immediate aftermath of brain injury. Eating fish oil containing the omega-3 pathway elongated DHA increases endocannabinoid levels in the brain. Oral administration of *Lactobacillus* increases the CB_2 receptors in intestinal cells, relieving symptoms of irritable bowel syndrome (McPartland, 2010). Some of the obstacles to cannabis research include the discomforting effects individuals may experience from THC (McCarberg & Barkin, 2007).

Cannabis and PTSD

Many people with PTSD enjoy and benefit from cannabis. This may be due to the part cannabinoids play helping the body to regulate the extinction of conditioned fear (Kamprath et al., 2011; Marsicano et al., 2002; Mechoulam, 2010) as well as the reduction of pain and anxiety. Both endocannabinoids in the brain and exogenous cannabinoids obtained from marijuana or hashish act on dopamine and decrease the reactivity of the amygdala to the fear response (Marsicano et al., 2002). Cannabis suppresses dream recall, thus reducing nightmares. One study found benefits to the use of nabilone, a synthetic cannabinoid, among PTSD patients who were experiencing poor control of nightmares after using standard pharmacotherapy (Fraser, 2009). Cannabis helps individuals focus on the present moment and thus reduces obsessive rumination on the past. Low-dose THC in cannabis appears to have anxio-lytic effects, whereas a high dose may be responsible for some of the anxiety-producing effects. Using low to moderate doses of cannabis while maintaining stable blood sugar levels maximizes positive effects for the treatment of PTSD (Mechoulam, 2010). Cannabis's subjective psychological effects vary depend-ing on the surrounding environment and the user's personality and history of use. Cannabinoids have been demonstrated to block spinal, peripheral, and gastrointestinal mechanisms that promote pain in headache, fibromyalgia, and irritable bowel syndrome (Russo, 2008b). THC decreases pain in fibromyalgia patients (Fiz, Durán, Capellà, Carbonell, & Farré, 2011) and stimulates beta-endorphin production. It is an anti-inflammatory with a potency similar to that of aspirin and twice that of hydrocortisone. Cannabis reduces levels of the inflammatory prostaglandin 2 (McPartland, 2010; Russo, 2002). THC is ef-fective as an analgesic, antiemetic, and appetite stimulant, and it shows some antispasticity effects (Spinella, 2001). Cannabidiol, a noneuphoriant phytocan-nabinoid common in certain strains of the plant, shares neuroprotective effects with THC; it inhibits glutamate neurotoxicity and displays antioxidant activity greater than that of ascorbic acid (vitamin C) or tocopherol (vitamin E) (Russo, 2008a). Chronic high doses of THC desensitize cannabinoid receptors, result-ing in the development of drug tolerance. Tolerance develops at varying rates and magnitudes in different brain regions—for example, it occurs faster and more strongly in the hippocampus as compared to the basal ganglia. This may explain why frequent users of cannabis develop tolerance to its effects upon memory loss but not to its euphoric effects (McPartland, 2010).

People with PTSD often experience migraine headaches, which are the re-sult of artery spasms combined with the overrelaxation of veins. These head-aches can be triggered for a variety of reasons; they may be due to stress, hormonal imbalances, shifts in neurotransmitter levels, food allergies, or en-vironmental stimuli and traumatic brain injury. Drugs used for the treatment of migraines generally target serotonin, though not very effectively, and they frequently produce side effects. The neurologist and cannabis researcher Ethan Russo (2002) suggests that cannabis is a safer alternative to many currently prescribed antimigraine drugs, providing both analgesic and antiemetic effects. THC inhibits the release of serotonin from the blood of migraine sufferers during an attack (Volfe, Dvilansky, & Nathan, 1985). Anandamide (AEA) po-tentiates the 5-HT1A serotonin receptor and inhibits the 5-HT2A serotonin receptors, resulting in therapeutic efficacy in acute and preventive migraine treatment (Russo, 2008b). The characteristic red eyes of the cannabis user are due to the dilation of arteries, which helps the migraineur.

Many of my clients have reported that cannabis lessens dissociation. This may seem paradoxical, because cannabis is also used as a mild dissociative drug. Yet some individuals who are already dissociated describe feeling more embodied by the heightened self-awareness of sensation and movement that cannabis facilitates. Many clients report the ability to reengage in exercise ac-tivities such as yoga, swimming, or running after using cannabis.

252 *Rhythms of Recovery*

STANDARDIZED CANNABIS MEDICINES

Sativex is a botanical extract used as an under-the-tongue spray; it is standardized to contain a 50:50 mix of THC and cannabidiol (CBD). Sativex is licensed in Europe and Canada for multiple sclerosis, neuropathic pain, and cancer-related pain (McPartland, 2010). Sativex has benefited many patients (though not all) experiencing severe chronic pain and sleep problems (Russo, Guy, & Robson, 2007). Synthetic THC has more side effects than cannabis. Cannabidiol balances THC-provoked anxiety and also contributes its own anxiolytic, antipsychotic, analgesic, anticarcinogenic, antioxidant, and neuroprotective effects.

While cannabis is far less addictive than nicotine, cocaine, heroin, or alcohol, some users can become dependent. The main consideration of excessive use of inhaled cannabis is its harmful effects on the lungs and sinuses, though moderate marijuana use (i.e., two joints a week) does not decrease lung function (Pletcher et al., 2012). The effects of inhaled cannabis on the lungs are lessened by using specialized vapor pipes or a cannabis tincture.

If individuals wish to reduce or eliminate their use of cannabis, they should evaluate its positive and negative effects and seek information about appropriate alternatives. Substituting the botanical kava and cranial electrical stimulation (CES) is effective for relief from pain, anxiety, and insomnia. Kava can alter consciousness and thus may serve as an excellent bridge or alternative self-medication option. I would advise, however, against replacing marijuana with pharmaceuticals.

Cannabis is generally contraindicated for patients with psychosis, though there is developing research suggesting a subgroup of people with schizophrenia experience a benefit via a "restorative" effect on neurotransmitter (NT) systems (Coulston, Perdices, Henderson, & Malhi, 2011). No deaths have ever been reported that were related to direct toxicity of cannabis. Synergistic effects with other sedatives, antiemetics, and analgesics may occur (Russo, 2002). Specific indications for use are best determined between client and practitioner to optimize the positive effects.

ENTHEOGENS

Ayahuasca, DMT (N,N-dimethyltryptamine), LSD, psilocybin/psilocin, MDMA (3,4-methlenedioxy-N-methlamphetamine), mescaline (peyote), ketamine, and ibogaine have all been researched for the treatment of depression (see Table 11.1). All of these substances act on receptors and neurotransmitters that influence mood, anxiety, sensory processing, and memory (Montagne, 2007). They alter the normal function of the nervous system and chemical transmission, engendering altered states and often transcendent or mystical experiences. *Psycholytic psychotherapy* refers to the integration of low-dose hallucinogens with psychoanalysis to activate and process memories and emotions (Passie, 2007).

Table 11.1 Spirit Molecules

Neurotransmitters	Amino Acids/ Nutrients	Botanicals	Foods	Entheogens
GABA	Glutamine, taurine, milk-derived neuropeptides. lithium orotate, phenibut	Valerian, hops, skullcap, green tea, kava	Walnuts, oats, spinach, beans, liver, mackerel	Fly agaric (*Amanita muscaria*) is a GABA(A) receptor agonist
Serotonin	Tryptophan, 5-HTP, B vitamins, esp B12, B6, niacinamide, folic acid	St. John's wort	Salmon, beef, lamb, figs, bananas, root vegetables, brown rice	LSD, psilocybin, DMT, ibogaine, ayahuasca
Dopamine	Tyrosine, DL-phenylalanine, B12, B6	Ginseng, fenugreek	Coffee, tea, eggs, pork, dark chocolate, ricotta cheese	MDMA/MDE, mescaline
Norepinephrine	Tyrosine	St. John's wort, holy basil	Meats, fishes, cheese	MDMA/ MDE, mescaline
Acetylcholine	GPC choline, phosphatidylserine, acetyl-L-carnitine, huperzine-A	Sage, *Bacopa monniera*, melissa, *Ginkgo biloba*, ashwaganda, *Huperzia serrata*	Eggs, liver, salmon, shrimp, nut butters, coffee	Scopolamine (contraindicated)

(*Continued*)

Table 11.1 (Continued)

Neurotransmitters	Amino Acids/ Nutrients	Botanicals	Foods	Entheogens
Glutamate	Glutamic acid	Gotu kola, kava, Passionflower	Caffeine, fermented foods, chicken, eggs, dairy	Ketamine, ibogaine
Endogenous opioids	Milk biopeptides	*Papaver somniferum*	Casein (milk), gluten (grains), spinach, fat, fasting	Ibogaine, *Salvia divinorum*
Cannabinoids	Fish oil, lactobacilli	Cannabis, hops	Hemp seeds/hemp oil	Cannabis

Source: Leslie Korn.

Ayahuasca

Ayahuasca (also known as *yaje, yage, hoasca*, and *caapi*), is a beverage with powerful psychotropic effects made of the *Banisteriopsis caapi* vine and other psychotropic plants, such as *Psychotria viridis, P. carthagenensis*, or *B. rusbyana* (Luna, 2011; Spinella, 2001). The name *ayahuasca* or *ayawaska* is from the Quichua (or Quechua) language and means "vine of the souls" (*aya* = spirit, *waska* = vine) and refers to both the beverage and the vine itself (Luna, 2011; McKenna, 2007). Some ayahuasca-using religious groups in Brazil call it *vegetal* or *santo daime*. *Daime* is the name used by the members of the Santo Daime Church in Brazil, and the Brazilian church União do Vegetal calls it *hoasca* and uses it as the Eucharist (Ott, 1995; Panneck, 2010).

The most abundant sources of DMT-containing plants are in South America, where indigenous peoples have used DMT in brews and snuffs to elicit visionary or shamanic experiences since precolonial times (Strassman, 2001). The use of ayahuasca goes back many centuries in South America, where indigenous tribes in the Upper Amazon, the Orinoco Basin, Colombia, and Ecuador have used it for spiritual-religious and medicinal purposes; its use spread to Peru, where it is used for healing (Luna, 2011). Winkleman (2007) suggests that that the use of ayahuasca in Amazonia in collective rituals helps to mediate two world views; the indigenous and the European (colonizer), with the ritual symbolizing a syncretic approach to acculturation.

Pharmacology

Ayahuasca's main hallucinogenic alkaloids are DMT (N, N-dimethyltryptamine) and β-carbolines (monoamine oxidase–inhibiting harmala alkaloids) (Spinella, 2001). DMT is a serotonin analog whose neuroendocrine effects include increases in growth hormone, β-endorphin, prolactin, corticotrophin, and cortisol (Spinella, 2001).

Pharmahuasca refers to capsules containing enough of the psychoactive components of traditional ayahuasca to mimic its effects (Ott, 1995). DMT (N,N-dimethyltryptamine, or N,N-DMT) is a potent psychedelic drug with short-lasting effects. DMT is found in plant and animal species around the world. It is theorized that the pineal gland, which is rich in serotonin, has the ability to convert serotonin to tryptamine, a critical step in DMT formation. Psychiatrist Rick Strassman (2001) proposes that near-death and mystical experiences are a result of DMT produced by the pineal gland. Strassman (2001) coined the term *spirit molecule* in reference to DMT, which is ubiquitous in humans, animals, and plants. Historically, evidence of the use of exogenous DMT has been documented at burial sites dated to the 8th century CE, and snuffs made from cohoba (*Anadenanthera peregrina*) were used in Colombia as early as the 1400s (Erowid, 2010a). The Sonoran desert toad *Bufo alvarius* secretes large amounts of the potent DMT-related hallucinogens

5-methoxy-N,N-dimethyltryptamine (5-MeO-DMT) and bufotenine from its parotid glands. This may be the "psychoactive toad" of Meso-American traditional medicine (Weil & Davis, 1994). The (mistaken) practice of licking toads to get high is rooted in this consciousness-altering search.

There may be a distant link between toad-licking rituals and the medicinal use of toads by present-day indigenous peoples of western Mexico, who rub oil on the toad and then rub the toad over areas of their own bodies affected by erysipelas. When this procedure is finished, the toad is washed, without which, it is believed, it will die, and is then released back into the wild.

Ayahuasca is often combined with traditional healing methods and psychotherapy as treatment for drug addiction (Mabit, 2002). Members of the Santo Daime churches Barquinha and União do Vegetal (UDV) have been evaluated psychiatrically and neurophysiologically by researchers who found that ayahuasca may reduce alcoholism and that it had no negative effects (Panneck, 2010). Over 70 *curanderos* (*curar* meaning "to cure or heal") use ayahuasca to treat drug addiction, giving patients the opportunity to look at their lives spiritually and to experience altered states of consciousness in a positive way (Mabit, 1996).

Using cannabis with ayahuasca is not advised for people predisposed to psychotic symptoms as it may produce negative reactions, including heart problems, anxiety, and psychotic episodes (dos Santos, 2011). Ayahuasca-derived harmine may act as an antidepressant in animals and humans (de Lima Osório et al., 2011). One double blind, placebo-controlled study on the use of ayahuasca demonstrated that panic and hopelessness were reduced during ayahuasca's acute effects, while state or trait anxiety was unaffected (Santos, Landeira-Fernandez, Strassman, Motta, & Cruz, 2007). Harmala alkaloids are contraindicated with the use of SSRIs and during pregnancy (Spinella, 2001). Studies suggest no negative effects from long-term usage of ayahuasca. One study identified physical and psychological improvement as compared with a control group (Mabit, 2007), and another study using the Addiction Severity Index with active users found no deleterious psychosocial effects such as those typically caused by other drugs of abuse (Fábregas et al., 2010).

Ayahuasca's legal status in the United States is often changing. The plants used to make the brew are generally not regulated, but the main psychoactive component, *N,N*-DMT, is a schedule I controlled substance. Certain ayahuasca-based religious groups, the Santo Daime Church and UDV, were recently approved by U.S. Courts for the legal use of ayahuasca in their ceremonies (Erowid, 2011).

Iboga

Iboga has been used for centuries in religious ceremonies and traditional medicine by the Gabon and Congo cultures (Lotsof, 1995; Spinella, 2001). The Fang peoples of West Africa say that the San people were the first to find the iboga shrub, *Tabernanthe iboga* in the rainforest and that the San ancestor, Bitamu, is contained within iboga (Rätsch, 1998). During the early 20th century the Fang people of Gabon in equatorial West Africa began using iboga, calling it Bwiti. The Fang Bwiti cult is a syncretic Neo-Christian religion in which the powdered iboga roots serve as the Eucharist (Ott, 1995). The bwiti cult and other iboga-using societies take iboga to make contact with the ancestors and "break open the head" (Schultes & Hofmann, 1979, p. 112). The iboga roots are yellowish in color and are traditionally scraped into a powder or made into an infusion for drinking (Schultes & Hofmann, 1979). In Gabon, hunters use small doses to stay awake and reduce thirst, hunger, and fatigue (Multidisciplinary Association for Psychedelic Studies [MAPS], 2003; Spinella, 2001). Members of the Bwiti religion use it at much higher dosages as a sacramental hallucinogen in rites of passage (Alper & Lotsof, 2007).

Ibogaine is an indole alkaloid that was first isolated from the roots of the *Tabernanthe iboga* plant in 1901 (Ott, 1995). It is also found in *Tabernanthe crassa* (MAPS, 2003; Popik, 1998). Ibogaine is a nonaddictive extract from the plant (Lotsof, 1995; Popik & Glick, 1996). Its active metabolite, noribogaine, is an atypical opiate that appears to alter the addiction circuit (Mash, 2010) by acting on both opioid and serotonergic receptors (Mash, 2010), which likely accounts for the elimination of opiate cravings and its hallucinogenic qualities, respectively. The effects of ibogaine are physically, psychologically, and spiritually profound (Mash, 2010), and both animal tests and human experiences result in an almost immediate elimination of symptoms of withdrawal and reduction in craving following the first ingestion. During an ibogaine treatment, individuals with opioid or opiate addictions experience a lifting of the physical symptoms of dependence within 30 to 45 minutes following ingestion. For some, this is when a visionary phase (MAPS, 2003) begins. Iboga may reduce a person's need for sleep in a discomforting way for a month or longer after the initial effects (Lotsof, 1995). Physiological effects include ataxia, a slight increase in blood pressure, and sometimes a decrease in pulse rate (Lotsof, 1995). Several treatments are often required for complete elimination of the addiction. There have been some case reports of death during use and there is concern about its potential to generate cardiac arrhythmia (Kovar et al., 2011).

Ibogaine is used in Europe and North America as a ritual hallucinogen for psychological insight or spiritual growth (Alper & Lotsof, 2007). Ibogaine was recently patented in the United States and has been studied for its use in treating addiction (Halpern, 1996).

Overall, iboga produces mild entheogenic effects, but the loss of ego associated with other entheogens, like LSD and psilocybin, does not occur. Discomfort may occur, usually caused by the subject fighting against the experience. This can be mitigated by having the client open his or her eyes to make the visions recede and by the presence and reassurance of the practitioner (MAPS, 2003). There are a number of clinics in the Caribbean countries, Mexico, and Europe where individuals may go for treatment.

Ketamine

Ketamine, also known as Special K or K, is 2-(2-chlorophenyl)-2-(methy-amino)-cyclohexanone, classified as a dissociative anesthetic and psychedelic (Kolp et al., 2007). It is not derived from a plant but is a drug used mostly as an anesthetic by veterinarians. It has been widely used recreationally for its psychedelic and dissociative effects, which include altered perceptions, vertigo, decreased motor function, enhanced sociability, and dissociation (Bergman, 1999).

Ketamine is typically bought as a powder and snorted or injected intramuscularly. Unlike other psychedelic drugs, ketamine shows a tendency to be slightly addictive psychologically, yet it has also been used to treat addiction in a controlled setting (Jansen, 2000). It is currently listed as a schedule III controlled substance. Vollenweider and Kometer (2010) conducted functional magnetic resonance imaging studies of people on ketamine, revealing increased signaling between neurons and increased growth of synapses, accounting for the experience of "boundlessness" and ketamine's antidepressant and anxiolytic effects. Ketamine's antidepressant effects take place within hours (Stern, 2010). Low doses are used as an antidepressant and as a "transpersonal " drug for the treatment of death anxiety (Kolp et al., 2007). In one study of treatment-resistant depression, participants receiving ketamine showed improvement of symptoms within hours, with one third of them experiencing lasting relief for a week (Zarate et al., 2006). There were some adverse effects that subsided within 1 to 2 hours (Zarate et al., 2006). The rapidity of response is an argument for ketamine in contrast to the weeks required for marginal response rates with SSRIs. Psychological and medical researchers emphasize that ketamine is a tool to be used in the context of psychotherapy as a facilitator of states of consciousness that advance healing; they do not suggest that it has benefits for the recreational user (Kolp et al., 2007). A ketamine-induced psychedelic experience is designed to be an adjunct to the psychotherapy and to induce a transpersonal peak experience (Krupitsky & Kolp, 2007). Ketamine psychotherapy when measured by the Minnesota Multiphasic Personality Inventory suggests that individuals become more confident, less anxious, less depressed and neurotic, and more emotionally open with treatment (Krupitsky & Kolp, 2007). Controlled clinical trials of ketamine for the treatment of alcoholism and heroin addictions found that 65% of patients remained sober for at least a year (Krupitsky & Grinenko, 1997). Both the alcohol- and heroin-using patients experienced less craving, anxiety, and depression as well as positive changes in attitudes toward themselves, others, and life itself, along with increased spirituality and sobriety (Krupitsky & Grinenko, 1997; Krupitsky et al., 2002; Krupitsky & Kolp, 2007). Ketamine is also used in small doses to treat pain and has been reported to produce lasting pain-reducing effects (Borsook, 2009), in particular for complex regional pain syndrome (Correll, Maleki, Gracely, Muir, & Harbut, 2004). When ketamine is injected intravenously at the anesthetic dose, the pain relief can last for months (Borsook, 2009).

Some adverse effects of ketamine include confusion, visual and perceptual changes, increased blood pressure, dizziness, and increased libido, all of which have been observed to subside within 1 to 2 hours (Zarate et al., 2006). There is some evidence that when ketamine is given during the acute phase of traumatic injury it might aggravate early posttraumatic stress reactions. Some people who have used ketamine extensively recreationally have experienced problems with the liver, kidneys, and urinary tract (Wood et al., 2011).

Mushrooms /Psilocybin

There are hundreds of hallucinogenic mushrooms, including *Psilocybe azteco-rum, P. Mexicana,* and *P. caerulescans* as well as *Panaeolus sphinctrinus, P. foenisecii,* and *Stropharia cubensis* (Spinella, 2001). Also known as mush-rooms, magic mushrooms, shrooms, and boomers, psilocybin mushrooms are found growing throughout the world, particularly in Mexico and Central America, where *Psilocybe aztecorum* and *P. mexicana* are used in religious ceremonies by the Aztec, Mazatec, Chinantec, Mije, Zapotec, Mixtec, and Mayan peoples (Spinella, 2001) (see Figure 11.2).

Most psychoactive mushrooms contain psilocybin (4-phosphoryl-DMT) or psilocin (4-hydroxy DMT), the two primary hallucinogenic alkaloids, as well as the less common baeocystin (Erowid, 2009; Spinella, 2001). Compared to LSD, psilocybe mushrooms are less potent and shorter-acting, and they provide

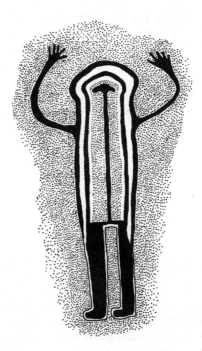

Figure 11.2 Mushroom spirit.
Source: Adapted from *The Shaman and the Jaguar: A Study of Narcotic Drugs Among the Indians of Colombia,* by G. Reichel-Dolmatoff, 1975, p. 190. © 1975 by Temple University Press.

a gentler "trip." Both psilocybin and psilocin act on the serotonergic system, like LSD. The effects of psilocybe mushrooms begin 30 to 60 minutes after ingestion and last from 4 to 6 hours.

Psilocybin's Effects on Psychological and Physiological Health

Psychologist Timothy Leary conducted early research on psilocybin in 1961. He used psilocybin to treat prisoners in Concord, Massachusetts, theorizing that the altered states engendered by the drug would lead to reduced levels of recidivism among the prisoners (Leary et al., 1965). An 18-month follow-up study showed that the prisoners' recidivism rate was 23%—much lower than the expected 65% (Forcier & Doblin, 1992). Psilocybin use is associated with profound spiritual experiences that have lasting effects (Griffiths, Richards, McCann, & Jesse, 2006). The psychological effects of psilocybin include shifts in mood, perception (visual), and perceived changes in time and space (Hasler, Grimberg, Benz, Huber, & Vollenweider, 2004) as well as loosening of ego-boundaries and geometric and complex visual hallucinations. One of my clients who had severe physical injuries and had been feeling hopeless took psilocybin and then described his experience as follows: "I was seeing the molecules that make up matter vibrating and glistening all around. I was witnessing the miracle of life and I realized that I best not squander what I have."

People who use subhallucinogenic doses of psilocybin or LSD to prevent or treat cluster headaches report efficacy, with only a single dose required for remission (Sewell, Halpern, & Pope, 2006). The authors suggest there might be mechanisms at work that are unrelated to the psychoactive components of psilocybin and LSD (Sewell et al., 2006).

Griffiths, Johnson, Richards, McCann, and Richards (2008) found no adverse effects from a clinical trial of psilocybin in a 14-month follow-up study; however, they advised of some potential risks, including panic and fear, exacerbation of psychiatric conditions, and long-lasting alterations of perception. Hasler et al. (2004) concluded that psilocybin given to healthy subjects is safe but advise against the use of psilocybin for those with cardiovascular conditions or hypertension.

LSD

LSD, also known as acid (D-lysergic acid diethylamide), is a well-known hallucinogenic chemical derived from the ergot (*Claviceps purpurea*) fungus, which grows on rye (*Secale cereale* L.). Ancient Celtic coins engraved with images of grain infected by ergot suggest the ancient use of this psychoactive substance (Rätsch, 1998). The ergot fungus was used in medieval times during childbirth and in the 18th and 19th centuries to stop bleeding, treat palsy, and induce abortions (Rätsch, 1998). Currently some homeopathic remedies use ergot preparations to treat migraines, menstrual cramps, and spasms (Rätsch, 1998). The Swiss scientist Albert Hofman accidentally synthesized LSD in 1938 when he was analyzing ergot.

LSD is used in a variety of experimental and clinical treatment settings for a variety of physical and mental illnesses including PTSD. LSD was used to treat Dutch World War II survivors of concentration camps with PTSD because it was believed that it allowed patients to remember and speak about the traumas they had experienced (Cohen, 1978). In 1956, Bill "W" (Wilson), the founder of Alcoholics Anonymous, took LSD under the guidance of a psychiatrist and had an intense spiritual experience, leading him to conclude that LSD could help others with alcoholism (Krupitsky & Kolp, 2007). LSD grew in popularity during the 1960s and was made illegal in 1968. It is now a scheduleI controlled substance.

The psychoactive effects of LSD begin within 20 to 60 minutes of ingestion and include increased energy, perceptual and visual changes, cognitive and physical changes, dilated pupils, occasional paranoia, insights and revelations, mood swings, and confusion (Erowid, 2010b). The types of responses are dose-dependent. Fadiman (2011), one of the first psychologists to research LSD, delineates the use of LSD for both immediate and long-term effects, suggesting that a high dose is used for spiritual growth, a moderate dose for a therapeutic response and a low dose for problem-solving. The effects last for 6 to 8 hours and the experience is usually followed by a come-down period of 2 to 6 hours

LSD is nonaddictive and no withdrawal effects have been reported (Erowid, 2010b).

MDMA

MDMA, commonly referred to as "ecstasy," is known as a psychedelic amphetamine. Ecstasy sold on the street, however, is rarely MDMA and should not be mistaken for it. It is unique in its effects, inducing feelings of empathy, euphoria, and positive emotions. MDMA is derived from safrole, an essential oil found in the sassafras root (*Sassafras albidum*) (Holland, 2001). Sassafras root is used as a stimulant tea by North American Indians (Rätsch, 1998) and was a main constituent of root beer until sassafras with safrole was banned in 1960 by the U.S. Food and Drug Administration. Due to MDMA's illegal status, sassafras oil is also controlled and rarely sold (Rätsch, 1998). MDMA is considered a nonsedating anxiolytic, an empathogen for its capacity to generate a sense of empathy, and an entactogen, from *tactile* = "touch" and *gen* = "creation," referring to a sense of "the touch within." MDMA was used privately in therapy in the United States and Europe before it became popular as a recreational drug (Holland, 2001), which in turn led to its criminalization in 1985 (Mithoefer, Wagner, Mithoefer, Jerome, & Doblin, 2011).

MDMA quiets down the amygdala, and the goal of MDMA therapy for PTSD is to decondition hyperarousal and anxiety in response to stimuli and also to increase empathy for self and others (Ruse, Jerome, Mithoefer, & Doblin, 2003).

Low doses of MDMA help people to be gentle with themselves, lower their defenses, and be open to the process of psychotherapy (Holland, 2001). The therapeutic dose is about 125 mg (Holland, 2000). MDMA is chemically similar to mescaline, which, along with MDMA, belongs to the family of phenethylamines (Holland, 2001). MDMA releases a flood of serotonin and dopamine and increases blood levels of the affiliation hormones oxytocin and prolactin (Jerome, 2004) leading to a profound sense of empathy (Johansen and Krebs 2009) and the potential to deepen trust in the therapist. It decreases activity in the amygdala and may facilitate an exploration of traumatic memories (Johansen & Krebs, 2009). Because MDMA also increases norepinephrine and cortisol, it might also enhance the rate of extinction learning (Johansen & Krebs, 2009).

The use of MDMA concurrent with psychotherapy with six women with chronic PTSD following sexual assault showed that low doses (50 to 75 mg) were safe psychologically and physically (Bouso, Doblin, Farré, Alcázar, & Gómez-Jarabo, 2008). MDMA has the potential to treat PTSD by reducing fear and anxiety, inducing states of openness and trust, improving the therapeutic relationship, and increasing the ability to remember things while being able to look at them with objectivity and compassion (Mithoefer, 2007). A study of MDMA and psychotherapy in people with chronic refractory PTSD resulted in resolution of symptoms, so that a large percentage of the group no longer met the criteria for PTSD (Mithoefer et al., 2011). Mithoefer, Wagner, Mithoefer, Jerome, and Doblin (2011) conducted a randomized controlled study on MDMA for patients with PTSD who had not responded to psychotherapy or medication. Results included a significant decrease in scores on the clinician-administered PTSD scale (Mithoefer et al., 2011).

MDMA-assisted therapy decreases or eliminates chronic hyperarousal and acute stress reactions to internal and external triggers. It gives individuals the opportunity to access very positive aspects of themselves, and enables them to deal with difficult feelings and memories (Mithoefer, 2007). As in the case of many consciousness-altering drugs, proper set and setting are essential to facilitating a therapeutic response versus acute anxiety and stress reactions. Holland (2000) suggests that MDMA can potentiate the recovery or reexperiencing of traumatic memories, thus emphasizing the role of an experienced therapist as a facilitator in preparation before, during, and after ingestion.

Research suggests that MDMA is safe to administer to humans in a controlled clinical setting and causes few adverse events (Jerome, 2004). The CYP2D6 enzyme metabolizes MDMA in the liver. It is deficient or totally absent in 5% to 10% of Caucasians and African Americans and 1% to 2% of Asians, suggesting that people without the CYP2D6 enzyme should refrain from taking MDMA (Holland, 2000). While there have been side effects in people using ecstasy recreationally, these effects are often due to the setting and the way in which ecstasy is used. Often illicitly purchased ecstasy pills contain other drugs such as speed, caffeine, and dextromethorphan sold as ecstasy or mixed in with MDMA. One adverse effect, hyperthermia, a dangerous and possibly lethal increase in body temperature, is usually caused by MDMA users who become overheated while dancing in hot clubs; it has not been observed to occur in subjects undergoing MDMA-assisted psychotherapy (Henry & Rella, 2001).

Peyote

> Peyote is the crossing of the souls, it is everything that is. Without peyote noth-
> ing would exist.
>
> —A Wixaritari man (quoted in Anderson, 1996, p. 15)

Peyote *(Lophophora williamsii)* is a cactus that grows in the deserts of Central
Mexico and as far north as Texas (Rätsch, 1998). *Péyotl,* the Nahua word,
means "furry thing" (Ott, 1995), referring to the tops of the cactuses. The fresh
or dried heads of the cactus, called "peyote buttons," are eaten or made into a
tea or a powder (Rätsch, 1998). Peyote preparations are bitter-tasting and dosages vary greatly (Rätsch, 1998). Common names include dry whiskey, divine
herb, medicine of god, péyotl, and híkuri. The major active ingredient is mescaline (3,4,5-trimethoxy-β-phenethylamine).

Archaeological digs in Texas have discovered peyote buttons as old as 6,000
years (Rätsch, 1998). The Cora, Rarámuri, Wixárikas, Tepecanos, and other
communities use peyote in religious rituals around which agricultural seasons
and spiritual life is organized. The Wixárikas use peyote, which they call híkuri,
for medicinal purposes—as a salve for pain, for scorpion stings, and to receive
messages from the gods (Anderson, 1996). Every October the Wixárikas make
a pilgrimage to the sacred land of Wirikuta, where the peyote grows. A successful journey will ensure abundant crops and good fortune (Anderson, 1996).
The Cora (they refer to themselves as Nayari) of western Mexico use peyote
to battle fatigue during all-night dancing ceremonies (Anderson, 1996). The
Rarámuri traditionally drink a peyote mixture to promote health and longevity,
and they chew peyote into a paste to be used topically for various ailments such
as snakebites, wounds, burns, rheumatism, and fractures (Anderson, 1996).

Peyote is used traditionally in Mexico to reduce fevers, for back pains,
and to promote lactation (Anderson, 1996). Peyote use was banned during
Spanish colonization and was severely punished by the Inquisition (Rätsch,
1998). However, the practices merely went underground; most of the communities live in high mountainous regions that are difficult to reach or control.
The influence of Christianity was absorbed into many of the indigenous communities' rituals. Over the past 40 years a new wave of community trauma has
affected most of these indigenous communities; forced relocation to access
land for drilling and mining, commodification, and sales of spiritual artwork
arising out of the peyote visions have been necessitated by increased poverty
and the demands of "spiritual tourism."

The use of peyote was spread to Native Americans by the Mescalero Apache
and the Lipan Apache of Mexico (Rätsch, 1998). Native Americans use peyote
to dispel bad spirits that are believed to be causing illness and also to treat diabetes, pain, colds, bites, alcoholism, headache, blindness, menstrual disorders,
and broken bones (Anderson, 1996).

The Native American Church (NAC) is a formally organized pan-Indian religion diffused directly from the older Mexican forms that transcends current borders. The NAC is based on the use of the peyote cactus as a sacramental medicine, which developed in the late 19th century in response to the trauma resulting from conquest of Native American communities (Calabrese, 2007). Membership in the NAC requires abstinence from alcohol and drugs and offers an important resource to participants who are detoxifying from alcohol. The use of peyote is part of a holistic communal ceremony during which the peyote spirit may illuminate an answer or knowledge about one's problems. As in the case of many psychoactive drugs used in the context of communal ritual with a supportive set and setting, participants undergo initiation with a guide who supports their vision of a fulfilling life without alcohol (Pascarosa & Futterman, 1976).

The NAC provides an indigenous alternative to Alcoholics Anonymous (AA), fostering positive cultural practices that support individual and group identity that also mitigate the ongoing effects of colonization and promoting health in areas beyond addiction (Prue, 2008). However, AA does not approve of the NAC's use of peyote (Prue, 2008). Halpern, Sherwood, Hudson, Yurgelun-Todd, and Pope (2005) conducted a trial with three groups of Navajo tribe members, one group that used peyote regularly, one group with past alcoholism, and one group with minimal substance use. The study consisted of a screening interview, the Rand Mental Health Inventory, and tests for cognitive and neuropsychological functions. The authors concluded that peyote use did not result in decreased psychological or cognitive function when American Indians were using it in a religious context.

There are more than 55 alkaloids in peyote, including mescaline, the main psychoactive alkaloid (Anderson, 1996). Peyote's psychoactive effects begin within 45 minutes to 2 hours following ingestion and last for about 6 to 9 hours (Rätsch, 1998). The peyote experience is similar to the visionary experiences facilitated by LSD and psilocybin. Before the initial effects begin, nausea and vomiting are common (Rätsch, 1998). The first phase, which lasts about 3 to 4 hours, is usually very uncomfortable, with effects such as headache, nausea, vomiting, a choking feeling, urgency to urinate, stomach cramps, tremors, anxiety, and fear (Anderson, 1996). The second phase is much more pleasant and includes feelings of euphoria, visions, and distortions in sense perception, as well as somatic effects. The use of peyote was made legal for church members in the United States in 1994.

Salvia

Salvia divinorum, also known as salvia, diviner's mint, and the shepherdess, is an herb of the *Labiatae* (mint) family from the Sierra Mazateca region of Southern Mexico. Salvia has been used historically by the Mazatec Indians in shamanic rituals and divination (Hanes, 2003). It is extremely rare in the wild because of its limited natural habitat, but many peoples continue to cultivate it around the world (Rätsch, 1998). Today, most of the Mazatec *curanderos* prefer to use psychoactive mushrooms for their rituals; however, salvia is used as a substitute in healing and divination, and some *curanderos* prefer salvia (Rätsch, 1998). Some 50 to 100 leaves are consumed in order to help the healers detect illness (Hanes, 2003). Salvia is used at low doses to treat headaches and pain and to rejuvenate the ill (Rätsch, 1998). Karl Hanes (2003), a clinical psychologist, used salvia in the treatment of several of his patients suffering from treatment-resistant depression, observing a decrease in depression, improved mood, and increased self-awareness (Hanes, 2003). In a small study of health subjects, Salvinorin A, the active compound of salvia, produced no side effects (Johnson, MacLean, Reissig, Prisinzano, & Griffiths, 2011). Yet others caution against the use of the pure compound, rather than the whole plant as traditionally used, due to the potential for dangerous side effects.

Salvia divinorum works on the opioid system and induces various effects including out-of-body experiences, time distortion, visual stimulation, the feeling of having become an inanimate object, and dissociation (Erowid, 2010c; Hanes, 2003). The effects of *Salvia divinorum* begin within the first minute after smoking, with an intensity of effects lasting 5 to 15 minutes and a return to normal after about 20 to 40 minutes (Erowid, 2010c). If consumed orally, the leaves of the plant must be kept in the mouth for 15 to 30 minutes in order to produce an hour of psychoactive activity (Hanes, 2003). Research has shown that in controlled settings it produces mild to strong hallucinogenic effects accompanied by mystical experiences similar to those produced by psilocybin. No side effects or toxicity with normal use has been reported (Johnson et al. 2011).

It is estimated that in the United States salvia is used by 2 million people (Johnson et al., 2011). It is legal in most states.

SUMMARY

Psychoactive plants and their derivatives may be either used or abused by people with PTSD. Understanding the use and abuse of specific plants will provide an opportunity to explore with clients their options for self-care and the role plants and substances may play in improving their well-being or in providing alternatives to destructive forms of self-medication. Though research into the medical and psychotherapeutic applications of psychoactive substances has been significantly dampened in the United States, especially following the surge in their use in the 1950s to 1970s, there is now renewed interest throughout the world in conducting research. This new interest will continue as new methods of treatment are sought and evidence for old methods is reacquired.

FINAL THOUGHTS

The experience of trauma is part of the human condition. When the conditions have been complex, trauma often involves exposure to evil, tearing the soul's fabric. This volume focuses on ways to help people who have been traumatized, whether accidentally, by "natural" forces, or by human hands. Because the essential life spark dims when people suffer from trauma, all that might ignite it from the natural world, including humans, animals, plants and the elements, should be engaged. These ways include forms of communication that call on our "ordinary" states of consciousness, such as talk, to ways of resonating that we don't as often cultivate in daily life or in the therapeutic milieu, including somatic empathy and the myriad of ways in which we tune in to the rhythms of others and help them to retune themselves.

Among many healing traditions of the world there is a saying that "where you find the disease, there you will find the cure"; thus where nature places poison ivy, so will you find the soothing leaves of the madrone and the manzanita. Once poison ivy enters the bloodstream, one sharpens the vision, scouts the land, and prays to steer clear of the brush, or, at the very least, to control and soothe subsequent outbreaks. But it always flows within. So it is with trauma. As clinicians, we walk along the path with our clients as guides to healing. The resolution of trauma is a lifelong process. Its rhythms ebb and flow according to where the developmental junctures and internal processes meet the external transits of life. I have explored some ideas here that address the nourishment provided by connection with others and nourishment by foods, plants, and "spirit chemicals." The scaffolding of spirituality, whether external or internal, also lends structure to an essentially solitary road through healing. Enhancing resiliency by engaging in new nontraumatic experiences reinforces a sense of competency and counteracts the dread and sense of foreboding that hovers over the victim's brow. Many survivors talk of finding purpose and meaning in their lives as a result of illness or trauma. Often they identify the gifts, talents, and stamina that adversity has, ironically, allowed them to mine. Many trauma survivors become "wounded healers" who, by virtue of their own suffering, become able to direct their passion, creativity, and wisdom to help others. They, like Guanyin, the Chinese bodhisattva in feminine form, "observe the cries of the world" and remain earthbound in order to assist others along the path of rediscovering their rhythms of recovery.

References

Aggarwal, B. B., Bhatt, I. D., Ichikawa, H., Ahn, K. S., Sethi, G., Sandur, S. K., . . . Shisho-
dia, S. (2007). Curcumin: Biological and medicinal properties. In P. N. Ravindran,
K. N. Babu, & K. Sivaraman (Eds.), *Turmeric: The genus curcuma (Medicinal and
aromatic plants: Industrial profiles)* (pp. 297–368). Boca Raton, FL: CRC Press.

Ahmadi, N., Hajsadeghi, F., Mirshkarlo, H. B., Budoff, M., Yehuda, R., & Ebrahimi,
R. (2011). Post-traumatic stress disorder, coronary atherosclerosis, and mortality.
American Journal of Cardiology, 108(1), 29–33.

Akhondzadeh, B. A., Moshiri, E., Noorbala, A. A., Jamshidi, A. H., Abbasi, S. H., &
Akhondzadeh, S. (2007). Comparison of petal of Crocus sativus L. and fluoxetine
in the treatment of depressed out-patients: A pilot double-blind randomized trial.
Progress in Neuro-Psychopharmacology & Biological Psychiatry, 31(2), 439–442.

Alarcon-Aguilar, F. J., Zamilpa, A., Perez-Garcia, M. D., Almanza-Perez J. C., Romero-
Nuñez, E., Campos-Sepulveda, E. A., . . . Roman-Ramos, R. (2007). Effect of Hibiscus
sabdariffa on obesity in MSG mice. *Journal of Ethnopharmacology, 114*(1), 66–71.

Alper, K. R., & Lotsof, H. S. (2007). The use of ibogaine in the treatment of addictions. In
M. J. Winkelman & T. B. Roberts (Eds.), *Psychedelic medicine: New evidence for hallucinogenic substances as medicine* (Vols. 1–2) (pp. 43–66). Westport, CT: Praeger.

Amber, R., & Babey-Brooke, A. M. (1966). *The pulse in Occident and Orient: Its philosophy and practice in holistic diagnosis and treatment.* New York: Aurora Press.

American Polarity Therapy Association. (1996). *Foundations of polarity therapy pro-
fessionalism standards for practice and code of ethics.* Boulder: Author.

Anda, R. F., Felitti, V. J., Bremner, J. D., Walker, J. D., Whitfield, C., Perry, B. D., . . . Giles,
W. H. (2006). The enduring effects of abuse and related adverse experiences in child-
hood: A convergence of evidence from neurobiology and epidemiology. *European
Archives of Psychiatry and Clinical Neuroscience, 256*(3), 174–186.

Anderson, E. F. (1996). *Peyote: The divine cactus.* Tucson: The University of Arizona Press.

Ang, D., Kesavalu, R., Lydon, J. R., Lane, K. A., & Bigatti, S. (2007). Exercise-based
motivational interviewing for female patients with fibromyalgia: A case series. *Clinical Rheumatology, 26*(11), 1843–1849.

Archana, R., & Namasivayam A. (1999). Antistressor effect of Withania somnifera.
Journal of Ethnopharmacology, 64(1), 91–93.

Ashton, C. H., & Young, A. H. (1999). SSRIs, drug withdrawal and abuse: Problem
or treatment? In S. C. Stanford (Ed.), *Selective serotonin reuptake inhibitors: Past,
present and future* (pp. 65–80). Austin: R. G. Landes.

Back, S. E., Sonne, S. C., Killeen, T., Dansky, B. S., & Brady, K. T. (2003). Comparative profiles of women with PTSD and comorbid cocaine or alcohol dependence.
American Journal of Drug and Alcohol Abuse, 29(1), 169–89.

Barach, P. M. (1994). *Guidelines for treating dissociative identity disorder in adults.* Skokie, IL: International Society for the Study of Dissociation.

Baum, E. Z. (1991). Movement therapy with multiple personality disorder patients. *Dissociation, 4*(2), 99–104.

Bayer, L., Constantinescu, I., Perrig, S., Vienne, J., Vidal, P. P., Mühlethaler, M., & Schwartz, S. (2011). Rocking synchronizes brain waves during a short nap. *Current Biology, 21*(12), R461–R462.

Becker, R. O. (1991). Evidence for a primitive DC electrical analog system controlling brain function. *Subtle Energies, 2*(1), 71–88.

Becker, R. O. (1992). Modern bioelectromagnetics and function of the central nervous system. *Subtle Energies, 3*(1), 53–72.

Becker, R. O., & Selden, G. (1985). *The body electric: Electromagnetism and the foundation of life.* New York: William Morrow.

Belenky, M., Clinchy, B., Goldberger, N., & Tarule, J. (1986). *Women's ways of knowing: The development of self, voice, and mind.* New York: Basic Books.

Bell, I. R., Schwartz, G. E., Baldwin, C. M., & Hardin, E. E. (1996). Neural sensitization and physiological markers in multiple chemical sensitivity. *Regulatory Toxicology and Pharmacology, 24*(1 Pt 2), S39–S47.

Benford, M. S., Talnagi, J., Doss, D. B., Boosey, S., & Arnold, L. E. (1999). Gamma radiation fluctuations during alternative healing therapy. *Alternative Therapies in Health and Medicine, 5*(4), 51–56.

Bennett, C. (2012). *Cannabis and the soma solution.* Walterville, OR: Trine Day Press.

Bergman, S. A. (1999). Ketamine: Review of its pharmacology and its use in pediatric anesthesia. *Anesthesia Progress, 46*(1), 10–20.

Berman, M. (1989). *Coming to our senses.* New York: Simon and Schuster.

Bernheimer, C. K., & Kahane, C. (Eds.). (1985). *Dora's case: Freud-hysteria feminism.* New York: Columbia University Press.

Bernstein-Carlson, E. B. (1994). Studying the interaction between physical and psychological states with the dissociative experiences scale. In D. Spiegel (Ed.), *Dissociation: Culture, mind, and body* (pp. 41–56). Washington, DC: American Psychiatric Press.

Bhattacharya, S. K., Bhattacharya, A., Sairam, K., & Ghosal, S. (2000). Anxiolytic-antidepressant activity of Withania somnifera glycowithanolides: An experimental study. *Phytomedicine, 7*(6), 463–469.

Bisbing, S. B., Jorgenson, L. M., & Sutherland, P. K. (1995). *Sexual abuse by professionals: A legal guide.* Charlottesville, VA: Michie.

Bittner, A. C., Croffut, R. M., & Stranahan, M. C. (2005). Prescript-assist TM probiotic-prebiotic treatment for irritable bowel syndrome: Randomized, placebo-controlled, double-blind clinical study. *Clinical Therapeutics, 27*(6), 755–761.

Blake, D. D., Weathers, F. W., Nagy, L. M., Kaloupek, D., Klauminzer, G., Charney, D. S., Buckley, T. C. (2000). *Clinician-administered PTSD scale (CAPS) instruction manual.* Boston: National Center for PTSD.

Blake, E. (2010). Naturopathic hydrotherapy in the treatment of fibromyalgia. In L. Chaitow (Ed.), *Fibromyalgia syndrome: A practitioner's guide to treatment* (pp. 289–302). New York: Churchill Livingstone.

Bloch, I. (1988). Physiotherapy and the rehabilitation of torture victims. *Clinical Management in Physical Therapy, 8*(3), 26–29.

Blumenthal, M. (1998). *The complete German commission E monograph: Therapeutic guide to herbal medicines.* Austin: American Botanical Council.

Blundell, S. (1995). *Women in ancient Greece*. Cambridge, MA: Harvard University Press.

Boon, S., Steele, K., & van der Hart, O. (2011). *Coping with trauma-related dissociation: Skills training for patients and therapists*. New York: Norton.

Booth, B., Mengeling, M.A., Torner, J., & Sadler, A.G. (2011). Rape, sex partnership, and substance use consequences in women veterans. *Journal of Traumatic Stress, 24*(3), 287–294.

Borsook, D. (2009). Ketamine and chronic pain: Going the distance. *Pain, 145*(3), 271–272. doi:10.1016/j.pain.2009.05.021

Boscarino, J.A. (2004). Posttraumatic stress disorder and physical illness: Results from clinical and epidemiologic studies. *Annals of the New York Academy of Sciences, 1032*, 141–153.

Bouso, J.C., Doblin, R., Farré, M., Alcázar, M.A., & Gómez-Jarabo, G. (2008). MDMA-assisted psychotherapy using low doses in a small sample of women with chronic posttraumatic stress disorder. *Journal of Psychoactive Drugs, 40*(3), 225–236.

Bradley, B.F., Brown, S.L., Chu, S., & Lea, R.W. (2009). Effects of orally administered lavender essential oil on responses to anxiety-provoking film clips. *Human Psychopharmacology: Clinical and Experimental, 24*(4), 319–330.

Bradwejn, J., Zhou, Y., Koszycki, D., & Shlik, J. (2000). A double-blind, placebo-controlled study on the effects of Gotu Kola (Centella asiatica) on acoustic startle response in healthy subjects. *Journal of Clinical Psychopharmacology, 20*(6), 680–684.

Bratmann, S., & Girman, A.M. (2003). Mosby's handbook of herbs and supplements and their therapeutic uses. St. Louis: Mosby.

Brattstrom, A. (2009). Long-term effects of St. John's wort (Hypericum perforatum) treatment: A 1-year safety study in mild to moderate depression. *Phytomedicine: International Journal of Phytotherapy and Phytopharmacology, 16*(4), 277–283.

Braud, W.G., & Dennis, S.P. (1989). Geophysical variables and behavior: LVIII. Autonomic activity, hemolysis, and biological psychokinesis: Possible relationships with geomagnetic field activity. *Perceptual and Motor Skills, 68*, 1243–1254.

Brave Heart, M.Y.H., & DeBruyn, L.M. (1998). The American Indian holocaust: Healing historical unresolved grief. *American Indian and Alaskan Native Mental Health Research: The Journal of the National Center, 8*(2), 60–82.

Bravo, J.A., Forsythe, P., Chew, M.V., Escaravage, E., Savignac, H.M., Dinan, T.G., . . . Cryan, J.F. (2011). Ingestion of lactobacillus strain regulates emotional behavior and central GABA receptor expression in a mouse via the vagus nerve. *Proceedings of the National Academy of Sciences, 108*(38), 16050–16055.

Brekhman, I.I., & Dardymov, I.V. (1969). New substances of plant origin which increase non-specific resistance. *Annual Review of Pharmacology and Toxicology, 9*, 419–430.

Bremner, J.D., Southwick, S.M., & Charney, D.S. (1991). Animal models for the neurobiology of trauma. *PTSD Research Quarterly, 2*(4), 1–7.

Brett, E.A. (1993). Classifications of posttraumatic stress disorder in DSM-IV: Anxiety disorder, dissociative disorder, or stress disorder? In J. Davidson & E. Foa (Eds.), *Posttraumatic stress disorder: DSM-IV and beyond* (pp. 191–204). Washington, DC: American Psychiatric Press.

Brewin, C.R., Rose, S., Andrews, B., Green, J., Tata, P., McEvedy, C., . . . Foa, E.B. (2002). Brief screening instrument for post-traumatic stress disorder. *British Journal of Psychiatry, 181*, 158–162.

Briere, J. (1995). *Trauma symptom inventory professional manual*. Odessa, FL: Psychological Assessment Resources.

Brilliant, J., & Berloni, W. (2003). *Doga: Yoga for dogs*. San Francisco: Chronicle Books.

Brown, D., & Fromm, E. (1987). *Hypnosis and behavioral medicine*. Mahwah, NJ: Erlbaum.

Brown, E., Hurd, N. S., McCall, S., & Ceremuga, T. E. (2007). Evaluation of the anxiolytic effects of chrysin, a Passiflora incarnata extract, in the laboratory rat. *American Association of Nurse Anesthetists Journal, 75*(5), 333–337.

Brown, L. S. (1994). *Subversive dialogues: Theory in feminist therapy*. New York: Basic Books.

Brown, L. S. (2008). *Cultural competence in trauma therapy: Beyond the flashback*. Washington, DC: American Psychological Association.

Brown, R. P., Gerbarg, P. L., & Ramazanov, Z. (2002). Rhodiola rosea: A phytomedicinal overview. *HerbalGram, 56*, 40–52.

Browning C. H. (1996). Nonsteroidal anti-inflammatory drugs and severe psychiatric side effects. *International Journal of Psychiatry in Medicine, 26*(1), 25–34.

Bryant, R. A., & Harvey, A. G. (2000). *Acute stress disorder: A handbook of theory, assessment, and treatment*. Washington, DC: American Psychological Association.

Bryant, R. A., Harvey, A. G., Dang, S., & Sackville, T. (1998). Assessing acute stress disorder: Psychometric properties of a structured clinical interview. *Psychological Assessment, 10*(3), 215–220.

Bryant, R. A., Moulds, M., & Guthrie, R. (2000). Acute stress disorder scale: A self-report measure of acute stress disorder. *Psychological Assessment, 12*(1), 61–68.

Buchanan, T. W., Kern, S., Allen, J. S., Tranel, D., & Kirschbaum, C. (2004). Circadian regulation of cortisol after hippocampal damage in humans. *Biological Psychiatry, 56*(9), 651–656.

Budzynski, T. H., Budzynski, H. K., Evans, J. R., & Abarbanel, A. (Eds.). (2008). *Introduction to quantitative EEG and neurofeedback: Advanced theory and applications* (2nd ed.). New York: Academic Press.

Buitrago-Lopez, A., Sanderson, J., Johnson, L., Warnakula, S., Wood, A., Di Angelantonio, E., & Franco, O. H. (2011). Chocolate consumption and cardiometabolic disorders: Systematic review and meta-analysis. *BMJ* 2011; 343:d4488 doi: 10.1136/bmj.d4488

Bullock, M. L., Culliton, P. D., & Olander, R. T. (1989). Controlled trial of acupuncture for severe recidivist alcoholism. *Lancet, 333*(8652), 1435–1439.

Burgess, A. W. (1981). Physician sexual misconduct and patients' responses. *American Journal of Psychiatry, 138*(10), 1335–1342.

Burke, N. J., Hellman, J. L., Scott, B. G., Weems, C. F., & Carrion, V. G. (2011). The impact of adverse childhood experiences on an urban pediatric population. *Child Abuse & Neglect, 35*(6), 408–413.

Burnett, B. P., Jia, Q., Zhao, Y., & Levy, R. M. (2007). A medicinal extract of Scutellaria baicalensis and Acacia catechu acts as a dual inhibitor of cyclooxygenase and 5-lipoxygenase to reduce inflammation. *Journal of Medicinal Food, 10*(3), 442–451.

Bystritsky, A., Kerwin, L., & Feusner, J. (2008). A pilot study of rhodiola rosea (rhodax) for generalized anxiety disorder (GAD). *Journal of Alternative and Complementary Medicine. 14*(2), 175–180.

Calabrese, J. D. (2007). The therapeutic use of peyote in the Native American church. In M. J. Winkelman & T. B. Roberts (Eds.), *Psychedelic medicine: New evidence for hallucinogenic substances as medicine* (Vols. 1–2) (pp. 29–42). Westport, CT: Praeger.

Cao, H., Liu, J., & Lewith, G. T. (2010). Traditional Chinese medicine for treatment of fibromyalgia: A systematic review of randomized controlled trials. *Journal of Alternative and Complementary Medicine,* 16(4), 397–409.

Carney, R. M., Freedland, K. E., Stein, P. K., Steinmeyer, B. C., Harris, W. S., Rubin, E. H., . . . Rich, M. W. (2010). Effect of omega-3 fatty acids on heart rate variability in depressed patients with coronary heart disease. *Psychosomatic Medicine, 72*(8), 748–754.

Carter, C. S., Ahnert, L., Grossmann, K., Hrdy, S. B., Lamb, M., Porges, S. W., & Sachser, N. (Eds.). (2005) *Attachment and bonding: A new synthesis.* Cambridge: MIT Press.

Cascella, N. G., Kryszak, D., Bhatti, B., Gregory, P., Kelly, D. L., McEvoy, J. P., . . . Eaton, W. W. (2011). Prevalence of celiac disease and gluten sensitivity in the United States clinical antipsychotic trials of intervention effectiveness study population. *Schizophrenia Bulletin, 37*(1), 94–100.

Cash, T. F., & T. Pruzinsky (Eds.). (1990). *Body images: Development, deviance, and change.* New York: Guilford Press.

Cash, T. F., & Smolak, L. (Eds.). (2011). *Body image: A handbook of science, practice, and prevention* (2nd ed.). New York: The Guilford Press.

Catherall, D. R. (1989). *Differentiating intervention strategies for primary and secondary trauma in posttraumatic stress disorder: The example of Vietnam veterans.* Chicago: Plenum.

Cavanagh, H. M. A., & Wilkinson, J. M. (2002). Biological activities of lavender essential oil. *Phytotherapy Research, 16*(4), 301–308.

Chaitow, L., Bradley, D., & Gilbert, C. (2002). *Multidisciplinary approaches to breathing pattern disorders.* New York: Churchill Livingstone.

Chalmers, J. (2007). Modern auricular therapy: A brief history and the discovery of the vascular autonomic signal. *Journal of Chinese Medicine, 84,* 5–9.

Chandler, C. K. (2011). *Animal assisted therapy in counseling.* New York: Routledge.

Charcot, J. M., & Goetz, C. G. (Trans.). (1987). *Charcot, the clinician: The Tuesday lessons.* New York: Raven Press.

Chi, Y. S., Lim, H., Park, H., & Kim, H. P. (2003). Effects of wogonin, a plant flavone from Scutellaria radix, on skin inflammation: In vivo regulation of inflammation-associated gene expression. *Biochemical Pharmacology, 66*(7), 1271–1278.

Chouinard, G., Beauclair, L., Geiser, R., & Etienne, P. (1990). A pilot study of magnesium aspartate hydrochloride (Magnesiocard) as a mood stabilizer for rapid cycling bipolar affective disorder patients. *Progress in Neuro-Psychopharmacology and Biological Psychiatry, 14*(2), 171–180.

Christianson, D. W., Mangani, S., Shoham, G., & Lipscomb, W. N. (1989). Binding of d-phenylalanine and d-tyrosine to carboxypeptidase a. *Journal of Biological Chemistry, 264*(22), 12849–12853.

Chu, J. A. (2011). *Rebuilding shattered lives: Treating complex PTSD and dissociative disorders* (2nd ed.). Hoboken, NJ: Wiley.

Chu, J. A., Frey, L. M., Ganzel, B. L., & Matthews, J. A. (1999). Memories of childhood abuse: Dissociation, amnesia, and corroboration. *American Journal of Psychiatry, 156*(5), 749–755.

Churchill, W. (1999). The crucible of American Indian identity: Native tradition versus colonial imposition in postconquest North America. In D. Champagne (Ed.), *Contemporary Native American cultural issues* (pp. 39–67). London: AltaMira.

272   *References*

Clare, D.A., & Swaisgood, H.E. (2000). Bioactive milk peptides: A prospectus. *Journal of Dairy Science, 83*(6), 1187–1195.

Clark, M.M., Hanna, B.K., Mai, J.L., Graszer, K.M., Krochta, J.G., McAlpine, D.E., . . . Sarr MG. (2007). Sexual abuse survivors and psychiatric hospitalization after bariatric surgery. *Obesity Surgery, 17*(4), 465–469.

Cleveland, A.J. (1995). Therapy dogs and the dissociative patient: Preliminary observations. *Dissociation, 8*(4), 247–252.

Cohen, D. (1978). LSD in Leiden. *New Scientist, 77*(1086), 175.

Cohen, H., Benjamin, J., Geva, A.B., Matar, M.A., Kaplan, Z., & Kotler, M. (2000). Autonomic dysregulation in panic disorder and in post-traumatic stress disorder: Application of power spectrum analysis of heart rate variability at rest and in response to recollection of trauma or panic attacks. *Psychiatry Research, 96*(1), 1–13.

Cohen, S. (1994). Psychosocial influences on immunity and infectious disease in humans. In R. Glaser & J.K. Kiecolt-Glaser (Eds.), *Handbook of human stress and immunity* (pp. 301–319). San Diego, CA: Academic Press.

Comas-Diaz, L., & Griffith, E.H. (1988). Clinical guidelines in cross-cultural mental health. New York: Wiley.

Cooke, B., & Ernst, E. (2000). Aromatherapy: A systematic review. *British Journal of General Practice, 50*(455), 493–496.

Coons, P.M. (1993). The differential diagnosis of possession states. *Dissociation, 6*(4), 213–221.

Coppen, A., & Bolander-Gouaille, C. (2005). Treatment of depression: Time to consider folic acid and vitamin B12. *Journal of Psychopharmacology, 19*(1), 59–65.

Correll, G.E., Maleki, J., Gracely, E.J., Muir, J.J., & Harbut, R.E. (2004). Subanesthetic ketamine infusion therapy: A retrospective analysis of a novel therapeutic approach to complex regional pain syndrome. *Pain Medicine, 5*(3), 263–275.

Coulston, C.M., Perdices, M., Henderson, A.F., & Malhi, G.S. (2011). Cannabinoids for the treatment of schizophrenia? A balanced neurochemical framework for both adverse and therapeutic effects of cannabis use. *Schizophrenia Research and Treatment, 2011,* 1–10. doi:10.1155/2011/501726

Courtois, C.A. (1988). *Healing the incest wound: Adult survivors in therapy.* Toronto: Penguin Books Canada.

Cox, C., & Hayes, J. (1999). Physiologic and psychodynamic responses to the administration of therapeutic touch in critical care. *Complementary Therapies in Nursing and Midwifery, 5*(3), 87–92.

Cox, R.H., Shealy, C.N., Cady, R.K., & Liss, S. (1996). Pain reduction and relaxation with brain wave synchronization (photo stimulation). *Journal of Neurological and Orthopaedic Medicine and Surgery, 17*(1), 32–34.

Crabtree, A. (1993). *From Mesmer to Freud.* New Haven, CT: Yale University Press.

Curi, R., Alvarez, M., Bazotte, R.B., Botion, L.M., Godoy, J.L., & Bracht, A. (1986). Effect of Stevia rebaudiana on glucose tolerance in normal adult humans. *Brazilian Journal of Medical and Biological Research, 19*(6), 771–774.

Cutler, M.J., Holland, B.S., Stupski, B.A., Gamber, R.G., & Smith, M.L. (2005). Cranial manipulation can alter sleep latency and sympathetic nerve activity in humans: A pilot study. *Journal of Alternative and Complementary Medicine, 11*(1), 103–108.

D'Adamo, P.J. (with Whitney, C.). (2001). *Live right 4 your type.* New York: Penguin.

Daniel, K.T. (2005). *The whole soy story: The dark side of America's favorite health food.* Washington, DC: Newtrends Publishing.

Danieli, Y. (1988). Treating survivors and children of survivors of the Nazi Holocaust. In F. M. Ochberg (Ed.), *Post-traumatic therapy and victims of violence* (pp. 278–294). New York: Brunner/Mazel.

D'Aquili, E. G., & Laughlin, C. D. (1975). The biopsychological determinants of religious ritual behavior. *Zygon: Journal of Religion and Science, 10*(1), 32–58.

Darbinyan, V., Aslanyan, G., Amroyan, E., Gabrielyan, E., Malmström, C., & Panossian, A. (2007). Clinical trial of Rhodiola rosea L. extract SHR-5 in the treatment of mild to moderate depression. *Nordic Journal of Psychiatry, 61*(5), 343–348.

D'Arcy, Y. (2011). Prescribing nonsteroidal anti-inflammatory drugs. *Nurse Practitioner, 36*(10), 8–11.

Davidson, J., & Foa, E. (1993). *Post-traumatic stress disorder: DSM-IV and beyond.* Washington, DC: American Psychiatric Press.

DebMandal, M., & Mandal, S. (2011). Coconut (Cocos nucifera L.: Arecaceae): In health promotion and disease prevention. *Asian Pacific Journal of Tropical Medicine, 4*(3), 241–247.

de la Fuente Arias, M., Franco Justo, C., & Salvador Granado, M. (2010). Efectos de un programa de meditación (mindfulness) en la medida de la alexitimia y las habilidades sociales. *Psicothema, 22*(3), 369–375.

de Lima Osório, F., Horta de Macedo, L. R., Machado de Sousa, J. P., Pinto, J. P., Quevedo, J., Crippa, J. A. S., & Hallak, J. E. C. (2011). The therapeutic potential of harmine and ayahuasca in depression: Evidence from exploratory animal and human studies. In R. G. Santos (Ed.), *The ethnopharmacology of ayahuasca* (pp. 75–85). Kerala, India: Transworld Research Network. Retrieved from http://issuu.com/researchsignpost/docs/rafael/1?mode=a_p

Delini-Stula, A., & Holsboer-Trachsler, E. (2009). Treatment strategies in anxiety disorders: An update. *Therapeutische Umschau, 66*(6), 425–431.

Demitrack, M., Putnam, F., Brewerton, T., Brandt, H., & Gold, P. (1990). Relation of clinical variables to dissociative phenomena in eating disorders. *American Journal of Psychiatry, 147*(9), 1184–1187.

Department of Health and Human Services (DHHS). (2011). *Complementary and alternative medicine: What people aged 50 and older discuss with their health care providers (AARP and NCCAM Survey Report).* Washington, DC: U.S. Government Printing Office.

de Saint-Hilaire, Z., Messaoudi, M., Desor, D., & Kobayashi, T. (2009). Effects of a bovine alpha S1-casein tryptic hydrosylate (CTH) on sleep disorder in Japanese general population. *Open Sleep Journal, 2,* 26–32.

de Santillana, G., & von Dechend, H. (1969). Hamlet's mill: An essay investigating the origins of human knowledge and its transmission through myth. Boston: David R. Godine.

Descilo, T., Vedamurtachar, A., Gerbarg, P. L., Nagaraja, D., Gangadhar, B. N., Damodaran, B., . . . Brown, R. P. (2010). Effects of a yoga breath intervention alone and in combination with an exposure therapy for post-traumatic stress disorder and depression in survivors of the 2004 South-East Asia tsunami. *Acta Psychiatrica Scandinavica, 121*(4), 289–300. doi: 10.1111/j.1600–0447.2009.01466.x

Dhuley, J. N. (2001). Nootropic-like effect of ashwagandha (Withania somnifera L.) in mice. *Phytotherapy Research, 15*(6), 524–528.

Didie, E. R., Tortolani, C. C., Pope, C. G., Menard, W., Fay, C., & Phillips, K. A. (2006). Childhood abuse and neglect in body dysmorphic disorder. *Abuse & Neglect, 30*(10), 1105–1115.

Dimpfel, W., & Suter, A. (2008). Sleep improving effects of a single dose administration of a valerian/hops fluid extract: A double blind, randomized, placebo-controlled sleep-EEG study in a parallel design using electrohypnograms. *European Journal of Medical Research, 13*(5), 200–204.

Dinan, T. G., Quigley, E. M., Ahmed, S. M., Scully, P., O'Brien, S., O'Mahony, L., . . . Keeling, P. W. (2006). Hypothalamic-pituitary-gut axis dysregulation in irritable bowel syndrome: Plasma cytokines as a potential biomarker? *Gastroenterology, 130*(2), 304–311.

Disch, E. (n.d.). Are you in trouble with a client? Unpublished handout. Boston Associates to Stop Therapy Abuse, Cambridge, MA.

Disch, E., & Avery, N. (2001). Sex in the consulting room, the examining room, and the sacristy: Survivors of sexual abuse by professionals. *American Journal of Orthopsychiatry, 71*(2), 204–217.

Dixon, J. (2008). *The biology of kundalini: Exploring the fire of life.* Raleigh, NC: Lulu Publishing.

Dobkin de Rios, M. (2002). What we can learn from shamanic healing: Brief psychotherapy with Latino immigrant clients. *American Journal of Public Health, 92*(10), 1576–1581.

Dolan, Y. M. (1991). *Resolving sexual abuse: Solution-focused therapy and Ericksonian hypnosis for adult survivors.* New York: Norton.

Donath, F., Quispe, S., Diefenbach, K., Maurer, A., Fietze, I., & Roots, I. (2000). Critical evaluation of the effect of valerian extract on sleep structure and sleep quality. *Pharmacopsychiatry, 33*(6), 239.

Dorn, M. (2000). Efficacy and tolerability of Baldrian versus oxazepam in non-organic and non-psychiatric insomniacs: A randomised, double-blind, clinical, comparative study. *Forsch Komplementarmed Klass Naturheilkd, 7*(2), 79–84.

dos Santos, R. G. (2011). Possible risks and interactions of the consumption of ayahuasca and cannabis in humans. In R. G. Santos (Ed.), *The ethnopharmacology of ayahuasca* (pp. 75–85). Kerala, India: Transworld Research Network. Retrieved from http://issuu.com/researchsignpost/docs/rafael/1?mode=a_p

Dossey, B. M., Keegan, L., Kolkmeier, L. G., & Guzzetta, C. E. (Eds.). (1989). *Holistic health promotion.* Rockville, MD: Aspen.

Dube, S. R., Anda, R. F., Whitfield, C. L., Brown, D. W., Felitti, V. J., Dong, M., & Giles, W. H. (2005). Long-term consequences of childhood sexual abuse by gender of victim. *American Journal of Preventive Medicine, 28*(5), 430–438.

Duran, E. (n.d.). Injury where blood does not flow. Retrieved from http://soulhealing16.com/yahoo_site_admin/assets/docs/Injury_Where_Blood_Does_Not_Flow2-10-1-1.287131055.rtf

Duran, E., & Duran, B. (1995). *Native American postcolonial psychology.* Albany: State University of New York Press.

Edwards, V. J., Holden, G. W., Felitti, V. J., & Anda, R. F. (2003). Relationship between multiple forms of childhood maltreatment and adult mental health in community respondents: Results from the adverse childhood experiences study. *American Journal of Psychiatry, 160*(8), 1453–1460.

Eidenier, H. O. (2000). *A clinician's view of Biotics research products* [Lecture transcript]. Rosenberg, TX: Biotics Research.

Eisler, R. (1988). *The chalice and the blade.* San Francisco: Harper.

Eliade, M. (1972). *Shamanism: Archaic techniques of ecstasy* (W. R. Trask, Trans.). Princeton, NJ: Princeton University Press.

Elias, G. A., Gulick, D., Wilkinson, D. S., & Gould, T. J. (2010). Nicotine and extinction of fear conditioning. *Neuroscience, 165*(4), 1063–1073.

Eliaz, I., Weil, E., & Wilk, B. (2007). Integrative medicine and the role of modified citrus pectin/alginates in heavy metal chelation and detoxification: Five case reports. *Forschende Komplementärmedizin, 14*(6), 358–64.Enig, M. G. (1996). *Proceedings from AVOC Lauric Oils Symposium: Health and nutritional benefits from coconut oil: An important functional food for the 21st century.* Ho Chi Min City, Vietnam: AVOC.

Enig, M. G. (2000). *Know your fats: The complete primer for understanding the nutrition of fats, oils, and cholesterol.* Silver Spring, MD: Bethesda Press.

Enig, M. G. (2006). *Eat fat, lose fat: The healthy alternative to trans fats.* New York: Plume.

Eovaldi, B., & Zanetti, C. (2010). Hyperbaric oxygen ameliorates worsening signs and symptoms of post-traumatic stress disorder. *Journal of Neuropsychiatric Disease and Treatment, 6*, 785–789.

Erdman, J., Oria, M., & Pillsbury, L. (Eds.), Committee on Nutrition, Trauma, and the Brain. (2011). *Nutrition and traumatic brain injury: Improving acute and subacute health outcomes in military personnel.* Washington, DC: The National Academies Press.

Ernst, E. (2007). A re-evaluation of kava (Piper methysticum). *British Journal of Clinical Pharmacology, 64*(4), 415–415.

Erowid. (2009). Psilocybin mushrooms: Basics. Retrieved from http://www.erowid.org/plants/mushrooms/mushrooms_basics.shtml

Erowid. (2010a). DMT: Basics. Retrieved from http://www.erowid.org/chemicals/dmt/dmt_basics.shtml

Erowid. (2010b). LSD: Basics. Retrieved from http://www.erowid.org/chemicals/lsd/lsd_basics.shtml

Erowid. (2010c). Salvia divinorum: Basics. Retrieved from http://www.erowid.org/plants/salvia/salvia_basics.shtml

Erowid. (2011). Ayahuasca: Legal status. Retrieved from http://www.erowid.org/chemicals/ayahuasca/ayahuasca_law.shtml

Evans, J. (1986). *Mind, body and electromagnetics.* Longmead, Great Britain: Element Books.

Everhart, J. E., Yeh, F., Lee, E. T., Hill, M. C., Fabsitz, R., Howard, B. V., & Welty, T. K. (2002). Prevalence of gallbladder disease in American Indian populations: Findings from the Strong Heart Study. *Hepatology, 35*(6), 1507–1512.

Fábregas, J. M., González, D., Fondevila, S., Cutchet, M., Fernández, X., Barbosa, P. C., . . . Bouso, J. C. (2010). Assessment of addiction severity among ritual users of ayahuasca. *Drug and Alcohol Dependence, 111*(3), 257–261.

Fadiman, J. (2011). *The psychedelic explorer's guide: Safe, therapeutic, and sacred journeys.* Rochester, VT: Park Street Press.

Fahrion, S. T., Walters, E. D., Coyne, L., & Allen T. (1992). Alterations in EEG amplitude personality factors and brain electrical mapping after alpha-theta brainwave training: A controlled case study for an alcoholic in recovery. *Alcoholism: Clinical and Experimental Research, 16*(3), 547–552.

Fallon, S., & Enig, M. (1999). *Nourishing traditions: The cookbook that challenges politically correct nutrition and the diet dictocrats.* Washington, DC: NewTrends.

Farley, M., Minkoff, J. R., & Barkan, H. (2001). Breast cancer screening and trauma history. *Women and Health, 34*(2), 15–27.

Farnsworth, N. R., Kinghorn, A. D., Soejarto, D. D., & Waller, D. P. (1985). Siberian ginseng (Eleutherococcus senticosus): Current status as an adaptogen. In H. Wagner, H. Z. Hikino, & N. R. Farnsworth (Eds.), *Economic and medicinal plant research* (Vol. 1, pp. 155–215). London: Academic Press.

Favazza, A. R. (1987). *Bodies under siege: Self-mutilation in culture and psychiatry.* Baltimore, MD: Johns Hopkins University Press.

Feily, A., & Abbasi, N. (2009). The inhibitory effect of Hypericum perforatum extract on morphine withdrawal syndrome in rat and comparison with clonidine. *Phytotherapy Research, 23*(11), 1549–1552.

Feinstein, A., & Botes, M. (2009). The psychological health of contractors working in war zones. *Journal of Traumatic Stress, 22*(2), 102–105.

Felton, C. V., Crook, D., Davies, M. J., & Oliver, M. F. (1994). Dietary polyunsaturated fatty acids and composition of human aortic plaques. *Lancet, 344*(8931), 1195–1196.

Ferdjallah, M., Bostick, F. X., & Barr, R. E. (1996). Potential and current density distributions of cranial electrotherapy stimulation (CES) in a four-concentric-spheres model. *IEEE Transactions on Biomedical Engineering, 43*(9), 939–943.

Feuerstein, M., Labbe, E. E., & Kuczmierczyk, A. R. (1988). *Health psychology: A psychobiological perspective.* New York: Plenum Press.

Field, T. (1985). Attachment as psychobiological attunement: Being on the same wavelength. In M. Reite & T. Field (Eds.), *The psychobiology of attachment and separation* (pp. 455–480). Orlando, FL: Academic Press.

Field T. (2000). *Touch therapy.* London: Churchill Livingstone.

Field, T., Diego, M., & Hernandez-Reif, M. (2010). Moderate pressure is essential for massage therapy effects. *International Journal of Neuroscience, 120*(5), 381–385.

Field, T., Hernandez-Reif, M., Hart, S., Quintino, O., Drose, L., Field, T., . . . Schanberg, S. (1997). Effects of sexual abuse are lessened by massage therapy. *Journal of Bodywork and Movement Therapies, 1*(2), 65–69.

Field, T., Lasko, D., Mundy, P., Henteleff, T., Kabat, S., Talpins, S., & Dowling, M. (1997). Brief report: Autistic children's attentiveness and responsivity improved after touch therapy. *Journal of Autism and Developmental Disorders, 27*(3), 333–338.

Field, T., Seligman, S., Scafidi, F., & Schanberg, S. (1996). Alleviating posttraumatic stress in children following hurricane Andrew. *Journal of Applied Developmental Psychology, 17*(1), 37–50.

Fine, A. (2010). *Handbook on animal assisted therapy: Theoretical foundations and guidelines for practice.* San Diego, CA: Academic Press.

Fisar, Z. (2009). Phytocannabinoids and endocannabinoids. *Current Drug Abuse Reviews, 2*(1), 51–75.

Fish, E. W., Sekinda, M., Ferrari, P. F., Dirks, A., & Miczek, K. A. (1999). Distress vocalizations in maternally separated mouse pups: Modulation via 5-HT(1A), 5-HT(1B) and GABA(A) receptors. *Psychopharmacology, 149*(3), 277–285.

Fisher, A. A., Purcell, P., & Le Couteur, D. G. (2000). Toxicity of Passiflora incarnata L. *Journal of Toxicology—Clinical Toxicology, 38*(1), 63–66.

Fiz, J., Durán, M., Capellà, D., Carbonell, J., & Farré, M. (2011). Cannabis use in patients with fibromyalgia: Effect on symptoms relief and health-related quality of life. *Public Library of Science One, 6*(4): e18440. Retrieved from http://www.ncbi.nlm.nih.gov/pubmed?term=%22Farr%C3%A9%20M%5BAuthor%5D

Flannery, R.B. (1987). From victim to survivor: A stress management approach in the treatment of learned helplessness. In B.A. van der Kolk (Ed.), *Psychological trauma* (pp. 217–229). Washington, DC: American Psychiatric Press.

Forcier, M., & Doblin, R. (1992). A long-term follow-up to Dr. Timothy Leary's 1961–1962 Concord state reformatory rehabilitation study. *Multidisciplinary Association for Psychedelic Studies*, 3(4), 3–5.

Fraser, G.A. (2009). The use of a synthetic cannabinoid in the management of treatment-resistant nightmares in posttraumatic stress disorder (PTSD). *CNS Neuroscience and Therapeutics, 15*(1), 84–88.

Frawley, D. (2001). *Ayurvedic healing: A comprehensive guide.* Twin Lakes, WI: Lotus Press.

Frawley, D., Ranade, S., & Lele, A. (2003). *Ayurveda and marma therapy: Energy points in yogic healing.* Twin Lakes, WI: Lotus Press.

Frecska, E., & Kulcsar, Z. (1989). Social bonding in the modulation of the phsyiology of ritual trance. *Ethos, 17*(1), 70–87.

Frederick, C., & Phillips, M. (1995). *Healing the divided self: Clinical and Ericksonian hypnotherapy for dissociative conditions.* New York: Norton.

Freedman, R. (1990). Cognitive-behavioral perspectives on body-image change. In T.F. Cash & T. Pruzinsky (Eds.), *Body images: Development, deviance, and change* (pp. 272–291). New York: Guilford.

Freud, S. (1955). Studies on hysteria. In J. Strachey (Ed. & Trans.), *The standard edition of the complete psychological works of Sigmund Freud* (Vol. 2, pp. 106–124). London: Hogarth.

Freyd, J.J. (1996). Betrayal trauma: The logic of forgetting childhood abuse. Cambridge, MA: Harvard University Press.

Fried, R., & Grimaldi, J. (1993). The psychology and physiology of breathing *in behavioral medicine, clinical psychology, and psychiatry.* New York: Plenum.

Friedlander, W. (1992). *The golden wand of medicine: A history of the caduceus symbol in medicine.* New York: Greenwood.

Friedman, M.J., Davidson, J.R.T., Mellman, T.A., & Southwick, S.M. (2000). Guidelines for pharmacotherapy and position paper on practice guidelines. In E.B. Foa, T.M. Keane, & M.J. Friedman (Eds.), *Effective treatments for post-traumatic stress disorder: Practice guidelines from the International Society for Traumatic Stress Studies* (pp. 84–105). New York: Guilford.

Fu, P.P., Xia, Q., Guo, L., Yu, H., & Chan, P.C. (2008). Toxicity of kava kava. *Journal of Environmental Science and Health, Part C: Environmental Carcinogenesis Ecotoxicology Reviews, 26*(1), 89–112.

Füssel, A., Wolf, A., & Brattström, A. (2000). Effect of a fixed valerian-hop extract combination (Ze 91019) on sleep polygraphy in patients with non-organic insomnia: A pilot study. *European Journal of Medical Research, 5*(9), 385–390.

Gaby, A.R. (2002). Intravenous nutrient therapy: The "Myers' cocktail." *Alternative Medical Review, 7*(5), 389–403.

Gagne, D., & Toye, R. (1994). The effects of therapeutic touch and relaxation therapy in reducing anxiety. *Archives of Psychiatric Nursing, 8*(3), 184–189.

Gagne, M. (1998). The role of dependency and colonialism in generating trauma in First Nations citizens: The James Bay Cree. In Y. Danieli (Ed.), *International handbook of multigenerational legacies of trauma: Group project for holocaust survivors and their children* (pp. 355–372). New York: Plenum.

278   *References*

Galanter, M. (1989). *Cults: Faith, healing, and coercion.* New York: Oxford University Press.

Gallagher, W. (1993). *The power of place.* New York: Poseidon.

Gartrell, N., Herman, J., Olarte, S., Feldstein, M., & Localio, R. (1986). Psychiatrist-patient sexual contact: Results of a national survey: I. Prevalence. *American Journal of Psychiatry, 143*(9), 1126–1131.

Gehlhaart C. (2000). *Healing for elders and institutions: Intentional touch therapy research project.* Lakewood, CO: Healing Touch International.

Gershon, M. (1998). *The second brain: A groundbreaking new understanding of nervous disorders of the stomach and intestine.* New York: HarperCollins.

Gilligan, C. (1982). *Different voice: Psychological theory and women's development.* Cambridge, MA: Harvard University Press.

Gilligan, C., & Richards, D.A.J. (2009). *The deepening darkness: Patriarchy, resistance, and democracy's future.* New York: Cambridge University Press.

Gilman, S. (1991). *The Jew's body.* New York: Routledge, Chapman, and Hall.

Gilman, S.L., King, H., Porter, R., Rousseau, G.S., & Showalter, E. (1993). *Hysteria beyond Freud.* Los Angeles: University of California Press.

Gimbutas, M. (1989). The language of the goddess. New York: Harper & Row.

Gleason, G. (1992). Mutual hypnosis. *Whole Earth Review, 75,* 28–30.

Global Commision on Drug Policy. (2011). *Report of the Global Commission on Drug Policy: War on drugs.* Retrieved from http://www.globalcommissionondrugs.org/Report

Goetz, C.G., Bonduelle, M., & Gelfand, T. (1995). *Charcot: Constructing neurology.* New York: Oxford University Press.

Goldberg, C. (1995, May 21). Betraying a trust: Teacher-student sex is not unusual. *New York Times,* p. 37.

Goldberg, N. (2005). *Writing down the bones: Freeing the writer within.* Boston: Shambhala.

Goldstein, B.D., Osofsky, H.J., & Lichtveld, M.Y. (2011). The Gulf oil spill. *The New England Journal of Medicine, 364*(14), 1334–1348.

Gonzalez, N.J., & Issacs, L. (1999). Evaluation of pancreatic proteolytic enzyme treatment of adenocarcinoma of the pancreas, with nutrition and detoxification support. *Nutrition and Cancer, 33*(2), 117–124.

Goodman, F.D. (1990). *Where the spirits ride the wind: Trance journeys and other ecstatic experiences.* Bloomington, IN: Indiana University Press.

Goodwin, R.D., Fischer, M.E., & Goldberg, J. (2007). A twin study of post–traumatic stress disorder symptoms and asthma. *American Journal of Respiratory and Critical Care Medicine,* 176(10), 983–987.

Green, B.L. (1990). Defining trauma: Terminology and generic stressor dimensions. *Journal of Applied Social Psychology, 20*(20), 1632–1642.

Green, E. (1990). Consciousness, psychophysiology and psychophysics: An overview (Unpublished paper). Topeka, KS: The Menninger Clinic.

Green, E., & Green, A. (1989). *Beyond biofeedback.* Fort Wayne, IN: Knoll.

Greene, B. (2011). *The hidden reality: Parallel universes and the deep laws of the cosmos.* New York: Knopf.

Gregory, R.L. (1987). *The Oxford companion to the mind.* New York: Oxford University Press.

Griffiths, R.R., Johnson, M.W., Richards, W.A., McCann, U., & Richards, B.D. (2008). Mystical-type experiences occasioned by psilocybin mediate the attribution of personal meaning and spiritual significance 14 months later. *Journal of Psychopharmacology, 22*(6), 621–632.

Griffiths, R. R., Richards, W. A., McCann, U., & Jesse, R. (2006). Psilocybin can occasion mystical-type experiences having substantial and sustained personal meaning and spiritual significance. *Psychopharmacology, 187*(3), 268–283. doi:10.1007/s00213-006-0457-5

Grodin, M. A., Piwowarczyk, L., Fulker, D., Bazazi, A. R., & Saper, R. B. (2008). Treating survivors of torture and refugee trauma: A preliminary case series using qigong and t'ai chi. *Journal of Alternative and Complementary Medicine, 14*(7), 801–806.

Grossman, F. K., & Moore, R. P. (1994). Against the odds: Resiliency in adult survivor of childhood sexual abuse. In C. E. Franz & A. J. Stewart (Eds.), *Women creating lives: Identities, resilience, and resistance* (pp. 71–82). Boulder: Westview.

Gunnar, M. R., & Donzella, B. (2002). Social regulation of the cortisol levels in early human development. *Psychoneuroendocrinology, 27*(1–2), 199–220.

Gunnar, M. R., & Vazquez, D. M. (2001). Low cortisol and a flattening of expected daytime rhythm: Potential indices of risk in human development. *Development and Psychopathology, 13*(3), 515–538.

Gutheil, T. G. (1989). Borderline personality disorder, boundary violations, and patient-practitioner sex: Medicolegal pitfalls. *American Journal of Psychiatry, 146*(5), 597–602.

Hagens, B. (1991). "Venuses," turtles, and other hand-held cosmic models. In M. Anderson & F. Merrell (Eds.), *On semiotic modeling* (pp. 47–60). New York: Mouton de Gruyter.

Hall, M. P. (1972). *Man: Grand symbol of the mysteries: Thoughts in occult anatomy.* Los Angeles: Philosophical Research Society.

Hallahan, B., Hibbeln, J. R., Davis, J. M., & Garland, M. (2007). Omega-3 essential fatty acid supplementation in patients with recurrent deliberate self harm: A double blind randomized controlled trial. *British Journal of Psychiatry, 190*, 118–122.

Halpern, J. H. (1996). The use of hallucinogens in the treatment of addiction. *Addiction Research, 4*(2), 177–189. Abstract retrieved from http://www.maps.org/newsletters/v06n4/06407abs.html

Halpern, J. H., Sherwood, A. R., Hudson, J. I., Yurgelun-Todd, D., & Pope, H. G. (2005). Psychological and cognitive effects of long-term peyote use among Native Americans. *Biological Psychiatry, 58*(8), 624–631.

Hampson, A. J., Grimaldi, M., Axelrod, J., & Wink, D. (1998). Cannabidiol and (−)Δ9-tetrahydrocannabinol are neuroprotective antioxidants. *Proceedings of the National Academy of Sciences of the United States of America, 95*(14), 8268–8273.

Hanes, K. R. (2003). Salvia divinorum: Clinical and research potential. *Multidisciplinary Association for Psychedelic Studies, 13*(1), 18–20.

Hanh, T. N. (1990). *The practice of mindfulness in psychotherapy (audio).* Boulder: Sounds True.

Harch, P. G., Andrews, S. R., Fogarty, E. F., Amen, D., Pezzullo, J. C., Lucarini, J., . . . Van Meter, K. W. (2012). A phase I study of low-pressure hyperbaric oxygen therapy for blast-induced post-concussion syndrome and post-traumatic stress disorder. *Journal of Neurotrauma, 29*(1), 168–185.

Harlow, H. F. (1961). The development of affectional patterns in infant monkeys. In B. M. Foss (Ed.), *Determinants of infant behaviour* (pp. 75–97). London: Methuen.

Harvey, M. (1990). *Proceedings from the trauma conference.* Boston: Harvard Medical School.

Hasler, F., Grimberg, U., Benz, M.A., Huber, T., & Vollenweider, F.X. (2004). Acute psychological and physiological effects of psilocybin in healthy humans: a double-blind, placebo-controlled dose–effect study. *Psychopharmacology, 172*, 145–156. doi:10.1007/s00213–003–1640–6

Heber, A.S., Fleisher, W.P., Ross, C.A., & Stanwick, R.S. (1989). Dissociation in alternative healers and traditional practitioners: A comparative study. *American Journal of Psychotherapy, 73*(4), 562–574.

Hemat, R.A.S. (2009). *Principles of orthomolecularism*. Urotext.

Henry, J.A., & Rella, J.G. (2001). Medical risks associated with MDMA use. In J. Holland (Ed.), *Ecstasy: The complete guide* (pp. 71–86). Rochester, VT: Park Street Press.

Herman, J.L. (1981). *Father-daughter incest*. Cambridge, MA: Harvard University Press.

Herman, J.L. (1990). Presentation at the trauma conference. Boston: Harvard Medical School.

Herman, J.L. (1992). *Trauma and recovery: The aftermath of violence-from domestic abuse to political terror*. New York: Basic Books.

Herz, R.S. (2009). Aromatherapy facts and fictions: A scientific analysis of olfactory effects on mood, physiology and behavior. International *Journal of Neuroscience, 119*(2), 263–290.

Ho, M.W. (1999, October). Coherent energy, liquid crystallinity and acupuncture. Talk presented to the British Acupuncture Society. Retrieved from http://www.ratical. org/co-globalize/MaeWanHo/acupunc.html

Hodge, D.R., & Limb, G.E. (2011). Spiritual assessment and Native Americans: Establishing the social validity of a complementary set of assessment tools. *Social Work, 56*(3), 213–223.

Hoffer, A. (1962). Niacin therapy in psychiatry (American lecture series). Springfield, IL: Thomas.

Hoffman, L., Burges-Watson, P., Wilson, G., & Montgomery, J. (1989). Low plasma B endorphin in PTSD. *Australian and New Zealand Journal of Psychiatry, 23*(2), 269–273.

Holick, M. (2003). Vitamin D deficiency: What a pain it is. *Mayo Clinic Proceedings, 78*(12), 1457–1459.

Holland, J. (2000). *Transcript of Lindesmith MDMA seminar* (3/30/00 NYC). Retrieved from http://weekendsatbellevue.com/PubEcstasy.html

Holland, J. (2001). *Ecstasy: The complete guide*. Rochester, VT: Park Street Press.

Hollifield, M., Sinclair-Lian, N., Warner, T.D., & Hammershlag, R. (2007). Acupuncture for posttraumatic stress disorder: A randomized controlled pilot trial. *Journal of Nervous and Mental Disease*, 195(6), 504–513.

Hollister, L.E. (2001). Marijuana (cannabis) as medicine. *Journal of Cannabis Therapeutics, 1*(1), 5–27.

Holmes, W.C., & Slap, G.B. (1998). Sexual abuse of boys: Definition, prevalence, correlates, sequelae, and management. *Journal of the American Medical Association, 280*(21), 1855–1162.

Holroyd, J.C., & Brodsky, A.M. (1977). Psychologists' attitudes and practices regarding erotic and nonerotic physical contact with clients. *American Psychologist, 32*(10), 843–849.

Hölzel, B.K., Carmody, J., Vangel, M., Congleton, C., Yerramsetti, S.M., Gard, T., & Lazar, S.W. (2011). Mindfulness practice leads to increases in regional brain gray matter density. *Psychiatry Research, 191*(1), 36–43.

Houghton, P.J. (1997). *Valerian: The genus Valeriana*. Amsterdam, the Netherlands: Harwood.

Houston, J. (1987). *The search for the beloved: Journeys in sacred psychology*. Los Angeles: Tarcher.

Howard, R. (1990). Art therapy as an isomorphic intervention in the treatment of a client with post-traumatic stress disorder. *American Journal of Art Therapy, 28*, 79–86.

Huang, L., & Obenaus, A. (2011). Hyperbaric oxygen therapy for traumatic brain injury. *Medical Gas Research, 1*(1), 21.

Hudson, T. (2011). Rhodiola rosea. *Emerson Quarterly, 2*, 14–15.

Hunter, D. (1985). Hysteria, psychoanalysis and feminism: The case of Anna O. In S.N. Garner, C. Kahane, & M. Sprengnether (Eds.), *The (m)other tongue: Essays in feminist psychoanalytic interpretation* (pp. 89–115). New York: Cornell University Press.

Ishak, W.W., Kahloon, M., & Fakhry, H. (2011). Oxytocin role in enhancing well-being: A literature review. *Journal of Affective Disorders, 130*(1–2), 1–9.

Ito, Y., Teicher, M.H., Glod, C.A., & Ackerman, E. (1998). Preliminary evidence for aberrant cortical development in abused children: A quantitative EEG study. *Journal of Neuropsychiatry and Clinical Neurosciences, 10*(3), 298–307.

Jacob, S.W., & de la Torre J.C. (2009). Pharmacology of dimethyl sulfoxide in cardiac and CNS damage. *Pharmacolgical Reports, 61*(2), 225–235.

Jacobsen, F.M. (1988). Ethnocultural assessment. In L. Comas-Diaz & E.H.E. Griffith (Eds.), *Clinical guidelines in cross cultural mental health* (pp. 135–147). New York: Wiley.

Jäger, R., Purpura, M., & Kingsley, M. (2007). Phospholipids and sports performance. *Journal of the International Society of Sports Nutrition, 4*, 5.

Jahn, R.G., & Dunne, B.J. (1983). *On the quantum mechanics of consciousness, with application to anomalous phenomena*. Princeton, NJ: Princeton University Press.

Jamal, M., Does, A.J., Penninx, B.W., & Cuijpers, P. (2011). Age at smoking onset and the onset of depression and anxiety disorders. *Nicotine & Tobacco Research, 13*(9), 809–819.

James, M. (2006). The gut-liver axis: Genetic and environmental influences on detoxification. In D.S. Jones & S. Quinn (Eds.), *Textbook of functional medicine* (pp. 562–580). Gig Harbor, WA: Institute for Functional Medicine.

Janoff-Bulman, R., & Frieze, I.H. (1987). The role of gender in reactions to criminal victimization. In R.C. Barnett, L. Biener, G.K. Baruch (Eds.), *Gender & stress* (pp. 159–184). New York: Free Press.

Jansen, K. (2000). *Ketamine: Dreams and realities*. Sarasota, FL: Multidisciplinary Association for Psychedelic Studies.

Jarrett, L.S. (1995). Chinese medicine and the betrayal of intimacy: The theory and treatment of abuse, incest, rape and divorce with acupuncture and herbs—part 1. *American Journal of Acupuncture, 23*(1), 35–51.

Jerome, L. (2004). *A review of research in humans and non-human animals* (MAPS' MDMA Investigator's Brochure: Update #2). Santa Cruz, CA: Multidisciplinary Association for Psychedelic Studies. Retrieved from http://www.maps.org/research/mdma/protocol/litupdate2.pdf

Jinfu, Z., & Xinha, J. (2008). Observations of diabetes mellitus treated by Chinese wudang zhonghe qigong (dynamic form). Retrieved from http://alternativehealing.org/Diabetes_qigong_therapy2.htm

Johansen, P. Ø., & Krebs, T.S. (2009). How could MDMA (ecstasy) help anxiety disorders?: A neurobiological rationale. *Journal of Psychopharmacology, 23*(4), 389–391.

Johnson, D. R., Feldman, S. C., Lubin, H., & Southwick, S. M. (1995). The therapeutic use of ritual and ceremony in the treatment of post-traumatic stress disorder. *Journal of Traumatic Stress, 8*(2), 283–298.

Johnson, M. W., MacLean, K. A., & Reissig, C. J., Prisinzano, T. E., & Griffiths, R. R. (2011). Human psychopharmacology and dose-effects of salvinorin A, a kappa opioid agonist hallucinogen present in the plant Salvia divinorum. *Drug and Alcohol Dependence, 115*(1–2), 150–155.

Jonas, W. B., & Crawford, C. C. (2004). *Healing, intention, and energy medicine: Science, research methods and clinical implications.* New York: Churchill Livingstone.

Joshee, N., Patrick, T. S., Mentreddy, R. S., & Yadav, A. K. (2002). Skullcap: Potential medicinal crop. In J. Janick & A. Whipkey (Eds.), *Trends in new crops and new uses* (pp. 580–586). Alexandria, VA: ASHS Press.

Kalichman, L. (2010). Massage therapy for fibromyalgia symptoms. *Rheumatology International, 30*(9), 1151–1157.

Kamprath, K., Romo-Parra, H., Häring, M., Gaburro, S., Doengi, M., Lutz, B., & Pape, H. C. (2011). Short-term adaptation of conditioned fear responses through endocannabinoid signaling in the central amygdala. *Neuropsychopharmacology, 36*(3), 652–63.

Kasper, S., Gastpar, M., Muller, W. E., Volz, H. P., Dienel, A., Kieser, M., & Moller, H. J. (2008). Efficacy of St. John's wort extract WS 5570 in acute treatment of mild depression: A reanalysis of data from controlled clinical trials. *European Archives of Psychiatry and Clinical Neuroscience, 258*(1), 59–63.

Katcher, A. H., & Beck, A. M. (1987). Health and caring for living things. *Anthrozoos, 1*(3), 175–183.

Kayıran, S., Dursun, E., Dursun, N., Ermutlu, N., & Karamürsel, S. (2010). Neurofeedback intervention in fibromyalgia syndrome: A randomized, controlled, rater blind clinical trial. *Applied Psychophysiology and Biofeedback, 35*(4), 293–302.

Keane, T. M. (1990). The epidemiology of post-traumatic stress disorder: Some comments and concerns. *PTSD Research Quarterly, 1*(3), 1–8.

Kelly, G. S. (2001). Rhodiola rosea: a possible plant adaptogen. *Alternative Medicine Review, 6*(3), 293–302.

Kerényi, C. (1959). *Asklepios: Archetypal image of the physician's existence.* New York: Pantheon.

Kerr, J. (1993). *A most dangerous method: The story of Jung, Freud, and Sabina Spielrein.* New York: Knopf.

Khalsa, S. B., Hickey-Schultz, L., Cohen, D., Steiner, N., & Cope, S. (2012). Evaluation of the mental health benefits of yoga in a secondary school: A preliminary randomized controlled trial. *Journal of Behavioral Health Services and Research, 39*(1), 80–90.

Khantzian, E. J. (1990). Self-regulation and self-medication factors in alcoholism and the addictions: Similarities and differences. *Recent Developments in Alcoholism, 8*, 255–271.

Kiecolt-Glaser, J. K., Malarkey, W. B., Cacioppo, J. T., & Glaser, R. (1994). Stressful personal relationships: Immune and endocrine function. In R. Glaser & J. K. Kiecolt-Glaser (Eds.), *Handbook of human stress and immunity* (pp. 321–339). San Diego, CA: Academic Press.

Kilts, J. D., Tupler, L. A., Keefe, F. J., Payne, V. M., Hamer, R. M., Naylor, J. C., . . . Shampine, L. J. (2010). Neurosteroids and self-reported pain in veterans who served in the U.S. military after September 11, 2001. *Pain Medicine, 11*(10), 1469–1476.

Kim, J.H., Desor, D., Kim, Y.T., Yoon, W.J., Kim, K.S., Jun, J.S., . . . Shim, I. (2007). Efficacy of alphas1-casein hydrolysate on stress-related symptoms in women. *European Journal of Clinical Nutrition, 61*(4), 536–541.

King, H. (1993). Once upon a text: Hysteria from Hippocrates. In S. Gilman, H. King, R. Porter, G. Rousseau, & E. Showalter (Eds.), *Hysteria beyond Freud* (pp. 3–90). Los Angeles: University of California Press.

Kirlin, M. (2010). Yoga as an adjunctive treatment for PTSD in Latina women: A review of the evidence and recommendations for implementation. School of Professional Psychology, Paper 133. Retrieved from http://commons.pacificu.edu/spp/133

Kirmayer, L.J. (1994). Pacing the void: Social and cultural dimensions of dissociation. In D. Spiegel (Ed.), *Dissociation: Culture, mind, and body* (pp. 91–118). Washington, DC: American Psychiatric Press.

Kirmayer, L.J., & Valaskakis, G.G. (Eds.). (2009). *Healing traditions: The mental health of aboriginal peoples in Canada.* Vancouver: UBC Press.

Kirsch, D.L., & Smith, R.B. (2004). Cranial electrotherapy stimulation for anxiety, depression, insomnia, cognitive dysfunction, and pain: A review and meta-analyses. In P.J. Rosch & M.S. Markov (Eds.), *Bioelectromagnetic medicine* (pp. 687–699). Mineral Wells, TX: Marcel Dekker.

Kleinman, A. (1988). *Rethinking psychiatry: From cultural category to personal experience.* New York: Free Press.

Kolp, E., Young, M.S., Friedman, H., Krupitsky, E., Jansen, K., & O'Connor, L-A. (2007). Ketamine-enhanced psychotherapy: Preliminary clinical observations on its effects in treating death anxiety. *International Journal of Transpersonal Studies, 26*, 1–17.

Koopman, C., Classen, C., Cardena, E., & Spiegel, D. (1995). When disaster strikes, acute stress disorder may follow. *Journal of Traumatic Stress, 8*(1), 29–46.

Korn, L. (1987). Polarity therapy: To touch the heart of (the) matter. *Somatics Magazine–Journal of the Bodily Arts and Sciences 6*(2), 30–34.

Korn, L. (1994, March). *Invited address: The bleeding heart.* Cambridge, MA: Lesley University.

Korn, L. (1996). *Somatic empathy.* Olympia, WA: Center for World Indigenous Studies, DayKeeper Press.

Korn, L. (2002). Community trauma and development. *Fourth World Journal, 5*(1), 1–9. Retrieved from http://www.cwis.org/fwj/vol5_1.htm

Korn, L. (2010). *Medicines from the jungle: Western Mexico.* Olympia, WA: Daykeeper Press.

Korn, L., Logsdon, R.G., Polissar, N.L., Gomez-Beloz, A., Waters, T., & Rÿser, R. (2009). A randomized trial of a CAM therapy for stress reduction in American Indian and Alaskan Native family caregivers. *Gerontologist, 49*(3), 368–377.

Korn, L.E., Loytomaki, S., Hinman, T., & Rÿser, R. (2007). Polarity therapy protocol for dementia caregivers: Part 2. *Journal of Bodywork and Movement Therapies, 11*(3), 244–259.

Korn, L.E., McCraty, R., Atkinson, M., Logsdon, R., Pollisar, N., & Rÿser, R. (2012). Heart rate variability, stress, depression and pain in American Indian dementia caregivers. Unpublished manuscript.

Korn, L., & Rÿser, R. (2006). Burying the umbilicus: Nutrition trauma, diabetes and traditional medicine in rural West Mexico. In G.C. Lang (Ed.), *Indigenous peoples and diabetes: Community empowerment and wellness* (pp. 231–277). Durham, NC: Carolina Academic Press.

Korn, L., & Rÿser, R. (2009). *Preventing and treating diabetes naturally: The native way*. Olympia, WA: DayKeeper Press.

Kornfield, J., & Hall, R. (1988a). *Touching the heart of healing, part one: Opening to acceptance (audio)*. Novato, CA: Access Group.

Kornfield, J., & Hall, R. (1988b). *Touching the heart of healing, part two: Path of the mindful heart (audio)*. Novato, CA: Access Group.

Kovar, M., Koenig, X., Mike, A., Cervenka, R., Lukács, P., Todt, H., Hilber, K. (2011). The anti-addictive drug ibogaine modulates voltage-gated ion channels and may trigger cardiac arrhythmias. *BMC Pharmacology, 11*(Suppl 2), A1.

Krenn, L. (2002). Passion flower (Passiflora incarnata L.): A reliable herbal sedative. *Wiener Medizinische Wochenschrift, 152*(15–16), 404–406.

Krieger, D. (1979). *The therapeutic touch: How to use your hands to help or heal*. New York: Prentice Hall.

Krieger, D., Peper, E., & Ancoli, S. (1979). Therapeutic touch: Searching for evidence of physiological change. *American Journal of Nursing, 79*(4), 660–662.

Kristal, H. J., & Haig, J. M. (2002). *The nutrition solution: A guide to your metabolic type*. Berkeley, CA: North Atlantic Books.

Kristal, H. J., & Haig, J. M. (2004). *Personalized metabolic nutrition: Practitioner's manual*. Mill Valley, CA: Personalized Metabolic Nutrition.

Krupitsky, E., Burakov, A., Romanova, T., Dunaevsky, I., Strassman, R., & Grinenko, A. (2002). Ketamine psychotherapy for heroin addiction: Immediate effects and two-year follow-up. *Journal of Substance Abuse Treatment, 23*(4), 273–283.

Krupitsky, E. M., & Grinenko, A. Y. (1997). Ketamine psychedelic therapy (KPT): A review of the results of ten years of research. *Journal of Psychoactive Drugs, 29*(2): 165–83.

Krupitsky, E., & Kolp, E. (2007). Ketamine psychedelic psychotherapy. In M. J. Winkelman & T. B. Roberts (Eds.), Psychedelic medicine: New evidence for hallucinogenic substances as medicine (Vol. 2, pp. 67–85). Westport, CT: Praeger.

Krystal, H. (1988). *Integration and self-healing: Affect, trauma, alexithymia*. Hillsdale, NJ: Analytic Press.

Kulka, R. A., Schlenger, W. E., Fairbank, J. A., Hough, R. L., Jordan, B. K., Marmar, C. R., & Weiss, D. S. (1990). *Trauma and the Vietnam generation*. New York: Brunner/Mazel.

Kulkarni, A. D., & Smith, R. B. (2001). The use of microcurrent electrical therapy and cranial electrotherapy stimulation in pain control. *Clinical Practice of Alternative Medicine, 2*(2), 99–102.

Kumar, A., & Singh, A. (2007). Protective effect of St. John's wort (Hypericum perforatum) extract on 72-hour sleep deprivation-induced anxiety-like behavior and oxidative damage in mice. *Planta Medica, 73*(13), 1358–1364.

Kuppurajan, K., Rajagopalan, S. S., Sitaraman, R., Rajgopalan, V., Janaki, R., & Venkataraghavan, S. (1980). Effect of ashwagandha (Withania somnifera Dunal) on the process of aging in human volunteers. *Journal of Research in Ayurveda & Siddha, 1*(2), 247–258.

LaDue. R. A. (1994). Coyote returns: Twenty sweats does not an Indian expert make. In N. K. Gartrell (Ed.), *Bringing ethics alive* (pp. 93–109). Binghamton, NY: Harrington Park Press.

Lake, J. (2007). Textbook of integrative mental health care. New York: Thieme.

Lakhan, S. E., & Vieira, K. F. (2008). Nutritional therapies for mental disorders. *Nutrition Journal, 7*, 2. doi:10.1186/1475–2891-7-2

Lakoff, R.T., & Coyne, J.C. (1993). *Father knows best: The use and abuse of power in Freud's case of Dora.* New York: Teachers College Press.

Landolt, H.P., Dijk, D.J., Gaus, S.E., & Borbely, A.A. (1995). Caffeine reduces low-frequency delta activity in the human sleep EEG. *Neuropsychopharmacology, 12*(3), 229–238.

Lapin, I. (2001). Phenibut (beta-phenyl-GABA): A tranquilizer and nootropic drug. *CNS Drug Reviews. 7*(4), 471–481.

Lawson, B.R., Belkowski, S.M., Whitesides, J.F., Davis, P., & Lawson, J.W. (2007). Immunomodulation of murine collagen-induced arthritis by N, N-dimethylglycine and a preparation of Perna canaliculus. *BMC Complementary and Alternative Medicine, 7*, 20.

Leary, T., Metzner, R., Presnell, M., Weil, G., Schwitzgebel, R., & Kinne, S. (1965). A new behavior change program for adult offenders using psilocybin. *Psychotherapy: Therapy, Research, and Practice, 2*(2), 61–72.

Lee, M.S., Yang, K.H., Huh, H.J., Kim, H.W., Ryu, H., Lee, H.S., & Chung, H.T. (2001). Qi therapy as an intervention to reduce chronic pain and to enhance mood in elderly subjects: A pilot study. *American Journal of Chinese Medicine, 29*(2), 237–245.

Levenson, R.W., & Ruef, A.M. (1992). Empathy: A physiological substrate. *Journal of Personality and Social Psychology, 63*(2), 234–246.

Levine, M. (1993). Current and potential applications of bioelectromagnetics in medicine. *Subtle Energies, 4*(1), 77–86.

Levinson, B.M. (1984). Human/companion animal therapy. *Journal of Contemporary Psychotherapy, 14*(2), 131–144. doi: 10.1007/BF00946311

Lewis, M.D., Hibbeln, J.R., Johnson, J.E., Lin, Y.H., Hyun, D.Y., & Loewke, J.D. (2011). Suicide deaths of active-duty U.S. military and omega-3 fatty-acid status: A case-control comparison. *Journal of Clinical Psychiatry, 72*(12), 1585–1590.

Lewis-Fernández, R. (1994). Culture and dissociation: A comparison of ataque de nervios among Puerto Ricans and possession syndrome in India. In D. Spiegel (Ed.), *Dissociation: Culture, mind, and body* (pp. 123–167). Washington, DC: American Psychiatric Press.

Li, J., Brackbill, R.M., Stellman, S.D., Farfel, M.R., Miller-Archie, S.A., Friedman, S., . . . Cone, J. (2011). Gastroesophageal reflux symptoms and comorbid asthma and posttraumatic stress disorder following the 9/11 terrorist attacks on World Trade Center in New York City. *American Journal of Gastroenterology, 106*(11), 1933–1941.

Liberman, J. (1990). *Light: Medicine of the future.* Santa Fe, NM: Bear.

Liedloff, J. (1986). *The continuum concept: Allowing human nature to work successfully.* Cambridge, MA: De Capo.

Lifton, R.J. (1979). *The broken connection: On death and the continuity of life.* New York: Basic Books.

Linde, K., Berner, M.M., & Kriston, L. (2008). St. John's wort for major depression. *Cochrane Database of Systematic Reviews, 2008*(4), CD000448.

Linde, K., Mulrow, C.D., Berner, M., & Egger, M. (2005). St John's wort for depression. *Cochrane Database of Systematic Reviews, 18*(2), CD000448.

Lisak, D. (1993). Men as victims: Challenging cultural myths. *Journal of Traumatic Stress, 6*(4), 577–580.

Lisak, D. (1995). Integrating a critique of gender in the treatment of male survivors of childhood abuse. *Psychotherapy, 32*(2), 258–269.

Liss, S, & Liss, B. (1996). Physiological and therapeutic effects of high frequency electrical pulses. *Integrative Physiological and Behavioral Science, 31*(2), 88–95.

Logan, B. K., & Jones, A. W. (2000). Endogenous ethanol 'auto-brewery syndrome' as a drunk-driving defense challenge. *Medicine, Science and the Law, 40*(3), 206–215.

Lotsof, H. S., (1995). Ibogaine in the treatment of chemical dependence disorders: clinical perspectives (a preliminary review). *MAPS, 5*(3), 16–27. Retrieved from http://www.ibogaine.desk.nl/clin-perspectives.html

Luna, L. E. (2011). Indigenous and mestizo use of ayahuasca: An overview. In R. G. Santos (Ed.), *The ethnopharmacology of ayahuasca* (pp. 1–21). Kerala, India: Transworld Research Network. Retrieved from http://issuu.com/researchsignpost/docs/rafael/1?mode=a_p

Lutz, A., Slagter, H. A., Dunne, J. D., & Davidson, R. J. (2008). Attention regulation and monitoring in meditation. *Trends in Cognitive Sciences, 12*(4), 163–169.

Luyer, M. D., Greve, J. W. M., Hadfoune, M., Jacobs, J. A., Dejong, C. H., & Buurman, W. A. (2005). Nutritional stimulation of cholecystokinin receptors inhibits inflammation via the vagus nerve. *Journal of Experimental Medicine, 202*(8), 1023–1029.

Lyoo, I. K., Demopulos, C. M., Hirashima, F., Ahn, K. H., & Renshaw P. F. (2003). Oral choline decreases brain purine levels in lithium-treated subjects with rapid-cycling bipolar disorder: A double-blind trial using proton and lithium magnetic resonance spectroscopy. *Bipolar Disorders, 5*(4), 300–306.

Lyttle, T. (1993). Misuse and legend in the "toad licking" phenomenon. *International Journal of the Addictions, 28*(6), 521–538.

Mabit, J. (2002). Blending traditions: Using indigenous medicinal knowledge to treat drug addiction. *Multidisciplinary Association for Psychedelic Studies, 12*(2). Retrieved from http://maps.org/news-letters/v12n2/12225mab.html

Mabit, J. (2007). Ayahuasca in the treatment of addictions. In M. J. Winkelman & T. B. Roberts (Eds.), *Psychedelic medicine: New evidence for hallucinogenic substances as medicine* (Vol. 2, pp. 87–105). Westport, CT: Praeger.

Mabit, M. (1996). Takiwasi: Ayahuasca and shamanism in addiction therapy. *Multidisciplinary Association for Psychedelic Studies Newsletter, 6*(3). Retrieved from http://www.maps.org/news-letters/v06n3/06324aya.html

Machoian, L. (2006). *The disappearing girl: Learning the language of teenage depression*. New York: Penguin.

MacIan, P. S., & Pearlman, L. A. (1992). Development and use of the TSI life event questionnaire. *Treating Abuse Today: The International News Journal of Abuse, Survivorship, and Therapy, 2*(1), 9–11.

Malchiodi, C. (2008). *Creative interventions with traumatized children*. New York: Guilford.

Mann, C. C. (2011). *1493: Uncovering the new world Christopher Columbus created*. New York: Knopf.

Marks, M., & Thayer, C. (1989). Engaging the somatic patient in healing through art. In H. Wadeson, J. Durkin, & D. Perach (Eds.), *Advances in art therapy* (pp. 169–180). Hoboken, NJ: Wiley.

Marlatt, G. A., Larimer, M. E., Mail, P., Hawkins, E., Cummins, L. H., Blume, A. W., . . . Gallion, S. (2003). Journeys of the circle: A culturally congruent life skills intervention for adolescent Indian drinking. *Alcoholism: Clinical and Experimental Research, 27*(8), 1327–1329.

Marshall, H. K., & Thompson, C. E. (1932). Colon irrigation in the treatment of mental disease. *New England Journal of Medicine, 207*, 454–457.

Marsicano, G., Wotjak, C. T., Azad, S. C., Bisogno, T., Rammes, G., Cascio, M. G., . . . Lutz, B. (2002). The endogenous cannabinoid system controls extinction of aversive memories. *Nature, 418*(6897), 530–534.

Martin-Baro, I. (1994). *Writings for a liberation psychology.* Cambridge, MA: Harvard University Press.

Marx, C. E. (2009, December). Abstract P-805. Presented at the American College of Neuropsychopharmacology (ACNP) 48th annual meeting, Hollywood, FL.

Mash, D. C. (2010). Ibogaine therapy for substance abuse disorders. In D. Brizer & R. Castaneda (Eds.), *Clinical addictions psychiatry* (pp. 50–60). Cambridge, UK: Cambridge University Press.

Massey, P. B. (2007). Reduction of fibromyalgia symptoms through intravenous nutrient therapy: Results of a pilot clinical trial. *Alternative Therapies, 13*(3), 32–34.

McCann, I. L., & Pearlman, L. A. (1990). *Psychological trauma and the adult survivor: Theory, therapy, and transformation.* New York: Brunner/Mazel.

McCarberg, B. H., & Barkin, R. L. (2007). The future of cannabinoids as analgesic agents: A pharmacologic, pharmacokinetic, and pharmacodynamic overview. *American Journal of Therapeutics, 14*, 475–483.

McCraty, R., Atkinson, M., & Bradley, R. T. (2004). Electrophysiological evidence of intuition: Part 1. The surprising role of the heart. *Journal of Alternative and Complementary Medicine, 10*(1), 133–143.

McCraty, R., Atkinson, M, & Tiller, W. A. (1993). New electophysiological correlates associated with intentional heart focus. *Subtle Energies, 4*(3), 251–268.

McCraty, R., Atkinson, M., & Tomasino, D. (2001). *Science of the heart: Exploring the role of the heart in human performance* (Publication No. 01–001). Boulder Creek, CA: HeartMath Research Center, Institute of HeartMath.

McCraty, R., Tomasino, D., Atkinson, M., & Sundram, J. (1999). *Impact of the Heart-Math self-management skills program on physiological and psychological stress in police officers.* Boulder Creek, CA: HeartMath Research Center.

McEwen, B. S. (2000). The neurobiology of stress: From serendipity to clinical relevance. *Brain Research, 886*(1–2), 172–189.

McEwen, B. S., & Seeman, T. (1999). Protective and damaging effects of mediators of stress: Elaborating and testing the concepts of allostasis and allostatic load. *Annals of the New York Academy of Sciences, 896*, 30–47.

McGrath, J. C. (2011). Posttraumatic growth and spirituality after brain injury. *Brain Impairment, 12*(2), 82–92.

McKenna, D. J. (2007). The healing vine: Ayahuasca as medicine in the 21st century. In M. J. Winkelman & T. B. Roberts (Eds.), Psychedelic medicine: New evidence for hallucinogenic substances as medicine (Vol. 1, pp. 21–44). Westport, CT: Praeger.

McPartland, J. M. (2010). Fibromyalgia and the endocannabinoid system. In L. Chaitow (Ed.), *Fibromyalgia syndrome: A practitioner's guide to treatment* (pp. 263–277). New York: Churchill Livingstone.

McPartland, J. M., Giuffrida, A., King, J., Skinner, E., Scotter, J., & Musty, R. E. (2005). Cannabimimetic effects of osteopathic manipulative treatment. *Journal of the American Osteopathic Association, 105*(6), 283–291.

Mechoulam, R. (2010). *General use of cannabis for PTSD symptoms.* Retrieved from http://veteransformedicalmarijuana.org/content/general-use-cannabis-ptsd-symptoms

Mechoulam, R., & Fride, E. (1995). The unpaved road to the endogenous brain cannabinoid ligands, the anandamides. In R. G. Pertwee (Ed.), *Cannabinoid receptors* (pp. 233–258). Boston: Academic Press.

Medin, A. E. (2010). Vinpocetine as a potent antiinflammatory agent. *Proceedings of the National Academy of Sciences, 107*(22), 9921–9922.

Medina, J. H., Viola, H., Wolfman, C., Marder, M., Wasowski, C., Calvo, D., & Paladini, A. C. (1997). Overview—flavonoids: A new family of benzodiazapine receptor ligands. *Neurochemical Research, 22*(4), 419.

Meichenbaum, D. (n.d.). Trauma, spirituality and recovery: Toward a spiritually-integrated psychotherapy. Unpublished paper, The Melissa Institute for Violence Prevention and Treatment, Miami, Florida.

Meltzer-Brody, S., Leserman, J., Zolnoun, D., Steege, J., Green, E., & Teich, A. (2007). Trauma and posttraumatic stress disorder in women with chronic pelvic pain. *Obstetrics and Gynecology, 109*(4), 902–908.

Meschino, J. P. (2001). Natural anti-inflammatory supplements: Research status and clinical applications. *Massage Today, 1*(12). Retrieved from http://massagetoday. org/mpacms/mt/article.php?id=10369

Messaoudi, M., Lefranc-Millot, C., Desor, D., Demagny, B., & Bourdon, L. (2005). Effects of a tryptic hydrolysate from bovine milk alphaS1-casein on hemodynamic responses in healthy human volunteers facing successive mental and physical stress situations. *European Journal of Nutrition, 44*(2), 128–132.

Metz, R. (1992). *Application of magnetic and polarity principles to life energy systems.* Santa Rosa, CA: Author.

Metzner, R., & Adamson, S. (2001). Using MDMA in healing, psychotherapy, and spiritual practice. In J. Holland (Ed.), *Ecstasy: The complete guide* (pp. 182–207). Rochester, VT: Park Street Press.

Mills, M. H., & Faunce, T. A. (1991). Melatonin supplementation from early morning auto-urine drinking. *Medical Hypotheses, 36*(3), 195–199.

Mintz, E. E. (1969). Touch and the psychoanalytic tradition. *Psychoanalytic Review, 56*(3), 367–376.

Mishlove, J. (1993). *The roots of consciousness: The classic encyclopedia of consciousness studies.* Tulsa, OK: Council Oak Books.

Mitchell, T. (2006, January). Theanine: Natural support for sleep, mood, and weight. *Life Extension Magazine.* Retrieved from http://www.lef.org/magazine/mag2006/jan2006_report_theanine_01.htm

Mithoefer, M. (2007). MDMA-assisted psychotherapy for the treatment of posttraumatic stress disorder. In M. J. Winkelman & T. B. Roberts (Eds.), *Psychedelic medicine: New evidence for hallucinogenic substances as medicine* (Vol. 1, pp. 155–176). Westport, CT: Praeger.

Mithoefer, M. C., Wagner, M. T., Mithoefer, A. T., Jerome, L., & Doblin, R. (2011). The safety and efficacy of ±3,4-methylenedioxymethamphetamine-assisted psychotherapy in subjects with chronic, treatment-resistant posttraumatic stress disorder: The first randomized controlled pilot study. *Journal of Psychopharmacology, 25*(4), 439–452.

Mollica, R. F., Wyshak, G., Lavelle, J., Truong, T., Tor, S., & Yang, T. (1990). Assessing symptom change in Southeast Asian refugee survivors of mass violence and torture. *American Journal of Psychiatry, 147*(1), 83–88.

Mollica, R. F., & McDonald L. (2004). Project 1 billion: Health ministers of post-conflict nations on mental health recovery. *UN Chronicle Online Edition.* Retrieved from http://www.thefreelibrary.com/Project+1+billion%3A+health+ministers+of+post-conflict+Nations+Act+on . . . .-a0114007100

Montagne, M. (2007). Psychedelic therapy for the treatment of depression. In M. J. Winkelman & T. B. Roberts (Eds.), *Psychedelic medicine: New evidence for hallucinogenic substances as medicine* (Vol. 1, pp. 177–190). Westport, CT: Praeger.

Montazeri, K., Farahnakian, M., & Saghaei, M. (2002). The effect of acupuncture on the acute withdrawal symptoms from rapid opiate detoxification. *Acta Anaesthesiologica Sinica, 40*(4), 173–177.

Moore-Ede, M.C., Sulzman, F.M., & Fuller, C.A. (1982). *The clocks that time us: Physiology of the circadian timing system.* Boston: Harvard University Press.

Moss, M., Hewitt, S., Moss, L., & Wesnes, K. (2008). Modulation of cognitive performance and mood by aromas of peppermint and ylang-ylang. *International Journal of Neuroscience, 118*(1), 59–77.

Movagegh, A., Alizadeh, R., Hajimohamadi, F., Esfehani, F., & Nejatfar, M. (2008). Preoperative oral Passiflora incarnata reduces anxiety in ambulatory surgery patients: A double-blind, placebo-controlled study. *Ambulatory Anesthesiology 106*, 1728–1732.

Moyers, B. (1993). *Healing and the mind.* New York: Bantam Doubleday Dell.

Muller, D., Pfeil, T., & von den Driesch, V. (2004). Valeriana officinalis—monograph. *Alternative Medicine Review, 9*(4), 438–441.

Multidisciplinary Association for Psychedelic Studies (MAPS). (2003). Ibogaine: Treatment outcomes and observations. *Multidisciplinary Association for Psychedelic Studies, 13*(2), 16–21.

Nadler, A., Kav-Venaki, S., & Gleitman, B. (1985). Transgenerational effects of the holocaust: Externalization of aggression in second generation holocaust survivors. *Journal of Consulting & Clinical Psychology, 53*(3), 365–369.

National Acupuncture Detoxification Association. (2010). *NADA Protocol: FAQs.* Retrieved from http://www.acudetox.com/nada-protocol/about-nada/12-faqs.html

Nelson, D.A. (2002). Gluten-sensitive enteropathy (celiac disease): More common than you think. *American Family Physician, 66*(12), 2259–2266.

Neufeld, K.M., Kang, N., Bienenstock, J., & Foster J.A. (2011). Reduced anxiety-like behavior and central neurochemical change in germ-free mice. *Neurogastroenterology & Motility, 23*(3), 255–264. doi: 10.1111/j.1365–2982.2010.01620.x

Ng, T.P., Chiam, P.C., Lee, T., Chua, H.C., Lim, L., & Kua, E.H. (2006). Curry consumption and cognitive function in the elderly. *American Journal of Epidemiology, 164*(9), 898–906.

Nixon, M.K., Cheng, M., & Cloutier, P. (2003). An open trial of auricular acupuncture for the treatment of repetitive self-injury in depressed adolescents. *Canadian Child and Adolescent Psychiatry Review, 12*(1), 10–12.

Norris, F.H., (2002). Psychosocial consequences of disasters. *National Center for PTSD Research Quarterly, 13*(2), 1–7.

North, C.S., Nixon, S.J., Shariat, S., Mallonee, S., McMillen, J.C., Spitznagel, E.L., & Smith, E.M. (1999). Psychiatric disorders among survivors of the Oklahoma City bombing. *Journal of the American Medical Association, 282*(8), 755–762.

Norton, D., Angerman, S., Istfan, N., Lopes, S.M., Babayan, V.K., Putz, . . . Blackburn, G.L. (2004). Comparative study of coconut oil, soybean oil, and hydrogenated soybean oil. *Philippine Journal of Coconut Studies, 29*(1&2), 1–5.

Nosova, T., Jousimies-Somer, H., Jokelainen, K., Heine, R., & Salaspuro, M. (2000). Acetaldehyde production and metabolism by human indigenous and probiotic Lactobacillus and Bifidobacterium strains. *Alcohol and Alcoholism, 35*(6), 561–568.

Novakovic, V., Sher, L., Lapidus, K.A.B., Mindes, J., Golier, J.A., & Yehuda, R. (2011). Brain stimulation in posttraumatic stress disorder. *European Journal of Psychotraumatology, 2*, 5609. DOI: 10.3402/ejpt.v2i0.5609

Novins, D.K., LeMaster, P.L., Jumper Thurman, P., & Plested, B. (2004). Describing community needs: Examples from the circles of care initiative. *American Indian and Alaska Native Mental Health Research, 11*(2), 42–58.

Ochberg, F.M. (1988). *Post-traumatic therapy and victims of violence.* New York: Brunner/Mazel.

Olasov-Rothbaum, B., & Foa, E.B. (1992). Cognitive-behavioral treatment of post-traumatic stress disorder. In P.A. Saigh (Ed.), *Posttraumatic stress disorder: A behavioral approach to assessment and treatment* (pp. 85–106). Boston: Allyn & Bacon.

Olff, M., Langeland, W., Witteveen, A., & Denys, D. (2010). A psychobiological rationale for oxytocin in the treatment of posttraumatic stress disorder. *CNS Spectrums, 15*(8), 522–530.

Ortmann, J., Genefke, I.K., Jakobsen, L., & Lunde, I. (1987). Rehabilitation of torture victims: An interdisciplinary treatment model. *American Journal of Social Psychiatry, 7*(4), 161–167.

Oschman, J.L. (2000). *Energy medicine: The scientific basis.* New York: Churchill Livingstone.

Ott, J. (1995). *The age of entheogens and the angel's dictionary.* Kennewick, WA: Natural Products.

Ott, J., & Wasson, R.G. (1983). The carved 'disembodied eyes' of Teotihuacan. *Harvard Botanical Museum Leaflets, 29*(4), 387–400.

Owen, G.N., Parnell, H., De Bruin, E.A., & Rycroft, J.A. (2008). The combined effects of L-theanine and caffeine on cognitive performance and mood. *Nutritional Neuroscience, 11*(4), 193–198.

Pace, T.W., & Heim, C.M. (2011). A short review on the psychoneuroimmunology of posttraumatic stress disorder: From risk factors to medical comorbidities. *Brain Behavior and Immunity, 25*(1), 6–13.

Palinkas, L.A., Petterson, J.S., Russell, J.C., & Downs, M.A. (2004). Ethnic differences in symptoms of post-traumatic stress after the Exxon Valdez oil spill. *Prehospital and Disaster Medicine, 19*(1), 102–112.

Panneck, J. (2010). *Spirituality and plant medicines: The future of modern psychotherapy.* Retrieved from http://www.examiner.com/alternative-religions-in-portland/spirituality-and-plant-medicines-the-future-of-modern-psychotherapy#ixzz1NsHrfvHI

Papadopoulos-Lane, C.A. (2010). *Cognitive appraisals, stress, and emotion about environmental contamination in the Akwesasne Mohawk Nation* [Doctoral dissertation]. Albany, NY: State University of New York.

Park, C.L., Cohen, L.H., & Murch, R.L. (1996). Assessment and prediction of stress-related growth. *Journal of Personality, 64*(1), 71–105.

Parker, G., Gibson, N.A., Brotchie, H., Heruc, G., Rees, A.M., & Hadzi-Pavlovic, D. (2006). Omega-3 fatty acids and mood disorders. *American Journal of Psychiatry, 163*(6), 969–978. doi: 10.1176/appi.ajp.163.6.969

Pascarosa, P., & Futterman, S. (1976). Ethnopsychedelic therapy for alcoholics: Observations in the peyote ritual of the Native American Church. *Journal of Psychedelic Drugs, 8*(3), 215–221.

Passie, T. (2007). Contemporary psychedelic therapy: An overview. In M.J. Winkelman & T.B. Roberts (Eds.), *Psychedelic medicine: New evidence for hallucinogenic substances as medicine* (Vol. 1, pp. 45–68). Westport, CT: Praeger.

Pasvogel, A.E., Miketova, P., & Moore, I.M. (2010). Differences in CSF phospholipid concentration by traumatic brain injury outcome. *Biological Research for Nursing, 11*(4), 325–331.

Paul, I.A., & Skolnick, P. (2003). Glutamate and depression: Clinical and preclinical studies. *Annals of the New York Academy of Sciences, 1003*, 250–272.

Pearlman, L.A. (2003). *Trauma and attachment belief scale*. Los Angeles, CA: Western Psychological Services.

Pelcovitz, D., van der Kolk, B., Roth, S., Mandel, F., Kaplan, S., & Resick, P. (1997). Development of a criteria set and a structured interview for disorders of extreme stress (SIDES). *Journal of Traumatic Stress, 10*(3), 16. doi: 10.1002/jts.2490100103

Peniston, E.G., & Kulkosky, P.J. (1992). Alpha-theta EEG biofeedback training in alcoholism and posttraumatic stress disorder. *International Society for the Study of Subtle Energies and Energy Medicines, 2*, 5–7.

Peniston, E.G., Marrinan, D.A., Deming, W.A., & Kulkosky, P.J. (1993). EEG alpha-theta brainwave synchronization in Vietnam theater veteran with combat-related posttraumatic stress disorder and alcohol abuse. *Medical Psychotherapy: An International Journal, 6*, 37–50.

Perez-Rodriguez, M.M., Baca-Garcia, E., Diaz-Sastre, C., Garcia-Resa, E., Ceverino, A., Saiz-Ruiz, J., . . . de Leon, J. (2008). Low serum cholesterol may be associated with suicide attempt history. *Journal of Clinical Psychiatry, 69*(12), 1920–1927.

Peters, L.G. (1994). Rites of passage and the borderline syndrome: Perspectives in transpersonal anthropology. *ReVision, 17*(1), 35.

Petkov, V.D., Yonkov, D., Mosharoff, A., Kambourova, T., Alova, L., Petkov, V.V., & Todorov, I. (1986). Effects of alcohol aqueous extract from rhodiola rosea L. roots on learning and memory. *Acta Physiologica et Pharmacologica Bulgarica, 12*(1), 3–16.

Petursson, H., Sigurdsson, J. A., Bengtsson, C., Nilsen, T. I., & Getz, L. (2012). Is the use of cholesterol in mortality risk algorithms in clinical guidelines valid? Ten years prospective data from the Norwegian HUNT 2 study. *Journal of Evaluation in Clinical Practice, 18*(1), 159–168.

Pfeiffer, C. (1988). *Nutrition and mental illness: An orthomolecular approach to balancing body chemistry*. Rochester, VT: Healing Arts Press.

Phillips, K.A. (2009). *Understanding body dysmorphic disorder*. New York: Oxford University Press.

Phillips, M., & Frederick, C. (1995). *Healing the divided self: Clinical and Ericksonian hypnotherapy for post-traumatic and dissociative conditions*. New York: Norton.

Picker, R.I. (1993). Cranial electrotherapy stimulation (CES). *Bridges, 4*(4), 7–9.

Pinkola-Estes, C. (1996). *Women who run with the wolves: Myths and stories of the wild woman archetype*. New York: Ballantine Books.

Pinkola-Estes, C. (2010). *Seeing in the dark: Myths and stories to reclaim the buried, knowing woman* [Audiobook]. Louisville, CO: Sounds True.

Pletcher, M.J., Vittinghoff, E., Kalhan, R., Richman, J., Safford, M., Sidney, S., . . . Kertesz, S. (2012). Association between marijuana exposure and pulmonary function over 20 years. *Journal of the American Medical Association, 307*(2), 173–181.

Plotnikoff, G.A., & Quigley, J.M. (2003). Prevalence of severe hypovitaminosis D in patients with persistent, nonspecific musculoskeletal pain. *Mayo Clinic Proceedings, 78*(12), 1463–1470.

Pope, K.S. (1988). How clients are harmed by sexual contact with mental health professionals: The syndrome and its prevalence. *Journal of Counseling and Development, 67*, 222–226.

Pope, K.S., & Vetter, V.A. (1991). Prior therapist-patient sexual involvement among patients seen by psychologists. *Psychotherapy: Theory, Research, Practice, Training, 28*(3), 429–438.

Popik, P. (1998). Pharmacology of ibogaine and ibogaine-related alkaloids. In G.A. Cordell (Ed.), *The alkaloids* (pp. 197–231). San Diego, CA: Academic Press.

Popik, P., & Glick, S.D. (1996). Ibogaine: A putatively anti-addictive alkaloid. *Drugs of the Future, 21*(11), 1109–1115.

Porges, S.W. (2011). *The polyvagal theory: Neurophysiological foundations of emotions, attachment, communication, and self-regulation.* New York: Norton.

Porter, R. (1993). The body and the mind, the doctor and the patient: Negotiating hysteria. In S. Gilman, H. King, R. Porter, G. Rousseau, & E. Showalter (Eds.), *Hysteria beyond Freud* (pp. 225–285). Los Angeles: University of California Press.

Poyares, D.R., Guilleminault, C., Ohayon, M.M., & Tufik, S. (2002). Can valerian improve the sleep of insomniacs after benzodiazepine withdrawal? *Progress in Neuropsychopharmacology and Biological Psychiatry, 26*(3), 539–545.

Price, C. (2005). Body-oriented therapy in recovery from child sexual abuse: An efficacy study. *Alternative Therapies in Health and Medicine, 11*(5), 46–57.

Price, C. (2007). Dissociation reduction in body therapy during sexual abuse recovery. *Complementary Therapies in Clinical Practice, 13*(2), 116–128.

Price, W.A. (2003). *Nutrition and physical degeneration* (6th ed.). Chicago: Keats.

Prousky, J. (2006). *Anxiety: Orthomolecular diagnosis and treatment.* Toronto: CCNM Press.

Prue, R.E. (2008). *King alcohol to chief peyote: A grounded theory investigation of the supportive factors of the Native American Church for drug and alcohol abuse recovery* (Doctoral dissertation, Publication #3336488). Lawrence, KS: University of Kansas Press.

Putnam, F.W. (1989). *Diagnosis and treatment of multiple personality disorder.* New York: Guilford.

Rao, M.S. (1968). The history of medicine in India and Burma. *Medical History, 12*(1), 52–61.

Raphael, B., & Wilson, J.P. (1994). When disaster strikes: Managing emotional reactions in rescue workers. In J.P. Wilson & J.D. Lindy (Eds.), *Countertransference in the treatment of PTSD* (pp. 333–350). New York: Guilford.

Rätsch, C. (1998). *The encyclopedia of psychoactive plants, enthnopharmacology and its applications.* Rochester, VT: Park Street Press.

Reader, A.L. (1994). The internal mystery plays: The role and physiology of the visual system in contemplative practices. *ReVision, 17*(1), 3–13.

Reite, M., & Capitanio, J. (1985). On the nature of social separation and attachment. In: M. Riete & T. Fields (Eds.), *The psychobiology of attachment and separation* (pp. 223–255). New York: Academic Press.

Reiter, R.J., & Robinson, J. (1995). *Melatonin.* New York: Bantam Books.

Ressig, C.J., Strain, E.C., & Griffiths, R.R. (2009). Caffeinated energy drinks: A growing problem. *Drug and Alcohol Dependence, 99*(1–3), 1–10.

Ricci, A., Bronzetti, E., Vega, J.A., & Amenta, F. (1992). Oral choline alfoscerate counteracts age-dependent loss of mossy fibres in the rat hippocampus. *Mechanisms of Ageing and Development, 66*(1), 81–91.

Robbers, J.E., & Tyler, V.E. (1999). *Tyler's herbs of choice: The therapeutic use of phytomedicinals.* New York: Haworth.

Rollnick, S., Miller, W.R., & Butler, C.C. (2007). *Motivational interviewing in health care: Helping patients change behavior.* New York: Guilford.

Roney-Dougal, S.M., & Vogl, G. (1993). Some speculations on the effect of geomagnetism on the pineal gland. *Journal of the Society for Psychical Research, 59*(830), 1–13.

Rosch, P.J., & Markov, M.S. (Eds.). (2004). *Bioelectromagnetic medicine*. New York: Marcel Dekker.

Roscoe, J., Matteson, S., Mustian, K.M., Padmanaban, D., & Morrow, G.R. (2005). Treatment of radiotherapy-induced fatigue through a nonpharmacological approach. *Integrated Cancer Therapy, 4*(1), 8–13.

Rossi, E.L. (1986). *The psychobiology of mind-body healing: New concepts of therapeutic hypnosis*. New York: Norton.

Rossi, E.L. (1999). Sleep, dream, hypnosis and healing: Behavioral state related gene expression and psychotherapy. *Sleep and Hypnosis: An International Journal of Sleep, Dream, and Hypnosis, 1*(3), 141–157.

Rossi, E.L., & Cheek, D.B. (1988). *Mind–body therapy: Methods of ideodynamic healing in hypnosis*. New York: Norton.

Rousseau. G.S. (1993). A strange pathology: Hysteria in the early modern world, 1500–1800. In S. Gilman, H. King, R. Porter, G. Rousseau, & E. Showalter (Eds.), *Hysteria beyond Freud* (pp. 91–221). Los Angeles: University of California Press.

Rowlands, D. (1984). Therapeutic touch: Its effect on the depressed elderly. *Australian Nursing Journal, 13*(11), 45–46, 52.

Ruckert, J. (1987). *The four-footed practitioner*. Berkeley, CA: Ten Speed Press.

Ruse, J., Jerome, L., Mithoefer, M.C., & Doblin, R. (2003). *MDMA-assisted psychotherapy for the treatment of posttraumatic stress disorder*. Retrieved from http://www.maps.org/research/mdma/treatmentmanual122303.html

Russell, A.L., & McCarty, M.F. (2000). DL-phenylalanine markedly potentiates opiate analgesia - an example of nutrient/pharmaceutical up-regulation of the endogenous analgesia system. *Medical Hypotheses, 55*(4), 283–8.

Russo, E.B. (2002). The role of cannabis and cannabinoids in pain management. In Weiner, R.S. (Ed.), *Pain management: A practical guide for clinicians* (pp. 357–375). New York: CRC Press.

Russo, E.B. (2004). Clinical endocannabinoid deficiency (CECD): Can this concept explain therapeutic benefits of cannabis in migraine, fibromyalgia, irritable bowel syndrome and other treatment-resistant conditions? *Neuroendocrinology Letters, 25*(1–2), 31–39.

Russo, E.B. (2008a). Cannabinoids in the management of difficult to treat pain. *Journal of Therapeutics and Clinical Risk Management, 4*(1), 245–259.

Russo, E.B. (2008b). Clinical endocannabinoid deficiency (CECD): Can this concept explain therapeutic benefits of cannabis in migraine, fibromyalgia, irritable bowel syndrome and other treatment-resistant conditions? *Neuroendocrinology Letters, 29*(2), 192–200.

Russo, E.B., Guy, G.W., & Robson, P.J. (2007). Cannabis, pain, and sleep: Lessons from therapeutic clinical trials of Sativex, a cannabis-based medicine. *Chemical Biodiversity, 4*(8), 1729–1743.

Russo-Neustadt, A.A., Beard, R.C., Huang, Y.M., & Cotman, C.W. (2000). Physical activity and antidepressant treatment potentiate the expression of specific brain-derived neurotrophic factor transcripts in the rat hippocampus. *Neuroscience, 101*(2), 305–312. doi:10.1016/S0306–4522(00)00349–3. PMID 11074154.

Rutter, P. (1991). *Sex in the forbidden zone: When men in power—therapists, doctors, clergy, teachers, and others—betray women's trust*. New York: Fawcett.

Rÿser, R.C. (2001). The invisible peoples: States governments, civil societies, and fourth world nations. *Social Development Review, 5*(2), 1–7.

Sachs, M. L, & Buffone, G.W. (1984). *Running as therapy: An integrated approach*. Lincoln, NE: University of Nebraska Press.

Sack, W. H., Clarke, G. N., & Seeley, J. (1995). Posttraumatic stress disorder across two generations of Cambodian refugees. *Journal of the American Academy of Child and Adolescent Psychiatry, 34*(9), 1160–1166.

Salamon, E., Kim, M., Beaulieu, J., & Stefano, G. B. (2003). Sound therapy induced relaxation: Down regulating stress processes and pathologies. *Medical Science Monitor, 9*(5), RA96–RA101.

Salmon, P., Skaife, K., & Rhodes, J. (2003). Abuse, dissociation, and somatization in irritable bowel syndrome: Towards an explanatory model. *Journal of Behavioral Medicine, 26*(1), 1–18.

Salzberg, S. (2011). *Real happiness: The power of meditation, a 28 day program*. New York: Workman.

Sansone, P., & Schmitt, L. (2000). Providing tender touch massage to elderly nursing home residents: A demonstration project. *German Nursing, 21*(6), 303–308.

Sansonese, J. N. (1994). *The body of myth: Mythology, shamanic trance, and the sacred geography of the body*. Rochester, VT: Inner Traditions International.

Santos, R. G., Landeira-Fernandez, J., Strassman, R. J., Motta, V., & Cruz, A. P. M. (2007). Effects of ayahuasca on psychometric measures of anxiety, panic-like and hopelessness in Santo Daime members. *Journal of Ethnopharmacology, 112*(3), 507–513.

Sarris, J., Kavanagh, D. J., Byrne, G., Bone, K. M., Adams, J., & Deed, G. (2009). The kava anxiety depression spectrum study (KADSS): A randomized, placebo-controlled crossover trial using an aqueous extract of Piper methysticum. *Psychopharmacology, 205*(3), 399–407.

Sartor, C. E., McCutcheon, V. V., Pommer, N. E., Nelson, E. C., Duncan, A. E., Waldron, M., . . . Heath, A. C. (2010). Posttraumatic stress disorder and alcohol dependence in young women. *Journal of Studies on Alcohol and Drugs, 71*(6), 810–818.

Sartori, H. E. (1986). Lithium orotate in the treatment of alcoholism and related conditions. Alcohol, 3(2), 97–100.

Scaer, R. C. (2001). *The body bears the burden: Trauma, dissociation, and disease*. Binghamton: Haworth.

Scaer, R. C. (2011). The whiplash syndrome: A model of traumatic stress. *Journal of Cognitive Rehabilitation, 18*(4), 6–15.

Scarborough, J. (1992). *Medical terminologies: Classical origins*. Norman, OK: University of Oklahoma Press.

Schellenberg, R., Sauer, S., Abourashed, E. A., Koetter, U., & Brattström, A. (2004). The fixed combination of valerian and hops (Ze91019) acts via a central adenosine mechanism. *Planta Medica, 70*(7), 594–597.

Schmitt, R., Capo, T., Frazier, H., & Boren, D. (1984). Cranial electrotherapy stimulation treatment of cognitive brain dysfunction in chemical dependence. *Journal of Clinical Psychiatry, 45*(2), 60–63.

Schmitz, M., & Jackel, M. (1998). Comparative study for assessing quality of life of patients with exogenous sleep disorders (temporary sleep onset and sleep interruption disorders) treated with a hops–valarian preparation and a benzodiazepine drug. *Wiener Medizinische Wochenschrift, 148*(13), 291–298.

Schore, A. (2003). *Affect regulation and the repair of the self*. New York: Norton.

Schrauzer, G. N., & Shrestha, K. P. (1990). Lithium in drinking water and the incidences of crimes, suicides, and arrests related to drug addictions. *Biological Trace Element Research, 25*(2), 105–113.

Schultes, R. E., & Hofmann, A. (1979). *Plants of the gods: Origins of hallucinogenic use*. New York: McGraw-Hill.

Schwarz, J. (1980). *Human energy systems*. New York: Dutton.

Seeman, T.E., Crimmins, E., Huang, M.H., Singer, B., Bucur, A., Gruenewald, T., . . . Reuben, D.B. (2004). Cumulative biological risk and socio-economic differences in mortality: MacArthur studies of successful aging. *Social Science & Medicine, 58*(10), 1985–1997.

Seicol, N.H. (1997). The consequences of cupping [Correspondence]. *New England Journal of Medicine, 336,* 1109–1110. Retrieved from http://www.nejm.org/doi/full/10.1056/NEJM199704103361520

Seligman, M.E.P., & Beagley, G. (1975). Learned helplessness in the rat. *Journal of Comparative and Physiological Psychology, 88*(2), 534–541.

Serpell, J. (1986). *In the company of animals*. New York: Blackwell.

Sewell, R.A., Halpern, J.H., & Pope, H.G. (2006). Response of cluster headache to psilocybin and LSD. *Neurology, 66,* 1920–1922.

Shafii, M., & Shafii, S.L. (1990). *Biological rhythms, mood disorders, light therapy, and the pineal gland*. Washington, DC: American Psychiatric Press.

Shalhoub-Kevorkian, N. (1999). Towards a cultural definition of rape: Dilemmas in dealing with rape victims in Palestinian society. *Women's Studies International Forum, 22*(2), 157–173.

Shannahoff-Khalsa, D.S. (2006). *Kundalini yoga meditation: Techniques specific for psychiatric disorders, couples therapy, and personal growth*. New York: Norton.

Shaw, A., Joseph, S., & Linley, P.A. (2005). Religion, spirituality, and posttraumatic growth: A systematic review. *Mental Health, Religion & Culture, 8*(1), 1–11.

Shay, J. (1992). Fluoxetine reduces explosiveness and elevates mood of Vietnam combat vets with PTSD. *Journal of Traumatic Stress, 5*(1), 97–101.

Shay, J. (1994). *Achilles in Vietnam: Combat trauma and the undoing of character*. New York: Simon & Schuster.

Shealy, C.N. (2006). *Life beyond 100*. New York: Tarcher.

Shealy, C.N., Cady, R.K., Wilkie, R.G., Cox, R., Liss, S., & Clossen, W. (1989). Depression: A diagnostic, neurochemical profile & therapy with cranial electrical stimulation (CES). *Journal of Neurological & Orthopedic Medicine & Surgery, 10*(4), 319–321.

Shealy, C.N., & Thomlinson, P. (2008). Safe effective nondrug treatment of chronic depression: A review of research on low-voltage cranial electrical stimulation and other adjunctive therapies. *Complementary Health Practice Review, 13*(2), 92–99.

Sheikh, A.A., & Sheikh, K.S. (1989). *Eastern and Western approaches to healing: Ancient wisdom and modern knowledge*. New York: Wiley.

Shen, Y.C., Chiou, W.F., Chou, Y.C., & Chen, C.F. (2003). Mechanisms in mediating the anti-inflammatory effects of baicalin and baicalein in human leukocytes. *European Journal of Pharmacology, 465*(1–2), 171–181.

Showalter, E. (1993). Hysteria, feminism, and gender. In S. Gilman, H. King, R. Porter, G. Rousseau, & E. Showalter (Eds.), *Hysteria Beyond Freud* (pp. 286–344). Los Angeles: University of California Press.

Silver, J.M., McAllister, T.W., & Yudofsky, S.C. (Eds.). (2011). *Textbook of traumatic brain injury*. Arlington, VA: American Psychiatric Association.

Singer, P., Shapiro, H., Theilla, M., Anbar, R., Singer, J., & Cohen, J. (2008). Anti-inflammatory properties of omega-3 fatty acids in critical illness: Novel mechanisms and an integrative perspective. *Intensive Care Medicine, 34*(9), 1580–1592.

Smith, E. (2003). *Therapeutic herb manual: A guide to the safe and effective use of liquid herbal extracts*. Williams, OR: Author.

Smith, M.A., Beilin, L.J., Mori, T.A., & Oddy, W.H. (2011). Essential fatty acids and mood: A systematic review of observational studies. *American Journal of Food and Nutrition, 1*(1), 14–27.

Smith, M.C., Stallings, M.A., Mariner, S., & Burrall, M. (1999). Benefits of massage therapy for hospitalized patients: A descriptive and qualitative evaluation. *Alternative Therapy for Health Medicine, 5*(4), 64–71.

Solomon, Z. (1995). Oscillating between denial and recognition of PTSD: Why are lessons learned and forgotten? *Journal of Traumatic Stress, 8*(2), 271–282.

Solomon, Z., Mikulincer, M., & Flum, H. (1988). Negative life events, coping responses, and combat-related psychopathology: A prospective study. *Journal of Abnormal Psychology, 97*(3), 302–307.

Southworth, S. (1999). A study of the effects of cranial electrical stimulation on attention and concentration. *Integrative Psychological and Behavioral Science, 34*(1), 43–53.

Spiegel, D. (Ed.). (1994). *Dissociation: Culture, mind, and body*. Washington, DC: American Psychiatric Press.

Spiller, R., & Shanahan, F. (2009). Gut microbiota and abnormal mucosal neuroendocrine immune activation. In E.A. Mayer & M.C. Bushnell (Eds.), *Functional pain syndromes: Presentation and pathophysiology* (pp. 337—360). Seattle, WA: IASP Press.

Spinella, M. (2001). *The psychopharmacology of herbal medicine*. Cambridge, MA: MIT Press.

Spinella, M. (2002). The importance of pharmacological synergy in psychoactive herbal medicines. *Alternative Medicine Review, 7*(2), 130–137.

Spinella, M. (2004). Herbal medicines and sleep. In M. Lader, D.P. Cardinali & S.R. Pandi-Perumal (Eds.), *Sleep and sleep disorders: A neuropsychopharmacological approach*. Georgetown, TX: Landes Bioscience/Eurekah.com.

Spitzer, C., Koch, B., Grabe, H.J., Ewert, R., Barnow, S., Felix, S.B., . . . Schäper, C. (2011). Association of airflow limitation with trauma exposure and post-traumatic stress disorder. *European Respiratory Journal, 37*(5), 1068–1075.

Stafford, B.M. (1993). *Body criticism: Imagining the unseen in enlightenment art and medicine*. Cambridge, MA: MIT Press.

Stargrove, M.B., Treasure, J., & McKee, D.L. (2007). *Herb, nutrient, and drug interactions: Clinical implications and therapeutic strategies*. St. Louis: Mosby.

Staudenmayer, H. (1996). Clinical consequences of the EI/MCS "diagnosis": Two paths. *Regulatory Toxicology and Pharmacology, 24*(1), S96–S110.

Steinberg, M. (1994). Systematizing dissociation: Symptomatology and diagnostic assessment. In D. Spiegel (Ed.), *Dissociation: Culture, mind, and body* (pp. 59–88). Washington, DC: American Psychiatric Press.

Stern, P.R. (2010). Antidepressant action of ketamine. *Science Signaling, 3*(136), ec259. doi:10.1126/scisignal.3136ec259

Spottiswoode, S.J.P. (1990). Geomagnetic activity and anomalous cognition: A preliminary report of new evidence. *Subtle Energies, 1*(1), 91–102.

Stone, R. (1986). *Polarity therapy: The complete collected works* (Vol. 1). Summertown, TN: CRCS Publications.

Stone, R. (1987). *Polarity therapy: The complete collected works* (Vol. 2). Summertown, TN: CRCS Publications.

Stoschitzky, K., Sakotnik, A., Lercher, P., Zweiker, R., Maier, R., Liebmann, P., & Lindner, W. (1999). Influence of beta-blockers on melatonin release. *European Journal of Clinical Pharmacology, 55*(2), 111–115.

Strassman, R.J. (1991). The pineal gland: Current evidence for its role in consciousness. *Psychedelic Monograph Essays, 5*, 166–205.

Strassman, R.J. (2001). *DMT: The spirit molecule*. Rochester, VT: Park Street Press.

Streeter, C.C., Whitfield, T.H., Owen, L., Rein, T., Karri, S.K., Yakhkind, A., . . . Jensen, J.E. (2010). Effects of yoga versus walking on mood, anxiety, and brain GABA levels: A randomized controlled MRS study. *Journal of Alternative and Complementary Medicine, 16*(11), 1145–1152. doi: 10.1089/acm.2010.0007

Strickland, C.J., Walsh, E., & Cooper, M. (2006). Healing fractured families: Parents' and elders' perspectives on the impact of colonization and youth suicide prevention in a Pacific Northwest American Indian tribe. *Journal of Transcultural Nursing, 17*(1), 5–12.

Sudati, J.H., Fachinetto, R., Pereira, R.P., Boligon, A.A., Athayde, M.L., Soares, F.A., . . . Rocha, J.B. (2009). In vitro antioxidant activity of Valeriana officinalis against different neurotoxic agents. *Neurochemical Research, 34*(8), 1372–1379.

Sunshine, W., Field, T.M., Quintino, O., Fierro, K., Kuhn, C., Burman, I., & Schanberg, S. (1996). Fibromyalgia benefits from massage therapy and transcutaneous electrical stimulation. *Journal of Clinical Rheumatology, 2*(1), 18–22.

Sussman, E. (1991). *The bleeding heart*. Seattle: University of Washington Press.

Tan, G., Dao, T.K., Farmer, L., Sutherland, R.J., & Gevirtz, R. (2011). Heart rate variability (HRV) and posttraumatic stress disorder (PTSD): A pilot study. *Applied Psychophysiology and Biofeedback, 36*(1), 27–35.

Tan, G., Rintala, D., Herrington, R., Yang, J., Wade, W. H., Vasilev, C., & Shanti, B. F. (2003, September). Treating spinal cord injury pain with cranial electrotherapy stimulation. Presented at the American Paraplegia Society Annual Meeting, Las Vegas, NV.

Tang, J.Y., Zeng, Y.S., Chen, Q.G., Qin, Y.J., Chen, S.J., & Zhong, Z.Q. (2008). Effects of valerian on the level of 5-hydroxytryptamine, cell proliferation and neurons in cerebral hippocampus of rats with depression induced by chronic mild stress. *Zhong Xi Yi Jie He Xue Bao [Journal of Chinese Integrative Medicine], 5*(3), 283–288.

Tart, C.T. (1994). Fears of the paranormal in ourselves and our colleagues. *Subtle Energies, 5*(1), 35–68.

Tart, C.T. (2009). *The end of materialism: How evidence of the paranormal is bringing science and spirit together*. Oakland, CA: New Harbinger.

Taylor, G.J. (1984). Alexithymia: Concept, measurement, and implications for treatment. *The American Journal of Psychiatry, 141*(6), 725–732.

Taylor, J.M., Gilligan, C., & Sullivan, A.M. (1997). *Between voice and silence: Women and girls, race and relationships*. Cambridge, MA: Harvard University Press.

Taylor, S.E., Klein, L.C., Lewis, B.P., Gruenewald, T.L., Gurung, R.A.R., & Updegraff, J.A. (2000). Biobehavioral responses to stress in females: Tend-and-befriend, not fight-or-flight. *Psychological Review, 107*(3), 411–429.

Tedeschi, R.G. & Calhoun, L.G. (2004). Posttraumatic growth: Conceptual foundations and empirical evidence. *Psychological Inquiry, 15*(1), 1–18.

Telles, S., Singh, N., Joshi, M., & Balkrishna, A. (2010). Post-traumatic stress symptoms and heart rate variability in Bihar flood survivors following yoga: a randomized controlled study. *BMC Psychiatry, 10*(1), 18. DOI: 10.1186/1471-244X-10–18

Terman, M., & Terman, J.S. (1995). Treatment of seasonal affective disorder with a high-output negative ionizer. *Journal of Alternative and Complementary Medicine, 1*(1), 87–92.

Terman, M., & Terman, J. S. (2005). Light therapy for seasonal and nonseasonal depression: Efficacy, protocol, safety, and side effects. *CNS Spectrums, 10*(8), 647–663.

Tiefenbacher, S., Novak, M. A., Lutz, C. K., & Meyer, J. S. (2005). The physiology and neurochemistry of self-injurious behavior: A nonhuman primate model. *Frontiers in Bioscience,* 10, 1–11.

Tiller, W. (1997). *Science and human transformation: Subtle energies, intentionality and consciousness.* Walnut Creek, CA: Pavior.

Tomes, N. (1994). Feminist histories of psychiatry. In M. S. Micale & R. Porter (Eds.), *Discovering the history of psychiatry* (pp. 348–383). New York: Oxford University Press.

Treanor, M. (2011). The potential impact of mindfulness on exposure and extinction learning in anxiety disorders. *Clinical Psychology Review, 31*(4), 617–625.

Trotter, C. (1992). *Double bind: Recovery and relapse prevention for the chemically dependent sexual abuse survivor.* Independence, MO: Herald House/Independence Press.

Ulbricht, C., Brendler, T., Gruenwald, J., Kligler, B., Keifer, D., Abrams, T. R., . . . Lafferty, H. J. (2005). Lemon balm (Melissa officinalis L.): An evidence-based systematic review by the natural standard research collaboration. *Journal of Herbal Pharmacotherapy, 5*(4), 71–114.

United States Association for Body Psychotherapy. (2009). *Definition of body psychotherapy.* Retrieved from http://www.usabp.org/displaycommon.cfm?an=1& subarticlenbr=9

Unschuld, P. (1985). *Medicine in China: A history of ideas.* Berkeley, CA: University of California Press.

Upchurch, D. M., & Chyu, L. (2005). Use of complementary and alternative medicine among American women. *Women's Health Issues, 15*(1), 5–13.

U.S. Department of Education, Office of the Under Secretary, Policy and Program Studies Service. (2004). *Educator sexual misconduct: A synthesis of existing literature* (Doc # 2004–09). Washington, DC.

van der Kolk, B. A. (1989). The compulsion to repeat the trauma: Re-enactment, revictimization, and masochism. *Psychiatric Clinics of North America, 12*(2), 389–411.

van der Kolk, B. A. (1994). The body keeps the score: Memory and the evolving psychobiology of post-traumatic stress. *Harvard Review of Psychiatry, 1*(5), 253–265.

van der Kolk, B. A., & Pelcovitz, D. (1999). Clinical applications of the structured interview for disorders of extreme stress (sides). *National Center for Post-Traumatic Stress Disorder Clinical Quarterly, 8*(2), 1–36.

van der Kolk, B. A., Perry, C., & Herman, J. L. (1991). Childhood origins of self-destructive behavior. *American Journal of Psychiatry, 148*(12), 1665–1671.

van der Kolk, B. A., Pynoos, R. S., Cicchetti, D., Cloitre, M., D'Andrea, W., Ford, J. D., . . . Teicher, M. (2009). Proposal to include a developmental trauma disorder diagnosis for children and adolescents in DSM-V. (Unpublished manuscript). Available from http://www.traumacenter.org/ announcements/DTD_papers_Oct_09.pdf

van der Kolk, B. A., Roth, S., & Pelcovitz, D. (2005). Disorders of extreme stress: The empirical foundation of a complex adaptation to trauma. *Journal of Traumatic Stress, 18*(5), 389–399.

van Dixhoorn, J., & Duivenvoorden, H. J. (1985). Efficacy of Nijmegen Questionnaire in recognition of the hyperventilation syndrome. *Journal of Psychosomatic Research, 29*(2), 199–206.

Vasquez, A., Manso, G., & Cannell, J. (2004). The clinical importance of vitamin D (cholecalciferol): A paradigm shift with implications for all healthcare providers. *Alternative Therapies in Health and Medicine, 10*(5), 28–36.

Veith, I. (1965). Hysteria: The history of a disease. Chicago: University of Chicago Press.

Villalba, V., & Harrington, C. (2003). Repetitive self–injurious behavior: The emerging potential of psychotropic intervention. *Psychiatric Times 20*(2). Retrieved from http://www.psychiatrictimes.com/showArticle.jhtml?articleID=175802309

Volfe, Z., Dvilansky, A., & Nathan, I. (1985). Cannabinoids block release of serotonin from platelets induced by plasma from migraine patients. International Journal of Clinical and Pharmacological Research, 5(4), 243–246.

Vollenweider, F. X., & Kometer, M. (2010). Opinion: The neurobiology of psychedelic drugs: Implications for the treatment of mood disorders. *Nature Reviews Neuroscience, 11*, 642–651.

Vuksan-Ćusa, B., Marčinko, D., Nađ, S., & Jakovljević, M. (2009). Differences in cholesterol and metabolic syndrome between bipolar disorder men with and without suicide attempts. *Progress in Neuro-Psychopharmacology and Biological Psychiatry, 33*(1), 109–112.

Wadeson, H., Durkin, J., & Perach, D. (Eds.) (1989). *Advances in art therapy.* Hoboken, NJ: Wiley.

Walker, M. (2001). Liver detoxification with coffee enemas as employed in the Gerson therapy. *Townsend Letter for Doctors and Patients, 216*, 46–50.

Walton, R. G., Hudak, R., & Green-Waite, R. J. (1993). Adverse reactions to aspartame: Double-blind challenge in patients from a vulnerable population. *Biological Psychiatry, 34*(1–2), 13–17.

Wang, C., Schmid, C. H., Rones, R., Kalish, R., Yinh, J., Goldenberg, D. L., . . . McAlindon, T. (2010). A randomized trial of tai chi for fibromyalgia. *New England Journal of Medicine, 363*(8), 743–754.

Wardell, D., & Engebretson, J. (2001). Biological correlates of Reiki Touch healing. *Journal of Advanced Nursing, 33*(4), 439–445.

Warner-Schmidt, J. L., Vanover, K. E., Chen, E. Y., Marshall, J. J., & Greengard, P. (2011). Antidepressant effects of selective serotonin reuptake inhibitors (SSRIs) are attenuated by antiinflammatory drugs in mice and humans. *Proceedings of the National Academy of Sciences of the United States of America, 108*(27), 11297. doi: 10.1073/pnas.1109215108

Wasson, R. G. (1980). *The wondrous mushroom: Mycolatry in Mesoamerica.* New York: McGraw-Hill.

Wasson, R. G., Hofmann, A., & Ruck, C. A. P. (1978). *The road to Eleusis: Unveiling the secret of the mysteries.* New York: Harcourt Brace Jovanovich.

Wasson, R. G., Kramrisch, S., Ruck, C., & Ott, J. (1988). *Persephone's quest: Entheogens and the origins of religion.* New Haven, CT: Yale University Press.

Waters, F. (1975). *Mexico mystique: The coming sixth world of consciousness.* Athens, OH: Swallow Press/Ohio University Press.

Watkins, J. G., & Watkins, H. H. (1990). Dissociation and displacement: Where goes the "ouch?" *American Journal of Clinical Hypnosis, 33*(1), 1–11.

Wattanathorn, J., Mator, L., Muchimapura, S., Tongun, T., Pasuriwong, O., Piyawatkul, . . . Singkhoraard, J. (2008). Positive modulation of cognition and mood in the healthy elderly volunteer following the administration of Centella asiatica. *Journal of Ethnopharmacology, 116*(2), 325–332.

Watts, D. L. (1995). *Trace elements and other essential nutrients: Clinical application of tissue mineral analysis*. Henderson, NV: Meltdown, International.

Wehr, T. A. (1992). In short photoperiods, human sleep is biphasic. *Journal of Sleep Research, 1*(2), 103–107.

Weil, A. T., & Davis, W. (1994). Bufo alvarius: A potent hallucinogen of animal origin. *Journal of Ethnopharmacology, 41*(1–2), 1–8.

Weill Medical College of Cornell University. (n.d.). The rise and decline of psychiatric hydrotherapy [Online Exhibit]. Retrieved from Oskar Diethelm Library Web site: http://www.cornellpsychiatry.org/history/osk_die_lib/hydrotherapy/default.htm

Weinberg, B. A., & Bealer, B. K. (2002). *The world of caffeine: The science and culture of the world's most popular drug*. New York: Routledge.

Weingarten, K. (2004). Witnessing the effects of political violence in families: Mechanisms of intergenerational transmission of trauma and clinical interventions. *Journal of Marital and Family Therapy, 30*(1), 45–59.

Werntz, D. (1981). *Cerebral hemispheric activity and autonomic nervous function*. (Doctoral thesis). San Diego, CA: University of California.

Wheatley, D. (2001). Stress-induced insomnia treated with kava and valerian: Singly and in combination. *Human Psychopharmacology, 16*(4), 353–356.

Whitbeck, L. B., Adams, G. W., Hoyt, D. R., & Chen, X. (2004). Conceptualizing and measuring historical trauma among American Indian people. *American Journal of Community Psychology, 33*(3–4), 119–130.

Wiechman Askay, S., & Magyar-Russell, G. (2009). Post-traumatic growth and spirituality in burn recovery. *International Review of Psychiatry, 21*(6), 570–579.

Williams, R. J. (1998). *Biochemical individuality*. New York: McGraw-Hill.

Wilson, E. S. (1993). Transits of consciousness. *Subtle Energies, 4*(2), 171–183.

Wilson, J. P. (1989). *Trauma: Transformation and healing: An integrative approach to theory, research, and post-traumatic therapy*. New York: Brunner/Mazel, Inc.

Wilson, J., & Lindy, J. (1993). *Countertransference in post-traumatic stress disorder*. New York: Guilford Press.

Wilson, J. P., & Lindy, J. D. (1994). Empathic strain and countertransference. In J. P. Wilson & J. D. Lindy (Eds.), *Countertransference in the treatment of PTSD* (pp. 5–30). New York: Guilford Press.

Wilson, J. P., Lindy. J. D., & Raphael, B. (1994). Empathic strain and practitioner defense: Type I and II CTRs. In J. P. Wilson & J. D. Lindy (Eds.), *Countertransference in the treatment of PTSD* (pp. 31–61). New York: Guilford.

Winkelman, M. (1990). Physiological and therapeutic aspects of shamanistic healing. *Subtle Energies, 1*(2), 5.

Winkelman, M. J. (2003). Psychointegration: The physiological effects of entheogens. *Entheos: Journal of Psychedelic Spirituality, 2*(1), 51–61.

Winkelman, M. J. (2007). Therapeutic bases of psychedelic medicines: Psychointegrative effects. In M. J. Winkelman & T. B. Roberts (Eds.), Psychedelic medicine: New evidence for hallucinogenic substances as medicine (Vol. 1, pp. 1–19). Westport, CT: Praeger.

Winkelman, M. (2010). *Shamanism: A biopsychosocial paradigm of consciousness and healing*. Santa Barbara, CA: Praeger.

Winkelman, M. J. (2011). *Neurotheology*. Retrieved from http://michaelwinkelman.com/neurotheology/

Wood, D., Cottrell, A., Baker, S.C., Southgate, J., Harris, M., Fulford, S., . . . Gillatt, D. (2011). Recreational ketamine: from pleasure to pain. *British Journal of Urology International, 107*(12), 1881–1884.

Xu, Y., Ku, B., Tie, L., Yao, H., Jiang, W., Ma, X., & Li, X. (2006). Curcumin reverses the effects of chronic stress on behavior, the HPA axis, BDNF expression and phosphorylation of CREB. *Brain Research, 1122* (1), 56–56. doi:10.1016/j.brainres.2006.09.009. PMID 17022948. edit

Yaffe, K., Vittinghoff, E., Lindquist, K., Barnes, D., Covinsky, K.E., Neylan, T., . . . Marmar, C. (2010). Posttraumatic stress disorder and risk of dementia among US veterans. *Archives of General Psychiatry, 67*(6), 608–613.

Yehuda, R., Engel, S.M., Brand, S.R., Seckl, J., Marcus, S.M., & Berkowitz, G.S. (2005). Transgenerational effects of posttraumatic stress disorder in babies of mothers exposed to the World Trade Center attacks during pregnancy. *Journal of Clinical Endocrinology & Metabolism 90*(7), 4115–4118.

Yehuda, R., Schmeidler, J., Elkin, A., Houshmand, E., Siever, L., Binder-Brynes, K., . . . Yang, R.K. (1998). Phenomenology and psychobiology of the intergenerational response to trauma. In Y. Danieli (Ed.), *Intergenerational handbook of the multigenerational legacies of trauma* (pp. 639–655). New York: Plenum.

Yokogoshi, H., Kobayashi, M., Mochizuki, M., & Terashima, T. (1998). Effect of theanine, γ-glutamylethylamide, on brain monoamines and striatal dopamine release in conscious rats. *Neurochemical Research, 23*(5), 667–673.

Zanarini, M.C., & Frankenburg, F.R. (2003). Omega-3 fatty acid treatment of women with borderline personality disorder: A double-blind, placebo-controlled pilot study. *American Journal of Psychiatry, 160*(1), 167–169.

Zarate, C.A., Singh, J.B., Carlson, P.J., Brutsche, N.E., Ameli, R., Luckenbaugh, D.A., . . . Manji, H.K. (2006). A randomized trial of an N-methyl-D-aspartate antagonist in treatment-resistant major depression. *Archives of General Psychiatry, 63*, 856–864.

Zatzick, D., Marmar, C., Weiss, D., & Metzler, T. (1993). Does trauma-linked dissociation vary across ethnic groups? *Journal of Nervous and Mental Disease, 182*(10), 576–582.

Ziegler, G., Ploch, M., Miettinen-Baumann, A., & Collet, W. (2002). Efficacy and tolerability of valerian extract LI 156 compared with oxazepam in the treatment of non-organic insomnia—A randomized, double-blind, comparative clinical study. *European Journal of Medical Research, 7*(11), 480–486.

Zink, N., & Parks, S. (1991, Fall). Nightwalking: Exploring the dark with peripheral vision. *Whole Earth Review*, 4–9.

Zotev, V., Krueger, F., Phillips, R., Alvarez, R.P., Simmons, W.K., Bellgowan, P., . . . Bodurka, J. (2011). Self-regulation of amygdala activation using real-time fMRI neurofeedback. *PLoS ONE, 6*(9), e24522. doi:10.1371/journal.pone.0024522

Index

deconditioning from 35; hyperarousal and 29

state-dependent response, depersonalization as 54

state-specific research 60

state-specific treatment 76

Staudenmayer 61

stereotypes, cultural 122, 128

still point 71

stimulants 226–8

Stone, Randolph 6, 88

story: client's trauma 118; as therapy 145–7

Strassman, Rick 8, 255

stress: biology of traumatic 28; definitions of major syndromes 111–17; diagnostic categories of traumatic 108; from fluorescent light 12; group 30–2; heart and 48–50; inescapable 33–4; perceived 28–9; *see also* posttraumatic stress; posttraumatic stress disorder

stress hormones 29–30

stress-induced analgesia 37

stress-inoculation training (SIT) 158

stress management groups 170

Stress-Related Growth Scale (SRGS) 130

stress response continuum of 28–30

Structured Clinical Interview for Dissociative Disorders (SCID:D) 66

Studies on Hysteria (Freud) 83

substance use/abuse: abstinence and 133; alcohol dependence 37, 42, 132–4, 238; assessment 132–4; chicken and egg treatment dilemma 133; policy 247; PTSD with 36

sugar: alternatives to refined 183–4; colon health and 192–3; detoxification from 238; natural sugar cane 185

suicidality 26, 57, 83, 85, 98, 104; low cholesterol linked to 198

Sun Dance 65

sun light 189, 213–14

surgery addiction 62–4

systematic desensitization 158

table salt 186

taboo, of touch 78–82; in psychology 82–5

TABS *see* Trauma and Attachment Belief Scale

Tai Chi 154

Tart, Charles 60

taurine 208

TBI *see* traumatic brain injury

telepathy 59

tend and befriend, female stress response 33

thatched roof houses (palapas) 1

theanine 227–8

therapist exercises: diaphragm bodywork technique 100–1; exploring role of ritual 172; postural/emotional empathy 148; *see also* clinician exercises

therapy: animal-assisted 106; art 154–5; derivation of term 145–6; goal of 68–9; hydro- 96; hypno- 162–3; light 165–6; MDMA-assisted 262; mind/body group 169–70; music and sound 166–7; previous 118–20; story as 145–7; therapeutic methods 149–75; verbal 149, 171–2; voice movement 154; *see also* body psychotherapy; healing; nutritional therapies; polarity therapy; psychotherapy; touch; treatment

Therapy Dog International 103

theta state 94

Thich Nhat Hanh 159

third eye 7, 8

thoracic outlet syndrome 45

Tibetan eye chart 11

time rhythms 13–16

tissue (hair) mineral analysis 138

toning exercise 167

torture victims, touch physiotherapy for 86–7

touch: of animal companions 102–7; attachment and 73–8; body consciousness and 76; cultural traditions of 74; diaphragm 101; first stage of 101–2; gentle massage 99; of Goddess 16; harmful behaviors eliminated by 98; healing mechanism of 86–7; hypnosis compared to 76–7; memories released by 91, 95, 99; overly directive 98–9; pressure continuum of 89; spinal column and 16; taboo of 78–85; as therapeutic 85–6

traditional medicine *see* complementary/alternative medicine; cultural traditions; natural medicine

trance 15, 57–60

trans fatty acids 198–9

transpersonal psychology 59–60, 168–9

trauma: ancient culture and 18; betrayal 168; environmental 15, 32; generic dimensions of 112; group stress and 30–2; historical 30, 129; human

314   *Index*

MENSANA PUBLICATIONS

CONTINUING EDUCATION FOR MENTAL HEALTH PROFESSIONALS

Routledge
Taylor & Francis Group
NEW YORK AND LONDON

An accredited continuing education component has been developed for this book by the author, in partnership with Routledge and Mensana Publications. The CE offer is worth 6 hours of continuing education credit, and may be purchased from the website below:

www.mensanapublications.com